A PASSION FOR
STEELHEAD

A PASSION FOR STEELHEAD

DEC HOGAN

Photography by the author, Ted Fauceglia,
Richard T. Grost, Walter Hodges, and Thomas R. Pero

Illustrations by Greg Pearson

WILD
RIVER
PRESS

Library of Congress Cataloging-in-Publication Data
    Hogan, Dec.
    A Passion for Steelhead/Dec Hogan.—1st ed.
    p. cm.
    ISBN 09746427-1-1 (hardcover)
    Steelhead fishing. 2. Fly fishing. I. Title.

    2006924271

Book and jacket design by Gregory Smith Design
Jacket photo by Keith Balfourd
Photographs of flies by Ted Fauceglia
Photographs of steelhead life history by Richard C. Grost
Fishing photos by the author and others

Published by Wild River Press, Post Office Box 13360, Mill Creek, Washington 98082 USA

Wild River Press Web site address: www.wildriverpress.com

Printed in China through Colorcraft Ltd, Hong Kong

10 9 8 7 6 5 4 3 2 1

DEDICATION

THIS BOOK IS DEDICATED to all of the men and women whom I've had the pleasure of guiding. You gave life to my dream. Thank You.

ACKNOWLEDGMENTS

I VIVIDLY REMEMBER SEEING THE PRINTED ARTICLE FOR THE FIRST TIME. The striking two-page opening spread jumped right off the glossy paper in my hands and into my psyche. The font was bold and captivating, the accompanying photographs and text laid out professionally—the whole presentation was extremely inviting. Without reading a single written word, the "eye candy" appeal alone was enough to validate the piece with my name on it as legitimate and worthy of an audience.

Elated with what I saw, I looked up from the pages of this new issue of *Wild Steelhead & Salmon* Magazine and directly into the eyes of the editor and publisher. "It's amazing that you could make something that took me only a weekend to write look so fantastic!" I said. Tom looked at me with a smile. "This article didn't take you a weekend to write, Dec," he said. "It took you 30 years."

That moment defined Tom Pero's understanding of and appreciation for those fortunate enough to write for him. Those words gave me confidence to continue communicating my love for steelhead through my growing interest in writing and photography. As an editor, at least for me, Tom has no rival. He knows rivers, fish, and the natural world. Most importantly, he knows me. His occasional "fixes" to my work are made as though, for the moment, he *is* Dec Hogan. He sometimes has a subtle way of inspiring me; other times he's in my face like a football coach, and I can't hardly wait to hang up the phone and get to work!

Writing this book has been an enormous effort. If life were such that 100 percent of my waking hours could have been devoted to it, it still would have been daunting, although accomplished with considerably less stress. But life isn't that way, and the completion of this ambitious project was made possible by Tom's undying patience coupled with his belief in me. Admittedly, there were times when I tested his patience, and I'm certain he had doubts about whether we would ever make it into the end zone. We did it, amigo. Thank you.

Three years ago, Tom and I had a vision of what *A Passion for Steelhead* should be, but it was the "two Gregs" who brought this book to life visually: Greg Smith who with incredible talent for design and graphic wizardry, painstakingly assembled all the parts and made them flow like one long, beautiful river of pictures and words. Greg Pearson is simply a magician with pencil and paper—his illustrations gracing these pages could not be more right on. Not only is Greg a superb artist, he's an accomplished, passionate steelhead angler and spey caster. Working with him was "two minds on the same page."

It seems only yesterday that I was dreaming of what it would be like to hook a steelhead on a fly. Now, after tens of thousands of hours on the water I not only have written a book about my experiences, but one of my true mentors—who at one time I thought of as an unreachable icon of the sport—has become a friend and has graciously written the Foreword. Bill McMillan is one of the all-time masters of steelhead fly fishing and a passionate soul. Through his writing he instills in his readers an indelible sporting ethic as it pertains not only to steelhead but to the river and its environment as a living entity.

A special thanks goes out to Pete Soverel, who is much more qualified than I to write about the steelhead's unfortunate peril and gloomy fate in the Afterword. Pete has allowed me to live peacefully with "blinders" in place.

To the talented photographers whose work we are all privileged to see in these pages—Ted Fauceglia, Rich Grost, and Walter Hodges—all I can do is look at your pictures in awe. A note of appreciation to Cameron Derbyshire and David Koopmans for their meticulous proofreading of the manuscript. And thanks to Dana Sturn at Speypages.com for help with the Asked and Answered chapter.

There are many other people to whom I owe gratitude. For fresh insight into the fascinating freshwater life of *Oncorhynchus mykiss*, thanks to dedicated biologist John McMillan of the Wild Salmon Center. And for sharing her knowledge about my favorite fish's life in the Pacific Ocean, Katherine Myers, Principal Investigator of the High-Seas Salmon Research Program at the University of Washington.

A sincere thank you to Nick Amato for publishing my early magazine articles and giving me a start. Steelhead writers Bob Arnold, Trey Combs, Roderick Haig-Brown, and Steve Raymond all have had an influence on me in some way. Lani Waller, wrote me a letter of encouragement in 1990 telling me that I have what it takes to succeed—I took it to heart, Lani! Jim Vincent of Rio and Tim Rajeff of Airflo who involved me in the testing of their awesome spey lines, thus forcing me to become a better caster in an attempt to give them the best possible feedback. Adam and Judy Tavender's generosity and hospitality allowed me to go nuts and "play" on the incomparable Dean River for seven years running. I can't thank George Cook enough for all he's done for my career— not to mention all the free comedy. Harry Lemire should be an inspiration for all those who have fished in his footsteps—he is for me. John Hazel, you are my brother and taught me more about guiding than you'll ever know; thanks, John, for all you've done for me. My parents independent of each other supported and encouraged my love of fishing and Nature throughout my life. Both always made me believe in myself: "You can do whatever you want to do, Declan, as long as you put your mind to it." For helping me to get and keep the ball rolling, thanks to Tom Darling, John Ecklund, John Farrar, and Tony Sarp. Then there are those special few, both living and deceased, who have in some way had an influence on my life as a steelheader: Enos Bradner, Wes Drain, Alec Jackson, Les Johnson, Walt Johnson, Mike Kinney, Al Knudson, Bob Stroebel, Ralph Wahl, and Jerry Wintle. For the most profound influence on my fly-tying skills and understanding—I don't even come close to his level of masterful skill—thank you to Steve Gobin. A special thanks goes to Battalion Chief Mike Adams and the rest of the Layton City Fire Department who showed support and keen interest in this project.

And to my fishing pals—without your friendship on and off the river there would be a void in my life. Thanks to: Keith Balfourd, Bob Budd, Charlie Gearheart, Scott Hagen; Marty, Mike, Monty, and Trevor Howard; Steve Kruse, Big Al Nagao, Scott O'Donnell, Beau Purvis, Gary and Rick Rawson, Brian Silvey, Ed Ward, and Tracy Whisonant.

At last, the biggest thank you goes to the love of my life, Amy Christensen. She patiently endured a "distant" Dec while I spent countless hours working on this monumental project. Even when I wasn't engaged in writing or posing for casting illustrations, etc., my mind was off wandering in steelhead country. Thanks for sticking by me, babe. Now we can go fishing! Brooke, Jenny, and Aspen—you can come, too.

DEC HOGAN
SALT LAKE CITY, UTAH
January 2006

CONTENTS

FOREWORD

I POINTED TO A DULL-COLORED BIRD, a little smaller than a robin, flicking its tail in the October sunlight along the shoreline of the Grande Ronde River. "There's a bird I may not have seen before—maybe a waterthrush," I said. "I'll have to look it up in the field book when we get back."

I expected no comment from the younger man who accompanied me as we walked through the golden sedges along the edge of a long steelhead run, black bluffs of basalt looming above us highlighted with crimson patches of sumac. Surprisingly few fly fishers are naturalists, particularly the new generation. So I was a little stunned with his contradiction: "Close. But it's a pipit."

I stopped to look at the "kid" more closely. He was in his late 20s, average height, square-built and in athletic prime. I was middle 40s, too portly for my own good at the time, and just beginning to gray. I'd tried to figure him out for two to three days, not sure what to think. It was his first year of guiding at Little Creek Lodge and my second year there teaching classes on fishing the floating-line methods for steelhead I began writing about in the early 1970s. On his first day of arrival, he came up to me with a question that seemed an incredible mix of naïveté, ego, and vulnerability all wrapped up into one. His face was earnest in expectation of an answer: "How do you become a famous steelhead fisherman?"

How does a person answer a question like that? Personally, I'd never considered fly fishing a particularly legitimate avenue to fame, and least of all that specialized little group trapped on the western edge of North America who fish rivers for steelhead. Why would anyone ask me about fame, for Christ's sake? I had lived life more or less a recluse—part-time work, occasional "dog-and-pony" programs, and the rare class or seminar that seemed to come in just the nick of time. Somehow I managed to pay delinquent taxes on my cabin, put a few groceries in a mostly vacant fridge, and sustain my volunteer work in conservation activism.

The kid was right. The bird was an American pipit. I knew it as soon as he said it. They aren't common along the rivers I've spent most of my life fishing in the Northwest. Someone who can identify an uncommon bird 100 feet away on the opposite side of a river with such cocksure immediacy is, well, a damned good observer. It's also the mark of a person who has pored over bird books in a devoted self-education at an early age. In fact, I later learned that he had constructed his own voluminous bird book at the age of 10 as a means of recording his early passion for birds, not steelhead.

The bird made my decision: I knew I liked Dec Hogan. That was back in 1991. I came to like him that much more in an annually renewed friendship during the next several years on the Grande Ronde. His perpetually open naïveté, boundless enthusiasm, and determination not only to learn, but to master, whatever set his mind afire charmed me as few human beings had for many years. Being with him, I could not help but feel young and more alive than I thought possible on rivers where our wild runs of steelhead had all gone to hell.

I suppose Dec learned some things about steelhead and steelhead fly fishing methods from me, but I also learned from Dec. This was particularly true of fishing two-handed rods.

In the early to mid-1970s, I was perhaps the first U.S. steelhead writer to recommend using fly rods longer than nine and a half feet. Although Roderick Haig-Brown described his 10½-foot Crown Houghton, 11-foot Wye, and General Money's two-handed rods in *The Western Angler* (1939) and *A River Never Sleeps* (1946), even in Canada with its British angling traditions the trend was toward smaller steelhead fly rods. For instance, Francis Whitehouse's *Sport Fishes of Western Canada and Some Others* (1945) had a section written by A.J. Milton regarding steelhead fishing in which 12- to 14-foot two-handed rods were described as providing great casting distances, but that a rod of 10 feet and nine and a half ounces would suffice and seemed to be his preference. W.F. Pochin's *Angling and Hunting in British Columbia* (1946) indicated that while two-handed rods were almost universally used for steelhead at one time, the trend was toward single-handed bamboo rods of six to nine ounces and nine to 10 feet in length.

The trend from the 1950s through the early 1970s was increasingly toward shorter fly rods as Lee Wulff's much-publicized fishing for Atlantic salmon using rods of six feet or shorter (or even no rod at all) gradually migrated West. But it was Haig-Brown whom I chose to emulate—more soul and less competitive bravado than Wulff. Because I learned my craft of steelhead fly fishing in complete isolation other than books, there was the freedom to experiment as my own heart chose without the coercion of other steelhead anglers to belittle, or otherwise compromise, my choices.

Nevertheless, I knew that Haig-Brown in the 1940s was outside the norm of U.S. steelhead fly-fishing practice in his continued application of tackle and methods learned for Atlantic salmon fishing as a youth in England. I was well aware of the literature, but it seemed to miss the point of the practicality of the older traditions. Furthermore, fly fishing is *supposed* to be an anachronism— a tradition of antiquated tackle choices to otherwise test mental ingenuity. Modern fly-fishing technology has often lost the point. The sport is designed to be difficult without attempting to attract new enthusiasts by dumbing it down, or by making it more "efficient."

The U.S. fly-rod recommendations from the fly-fishing literature regarding steelhead increasingly included shorter rod lengths from 1938 to 1971:

1938, Ray Bergman's *Trout*—nine to nine and a half feet

1946, Frank R. Steel's *Fly Fishing*—nine to nine and a half feet

1948, Syl MacDowell's *Western Angler*—nine to nine and a half feet

1948, Claude M. Kreider's *Steelhead*—nine to nine and a half feet

1952, Enos Bradner's *Northwest Angling*—nine to nine and a half feet with a growing minority using rods of eight to eight and a half feet

1954, Clark C. Van Fleet's, *Steelhead to a Fly*—eight and a half to nine feet

1971, Trey Combs's *The Steelhead Trout*—seven and a half to nine and half feet.

In the 1960s and early 1970s, the steelhead fly-fishing literature sometimes belittled anything longer than eight and a half to nine feet as "unsporting" behemoths. As Trey Combs described in *Steelhead Fly Fishing* (1991), "I recall a famous fishing writer of the period stating that there was no excuse for any rod to be more than eight feet."

When I recommended 10- to 11-foot single-handed rods for larger winter steelhead rivers in an article I originally wrote in 1974 (published as "Fine Techniques of Steelhead Fly Fishing," *Salmon Trout Steelheader*, June–July 1975, and later in *Dry Line Steelhead and Other Subjects* in 1987) along with the consideration of two-handed rods, it was going against the current. Led by the exploits of Lee Wulff with Atlantic salmon, John Fennelly in *Steelhead Paradise* (1963) described how he first came to the Skeena River drainage in 1951 with a seven-foot fly rod. However, it proved of little use on the big waters and in subsequent trips he came to rely on a nine-and-a-half-footer. Nevertheless, he described two-handed rods as recommended for Atlantic salmon rivers as "old-fashioned 'telegraph poles'" when it came to steelhead.

By 1967, even Roderick Haig-Brown had shifted to smaller rods for steelhead. In "Winter Steels and the Fly" (*Outdoor Life*, November 1967, Volume 140, Number 5), he advocated a nine-foot rod with a 9-weight line, and as early as *Fisherman's Summer* (1959) he advocated an eight-foot four-ounce bamboo rod for dry-fly work on Vancouver Island summer steelhead rivers. While I found the latter a practical tool for summer fish on smaller rivers, for winter steelhead I chose to continue the vein of experiment chosen by the younger Haig-Brown of the 1940s.

When my 1975 article came out, the only two-handed rods available in the U.S. were those from used bamboo rod dealers with quite high price tags (remember that $300 to $400 then equaled more than $1,000 now). They had remained in use on Canadian Atlantic salmon rivers through the 1950s and into the 1960s. I longed for one. Sometimes I fished the 12½-foot Payne my friend Dave Ulrich decided to purchase—and I could only envy—in 1974. It was great fun to wade the Washougal River clumsily trying to teach ourselves to spey cast with a two-handed fly rod—the likes of which may not have been seen on the rivers of Oregon and Washington since Rudyard Kipling fished the Clackamas in 1889. In 1975, Dave purchased a 14-foot Thomas that he liked even better.

I later learned that in 1977 Chuck Doke of Portland persuaded Hardy to make him the complete three-rod set of 12-foot single-handed cane rods A.H.E. Wood used with his greased-line method on the River Dee in Scotland. Chuck let me cast one of these when we met one day on the Washougal.

However, the small rivers I typically fished did not justify a rod longer than 10½ feet, so I lived well enough without a two-handed rod until 1989 when The Orvis Company offered me the gift of a 13½-footer. I was traveling more and occasionally fished large rivers in winter where a double-handed rod had obvious advantages for fishing a floating line and the large 3/0 to 6/0 flies I preferred in those conditions.

By 1989, many Northwest steelhead anglers had shifted to increasingly long rods. This included growing numbers who were using two-handers on our larger rivers. Mike Maxwell of Vancouver, British Columbia, was teaching a renaissance in spey casting on Canadian steelhead rivers by the 1980s. Spey casting had been part of Mike's angling instruction as a youth in England.

Al Buhr of Salem, Oregon, was in the forefront of bringing two-handed rods to U.S. steelhead rivers. He began making his own by piecing together parts of the longest glass and graphite rods he could find for fishing the Santiam and the Snake rivers in the early 1980s. By the mid-1980s, Al was consulting with Jimmy Green to improve on two-handed rod design and use.

But I was no longer young. I quickly learned the humility of "you can't teach an old dog new tricks." Although I taught myself to spey cast with a single-handed rod in the late 1970s by following a verbal description provided by Haig-Brown (combined with some photographs of him doing so single-handed), for some reason when I used two hands it would not come together. Although I could spey cast a sufficient length of line to fish effectively, it sometimes took me half a dozen casts to do so if there was any adversity—even a minor breeze. What's worse, it never felt comfortable. I was denied the joy of the casting–wading rhythm that had been integral to my fishing.

By the last year Dec and I were together on the Grande Ronde in 1994, he was a master of spey casting. As I watched Dec's grace, line easily curling out 100 feet, I asked if he could perhaps analyze my own ineffectual spey casting. By then I also had a lovely, limber 13½-foot Sage for a 7/8 line for summer and fall water on larger rivers. Without belittling me, he gently tried to show me how to improve. Nevertheless, as so often when it came to direct teaching, I could not pick it up. Mine was a long history of learning by trial and error, not through word or example.

In the spring of 1995, Mike Garoutte and I traveled from La Grande, Oregon, to meet Dec for a couple of days together on the Skykomish, Sauk and Skagit. Mike had shifted to a two-handed rod and had picked up spey casting very quickly thanks to Dec's example on the Grande Ronde. Fishing was not good. Mike was the only one to briefly hook a fish. It was a typical Puget Sound spring: windy, cold and wet. I gamely stuck with the two-hander, determined to learn the graceful ease of the spey rhythm but absolutely failed.

This was particularly frustrating. My own writings more than 20 years earlier had spurred the initial interest in and gradual acceptance of long fly rods again on steelhead rivers. Mike had become a master of the two-handed spey cast within months while I had struggled with it for years. I felt like a broken little boy and sometimes swore I would not touch a two-handed rod ever again. Why go through this frustration? I had caught steelhead, well over 1,000 of them, with long, single-handed rods and a floating line for 34 years.

But I could not let it go. The vision of watching Dec and Mike fish with such grace and ease kept my stung pride in check. And there was something else—the example of Dec's perpetual joy of heart, no matter the difficulty of something he had set his mind to. More than anything else I tried to learn that invulnerable joy that shielded Dec.

My own enthusiasm had spiraled into despondency as the list of rivers nearly vacant of wild fish grew. In fact, between 1994 and 1998, I had nearly ceased fishing for steelhead. I fished only during two seven-week stints with the Wild Salmon Center's Russian–American scientific expeditions to study steelhead on Russia's Kamchatka Peninsula, and on the occasional local outing to renew old friendships. The loss of wild steelhead in the rivers where I had spent my youth and young adulthood with such joy had virtually broken me inside. I could no longer justify fishing over such depletion of a wild resource. In that loss I had become a nomad, looking for some less fragile meaning to life than steelhead and steelhead rivers.

In an odd irony, in Dec Hogan's last few years before leaving the Skagit River when its steelhead runs finally plummeted into depletion, I ended up moving there. My wife and I were searching for a rural home outside Seattle's sprawl; she to have seclusion and chickens, and me to find some proximity to Nature and inner peace after having left behind my Washougal River cabin in the summer of 1996. We had not found what we wanted after several months of looking.

...

It was one of those rare early springs with more sun than rain. By St. Patrick's Day of 1998, the wild cherry were in full blossom and the morning sunlight drew me to my first day of fishing in months. After several hours of lazy fishing along the broad gravel bars of the Sauk River, I decided to explore the Skagit. I came on a "House for Sale" sign leading down a gravel road through a tunnel of 100-year-old maple limbs draped in moss. Inquisitive, I followed. There it was: seclusion itself—an old dilapidated house, modest acreage, view of the valley hills, and 100 yards from the doorstep perhaps the largest remaining river in the lower 48 with near pristine water quality. More to the point, it was in our price range.

The daily proximity to one of the Skagit's immense steelhead runs could not be ignored. That winter I fished almost daily. My body finally came to understand the needs of double-handed spey casting using a 15-foot two-handed rod built for me by master craftsman, Kerry Burkheimer. It was my first winter in nearly 15 years of once again experiencing the gift of remarkable steelhead fishing. It had been a long time, and it quickly died. The wild steelhead throughout Puget Sound crashed the very next winter, 1999–2000. The depletion has persisted to this day with the imminent probability that Puget Sound steelhead will be listed under the Endangered Species Act, just as had occurred with the steelhead I had left on the rivers of my youth, the Wind and the Washougal.

. . .

Most people come to steelhead fly fishing as a test of overcoming its notoriety for difficulty. The sport would not have the same fascination if it came easily. For the same reason, those who succeed tend to be driven personalities who express themselves in differing ways. Some steelhead fly fishers, as with some mountaineers, tend to eventually become like seekers of religious experience—hair shirts, seclusion in caves or huts, distancing from the accepted norm of social inclusion to find some higher meaning. For others, steelhead fishing is strictly the quest of the thrill of the great yank, forever unexpected, yet forever anticipated, from an animal concealed by the blank stare of broad water. There are others who are purely competitive and who like the challenge of equaling or bettering what those who have preceded them have done . . . strictly a numbers game of notches on the handle of gun. And there are still others who simply enjoy being a part of small circle of people who pursue something difficult. Those who have been steelhead fly fishers for 40 to 50 years may have gone through this entire gamut of motives.

I had a friend who came to take up, excel at, and then cease to fly fish for steelhead—all within the span of 10 years. He was a remarkably gifted man, a fine athlete, and artist in oils, charcoal, pen and ink. He was a decade older than I; watching me fly fish had been his initial impetus to shift from bait fishing to fly fishing. It was staggering to watch him exceed facets of the sport beyond what I was capable of. And then he simply walked away from steelhead rivers, just like Jim Brown and Rocky Marciano walked away from professional football and boxing at the peak of their games.

I had not seen my friend in three to four years. Then one day he bicycled past the soccer field where my son was playing. I hailed him. We exchanged trivialities for a few minutes and then got down to what needed to be said. He explained it something like this:

I took up steelhead fly fishing because of the thrill—I used to see it on your face when you would tell me of your most recent experience when we saw each other along the river. Bait fishing was not providing that kind of thrill.

After the Russians put Sputnik up, there was a great interest in stimulating scientific advancement. As part of that the Coast Guard sent missions to the Antarctic. I volunteered to be a part of that as a skin diver. We went out beneath the ice in wetsuits to collect differing sets of information. Every dive was a thrill—life and death separated by a fine line.

When I married, I wanted to sky dive, but my wife made me promise to wait until after the children were raised and out of the house. Three years ago our last went to college. I reminded her of that promise. So I began sky diving at age 50. I have now made more than 200 jumps. Every jump out that plane door is a guaranteed thrill. Three times I have had to cut myself out of my harness due to tangled shrouds in order to effectively release my emergency chute.

It used to be that steelhead fly fishing provided all I needed. It did not happen every day, but there were many days when steelhead could provide that level of thrill—not life and death, but that same sort of emotional jolt. But steelhead have become so few that the thrills became too few and too far between.

My friend could not have known how grateful I was for that conversation. I had long admired him for so completely excelling at whatever he decided to do. But I had never really understood him. Despite the many times we sat and talked along the river for an hour or so to compare our steelhead experiences over the days or weeks in between visits—or some of the interesting observations of fish, animals, or bird life we had made—he knew me more than I had ever known him. My friend was driven by the sheer power of that one moment of electric thrill a steelhead can somehow generate.

I remember the first steelhead I ever caught. I sat on the river bank and shook for 15 minutes. Two years later I hooked my first on a fly and sat and shook all over again. The quest for that repeated thrill drove me to the river an average of 300 days each year in my first 10 years after moving to the Washougal River in 1970. For love of steelhead, I was a mess.

During our first autumn together on the Grande Ronde, Dec Hogan was a vision of a man in the midst of having been bitten by steelhead thrill. It burst out of him, hovering like an aura, radiating like the flame of the Holy Ghost over each of the 12 Apostles. I wanted to laugh with him, cry for him, and slap his back twice—once to congratulate him, and once to bring him to his senses not unlike the birthing of an infant held by the feet and still covered in his mother's blood.

A passion for steelhead is a hard ride. It is all consuming. God help the woman, man, or child who hopes to compete for some small claim to the passion in the angler so stricken.

Be that as it may, my hard ride is over. My love of steelhead and steelhead rivers remains, but it is no longer one of great passion. It is tempered by a profound sorrow of having lost something so great that it somehow freed me to larger visions. Janis Joplin once sang a song whose lyrics were likely beyond her youthful knowing before she died: "Freedom's just another word for nothin' left to lose. . . ." Then again, maybe she did know. If there is one vision that symbolizes passion, it is that of Janis Joplin . . . fists clenched, breasts flying at any constraint, hair a whirling frenzy.

I remember the vision of a friend on a small, unheralded tributary of the Skeena River in October of 1985. In five days of fishing together on the Copper River, he had effectively risen many large steelhead, somewhere around 40. He was just learning to fish surface flies after several years of catching steelhead subsurface. Up they came, mouths gaping wide—some of them chasing across the river with rise after rise. He could not contain his excitement. Most of the rises were missed or those hooked somehow lost. He stood on one rock and missed or lost nine large steelhead in the space of 15 minutes.

On our last day we diverted to a smaller stream in hopes that a change in water might break his spell. As his Bomber waked across the glacial-tint of turquoise water, a steelhead took it down with such violent suddenness that it hooked itself well. A very large and very bright steelhead tumbled end-over-end through the air and shot out the tailout of the pool with the line noisily melting off the reel spindle. Suddenly the line-to-backing knot somehow wedged in the cobble of the tailing's shallows. The ratcheting reel went quiet. There was a brief moment of forest silence in the gray drizzle of rain. Then he went into dementia—every pent-up passion of his 35 years loosed. He twirled in frenzied pirouettes, his 10-foot graphite rod beating the water into a 20-foot circle of white froth in the perfect storm of himself, his wool hat flying from his head in the self-inflicted melee as it floated away, gradually sinking into the opaque blue water. His curses had been in perfect time with each hit of the rod on the water—the precise words unimportant and long ago forgotten, but a veritable song. He finally stopped, breathing heavily from the incredible exertion of the episode. I had never seen the equal of the physical intensity that came out of him, save for some of those performances by Janis Joplin under a full head of steam.

To know real freedom one has to lose everything that had provided one's past base for meaning. Freedom is not a cuddly friend. It is the awe of having fallen off into nothingness. It is what Zen and Taoist monks have found, and what ancient shamans once found in their psychotic flights into the universe. The hard part is to come back—what the early astronauts called re-entry. Re-entry means to try to find meaning once you have seen the vast fearful awe of complete freedom at the end of passion's rocket ride.

For me, the meaning to life is no longer that of steelhead fishing, but of trying to save steelhead populations and steelhead rivers. For more than 30 years, steelhead provided me love for life in a culture where I could not otherwise find it. Steelhead gave me all they had to give. My life was consumed with taking what they provided. In my loss of that, in my facing the awe of freedom's void, I have come back with the duty of a mission: to try to give back to steelhead some small semblance of what they gave me. It all began with a passion for an animal, for the sport of pursuing that animal, and it has ended very different than it began.

In this book, Dec Hogan has written about his passion for steelhead. I would have been disappointed if he had chosen otherwise. It is the best of who Dec is—a man whose joy for the sport remains forever undiminished. Dec is one of the true masters of steelhead fly fishing, and is perhaps the best one-on-one instructor I have ever met in conveying the ability to successfully catch steelhead. What has made him so effective at conveying this ability in 15 years of guiding has been his aura of impassioned enthusiasm. Time and again in our few years on the Grande Ronde, it was Dec's clients who were invariably the high rods. It occurred too often to be luck. I came to understand that Dec was somehow able to enlarge his own aura of enthusiasm to include even the most unlikely personality to succeed. It was solely his own enthusiasm that kept his clients on the water that extra hour, or to make the extra effort of a difficult wade, or the necessary persistence with a surface fly to bring his anglers back to the lodge at the evening table bubbling over with the thrill of their successes.

Those who learn this enthusiasm, this passion for steelhead, will not only succeed but will likely excel in this sport of a thousand casts. However, as the saying goes, beware of what you wish for— it can be a hard ride. It's a sport that can both fill and break your heart.

I leave the rest to Dec.

BILL McMILLAN
CONCRETE, WASHINGTON
January 2006

A MIGRATORY
WONDER

BY THOMAS R. PERO

SECONDS AFTER 10 P.M. ON A SOFT EVENING IN EARLY JULY, as the amber light dims to satin gray, an insignificant blob of transparent orange plasma rises from the darkness of an underwater gravel cave. For the first time in its life, it kisses the transparent ceiling of its home. The creature looks absurd. Its stark eyes are enormous, wildly out of proportion with its gelatinous body, the size of a pencil eraser. Yet a feeble spinal cord is visible. Weightless and helpless against the hard-pressing current, the tiny blob panics. Instantly, it dives back to the safe haven it has known since the summer solstice, weeks earlier, when it struggled to break through the rubbery coating of its self-contained food capsule. The egg was one of more than 3,000 its mother—a lustrous 14-pound silver female steelhead—shot spasmodically into the shifting gravel on a sunny spring day amidst an orgy of churning silver and red bodies straining for immortality in the glass-clear current of this Pacific Northwest coastal river.

Mykiss is lucky. Already half the eggs formed in his mother's womb are dead. Some escaped the drifting clouds of milt emitted from the gang of male steelhead, tumbling to the cold, rocky river bottom unfertilized. Some were eaten by voracious juveniles of their own species or adult trout before they reached the gravel. Some were swept downstream to oblivion. Some never hatched, smothered by silt, covered in fungus, or left to freeze in the killing air by a sudden episode of receding water. A number of his potential brothers and sisters had been born with strangely twisted bodies—scoliosis—the unhappy consequence of bad genes. These deformed fishes would soon perish. Others emerged in water that grew too warm. Their bodies developed too quickly, not having enough time to form adequately. They had fewer vertebrae than Mykiss. These too were doomed, as were the alevins destined to emerge from the gravel later, in August or even September: They will not be strong enough to survive the flood.

At first, with his yolk sac still attached, the alevin was highly vulnerable. Instinctively, he gravitated away from the light, keeping his underside pinned against the gravel, head facing into the micro-current. Water passing through his mouth and gills brought diatoms and other microscopic food into his developing stomach, triggering the desire to ingest nourishment.

Day by day, Mykiss grows bolder. Forays to the surface and explorations outside the egg pocket where he first felt life are more frequent, although still under the cover of darkness. He is a cautious little creature. Touches of color begin to appear on his hardening body—green on his topside or dorsal, a blush of silver along his flanks. One day a spot appears. Two days later, another. He is looking less awkward. He is slowly absorbing the shrinking orange yolk sac that has nourished him for months. Mykiss is becoming skinnier and longer. By early August his family lineage is obvious: He looks like a sliver of rainbow trout, complete with faint red stripe, spotted back, miniature fins, and bulging eyes at the front of a tiny head. Now he is a fry.

His newfound identity comes at a perfect time: the convergence of the lunar and solar cycles. Summer days in the northern rain forest are long and golden. The earth is warm. Everything is blooming. The sun streams through lush, green stands of vine maple and alder, spotlighting the water in moving mosaics of light. The river is alive. Mayfly nymphs and caddisfly larvae writhe in the gurgling riffles. Long-legged waterbugs skate across slick shallows. Mottled-winged caddisflies ricochet across the glassine pool. The bubbly flow is filled with an endless stream of tidbits with good things to eat. For Mykiss, his eyes fixed on the gleaming surface, the temptation is too great to resist. His compulsion is to eat. He spends more and more time in the open during daylight. Still, he dares not to go far. He stays in water only an inch or two deep, around rocks the size of golf balls. He meets other juvenile steelhead, some from his own redd, others from nearby. He meets other fishes: coho salmon about his size but noticeably different. At almost an inch in length, Mykiss can outswim the

salmon, even though they were spawned before he was, last winter. They are less agile. They move awkwardly, their tails propelling their bodies like stiff rudders. Mykiss's lithe body moves sinuously like a snake's. The salmon crowd together in concentrations.

One evening in the reflection of the Sturgeon Moon, Mykiss is foraging on the periphery of a school of coho fry. He sees very well at night. Without warning, the shallow water erupts as a predator a thousand times his size crashes jaws-open into the school, sending the sheet of fry fleeing in terror. It's a spawned-out cutthroat trout, emaciated and starving, who just finished spawning. It hits the shallows so hard that it beaches itself momentarily before flopping back and disappearing with a noisy splash into the night.

Despite the terrifying episode, day and night Mykiss and his spawnmates stick to the river's wavering edges. They hover over small cobble, drawn to darker rather than lighter backgrounds. This affords them protection against dreaded enemies from above—elegantly stalking herons, dipping and dodging water ouzels, dive-bombing kingfishers darting through the

willows in a chattering blue whir—but not from bottom-lurking sculpins, seen frequently with salmon fry sticking out of their horny toad-like mouths.

To make it though their first summer, the little steelhead must have a home. Some of them pick placid backwaters, others dancing riffles or streamy glides. The character of the water they choose determines what they will eat during their time in fresh water, and perhaps how they will key to food for the rest of their lives. The fish taking up residence in moving water feed on aquatic insects drifting with the current, dashing up, being carried, then wheeling around to the bottom and refuge. Mykiss chooses a more solitary spot at the shallow side of a pool near a bank, where the tips of long green grasses trail gently in the water. The water is quieter here. He sees out of his water world with exceptional clarity. He eats some of the same mayflies and caddisflies, but also learns in short order to relish the shiny ants and juicy inchworms that announce their arrival with a delicate dimple.

Whatever their feeding strategy, the juvenile steelhead share one trait: they all look up at the water's surface, toward the atmosphere that is the source of ever-changing light and the source of their next mouthful. Practically every hour of every day during the coming weeks and months, they take sustenance through this magic looking glass.

Mykiss successfully makes it through his first summer, one of only 300 remaining from the original 1,500 that emerged from the gravel. By the autumn solstice, he has doubled in size. He is stronger and surer. But his placid pool is a place of low energy in summer, an hospitable habitat offering few clues to the coming cataclysm.

The last week in October the heavens collide and the rains start. The sky wails for days, unceasing. The river rises, triggering the young steelhead to migrate. Of his 300 brothers and sisters, 100 swim downstream, toward the broad alluvial riffles of the lower river. They are committing suicide: By the hour

the flow in these once-calm, sweeping bends multiplies in velocity—in 24 hours from 50 cubic feet per second in a stream knee-deep and 20 yards wide to a torrent of 4,000 cfs and 60 yards wide. The current is so swift no human can stand upright in it; the new river is bank-full and a dozen feet deep. The recast river is raging. The wrath of the native people's mythological Thunderbird—high in the snowcapped crags 10,000 feet above the rain forest hurling lightning bolts—plays out his legendary feud with Whale, sending a ferocious wall of brown water carrying giant boulders and trees 10 feet in diameter down to windlashed gray beaches and into the churning whitewater sea beyond.

Then the violence subsides as the storm passes. The river recedes. In the steaming morning sunshine, a raven's guttural call echoes through the dank forest. Thousands of dead juvenile steelhead and salmon fry hang like glittering ornamental tinsel from streamside alder and cottonwood shoots, their high-and-dry branches still bent downstream in tribute to the river's supremacy, festooned with sodden clumps of yellow and green leaves. Two days later not one fish remains, a feast for the river's alert avian cleaning crew.

Mykiss fares better. During summer his body has grown hydrodynamic. He sports a distinctly spotted, white-tipped dorsal. His adipose fin is outlined in black. His head is slightly blunt, eyes bulging. In the face of rising water, he makes a fateful choice to swim upstream. He does not make this decision capriciously, as an individual in historic isolation from this population. Generations before him who turned into the flow and lived to spawn successfully in numbers greater than steelhead that went in other, less-rewarding directions have armed Mykiss with a built-in genetic compass—Evolution 101. As the river floods and the channel widens, he stays course in the shallows, negotiating tumbling sticks and debris, passing rushing tributaries large and small. Instinctively, the diminutive steelhead makes his way progressively upstream along thin edges of current. Midstream the boiling, dirty current surges. He swims indomitably. He is moving headfirst against a rapidly rising river toward safe haven high in

the system, where the gradient is steeper and where large strewn boulders anchoring the cobble streambed are less affected by the volatility of sudden hydraulic hurricanes. In five days, Mykiss travels an astonishing 32 miles. He is only three and a half inches long. And he is not alone—he and his 200 redd-mates are part of a massive hidden upstream migration of fry seeking winter security far from their natal gravel; some relocate as far as 50 miles from where they hatched. Many more perish than survive the journey. Now they are only 40.

Mykiss finds himself up a narrow canyon in a strange tributary in a miniature pool scoured by decades of mountain runoff water rushing under and around the fallen trunk of a half-hollow cedar, long ago collapsed in a carpet of sword fern. The flow is high and green, slightly cloudy. Overhead a thick canopy of Sitka spruce, western hemlock, and red cedar dampens the rain and diffuses the seasonally dimming sun. The water is cold and getting colder. He is not alone. Near a tangle of underwater exposed roots lie a half dozen charcoal-colored coho salmon wearing botches of white fungus. Mykiss smells them, and it excites him. The eggs in the bellies of the females—strays at the mercy of the current—will be his last easy nourishment for a long time. When the spawned-out coho lie dead and rotting in the frigid flow, his metabolism slows to a virtual halt. He burrows slowly into the gravel substrate, finding comfortable sanctuary in pockets among the rocks. He settles into one of these fish apartments in nearly total darkness. During the days ahead, his body temperature lowers, degree by degree. He grows still. It is December. For the next two months, Mykiss gains no weight. His metabolic supply barely meets the demand during this time of relative famine. Essentially, he hibernates.

Overhead the forest that is part of the steelhead's world is plunged into the great winter water cycle. An ancient spruce 23 feet around at the base and soaring 158 feet in elevation stands over the stream, its roots covered with fern and fungal mats. Club moss hangs like green witches' hair in garlands from rough, scalloped bark. The spruce has stood sentinel for 600 years, a long life for any tree in the ever-shifting riparian zone. Day after day sheets of rain driven inland from the roiled Pacific pound the dark wooded valley. High upstream where the treeline stops and the wind-ravaged, nutrient-deprived Douglas firs clinging to granite resemble Bonsai miniatures, the precipitation turns to swirling crystal, piling blanket upon blanket of snow on to the glaciers where the river is born.

. . .

On a day in late February the renegade sun reappears. It casts a thermal spotlight on the gigantic spruce, the first sunlight in weeks. The waves excite the molecules of ocean-borne water clinging to every needle, igniting the process of photosynthesis. The evaporating moisture steams upward toward the blue sky. In one day, the enormous pine transpires more than a ton of water into the atmosphere. More than 100 inches of rain has fallen.

As winter wanes, daylight grows longer and stronger. The water warms. The tiny fish that imprisoned themselves several months ago now begin appearing infrequently during the day—one popping out of the gravel here, another from near a large boulder over there. But the pool that was 200 feet long in full flow when Mykiss and his cohorts arrived last November is now shrunken and clear, Lucite-still. The fish are confined to a 50-foot puddle and a barely moving riffle upstream; downstream is blocked. By day a pair of water ouzels incessantly scours the shallows and riffled pockets for fish, bobbling and diving from their moss-rock perches, feeding themselves as their reproductive time nears. The 17 steelhead fry must survive. To live they must eat. Those who

decide to venture from cover only when night envelopes the rivulet are safest, while the one who risks feeding in daylight—to grab a tempting *Baetis* mayfly one bright March morning, for instance—grows a bit faster. He develops a higher fat store. He gives himself a head start on the coming spring and summer growing season.

On a spring evening, young Mykiss feels restless. He is keenly alert. His home is filled with rushing, well-oxygenated water. Food is plentiful. He swims downstream out of the pool and disappears around the bend, gone forever. Three miles downstream, where the tributary joins a larger stream, he comes upon a startling scene: an active spawning bed occupied by several late-winter-run steelhead. He sees other parr hovering about the periphery. Many look like him. Others look like miniature adults with the distinctive outline of a steelhead and black bands on their tails. Their eyes are smaller in relation to their bodies. Their flanks display dues hues of purple and pink. A touch of silver is noticeable on their gill plates.

Mykiss has learned to be wary of anything larger than he is—anything that might eat him. But he quickly realizes the attention of his larger cousins is not on him. The oversized parr carry the genetic capacity to grow rapidly, a robust lineage that drives them to sexual precociousness. Most have viable milt and the desire to join in on the action. They likely were spawned the previous year in January or February and then hatched in March. This jumpstart gave them a big advantage over those later-spawned fish that didn't become alevins until July or August. They are large for their age, and require only one or two years to mature, although most take two. Despite their advanced development, none of these juveniles is ready to migrate to sea. They are too high in the watershed. They still have another year in fresh water before they move onto the next phase of life and become smolts.

Mykiss does not feel their compulsion to spawn. He moves in behind the mounds of kicked-up gravel to satisfy another craving: food. As the nine-pound female steelhead excavates gravel, she creates drift—insects of all sizes peppering the mists of sediment fines and algae washed loose and drifting downstream in the current. Mykiss finds the bugs easy pickings. He relishes the stray eggs, including a few from a nearby cutthroat redd.

When the April spawning party is over, Mykiss continues his search for summer habitat—a place where he'll be safe during the coming months and enjoy a steady stream of nourishment. He selects a pool where large speckled mayflies are hatching. Chunky chocolate and orange *Pteronarcys* stoneflies are crawling out of their shucks on waterworn, blackened volcanic rocks. The river has warmed to 45 degrees. His metabolism accelerates. Sometime in May, after three or four weeks of continuous feeding, he builds up sufficient fat reserves to allow him to resume growing. He's a solid little fish now, his length increasing steadily by a quarter of an inch with each passing month. His head is noticeably longer. His eyes are less pronounced.

Mykiss has survived the hardest time. But this is still an important summer. And our little steelhead and his friends are living lavishly. They have lots of food and they are good swimmers. They're feeding on a plethora of aquatic insects—mayflies, caddisflies,

stoneflies, midges—and weeks-old juvenile fish now emerging in late May and early June, including the occasional steelhead. A tremendous range of food is available. They are opportunistic. Whatever they can eat, they will eat: tadpoles, tiny frogs, inchworms, beetles, grasshoppers, and—with the first big burst of warmth—carpenter ants flying around in swarms. At times the sky seems to be raining food.

Mykiss's stomach is nearly always full. He's large enough now that most other juvenile fishes don't view him as prey, but he must still watch out for the occasional ravenous cutthroat with an appetite that outpaces its ability to swallow. Over the course of spring and summer, Mykiss grows from three and a half inches to six inches long, almost double in length. There's another interesting dynamic.

Suddenly he decides to move downstream. Perhaps he is curious about whether there are more spawning fish. Perhaps it's a social calling too, to seek larger juveniles and adult steelhead. He senses that in some way he is related to them.

Now the torrents of spring have subsided. The river has dropped to its benign summer level. By July the water temperature reaches 50 degrees Fahrenheit. By August, 55 to 57 degrees—even 60—feels good to Mykiss. At this deliciously warm time of year, all the young steelhead are very active, feeding and swimming, swimming and feeding. They're social and gregarious, not as interactive as salmon, but nonetheless excited. They nip at each other. They chase each other. Although they are competing for food, at times in groups of three or four they line up

in a riffle. At other times they line up behind each other, learning to hold positions in the moving water the way a school of tuna or mackerel swims, or geese fly. They use the hydraulics—the velocity and subtleties of flow—to station themselves behind and in front of each other. They hold for a minute, sometimes only seconds, before breaking rank. They're too antsy to sit in one place for too long, with the exuberance of a puppy or a wide-eyed child. Freed from their winter confinement, the growing steelhead now enjoy freedom to explore hundreds of square feet of water, trading places back and forth between channels.

Mykiss goes swimming. He heads upstream. He's on a mission for food—every minute. That is the key to his youthful behavior. While sex will drive him at a mature age of five or six when he comes back from the ocean, an insatiable craving for calories is driving him now. During this second summer of life, he's constantly on the prowl for food. Thus far his diet has been a random mixture of aquatic and terrestrial insects—anything that lives in the woods and falls out of the trees and is awkward in the water makes a tempting target. But it takes him dozens of miniscule mayflies to obtain the same amount of protein he gets from sucking under a single kicking grasshopper. Economy of effort is important in the wild. No one

has to teach him this.

Mykiss turns up a small cascading creek and hits the jackpot. On the upstream side of a cluttered heap of old and new beaver sticks partially blocking the creek's width, a caterpillar nest hangs from an overhead alder sapling. No sooner does he pull into the diminutive pool but one of the resident caterpillars drops onto the surface with a *plop*. It's round, fat and puffy, and wiggles in a seductively helpless manner. Mykiss makes a mad dash for the squirming creature and gobbles it greedily. The terrestrial landscape is so large and the aquatic so small that for climbing, crawling, clinging insects it's like trying to cross a gravel road—the bugs are continually falling off the leaves while trying to get to the other side. When Mykiss was in the wider river, he fed mostly on aquatic insects, because it required extra effort for him to hang out along the edges searching for larger food. It also exposed him to greater danger and made him nervous. Now he sits serenely under a glassine conveyor belt of morsels that never stops delivering.

By his second October, Mykiss is seven inches long. He has prospered from a bountiful summer. Now with colder nights, the bounty of food has diminished. Far fewer terrestrial insects are falling in the water and drifting down to him. He shifts the bulk of his daily consumption to aquatic insects, and is particularly aroused by the outsized October caddisflies with their burnt-orange bodies skating across and enlivening the pools each afternoon.

The young steelhead troupe is down to 15 members. One was lost to disease. A tall and leggy heron picked off another. The survivors are well-prepared to endure this year's autumn coming flood. They made it through their first one when they were frail and vulnerable. Now they are in nursery habitat of their own choosing and an environment to which they have acclimated. They have a choice: stay put or move. If the choice is migration, do they go downstream or upstream? Their instincts might tell them that the place where they managed to survive their first winter wasn't adequate—they must prepare themselves better. The carrying capacity might be

it's his refuge now. November brings another round of spawn-laden coho salmon to him. He is considerably larger and more dominant this year. He is swifter. When other steelhead parr wander into his territory, he wastes no time aggressively chasing them away, sometimes even eating them. This winter he continues feeding. He doesn't hibernate as he did during the first flood, cowering among the dark spaces in the gravel. Now he's out and about during daylight. He still relies strongly on log jams and boulders for cover but, spurred by increasing testosterone, he forages actively. Along with feeding on stray eggs, he turns on other fish that are also feeding on eggs. He continues building muscle and fat reserves. When the spawning coho are dead and gone, he selects a nocturnal habitat. He doesn't want to expose himself during the day continually. He has observed other fish leave the

limited. There might be too many fish within that piece of habitat, with a whole new crop of fish hatched this year joining them. Each one is a competitor, for space and for food. The thing Mykiss and his friends have going for them is their size. The adults are finished spawning and have disappeared. Nearly all the older parr became smolts and swam to sea. Now Mykiss and his friends are tops. They are temporal princes of the realm.

Mykiss decides not to embark on another long migration. Instead, he feels safe in the tributary he discovered last summer. It was his meal ticket then;

gravel and never come back—a cause for alarm in his unrelenting eat-or-be-eaten world. Mykiss himself has had a close encounter or two by making the mistake of carelessly poking his head out to see what was going on during the day. When a 15-inch cutthroat shot right at him, instead of engulfing Mykiss, the predator ate the parr directly behind him. The experience was indelible. It didn't quell his curiosity, but it reinforced the vital lesson of risk versus reward.

Compared with last winter's sullen time of reclusive fasting, Mykiss's diet is markedly expanded. He has developed a taste for sculpins. He knocks bugs off

rocks. And he has learned to root around for case-spinning caddisflies, sticking his nose into the slim crevices between rocks and hammering away to get at the tasty larvae. Best of all are the periwinkles, which he roots out tail-up and nose-down, with his sides glinting like a whitefish. He devours each crunchy periwinkle, case and all, digesting the good stuff, and leaving the case for excrement.

. . .

The gold-green blush of the cottonwoods and the alders and the melody of the song sparrow signal the arrival of another spring. Mykiss feels different. He senses that he is no longer where he's supposed to be. He feels trapped. He has a yearning to leave this

place. The instinct to travel becomes overwhelming.

During these last several weeks of warming water temperatures, growing daylight, and renewed stirrings of life in and out of the river, Mykiss has added a full inch to his length. He is now a lean and streamlined eight inches. His head is shaped like a bullet. His tail is firm and narrow, his fins pronounced and triangular. His back is darker. His glands excrete a chemical substance called guanine below his skin, masking the vertical-bar mottled markings and scattered spots that helped camouflage him in his freshwater sanctuary with a fine silvery coating—looking as if it were delicately spray-painted on. His scales loosen, some falling off in anticipation of dramatic spurts of growth to come.

The physical transformation is startling. Nature is preparing him for a new life in a whole new world.

On the night of April 10, under a dark sliver-moon sky and triggered by a warming freshet, he begins his journey. As he descends the tiny headwater creek, gradually making his way over its pebbly riffles, he meets another steelhead smolt. They become traveling partners. They are in no great rush, swimming a couple hundred yards and then pausing for an hour or two in a comfortable lee of a current-splitting basalt boulder, under a curtain of shimmering bubbles. During the next few days, they are joined along the way by four others, all silvery like Mykiss and all driven by the same cellular wanderlust. The half-dozen young steelhead share a bond. They are survivors. They are the precious distillation of nature's cruel crucible. They are the future of this vanishing race of noble sea-going fishes.

Two miles from where Mykiss set out last week, the group of smolts enters a larger tributary stream leading to the river, still some 14 miles downstream. The stream runs 10 to 20 feet wide, several feet deep, and filled with medium-size boulders and branches clogged with mats of gray and brown rotting leaves. It gathers strength from countless rivulets pouring in from the fern-laced banks and from springs bubbling up through watercress. The smolts travel by night, to sleigh-bell choruses of green tree frogs. They are still feeding heartily. They swim past swamps of pink-flowering salmonberry bushes and sprouting green and yellow skunk cabbage. They progress by fits and starts. One week later they hit the main stem of the river. Now it's a race.

Most outmigrating juvenile Pacific salmon, typically smaller than juvenile steelhead, swim downstream tail-first. They back down at a moderate pace. Not steelhead. True to their nature, Mykiss and friends plunge head-first into the green, swirling current of the main river and zoom straight downstream. The first day they clock nine miles, the second day 11. Every now and then one fish takes the lead and the others swim behind—or two take the lead and four ride behind. They switch back and forth, dizzy adolescents on a wild rapid ride. The flow is strong so the going is easy, thanks to this winter's exceptionally deep snowpack and its offspring melt now powering the river toward the Pacific. Last year the smolts wouldn't have had things so easy. Last year's snowmelt was below normal. The schools stopped frequently at the heads of shallower, slower-moving riffles, lying there hungry, waiting for food, unwittingly offering themselves up as prey. This time of year,

otters are teaching their pups how to fish. Spying ospreys circle overhead. And mergansers along the river are hatching hundreds of ducklings. While it's difficult for a merganser to kill a seven- or eight-inch fish, they can do it, particularly when a flock of 15 to 20 birds circles a school of smolts like a commercial purse seiner, forcing little chance of escape. But with this year's swift, steady flow, traversing 40 miles of twisting and turning river, Mykiss and his five traveling companions make it to the estuary alive—almost.

A mile above tidewater one of the smolts—the only one larger than Mykiss—spies a small, brightly colored insect. It's acting oddly, alternately drifting with and struggling against the current. It is enticing. Irresistibly the smolt breaks ranks and grabs the bug. It's so easy to take. The young steelhead that has been the strongest and has survived with relative ease is now a victim of his own prowess. The demonic superbug pulls him across the current against his thrashing will and rudely wrenches him out of the water. Although an invisible force throws the smolt back into the water with a splash, he is scarred by human finger prints. Scales are missing and his organs

smashed. His eyes are popped out and he is bleeding profusely. Mykiss and his fleeing friends can't wait. As they continue swimming downstream they see a few more smolts belly up on the bottom. Nature isn't always predictable; sometimes outcomes are random. Not always the largest or strongest survive—the smaller smolts avoided the fisherman's lure because they weren't quite as aggressive.

The school hits the estuary running. And they are stopped cold. They hit the critical transition zone where fresh water collides with salt. The freshwater current of the river is lighter and stays on top, stratified over the intrusive salt water like a spreading surface apron. The denser salt water lies underneath in the shape of a wedge. The seawater off the mouth of the river is a solution of 30 parts per million salinity. Mykiss can't take it. He has spent every day of his life absorbing fresh water into his tissues and excreting non-essential salts as dilute urine. Straight seawater is toxic—it will suck fresh water out of him and his body will dehydrate. Mykiss is trapped. The salt wedge below forces him to stay in the upper water column along the edges. He's in big trouble.

Waiting for Mykiss is a lethal welcoming committee of gulls, terns, pelicans, cormorants, scoters, and seals. Everyone wants to eat him. While desperately trying to dodge beak and fang, he urinates constantly, trying to rid his body of the additional salt he is taking in through osmosis from the brackish water. Then magic happens. His whole metabolism shifts. His blood chemistry reverses itself. His kidneys start removing salt from his bloodstream in steadily increasing concentrations. Over the course of 24 hours he gradually acclimates—10 parts per million salinity, 12 parts, 15 parts . . . . Upon completion of this extraordinary metamorphosis, Mykiss excretes highly concentrated salt water though his gills and urinary tract while retaining fresh water. His body has become its own miniature desalinization plant. The internal transformation complete, he is now a fully functioning creature of the sea, able to live and breathe in the saltwater environment. The largest ocean on earth beckons. From this moment forward, he is a swimming and eating marine machine.

. . .

Mykiss is swept buoyantly into an amazingly fertile habitat. Long days of bright sunlight have stimulated the coastal shallows. Clouds of microscopic blooming phytoplankton and feeding zooplankton in enormous schools choke the upwelling water. He opens his mouth to an immense marine buffet, sucking water through his gillrakers to filter out the hidden food. He starts swimming north, guided by a combination of genetics, intuition, and a sonar system that remains undeciphered by humans.

During the migration, he encounters many new and interesting things to eat: tiny, inch long, transparent squid, shrimp, barnacle larvae, and orange swarms of tasty larval Dungeness crab. Mykiss spends just enough time in the near-shore area to reach a foot in length. His extended time developing in fresh water gives him an advantage over young chum and pink salmon migrants, for instance, which must spend months instead of weeks nurturing in coastal waters, exposing the vulnerable salmon to near-shore predation for longer periods. Now that he is capable of fending for himself in the open ocean, the young steelhead is drawn by the northward-flowing Alaska Current, carrying nutrient-rich water from the North Pacific Current flowing across the ocean from Asia.

Mykiss sees increasing numbers of fish his size and smaller—schools of other steelhead smolts as well as coho and chinook salmon, all escaping from their rivers and entering Poseidon's domain by the collective millions. In one month he goes from headwater

hermit to socialite of the sea. Many of the other steelhead he passes look odd. They are larger than he is, but they are skinnier and don't appear as fit. Many are missing scales and fins. Mykiss is used to sharing space with wild, quicksilver fish as taut and lean as he, sculpted by the raw elements. Now he is in competition with millions of soft, coddled hatchery fish. They act differently, too. They're in huge, uncoordinated schools of hundreds of individuals while he is in a tight group of several dozen natives from the neighborhood. Mykiss keeps swimming. Within a week, he and his fellow travelers are 500 miles away in the middle of the Alaskan Gyre, a great circular marine current caused by the current they rode here on turning back on itself counterclockwise in the center of the Gulf of Alaska. They spend the summer and early autumn foraging in waters north of 50°N latitude and between 125°W and 165°W longitude. They learn to focus on the strong eddies two to 200 miles across scattered throughout the gulf. The eddies concentrate prey—juvenile rockfishes, northern anchovy, threespine stickleback, Pacific pomfret and smelt, chinook salmon smolts, Pacific herring and sardines, juvenile Atka mackerel spawned in the subarctic coral gardens, and gonatid squid. But the ocean is a brutal environment. One by one, the free-ranging steelhead meet their demise. Some are lost to the powerful currents while others are eaten or wounded. As he has all his life, Mykiss learns from observation to stay away from anything that appears threatening. As always, much of the mortality is chance. And once again, Mykiss is lucky.

In September the waters in the Gulf of Alaska begin to cool. Storms bring intense wind and precipitation that cause downwelling, quickly diminishing levels of topwater nutrients, and sending the pelagic food-chain predators in search of fresh feeding grounds. Mykiss is among them. He heads southeasterly, leaving the chilling waters for temperatures more to his—and his prey's—liking.

. . .

For miles away he hears them. Then he smells them, and finally he see the wakes and the surface commotion caused by the grenadines and northern fur seals and Dall's porpoises—a feast awaits.

Mykiss has survived his first winter at sea. In the fading spring light, thousands of jet-propelled fleshy torpedoes four to eight inches in length suddenly fill Mykiss's overhead world. The vast school of commander or armhook squid stretches more than a mile. In the slanting sun, their topwater forms appear larger than life. Their muscular reddish-brown bodies tinged with iridescence and ivory glow like fiery gems. They are everywhere, blanketing the surface. They are exquisite creatures, with eight arms and two tentacles arranged in pairs. The food-capturing tentacles are covered with 20 rows of suckers—modified into hooks on the females. These ubiquitous animals are carnivorous. Horny beaks kill and tear their prey to pieces. Wing-like rear fins make up half their mantle length. They have an internal balancing organ called a satocyst that aids in their graceful movement while maintaining equilibrium. They have a specialized foot or hyponome that acts as a siphon. It allows them to move by expelling water under pressure—nature's original jet propulsion. This flexible, locomotive strategy controls their dynamic balance. They roam the depths of the Pacific Ocean by day, descending thousands of feet into the abyss. At night they ascend to the surface to feed by starlight.

All the steelhead must do is swim up behind one of these delectable, protein-packed crustaceans and inhale. The sleek little squid are fast, but he is faster. After swallowing each one whole, he takes a satisfying turn down and away, in a slow-motion, predatory pirouette.

The whole ocean is erupting. Mykiss devours nine succulent squid in one hour. His belly is so full

he feels bloated. Tentacles hang from his gullet. He can't fit another. He is thoroughly sated. The water temperature is perfect—warm enough for rapid metabolism but not so warm that precious energy is wasted. His highly efficient digestive system goes to work turning calories to muscle.

. . .

During his first year at sea, Mykiss has grown from a slim, sprite seven inches in length flushed precariously into the treacherous estuary of his birth river to a robust 22-inch oceanic predator in top killing form. He is some 3,000 miles from his natal stream. No species is his equal. He is ecologically and geographically out there. Through a continuum of distant gales and waves, sunshine and calm, he is a singular chrome hunter in a sea of sapphire. He swims a broad longitudinal range—to 150°E on the continental shelf of Asia—but a relatively narrow latitudinal band. He roams from 40°N to 44°N, mostly south of the central and western Aleutians. The swift little fish from the little creek is a world traveler. During the two additional years that Mykiss explores the North Pacific, he approaches the Kamchatka Peninsula of Russia and the Japanese islands. He moves purposefully with the seasons, tracing immense circles over hundreds and thousands of

miles. Because Mykiss cannot regulate his own body temperature, he follows a comfort zone of 45 to 53 degrees Fahrenheit. This sends him northward and westward spring through summer; southward and eastward autumn through winter. Occasionally he encounters schools of Pacific salmon and other solitary steelhead. He sees the spectacle of whales. More than once his length is illuminated by the reflected flames of the aurora borealis.

Like a jaguar in the jungle, Mykiss feeds most actively during periods of low light, when his prey is most exposed. He seldom makes deep vertical dives, preferring to swim and rest in the upper 10 to 30 feet of the stunning clear blue water of the North Pacific— living virtually on the surface just as he did during his freshwater summers. He is majestic. Like a red-tail hawk riding the thermals, he glides gracefully above a third of all the liquid water on the planet, over submerged mountains and ridges and trenches that plunge as far as 35,830 feet into the inky lightless depths.

He is as opportunistic as ever. An indiscriminate mixture of finfishes and squid make up 98 percent of the bulk in his diet, but he'll eat just about anything. On the edge of the Sea of Okhotsk off the Kuril Islands stretching from Hokkaido to the southern tip of Kamchatka, he finds himself looking up at a Tiffany's filigree of thousands of floating butterflies and hawk moths that a violent storm over the water had slammed to their deaths. *Slurp, slurp, slurp*—he savors the exotic treat.

Mykiss is 30 inches long. He is in supreme physical shape: hard thick shoulders, broad shiny sides, vivid white belly, and long Roman gunmetal snout.

His pure white jaws—the lower slightly hooked and curling up—are edged slightly with charcoal. Liquid black opals stare out of lighter recessed eye sockets surrounded by handsome dark accents. His cheeks and nose are elegantly polished in a ragged-edge layer of silver that appears to have been air-brushed on. His gill plates are blushed with faint pink. The upper third of his body including his back is heavily spotted against a background of dark marine gray-green, almost black. The edges of the diamond-shaped scales on this dark surface are touched with silver, creating a latticework effect—when he turns, his whole body shimmers. The radiating rays on his square, compact tail have lines of dark, oval spots, each spoke dressed finely in silver. His fins are sharp and flawless and nearly transparent. Mykss is impeccably dressed for nature's own dazzling black-and-white gala. He is luminescent.

As his third rollicking summer at sea comes to a close, his stirring hormones tell him it's time to come home. His thyroid gland begins producing increasing levels of thyroxine, increasing his heart rate and sending super-oxygenated blood to his muscles to power his drive across the ocean.

His return to the river is no accident—it is what makes steelhead so wondrous. The magnetic iron particles in Mykiss's lateral lines and in his head provide him with a built-in compass to navigate the earth's magnetic field. His migratory map is as dependable as the internal devices that guide a ruby-throated hummingbird from Gaspésie to Guatemala or a monarch butterfly from Mexico to Michigan. Although waves and wind and clouds may send him temporarily off track, it's not for long. The navigational instruments nature provided him are true. He swims during the day, using the sun's position to stay his course. At night he stops or slows, when his movement is primarily by drift or tidal current. By day he swims at a speed of one body length per second. His average straight-line travel from feeding grounds on the high seas back to North America is just over 20 miles per day. He continues feeding voraciously, growing six additional inches and packing on as many pounds from mid-summer through autumn. Over five months, he swims with remarkable precision almost directly back to the point where he left the coast more than half his life ago. Our marathon swimmer hits the continental shelf off British Columbia and then heads south. During the last leg of his journey, his intake of energy shifts from producing stores of fat to growth of his gonads—to producing milt sacs.

As Mykiss makes his way down the coast, his highly sensitive body pumped up by thyroxine detects changing currents, temperatures, and levels of salinity. From freshwater rivers coming off the mountains, a big New Year's storm has pushed broad plumes of silt up to 40 miles offshore. Mykiss notices the water is murkier. It's also noisier and there is more traffic. Along the way other steelhead—all males—have joined him. As they scent exciting mineral traces from their embryonic rivers, they peal off and head inland.

Now his compass is liquid. He is smelling his way home. Every cell in his body is on high alert. Then he senses it: his own river. The moment is electric. There is no mistaking it as he tastes the estuary's unique cocktail of melding waters. The nerves connecting his olfactory lobes with his brain tell Mykiss that he's home. For two changes of tide, he and four other steelhead who share his final destination pace nervously up and down the coast, covering the same several hundred yards. They feel their bodies re-acclimating physiologically to live in fresh water. Their anxiety, however, is more than aqueous re-entry jitters. Three California sea lions, each weighing as much as a torpedo, have formed a triangular trap. Two of the enormous beasts are moving back and forth across the river's outflow, driving their prey toward a third lion that has positioned itself toward shore. To the returning steelhead, caught off-guard from years of foraging relatively attack-free in the spacious clarity of the western North Pacific where they were the piscivorous predator, the stench of the blubbery mammals is terrifying.

There is no turning back. Catching a steelhead is not easy for a sea lion, but the storm runoff makes it difficult for the fish. They can't see any more than two to three feet ahead. The lack of visibility provides the giant mammals an opportunity for success. Mykiss breaks the tension and heads into the murky current like an airplane on autopilot making its final descent through thick fog. His four companions follow. In a flash a lion locks onto one of the steelhead in its savage jaws and takes a murderous bite out of the fish's back, cutting its vertebrae in half and throwing the unfortunate fish three feet into the air in a bloody spray of glistening crimson. The rampaging lions bob to the roily surface simultaneously and start talking excitedly among themselves in deep guttural yelps, a primordial celebration of carnivores under the Wolf Moon.

Mykiss powers up the oncoming flow, away from the deadly gauntlet of sea lions, only to face another obstacle: monofilament screens called gill nets, placed strategically on the inside of shallow bends to

intercept steelhead swimming upstream to spawn. A fish comes upon the net, 30 feet long by perhaps eight feet deep, contracting and expanding in the current like a sheet in air unfurling in slow motion, suspended from the surface of the water by battered Styrofoam floats. The fish attempts to pass though the net, poking its head into the mesh. When it tries to back out the strong, thin filaments snag its gill covers. The ensnared fish tries to break free of the net by thrashing and twisting. Keying in on the frenzied struggle, hungry seals frequently move in and execute the gasping victims. The effect is diabolical. A few smaller fish propel forward and eventually work their way through the mesh, their bodies scarred and their dorsal fins rubbed raw. The larger fish drown.

Fortunately for Mykiss, the conditions that allowed the behemoths lurking at the mouth of the river to make sashimi out of his cohort have effectively disabled the nets. Floating debris has put most out of commission and swept others ineffectually into eddying backwaters. Mykiss enters fresh water at exactly the right time. Next week's wave of tide-runners won't be so lucky.

He is the equivalent of a prize racehorse in his prime, fluidly taking the inside bends, wasting no energy unnecessarily bucking the heavy current when the soft water on the edge makes his way so effortless. He takes the path of least resistance. He cuts across a flooded meadow and through a stump-studded clear cut where the boisterous watercourse has overflowed its banks. It's as if he has swum this river 1,000 times. When he comes to a split channel, he unerringly

trench she expands to the sides. These are very long and forceful digs—an exhausting effort that takes a toll on her body. Because she is one of the first to spawn this year, she is working compacted gravel. Fish that follow her and spawn later in the year will have the benefit of gravel has already been loosened. She works arduously to remove silt from her nest. In the process she scours algae off the rocks, giving them a clean polished look.

While she digs, Mykiss comes up beside her. He tries to stimulate her by shuddering, sending a signal to the other fish that this is spawn time. The others are not sure when she's going to drop her eggs. They pulse toward her flank. When Mykiss turns and chases one of the interlopers, another fish rush in and take his place, even though the female is not ready. When the dominant Mykiss comes back a minute or two later, the sneak scoots away.

It takes her three days to make the redd ready. She works outward from the trench to create her first egg pocket, sinking down and touching the gravel delicately with her lower body and fins, measuring for proper depth and width. When she is satisfied with her excavation, the female dips down into the depression in the gravel. Mykiss moves close to her. Immediately he is joined by a small group of parr, and then the other sneaker adult males all shoot in together. She arches her back and drops to the bottom. He moves toward her with his mouth gaping, instantly ready to releases his sperm. The whole time he is shuddering. He's keeping a constant eye on the female, trying to stimulate her and excite her.

Sometimes he brushes softly over her back, barely touching her. He is at the height of sexual fervor—so excited that he often thinks she is laying eggs when she's not. There are many false matings.

He is watching her face. Her facial expression is his signal to make his move. When her mouth opens wide, he is instantly alongside her. She arches her back and thrusts her anus downward into the gravel, releasing a stream of 168 yellowish orange eggs, simultaneously enveloped in a cloud of milt. The satellite males, most of them two-salt fish from six to 11 pounds, don't use her cutting action as their cue. Instead they focus on Mykiss. After he has fertilized her eggs, the sneaks rush in and release their milt in a frenzy. Suddenly one screwball sneak turns and bites the female. The big guy swings around to settle

the matter, quickly chasing him and the others away.

Hour after hour, with Mykiss glued to her side, she creates a dozen new pockets, laying 100 to 300 eggs in each spurt. Sometimes a pulse is into an individual egg pocket and sometimes it's into a larger extended egg pocket. Most of the eggs find their way down into the interstitial space among the gravel, a kind of a matrix into which the eggs drop. But she isn't taking any chances. Once the female creates her first egg pocket, she works in an upstream direction, the gravel from each new pocket successively and neatly burying the eggs in the previous one. As she works forward, gravel gets pushed backward, building up like a weld layer. Although she initially buried each spurt of eggs in a few inches of gravel, at the end of the prolonged flurry of passionate activity, her eggs end up protected under a full foot of gravel. The resulting hump catches clean, oxygenated water and sends it filtering downward to meet the water already percolating from below.

Because it's early in the season, she deposits all her eggs in one redd, three feet wide by three feet long. The tiny steelhead that emerge later will be like a nuclear family. As spring draws on, and as competition becomes more intense and space more limited, one female spawner might have to swim long distances to find unoccupied gravel. She might scatter her eggs in different redds hundreds of yards from each other, hedging her bet. This is not an altogether negative outcome. Survival over time in the harsh flow regime of a rain forest may ultimately favor the genes of the fish that deposits her eggs in multiple redds.

It's a quick process—two nights and she's done. Once the female steelhead is finished dumping her eggs, she settles down into a choppy bucket behind a downstream rock. She rests there for 14 hours. She is now a kelt. She has lost almost all her eggs. She has shrunk from 14 pounds to a skinny nine pounds.

Her act of spawning is not a non-commutable sentence to die. If she can make it back to the healing sea, she might survive—between one and two of every 10 post-spawn females in this relatively short coastal river are rejuvenated and come back. She might live to spawn a second time. Some kelts drop back to the ocean individually, others out-migrate in schools. Early-spawning females in February normally make the journey alone and at night. Her chances of survival though depend on luck as well. If caught by an angler, her dwindled energy reserves may lead her to the river bottom to hide under a Volkswagen-size boulder as a last resting place. Or she might be caught in a gill net, or chased and eaten by a school of otters targeting the weakened kelts. Nonetheless, she has a chance. It will take her only a day or two to run the 20 miles back to the Pacific Ocean.

Maybe Mykiss's first spawning partner has enough left in her. A little spurt of energy combined with a soothing rain that day or a little snowmelt could send her on her way. And she might make it safely downstream.

. . .

Mykiss wants more and more sex. By late February he has assembled a harem, going furiously back and forth among multiple redds. The enormous spawning bed is a continuous 45 feet long and a dozen feet wide, featuring individual redds connected like beads on a chain and a parade of a half-dozen fertile females plying the excavated gravel at any one time.

He is unmistakably the dominant male in this 100-square-yard stretch of river—his imperial territory. Although he's showing wear, he is in good enough shape to keep most other males at bay simply by his intimidating presence. He patrols a mile and more upriver and down, at times chased out by other males lording over their beds and entourage of spawners. He picks fights with other dominate males. Others over which he knows he has a superior advantage he ignores. And he knows to leave alone others larger and more spirited than he.

He has been back home in the river for three weeks. He is robust. With large elongated head, dramatic red stripe down each side, spotted green back and graying belly, he looks different from—and attractive to—the females he seeks. Yet his peak is short. Mortality stalks him. Mykiss has now mated with seven different females. Each mating saps irreplaceable strength from him. Simultaneously, the warming water temperature increases his metabolism and accelerates the breakdown of his tissues. He does not regenerate milt. Although he has a finite reserve, he won't use it all.

In early February when he first spawned, there were few females. Potentially competitive males were dispersed. Now in early March, each tide brings new spawners. His fins are tattered. Scars adorn his body from fights with other male steelhead. These are mostly mock fights engaged to intimidate, but each takes an incremental toll. Mykiss must worry not only about fresh-run males nearly his equal but also four or five sneaker males half his size. A swarm of parr hangs around the redd just downstream. These juvenile steelhead are a mixed bag: Some are there to spawn precociously, some to eat eggs, and some to consume the drift of insects caused by excavation as he did

during his youth. But he pays scant attention to any fish shorter than 15 or 16 inches—these resident rainbow and cutthroat trout won't enter the reproductive fray until late spring.

By early April, Mykiss has mated with 19 females, outlasting all of his tide-running partners. A month and longer ago almost all his spawning was under the cover of darkness. Now more and more he spawns during daylight hours. The light of day reveals a shocking degradation: His body is covered in open sores and fungus. He can't see very well. Using his lateral line as defense, he can't shudder as quickly or as threateningly. His gills are full of leeches. He is constantly shaking his long, ugly head to rid himself of the torturing parasites. His energy is fading. Yet he obsessively pursues his biological imperative. He has positioned himself 50 feet downstream from a 12-pound female busily cutting redds. Mykiss is panting. For the first time in his life he's having difficulty getting enough oxygen through his gills and into his bloodstream. The fat, well-fed rainbow trout he sees finning vibrantly off to the side isn't condemned to an almost certain death after this spawn. The trout's life is sustainable, a cruel reminder that Mykiss has invested all his energy in five years of spectacular growth for what—this ignominious end? He watches other adult males much smaller than he take turns stimulating the female. Despite his obvious deterioration, the female realizes he is still the dominant male. His superior genes are most desired. The whole reproductive hierarchy hangs in the balance. She won't release her eggs until he is alongside her.

Slowly his tired, undulating form makes its way to the beacon of clean gravel. Out of nowhere a chrome male with flaring crimson gills charges the spawning bed. Mykiss hadn't paid attention or he would have seen the newcomer ease into the tailout earlier this afternoon. He is 35 inches in length—an inch shy of Mykiss but bright with all the energy of the sea. He hits Mykiss head on, pounding his left flank and biting Mykiss severely on the caudal. Every other fish within yards scatters in an explosion of water and gravel and silt. For the first time since he was a smolt weighing mere ounces, Mykiss is outclassed. His ability to defend the territory is no match for the challenging male's aggressive vigor. He battles vainly with what little remains of his once-mighty strength. His will falters. His body fails him. Stripped of his primacy, he is not allowed even the role of a sneaker. He is relegated to voyeur. His last sexual experience is watching the new monarch take his place in the center of the spawning bed, convulsing with the ripe female in a

shower of eggs and milt.

Mykiss slowly works his way downstream, finding a strip of soft water where he might rest in comfort. He is a sullen specter—his glorious 18-pound hunk of solidity now reduced to a flaccid 13 pounds. His stomach is shrunken. His pallid skin is riddled with open wounds. Fungus covers his head, now twisted and grotesque. He feels parasites insidiously draining the last of his blood. Although his species is physiologically capable of returning to sea for cleansing rejuvenation, like 99 out of 100 spawned-out male steelhead he is overwhelmingly beaten. The ordeal has devoured him. He cannot muster the strength to deliver what the unforgiving river demands. In a futile attempt to relieve himself of the leeches and mites infesting his gills and throat, with a final burst of energy he clears the water in a series of frantic last-rites leaps. He can't control his swim bladder any longer. His vital equilibrium is gone. He has lost his sense of up and down. He jumps clumsily and his body smashes the smooth surface of the pool once, twice, thrice—seven times in a row. Everything feels different, no longer synchronized, an unceasing pressure. He cannot see. Darkness swallows him. In weeks he

has gone from homecoming luminary to death-masked detritus.

The rotting, emaciated carcass sinks slowly through six feet of water until the fine silt bottom of the river touches his frayed and muted pelvic fins. His gills flushed of color tremble. He lies barely conscious, rocking imperceptibly back and forth to the rhythm of the gentle current. He resembles a dirty disintegrating rag waving weakly on the bottom. The slight flow tips him over. He rights himself, woozily pulling back desperately for one more fleeting moment of life—and so on back and forth for six hours. At last he rolls over and gives in. Three-quarters of a mile from the patch of bright gravel where he was laid five springs ago, his life is finished, the odyssey complete. The river that conjured him is now his crypt.

Above water, the riverbank is festooned in a confetti-burst of bright yellow marsh marigolds. An eagle blinks. Upriver and down, in countless promising pockets of clean scattered gravel, more than 50,000 translucent eggs bearing the distinct genetic imprint of this migratory wonder lie waiting.

FIRST CAST

STONYFORD, CALIFORNIA, WAS THE PERFECT PLAYGROUND for an adventurous, Nature-loving little boy. There were ponds, creeks, mountains, and deer-filled valleys. Every rock and log I turned over revealed some slithery or crawly surprise. We came to Stonyford from the East Coast when I was six years old. I'm not sure of the exact story, but I think it had something to do with my father's need to head west and sow his wild oats. Little did I—or he—know at the time what an impact it would have on my life. My exposure to this foothill country of northern California quickly transformed me into a lizard-chasin', snake-catchin', bird-watchin' addict.

At age six, everything a child sees and hears is new, exciting, and mysterious. I can distinctly remember when I saw my first jackrabbit. My dad, my younger sister, and I were riding in the car when Dad shouted, "Look, a jackrabbit!" There he was, this tall, extremely long-eared rabbit standing as frozen as a statue in a small, manzanita bush-covered draw. Just the name jackrabbit was mysterious to me. I am certain it was at that very moment in my life that I became passionate about the wild world. I remember lying in bed that night, fixated on the image of that little rabbit.

It seemed that every day I experienced a new first: my first deer, my first red-tailed hawk, my first coyote. It was an exciting time of discovery. Then Dad took me fishing.

Dad had access to several small- to medium-sized private ponds full of largemouth bass and bluegill. We normally headed to the ponds in late afternoon and positioned ourselves for the spectacle to unfold just before dark. It rarely disappointed. I remember the two of us sitting there in the little rowboat we had dragged through the thick stand of cattails and tule reeds that surrounded our chosen pond. It was dead calm and quiet. Occasionally a deer appeared on a nearby hillside and the odd dragonfly buzzed by our boat. Red-winged blackbirds were abundant, and as the sun began to set the brightly plumaged males began vibrant territorial calls. *Oak-eh-lee.*

Before long, dragonflies of many colors filled the air, racing across the pond in every direction. Bats suddenly appeared, flying erratically, in pursuit of the dragonflies. Once in a while one collided with our rod tips. Back in the tules, bullfrogs sounded off in deep baritones. First one, then another, until a virtual chorus exploded. American coots joined the concert, adding all sorts of odd, coot-like sounds. Mixed in with this seemingly chaotic crescendo of sight and sound were the bass, there to capitalize on all of the activity on the living surface of our little pond. *Kasploosh!* We heard them attacking frogs, blackbirds, dragonflies—anything that swam through or came near the water fell victim. Dad and I even witnessed a bass trying to engulf a young muskrat one summer evening. Needless to say, amidst all this natural fury, fishing was easy. The bass pounced on practically anything we cast to the water's surface. I remember him laughing out loud sometimes when the pond's frenzy was almost too much to absorb all at once: just Dad, me, the bats, the birds, the bugs, the frogs, and the fish. For me, it was an indelible experience.

The three-mile nighttime drive out of the ponds through hilly range-cattle land was nearly as exciting as the fishing. I was alert and attentive, scanning the dirt road as our headlights revealed coyotes, gray fox, deer, mice, rabbits, raccoons, skunks, opossums, owls, and—if we were really lucky—a rattlesnake. The snakes were the best because Dad always stopped the truck so we could get out and mess around with them a bit. We never harmed one. And one never harmed us.

My parents divorced in 1970. Two years later I went to live with my mother. Dad stayed in Stonyford. To this day when I visit, if the timing is right, we return to our secret bass ponds.

When I went to live with Mom, I brought my desire to be fishing all the time with me. As she searched for a career to adequately pay the bills, it seemed we were always moving. By the time I graduated the sixth grade, I had attended five different elementary schools in various parts of California. Along the way I learned that anywhere we went, I could adapt. There was always some kind of fishing. Whether in creeks, lakes, ponds, golf-course water hazards, or irrigation canals, I was able to find fish. I didn't care what kind of fish they were. I learned to catch bass, bluegill, crappie, trout, catfish, carp—you name it. We lived in Huntington Beach for a while when I was in the fifth grade. This is when I got my first taste of saltwater fishing, mostly for smelt, sting rays, and small sharks. I rode my bike to fish the harbor before and after school nearly every day.

One day at school during the lunch hour I overheard a kid say, "Yeah, my dad and I are going fishing over Christmas vacation." I heard those words as sharply as a coyote hears a distressed rabbit. I ran over to him.

"Fishing?" I blurted out. "Where?"

"We go up north and we catch steelhead," he said. Steelhead? I didn't know what the word meant, but it filled me with intrigue. STEELHEAD. I collected myself and continued the interrogation of my new friend.

"Where do you fish for them?" I asked.

"Oh, in northern California near a town called Eureka," he answered. "It's near the redwood forest." I knew what that country looked like; I had been there on a family vacation. Looking at those rivers with my 10-year-old imagination, they seemed so mysterious and formidable. They were huge and green, cold and wild, and magnetic. When this boy told me he was fishing those rivers to catch a fish called steelhead—even though until moments before I had never heard the word and certainly had no idea what one looked like—it all made sense to me, right then and there. Steelhead.

Every day during that Christmas vacation I thought about the kid and his father and what they were experiencing on those cold, dark rivers. I pictured them bundled up in heavy jackets and wool caps catching steelhead hand over fist. Before I knew it, vacation was over. Now my main mission back at school was to find the boy and hear about his grand adventure. When I finally caught up with him, I asked excitedly, "Well, how was it—your steelhead trip?"

"We didn't catch anything," he said.

Although I was a little disappointed, his admission of failure didn't dampen my interest. Maybe it even spurred my interest. "Why didn't you catch them?" I asked.

"I guess I didn't tell you this before, but steelhead are really hard to catch," he said. I then asked him what steelhead were like. He said, "They look like salmon, but they're kind of a trout, and they're about this big," holding out his arms as wide as they stretched. "And they're really hard to catch, and

pick me up, I never was ready to leave. I could have stayed and fished all night. I also joined the Boy Scouts. Every month found us at some high-altitude lake or stream, including week-long summer backpacking trips to the High Sierra Mountains. There, I found beautiful, clean mountain lakes and streams full of lively trout of all colors and species: rainbows, brookies, browns, and vibrantly colored golden trout. Here at age 13 I caught my first fish on a fly. Up to that point I had fished with spinning rods and lures.

To hold and cradle a living, breathing animal so vibrant and alive is both an honor and a privilege never to be taken for granted.

when my dad catches one he gets really excited."

That first, fleeting, second-hand encounter with steelhead never left me. An idea was planted. Someday I knew I'd fish for steelhead.

In the meantime, I kept fishing and dreaming. We moved a couple more times: new schools, new friends, and new fishing opportunities. The Santa Monica and Malibu piers became regular weekend haunts. My mom drove me down in the morning and dropped me off. When she returned in the evening to

Occasionally I fished with bait but never enjoyed it the way I did lure fishing. I needed to be moving and busy. Even at a young age, reading the water, making the right cast, and controlling the lure came naturally to me. When I fished with bait, I never felt I was really fishing. It was more like I was simply waiting for a fish to swim by and happen upon my bait. Too much chance. I wanted to make things happen.

My favorite lure in the high-mountain lakes was a black Panther Martin spinner, with yellow spots. I had some others that I seldom used. I figured if they wouldn't take my Panther Martin, they just weren't biting. That is, until the last bit of daylight crept off the lake and the fish began to rise like crazy. There were fish visibly feeding everywhere, but I couldn't get them to bite. This was frustrating! I did well in this same spot during the day, when I hardly ever saw a trout break the surface. It was obvious to me that the trout were gorging themselves on some kind of little bug. I knew what I needed to do. I had little knowledge of fly fishing, but I knew fish and fishing. The only way to catch these fish was with a fly.

I talked my mom into buying me an inexpensive fly-fishing outfit. The next time I returned to those lakes, my hunch came true. The flies worked. I knew nothing about casting, but I figured out enough to get the line out there, however ungracefully. Good enough to fool the trout anyway. I was thrilled with my new discovery. It was extremely satisfying to know that my ability as an angler was expanding. Through my teenage years, the fly rod was a tool that came out only when I felt it necessary. I enjoyed using it at times, but my enthusiasm was for fishing in general. Methodology was not important to me. I was after what was most effective.

After attending one year of college in southern California, I decided to change schools and head back north. Now I was a young adult with a driver's license, which opened up a whole new world of angling opportunity for me. I still wasn't much of a fly fisher, concentrating on bass, bluegill, crappie, and catfish. I was still intrigued by the mystical allure of steelhead, but the rivers seemed so far away. I didn't know anyone who fished for steelhead and never heard anyone speak of them. That is, until one day when I was hanging out with my step-uncle, Ken.

A friend of Ken, whom I had briefly met several times before, stopped by to invite Ken on a fishing trip. Marvin was his name, a full-blooded Native American who had family living on the Hoopa Reservation on the Klamath River.

"Hey, Ken, the steelhead are in up on the Klamath!" was Marv's greeting.

Did he say what I thought he said? I thought to myself. I had not heard that word uttered since the fifth grade. And I certainly never heard it from Uncle Ken. Actually, judging by the look on Ken's face, I don't believe he knew what Marv was talking about. I chimed in, "You mean steelhead—you fish for steelhead?" Marv explained that he traveled to the Klamath once a year in the fall when his family let him know fishing was good. He was highly excited, I

could tell, telling Ken to pack his bags and that he wouldn't regret it. He said the steelhead were "half-pounders," young fish that spent only a few months in the ocean but were a kick in the pants to catch. He said there was also an opportunity to catch larger adult steelhead while fishing for the half-pounders. I stood there wishing, hoping, and praying for an invitation. Marv must have read my face, because I remember him saying, "Declan, you like to fish, don't you?"

"Heck, yes, it's what I live for!" I shouted back.

"Then you should come, too," he replied.

Oh, baby, I'm going fishing for steelhead!

We left early the next morning and trekked north four hours to the Klamath. I packed my biggest spinning outfit, my tackle box and a sleeping bag. Marv said the best way to catch a steelhead was by drifting nightcrawlers along the bottom of the river. I didn't care how we fished for them.

Because of Marv's heritage, we were permitted access to the reservation water. Not far from tidewater the deep, green river looked massive. We drove our truck right onto a large gravel bar along the river where we would camp and fish for the next three days. I didn't know anything about fishing a large river, of course, but I was a competent, confident angler. Ken and Marv began setting up camp and talking to some of Marv's relatives. I couldn't take my eyes off the water. I knew the right thing to do was to help set up camp, but my 19-year-old enthusiasm took over, and I hurriedly began rigging my rod. I didn't feel too badly, though: Ken and Marv were already into their beer, shooting the bull in a circle of friends.

Rigged up, nightcrawler firmly impaled on my size 2 bait hook, I made a long, random cast slightly quartering upstream into the Klamath's muscular current. What happened next was so nearly unbelievable that until this moment I have had the nerve to share the tale with only a few close friends: My weight found the bottom of the river and began ticking along for several yards when it abruptly stopped. I instinctively knew something good was happening. Then it started pulling hard. Really hard. For a split second I started to panic. "Think," I said aloud to myself. "This has got to be a steelhead." *Stay calm. You know what you're doing. Let him run. . . .*

He kept pulling and fighting. That's when I yelled to Uncle Ken and Marv that I had one on. They came clambering over the sun-bleached gravel bar shouting words of encouragement. I had the fish nearly beached when Marv started yelling: "You caught a real one, Declan. Oh, yeah! It's a real one all right."

Shaking from adrenal overload and sporting a smile the size of Texas, I asked Marv what he meant by real one. "That's no half-pounder, buddy—look at the size of him! You caught yourself an adult steelhead," he said.

The steelhead of my dreams weighed six pounds. I had hooked him on the very first cast I ever made for steelhead.

During the next couple of days, we hooked dozens of squirrelly little half-pounders, hard-bodied chrome steelhead in miniature. They were a blast to catch and it didn't take long before I put those nasty nightcrawlers to rest. I found that the fish responded more aggressively to spoons and spinners anyway.

Like the too-soon ending of a captivating movie, our trip was over. The fish I caught on my first cast was the only adult steelhead any of us saw during three days of hard fishing, and from that day on I wouldn't have wanted it any other way.

Less than a year after meeting my first steelhead, I decided that college life wasn't doing it for me. Still wanting to do something adventurous and productive, I found myself intrigued by the romance of seeing the world. There was only one branch of the service that piqued my interest: the U.S. Navy.

I'm not certain how destiny works; maybe it's something we subconsciously create. But of all the places on the globe I could get orders to, I was sent to Whidbey Island in Washington State, right in the heart of Northwest steelhead country. I had it made. I was in a naval air squadron—A6-E attack bombers—which meant I was land-based until we would deploy on an aircraft carrier for six months at a time. I had the best of both worlds.

Whidbey Island, and all of northwestern Washington for that matter, is breathtakingly beautiful. The large island nestled in the Puget Sound's biologically rich, peaceful waters is geographically part of the San Juan Islands. Douglas fir, western hemlock, and western red cedar dominate the water-enshrouded landscape. In addition to being a dedicated Navy man, there was a lot to learn and to explore on the recreational side of things. During the course of my four-year tour of active duty, I became thoroughly hooked on fly fishing.

There was a fabulous fly-fishing-only lake only four miles from the base where I spent a great deal of my off-time. There were several other lakes I visited from time to time, but Pass Lake with its fly-only regulation had the biggest, hardest-fighting trout. I capitalized on the area's myriad sporting opportunities and rabidly pursued nearly all there was to offer: I

went crabbing, clam digging, salmon fishing, duck and pheasant hunting. I even shot my one and only deer on Whidbey Island—an experience I needed to try but didn't really excite me too much.

I learned that in the spring and early summer sea-run Dolly Varden and cutthroat trout could be caught by fly fishing from the beach as they fed close to shore on candlefish. There was so much opportunity within in a five-mile radius of the navy base that was so fun, new, and exciting to me that for the first couple of years I never traveled far to get my fix.

I was definitely aware that I was in the land of steelhead, but I was on an island with no rivers. All the people I associated with were also from other states. They had no knowledge of steelhead. Mostly I fished alone. Occasionally I invited a Navy buddy along who expressed an interest in fishing, but he usually turned out to have a different sporting ethic than I. The objective of each outing seemed to be consuming large quantities of beer and killing everything in sight.

I couldn't stand it any longer. I began researching local steelheading opportunities. Checking with the local sport shops on the Island didn't do me much good as they were really geared toward the local stuff. But when I did inquire, the same names would pop up: "Steelhead? You need to go to the Skagit, Stilliguamish, or Skykomish rivers for steelhead." They were exotic names that seemed far away. But they weren't.

The Skagit near Mount Vernon was only a 40-minute drive from the base. One winter day I drove up to check it out. I found a huge river. Through my eyes it looked about the size of a small Mississippi. I couldn't imagine where any sane human being could fish from shore or by wading. As I drove upriver looking for fishermen, I spotted the occasional small shack right on the banks of the Skagit, with scattered cars and trucks parked along the road near them. Upon closer observation, I saw fishing rods, with lines out, placed in holders in front of the shacks. I was puzzled—there couldn't be catfish in this cold, northern river!

I hiked down to talk with the occupants. The anglers I encountered weren't exactly the friendliest people I had ever met. Nor did they come across as overly bright. I screwed up my optimism and with a big smile asked, "Whatcha' fishin' for?" They looked at me as if I wasn't too bright either. One crusty dude quietly muttered, "Steelhead."

My heart picked up its pace.

"Do you have any I can see?" I asked eagerly.

"Got a couple in that ice chest over there—take a look," the dude offered. I ran over to the huge chest and lifted the lid. Lying before me were two beautiful silver fish, eyes staring coldly blank. But the power of these steelhead radiated from their thick bodies and broad tails. I was taken by them. I was even intimidated by them in a strange sort of way. Those big, wild winter-run steelhead startled me. At that instant I

I went straight to the nearest library to look for books on steelhead fishing. I was surprised at how much I found. There had evidently been a lot written about the subject. This was a good sign. I grabbed the whole row of books and pamphlets with the word steelhead in their titles. I sat down at a table and spent the next five hours in another world, completely absorbed in what was quickly becoming my new

Pure platinum brilliance radiates onto the river's surface. Even the small ones are larger than life. All should be released.

knew that somehow my life was changed. I quietly closed the ice chest turned to the men in the shack, thanked them, and walked away.

Normally, upon such a discovery I would have drilled those guys with question after question, and probably would have even been fishing right beside them the next day! Not this time. This was different. What I had just seen muscled its way in to my soul. It was too personal to discuss with strangers. I needed time to think this one over.

obsession, my purpose for living.

When I learned that you could fly fish for steelhead, I nearly screamed. The proposition gave me a feeling I had never felt in all my years of fishing. It was exciting and spooky at the same time, with undertones of the mystical. Every new page was a revelation. The photographs and illustrations of fish, fishermen, flies, and tackle had me in their grasp. I couldn't believe what I was seeing. Eventually coming out of my trance, I checked out as many books as the

librarian allowed. I drove home with one eye—well, half an eye—on the road, and my real concentration on the open books propped open on the passenger seat.

In addition to a couple of books filled with pictures of gear fishing for steelhead, by good fortune I had in my possession several books that much later I came to realize were classics—seminal writings on the subject of steelhead fishing with a fly: *Steelhead to a Fly* by Clark Van Fleet (1954), *Northwest Angling* by Enos Bradner (1950), *A River Never Sleeps* by Roderick Haig-Brown (1944), and *Steelhead Fly Fishing and Flies* by Trey Combs (1976). I read them over and over every chance I got. I was enamored not only of what appeared to be a magnificent animal—the shining steelhead—but equally impressed with the sense of lore, tradition, and sporting ethic that came through so vividly in the words of the men who had written these books. They were clearly passionate about this stuff.

Everything about steelhead fishing now enchanted me: the landscape, geography, and climate of the rivers, as well as their poetic names; the sleek and sexy flies with their seductive names; the hefty tackle required, compared to trout fishing; the special angling techniques; and, of course, those unbelievable river-returning oceanic steelhead.

A change had come over me. I felt it deeply and profoundly. It was as if I had found a new religion, and in my heart I had become a disciple of the steelhead and everything associated with it.

As soon as I was able, I went out and purchased a rod, reel, and line to catch a steelhead on a fly. I bought a nine-and-a-half-foot 8-weight Loomis graphite rod and a Scientific Anglers System II reel, a 13-foot type IV sink-tip line, and some Maxima leader material. I already had a bunch of flies. I had feverishly tied them onboard the aircraft carrier U.S.S. *Kitty Hawk* cruising the Indian Ocean.

There was one key issue to be resolved in my new quest: I still wasn't exactly sure just where to take all this equipment. Although I had spent a great deal of time reading about steelhead, I still hadn't met anyone who actually fished for them. That changed one day when I dropped in to my favorite sporting goods store, Ed's Sport Shop in Mount Vernon right on the lower Skagit River. It was the store where I bought my new equipment. Owned by Kim Weymouth, the shop had everything from duck and goose decoys and crab nets to salmon and steelhead gear. Ed's had plenty of fly tackle, but there really wasn't anyone working there who was particularly knowledgeable about fly

fishing. Until that day.

I was looking at some fly-tying material hanging on the wall when I was approached by a small-framed and balding man in his late forties. He was super friendly.

"Charlie, Charlie Gearheart," he said in a distinctly southern—if not hillbilly—accent as he extended his hand. He told me he had just started working part-time in the shop to help build the fly-fishing department. He said he played music the rest of the time. When I asked about his accent he said he was originally from Kentucky. He had made his way out to Washington for the fishing. I could tell this guy was extraordinarily cool and wise, and that I could learn much from him. I told him that I was seriously into fly fishing. And then he popped the question.

"You do any steelheading?" he asked.

I felt myself tense up. I really didn't want to say no.

"Well, I haven't yet, but I've got all the gear and I've been reading about it. It's something I really want to do," I replied. "How about you?" I asked.

With a big smile and a chuckle he said, "Oh yeah, it's mainly all I do. Caught a real nice one last night—'bout 12 pounds."

"You did? Where?" I asked incredulously.

"Up on the Sauk River. Only had an hour to fish. She was a beauty," he replied.

"What fly did you catch it on?"

"A purple marabou."

My mind instantly took me to the Sauk River, seeing my new friend Charlie kneeling at river's edge just before dark, releasing his big chrome-bright steelhead. He was all smiles yet all knowing. I could feel his experience at this. I couldn't believe that I was finally in the presence of a real steelhead fly fisher! Charlie explained to me that the Skagit River and its principal tributary, the Sauk, had a special catch-and-release season each year in early spring. He said the fishing was fabulous for large wild steelhead. I believed him. Hell, he just ran up there for an hour last night and caught one 12 pounds! I was going crazy inside.

"If I go up there tomorrow, would you point me in the right direction?" I asked.

"Oh, Dec, I'd love to, but you're too late. The season closed yesterday." Today was the first day of May. *Aaaagh!* Why didn't I find out about this earlier? I played it relatively cool in front of Charlie. He had the answer I was praying for. He went on to tell me that I could get started fishing for summer-run steelhead on the Stilliguamish River in June. I had read a lot about the North Fork Stilliguamish in Enos

Bradner's book, *Northwest Angling*. The river's fly-fishing-only water was legendary. I had learned it was an important place in the history and development of the sport. For the next hour, Charlie and I had a great conversation. When I left, I knew I had truly made a new friend.

The next month was a torturous one. The Skagit was closed, and Charlie said the Stilliguamish wouldn't be open until June. My debut as a steelhead fly fisher would have to wait. In that time, my four-year tour with the Navy was up and I was honorably discharged. I took a job with the Boeing Company in Everett. My wife and I bought a house in Mount Vernon close to Ed's Sport Shop and the Skagit River.

As soon as June hit, I was in the shop talking to Charlie. He must have taken a liking to me because he told me in remarkable detail about a small slot on the "Stilly" that always held a steelhead. If I went there and fished it properly, he said, I'd catch one. Those words of confidence were almost too much to handle. I was off and running, headed to the Stilly. Charlie's last words to me were, "Let me know."

Once on the river, Charlie's directions led me right to the spot. It was a big, wide, shallow flat—featureless water between two runs. He said there was a deep, narrow slot on the far side. I literally ran down there and started looking for the magic spot by wading in at the top of the flat. As I started wading downstream I didn't see anything, so I worked my way across farther and farther. Stepping along and peering at the far bank for any sign of deeper water, I began to doubt that I was in the right place. Finally the water began to deepen a bit. I guessed this must be it. Nervously I sent my purple marabou on its first cast. My line swung around. I stepped and made another cast—just like my books and Charlie had said.

I kept working down, but my instinct told me something wasn't right. The water didn't feel "fishy" to me. I kept fishing. Who was I to say what fishy was? This was my first time steelheading! Suddenly the water deepened dramatically. The place reeked of fish. My heart started racing. And I remember saying out loud, "This is it." I slowed my pace to a crawl and brought all my powers of concentration to bear. For the moment I forgot that I'd never done this before. I was finally fly fishing for steelhead.

I pounded the tiny piece of water for too long; nothing but my ignorance kept me at it. Charlie said I would catch one, and I believed him. I kept casting and casting to what appeared the most likely section of the slot. On one of my endless casts-and-swings, my line stopped. I didn't feel anything, particularly.

The fly simply stopped. I pulled up on the rod and felt weight. It started to move away, taking my line with it. I panicked and pulled back hard with the rod. I felt terrific power and weight. *It's a fish! This can't be!* And then it was gone. Oh, how I wanted it back. But wait a minute: I just hooked a real steelhead. On a fly. On *my* fly. On the storied North Fork Stilliguamish. Under snow-capped mountains in the Pacific Northwest. This is how it feels. This is how it's done. I was fishing now, baby!

I fished the slot for another half hour with dimming confidence. I couldn't keep my mind off what had just happened and desperately needed to tell someone. I called my buddy, Scott O'Donnell. I met Scott in the Navy. He was from Massachusetts. The guy would do anything and go anywhere. But mostly he liked do the things I liked to do: fish and hunt. I got him hooked on fly fishing and immediately created a monster. He and I were constant companions. We fished and hunted ducks and explored together like wild men.

That night I talked Scott's ear off for an hour. The next day when I got home from work he was waiting for me, insisting we head up to the Stilly and my secret slot. Who was I to argue? We loaded up and headed out. I cannot recall what kind of gear Scott had at the time, but I'm sure he didn't have any proper steelhead equipment yet. No matter, he would have fished a 2-weight that night.

We hoofed it down to the river. Once on the water, I excitedly explained to him where I hooked up the previous evening. He stopped my jabbering and said, "Well, what are you waiting for? Go for it. Go catch your steelhead!" I waded out well above the spot and started to cast. Working down the run I could see the tip of my graphite rod quivering as my adrenaline-loaded torso transmitted its surplus through my hands. I was bursting, thinking how thrilled I was to be right in this spot on this very day when . . . WHAM! I was hit so hard I could almost hear it. It felt like thunder and moved like lightning. I was stunned as the big fish peeled line off my reel faster than I ever thought possible. Then it exploded out of the river well below me. I was awestruck. I started screaming to Scott, "I'm doin' it, I'm doin' it!" Conscious of my uncontrollable shouts, the words I heard were clearly defining this moment—all my dreaming, fantasizing, and visualizing since the fifth grade were manifested in this single magical event.

Then I fell in.

Fish still attached, camera thoroughly dunked and presumably dead, I stood up, took a deep breath and continued reveling in my good fortune. The steelhead made a few more runs and soon I had her in the shallows. What I saw amazed me. She was fairly transparent as she circled around in less than a foot of water. The most visible thing I could see was the purple marabou hanging off the side of her jaw. Then she rolled on her side revealing absolute platinum brilliance from head to tail. She was spectacular. Her missing adipose fin let Scott and me know she was of hatchery origin. It was her only blemish. I could have kept her, but there was no possibility of killing my first fly-caught steelhead irrespective of her birthplace. She swam back to sanctuary, disappearing into the brown, olive mosaic of the Stilly's rocky bed.

Scott and I looked at one another, knowing we had just encountered something so privileged, so top secret, an ethereal feeling consumed us both. We were momentarily speechless. Then we simultaneously erupted in a gigantic bear hug. We both started talking loudly over each other, describing the instant emotions we both felt about what had just happened. A half-hour later I hooked and landed another, this time a colorful wild buck still in the river from last winter. This was fishing on a different plane. I had found Nirvana.

I was obsessed. I fished the Stilliguamish before, after—and sometimes during—work nearly every day for the rest of that summer and autumn. I caught a bunch more steelhead, each one an event complete with its own theatrical story. I was there when Scott

My buddy Rick Rawson getting a big ol' steelhead smooch! Life is good when the river's in shape and the fish are bitin'.

The sun struggles to break through dense fog blanketing the Skykomish. The experience is enhanced by such conditions.

landed his first steelhead, and even went fishing with Charlie several times. I rapidly learned the river by honing my skills in episodes of tactical trial and experimentation. I had my favorite spots, but every bend of that river beckoned exploration.

Winter came. I turned my attention to the enormous, powerful Skagit River to the north. At first the river mystified me. For what seemed like too long, I caught nothing. Each time I waded out I came back empty. Finally, on the last day of March during the catch-and-release season, I hooked and landed my first Skagit fish: a glorious buck of about 12 pounds. That unbelievable spring is still deeply etched in my memory. Scott and I and our newest friend, Ed Ward from Michigan, hooked and played many of those beautiful Skagit wild steelhead, bonding a friendship to last a lifetime.

I was still working at Boeing, building 747 aircraft. But I had steelhead dangerously on the brain. I knew I needed to get out of there and somehow figure out a way to spend my days on the river. I knew what I really wanted to do was get paid to play. It was frustrating. I began offering fly-fishing clinics to Boeing employees for a small fee, posting flyers on the factory bulletin boards. They were an instant success. I organized several clinics with as many as 30 attendees. Then one day in May, Charlie called and asked if I would be interested in guiding a man who was in town on business from South Africa. He had one day to fish and wanted to try for steelhead. The Stilly was now open in May and fishing for wild spring steelhead had been good. Nervously, I said I'd do it. The guy caught two fine steelhead, and I experienced one of the most rewarding days of my life. I'd become a steelhead guide.

I let the resident dean of Skagit fly-fishing guides, John Farrar, know that I wanted to start guiding. He promptly gave me a couple of sports for a day in April of 1989, which turned into two days because they had so much fun on the first. Maybe my enthusiasm was rubbing off. I knew I still had much to learn, but I also believed that I knew enough—and was dedicated enough—to show people a good time. And I'd give them a legitimate shot at a steelhead on the fly.

In April of 1990, with John's help and recruits from my Boeing clinics, I guided quite a few days. I also had secured a job guiding in Alaska at Katmai Lodge on the Alagnak River during the coming summer. I left the guaranteed paycheck behind and exuberantly jumped waist-deep into my new career as a professional fly-fishing guide.

My career on the water took off after an exciting and educational summer in Alaska. While guiding fly fishers after trout or salmon, I was also on a personal mission to build a steelhead-fishing cliental, which I accomplished. I sold my steelhead seasons well and started taking people steelheading from all over the country and even Europe. Many of them became regulars, booking the same days year after year.

I worked in Alaska a total of four summers. The rest of the year I guided steelhead anglers during winter and spring among the Skagit, Sauk, Skykomish and Stilliguamish rivers in Washington. In autumn I guided on the Grande Ronde River in Oregon. I worked the Ronde from the fall of 1991 through the fall of 1994 and then switched to Oregon's Deschutes River. I had become a bona fide steelhead guide. My dream had come true—I was getting paid to play.

More opportunities came my way when Nick Amato of Amato Publications in Portland asked if I would write articles for them. That was in 1993 and since then, at one time or another, I have written for every one of their several publications. Then, when Tom Pero moved to Seattle, I started writing and taking pictures for his beautiful new magazine, *Wild Steelhead & Atlantic Salmon*, and began a long working relationship with Tom and his ever-evolving publications. I befriended George Cook of Sage and taught fly-casting schools and clinics for them. The list goes on.

Through all of my professional success, one thing remains constant: my true love, devotion, and passion for steelhead. I have hooked hundreds of steelhead myself and have guided other anglers to hundreds more. I can honestly say that with each and every one, my heart still races and my hands still shake.

FLIES

THAT TAKE STEELHEAD

FLIES TIED BY DEC HOGAN

THE STEELHEAD FLY IS THE THING THAT SETS THIS UNIQUE form of angling apart from others. Even the largest of flies are not heavy enough to be cast by conventional tackle and fished with conventional methods. Fly rods and lines are specifically designed and engineered to cast and present these near-weightless lures to a wide range of distances. The weight that carries the fly is built into the fly line—technically we are casting the line with the fly simply going along for the ride.

Fly casting in the hands of a skilled caster ranks one the most graceful spectacles in sport. Casting in itself is an art form to be admired and appreciated. Coupled with the art of fly casting is the fly itself. Flies are the very symbol of our sport. I can comfortably say, without reservation, that steelhead and Atlantic salmon flies are the most beautiful, elegant flies in all angling.

Essentially, flies for steelhead are not explicit imitators of a natural life form. Rather, they suggest life. Steelhead and Atlantic salmon share similar life histories and behaviors; at times, both show a willingness to move to and take just about any fly that swings across the current. Neither animal is in the river to feed. They are there to spawn. Growth takes place in the ocean while they feed heavily on a wide variety of rich marine life. Once in the river, it is not clearly understood why steelhead take flies, bait, or lures. There are many theories, some of which I have difficulty agreeing with. I've heard it theorized that they take flies because they are mad, curious, or playful. These are primarily human emotions that I don't believe can, or should, be applied to cold-blooded creatures. I believe that the steelhead is an animal of instinct that reacts due to repetitive conditioning for its survival: See food and eat it. Therefore, I believe steelhead take flies due to an inherent conditioned response—they just can't help themselves. Roll a knitted ball past a resting cat and nine times out of 10 the cat will lash out and grab the ball. The

A selection of flies spawned from the Coast Orange design. Any style of fly lends itself well to modifications and subtle changes.

cat has no intention of eating the ball but is conditioned through years of evolution to catch small animals scurrying away. When in bear country the number one rule is, "Don't run from the bear!" Again, the bear may have had no intention of attacking, but as soon as it sees an animal running from him the chase and kill response is triggered.

Later in this chapter I'll discuss the steelhead's oceanic forage, but in the meantime suffice to say it's an exceedingly varied diet. To our advantage, the steelhead's aggressive nature allows us freedom to tie and fish just about anything we want. Borrowing from Atlantic salmon angling techniques and traditions, steelhead flies are similar to and certainly interchangeable with salmon flies. In fact, the influence supported by salmon flies is so prevalent that I've often wondered about the form in which steelhead flies would have evolved if Atlantic salmon did not exist. We'd probably all be fishing leeches and Woolly Buggers. Instead, only some of us are. I'm grateful for the simple to complex elegance of the salmon fly and its fitting adaptations to steelhead angling.

Flies add greatly to the overall aesthetics of our glorious sport other than simply being a lure for tempting a fish. Appreciation for sport and Nature are often reflected in the flies one carries and fishes. Deep respect and admiration for the animal and its environment come through in a well-tied fly, telling me a lot about its owner. Ugly flies have no place in steelhead fishing, but I do believe beauty truly does lie in the eye of the beholder. I would never turn my nose up at a fly tied by someone with meager tying skills. Neither does the forgiving steelhead. To me, the only "ugly" steelhead flies are those tied with rubber-legs, excessive amounts of flash, and cheap plastic materials (the Squamish Poacher, a prawn fly tied with fluorescent surveyor's tape comes to mind). Fortunately, most people who have made a commitment to the sport enjoy and appreciate flies to the degree I'm trying to convey. Tying flies keeps us close to our sport. I thoroughly enjoy time spent with friends as we tie flies while waiting for the river to come back into fishable shape. Peering into foreign fly boxes is always fun. I'm much more interested in what's in someone's fly box than what kind of rod and reel he is using. We decorate our lives with flies, sticking them in random holds in our homes, offices, and vehicles. We keep them close to us to remind us of our passion and to invite others to share who we are.

My brother-in-law, Marty Howard of Heber, Utah, lives hundreds of miles from the nearest steelhead river. Yet he is a bona fide steelhead junkie and a damn fine angler. He ties more flies—and more beautifully—than I ever could imagine. Because of geographical constraints, his steelhead fishing is limited. So what does he do to connect with his sport? He ties flies, of course. He's rarely without a box filled with radiant steelhead patterns. No telling where or when he'll whip one out for show and tell.

A well-tied fly enhances the magic of hooking a steelhead. I remember vividly the moments when I hooked my first steelhead using flies tied with certain seductive materials, and specific beautiful patterns. Knowing that the fish moved to my very personal offering is a joy.

There are certain parameters to consider when selecting what fly to fish. By and large, the latitude in meeting those considerations is wide. Confidence in the selected fly and sound presentation far outweigh the importance of the actual fly. When I was a budding steelheader, the flies I saw in most books were what I call standard classics: a tail, a ribbed chenille or wool body, a collar hackle, and a calf or bucktail wing. The Skunk, Green-Butt Skunk, Skykomish

Sunrise, Polar Shrimp, Thor, and Purple Peril—to name a few—appeared in every bit of literature I saw. All these flies are basically the same, but in different colors. I caught my first steelhead on a simple purple marabou because my friend Charlie told me with such conviction that it would work that my confidence in the fly was instantly overflowing. It did work. My faith was so rooted in purple marabous that for a long time I felt insecure fishing anything else, even though right there in front of me were volumes of literature stating that all these other patterns were the industry standards—other peoples' confidence flies. Eventually I got up the nerve to stick with something other than a marabou fly long enough to hook a steelhead. Then another and another.

When I began to accept that steelhead would take many different patterns, I went berserk. I was already enamored with steelhead flies. Now I had the confidence to fish anything that suited my fancy. I set out to see how many different patterns I could get a steelhead to grab. For however long it took, I would hook a fish on a certain fly and then change to something different. During that time I hooked steelhead on 104 different patterns! Needless to say, what I learned from that experience is something I still draw on today. Occasionally, when fishing is really productive, I still play the let's-see-how-many-flies-I-can-take-'em-on-in-a-day game.

If you are a newcomer to the sport and are confused as to what fly to use, trust me and stick with a fly that appeals to you. It will work. Beginners too often spend more time fussing over what fly to use than learning how to read and fish the water properly. As you gain skill and experience, you will find peace in knowing you've selected the right fly.

Within the steelhead's range, from region to region and river to river, local flies may incorporate a specific size range or style of flies. Much of this is born of traditions passed on by generations of anglers. This too is a result of the confidence factor. I never check with locals to inquire what specific flies are working in a given area. I know steelhead behavior and river conditions, and have found that steelhead are steelhead wherever I travel. Conditions vary: That's what determines the fly I select.

Carefully selecting flies to meet the prevailing conditions can be very rewarding. Self-gratification comes when you know that other flies may have worked, but you made your decisions based on prior experience and knowledge of what personally feels right under the given conditions. These conditions include—but are not limited to—river size and color,

TRAGOPRAWN

I LOVE PRAWN-STYLE PATTERNS which I guess you can say are all variations and derivatives of the famous General Practitioner. The GP was tied originally for Atlantic salmon but has found an important place in steelheading. My Tragoprawn is nothing more than another variation on the GP. Being creative at the vise, utilizing unusual or rare feathers and material, is recreation in itself. The Tragoprawn is one of dozens of various prawn patterns I tie and fish. No one works better than another at taking steelhead—it's more for me than the fish.

TRAGOPRAWN

HOOK: Alec Jackson spey

FEELERS (TAIL):
Orange polar bear or substitute, sparse

BODY: Four to five sections of orange seal fur dubbing or substitute

RIB: Fine oval gold tinsel

HACKLE OR LEGS:
One turn of dyed orange guinea at the joint of each body section and after last section as a beard. Hackle should be tapered from large to small toward the hook-eye.

EYES: Plastic bug eyes

SHELLBACK:
Tragopan pheasant breast feathers

COLLAR: Orange seal fur dubbing

water temperature, weather, amount of fishing pressure, time of year, steelhead migration, and geographical location. Geography and migration have the biggest influence on the size and styles of flies I fish on my favorite rivers. My rivers come in two categories: coastal and inland. Separating the two is primarily the tidal influence of coastal rivers and the behavioral differences between steelhead fresh in from the ocean and those that have been in the river for some time. It is important to note that it's better to think in terms of conditions rather than of season. Seasonal changes are not always consistent from week to week, month to month, or year to year. I've experienced many February days when river conditions more

closely resembled late spring than that of a typical winter day. I've also seen consistently easy fishing with floating lines and small flies on a warm September river quickly turn to big-fly sink-tip fishing hoping to get a fish every other day with the sudden onset of a massive, wet, cold front. Fortunately, seasonal conditions remain fairly constant and dependable

JUNGLE COCK ROCK

THE FIRST JUNGLE COCK ROCK basically tied itself. I loved the look of the body feathers of the gray jungle fowl and couldn't resist tying with them. After a bit of contemplation, it became apparent that the feathers would prove most effective if they simply stood on their own. This fly has been a proven killer under a range of water temperatures, provided the river is running clear. The first fish I hooked on a JCR was on an October day while fishing the Stilliguamish River. My friend Scott O'Donnell watched the spectacular aerial show from a high cut-bank overlooking the pool. Scott yelled out, "Rock 'n roll man . . . rock 'n roll!"

JUNGLE COCK ROCK

HOOK: Alec Jackson spey

BODY: None

UNDERWING:
Small bunch of dyed orange squirrel rail extending beyond hook bend and cocked slightly, followed by a few strands of orange polar bear hair or substitute, uneven and well beyond the bend; should be sparse.

HACKLE: Dyed orange pheasant rump feather tied in by tip, followed by a dyed black pheasant rump feather tied in the same manner.

WING: Brown-tipped flank feather from jungle cock, one from each side of neck, tied on each side of the hook extending just beyond hook.

COLLAR: Black and white feather from the base of the jungle cock neck, tied in by tip and folded, two turns.

CHEEKS: Cheeks of jungle cock are optional (fly pictured without).

throughout the year. However, it does pay to be prepared when dealing with Nature.

I fish for steelhead throughout the year, meeting the demands and varied conditions of all four seasons. In winter, spring, and summer, the rivers I fish are in close proximity to salt water with steelhead at various stages of migration and sexual maturity. Steelhead fresh in from the ocean can appear on any given day. Irrespective of river conditions, all these fish have one thing in common: They are not far removed from life in the ocean.

Because there is no definitive answer as to why steelhead take flies and lures once in our rivers, one

thing is certain: They do. If we knew nothing of their life history, we could just as easily knot on a fly and go to work trying to catch one. But I believe that their

AKROYD

THE FAMOUS AKROYD comes from Scotland's River Dee and is the flagship of the dee-style flies. The first thing you notice about my dee flies is that they are unorthodox in how the wing is tied in. I tie more of a spey-style wing—it's just my personal preference. The Akroyd is complicated to tie but worth the effort. Not only do I get great satisfaction in fishing such an elegant fly, it is so life-like in the water that steelhead can't resist.

AKROYD

HOOK:	Alec Jackson spey
TAG:	Silver tinsel
TAIL:	Golden pheasant crest, over which are golden pheasant tippets half as long as crest.
BODY:	Rear half—yellow or light orange seal, ribbed with oval silver tinsel and palmered with yellow hackle.
	Front half—black floss wound with oval silver tinsel and palmered with black spey hackle.
WING:	Two narrow strips of turkey wing feathers
THROAT:	Teal flank
CHEEKS:	Jungle cock set low and drooping

life spent at sea has a great deal to do with why we can hook them. Certainly there's a lot of mysticism involved with our pursuit; personally, I prefer it that way. Knowing as much as we can about steelhead and their behavior perhaps can make us more cognizant anglers and at the very least make the overall experience that much more gratifying.

How I Design My Flies

Upon researching the marine diet of steelhead, I was confronted with a startling surprise. I always assumed, as do many avid steelheaders, that shrimp is of major importance to the steelhead's diet. Look at all the fly patterns tied to imitate prawns. Yet according to studies reported by the International North Pacific Fisheries Commission, large shrimp and prawns are not even mentioned. Small shrimp-like

crustaceans and tiny amphipods make up an insignificantly tiny percentage of their diet, primarily among juvenile fish when they first hit salt water. Finfishes and squid are of significantly greater importance, namely, the Atka mackerel and gonatid squid. The Atka mackerel is not the tuna-like mackerel one commonly thinks of. Rather, the species is a member of the pollock and greenling family—it's perch-like.

An important food fish inhabiting the North Pacific, the Atka mackerel is a schooling fish of remarkably colorful brilliance. Adults and juveniles alike possess heavy vertical barring along their sides with brownish-olive, yellow, orange, and dark-green the predominant color pattern. In one study, Juvenile Atka mackerel were the most important species in the steelhead's diet, accounting for half of their total marine consumption. The next most important food source is the gonatid squid. This squid is of moderate size,

research that I've never heard discussed among anglers during all our entertaining, philosophical arguments about why steelhead take flies and why we tie the flies we do: Everything the steelhead eats in the ocean is a schooling organism. Our fly is out there by itself. Hmmm. Remember, there's a lot of unanswered questions surrounded by a ton of mystique.

We do know with much certainty that steelhead are voracious feeders rapidly growing on a diet of fish, squid and a variety of other marine life. This is what

Sitting at Roderick Haig-Brown's desk in Campbell River, British Columbia. From early on, Haig-Brown's thoughtful, insightful writing had a profound influence on me. I believe he should be required reading for all those who venture to the river.

creamy in color, and somewhat translucent with brown to purple spotting and blotching. The reports also revealed that steelhead at sea feed in measurable quantities on northern anchovy, chinook salmon smolts, smelt, three-spine sticklebacks, and various crab and snail larvae.

This knowledge isn't necessarily going to change my approach to fly selection, but it confirms my belief that steelhead are conditioned to eat a wide variety of food sources. Although, just for fun, I will experiment in tying some flies utilizing the Atka mackerel color scheme!

One thing came to my realization during my

they are conditioned to react to and ingest. It's also the reason we tie and select the flies we do. I see the river as an extension of the ocean. The fish swim right in having just fed every day for one to several years on oceanic food. I want my flies to resemble just that: oceanic steelhead chow.

All the flies I fish from winter through early summer are meant to resemble marine life forms—creatures that exist in the wild in an amazing array of colors from the brightest of reds to near-black, some so transparent they are barely detectable to the human eye. Some have tentacles, some sharp-rayed fins. They come distinctly striped, spotted and mottled in

BLACK DRESS

I FISH THE BLACK DRESS during the last hour of failing light on the high-desert tributaries of the Columbia River. But more often I use it as a follow-up fly to a missed "player." Dressed in smaller sizes, the Little Black Dress usually turns the trick.

BLACK DRESS

HOOK:	Alec Jackson spey or Tiemco 7999
TAIL:	Dyed red golden pheasant crest
BODY:	Black seal fur dubbing
RIB:	Oval silver tinsel
HACKLE:	Black saddle
WING:	Black polar bear or substitute

two or more pigments. Most have trademark shining eyes, plainly visible to anything wishing to make a meal of them. Many species are iridescent. Upon close examination, no matter how odd-looking out of the water, in their natural environment their body parts seem to move as one. They are highly animated, adorned with multiple appendages that pulse and move. These are the qualities I try to incorporate in the design and construction of my flies. I believe steelhead react to them as a conditioned response that is genetically predisposed for marine survival.

The shape of a fly designed to look like an escaping fish or propelling squid is of critical importance. The answer is easy: this universal shape is oval or tear dropped. As my friend Ed Ward says, "If your fly isn't square, you're probably fine." I believe shape, size, and movement are more important than color. I don't believe steelhead are particularly concerned with color because they see most of their prey silhouetted against the sky as they ambush from below, often in low atmospheric light. Color schemes in fly selection become of use to the angler as river conditions and water clarity vary. The fish simply must see your fly.

Before we continue discussing shape and movement, I wish to make clear that presentation of the fly is the most critical element in triggering a strike from a steelhead. Every inanimate object in the river drifts, tumbles, or floats as it is swept downstream with the pull of the current. Animate objects such as insects, fish, and crustaceans typically move upstream, downstream, or crawl along the bottom. Lateral movement by these organisms certainly does occur, particularly with fish, but it's usually quick and short in duration. Insects that inhabit the sturdy flow preferred by steelhead aren't strong enough to swim directly sideways to the current. Therefore, steelhead are not accustomed to seeing objects, whether living or non-living, swimming powerfully and steadily across current. It's rare that anything in the river exhibits such behavior. A fly tethered to the angler's leader swims powerfully, sending out a beacon as it makes its way in a direct path to shore. This alone, irrespective of fly pattern, is usually enough to get a response from an active steelhead. Add color and movement to the fly's construction and the steelhead can't resist.

When we talk about movement in flies, we are talking about a requirement for materials that pulse and undulate in the current. Remember the highly animated squid? Simply put, movement within the fly is a good thing. A very good thing. So is detail and contrasting color. Detail and movement are particularly important in clear-water conditions. The clearer the water, the more time the steelhead has to scrutinize and become suspect of the fly's authenticity. This is where speys, dees, Intruder, and General Practitioner-style flies work at their maximum efficiency. As visibility decreases, detail is lost and the fly is in the steelhead's window of vision for a shorter time. The steelhead's response time is quick and sudden as when someone tosses an object your way and sharply says, "Think fast!" you may not have any notion of what the object is—it could be a set of car keys, it could be a tarantula—but your ready hands and mind instinctively react to catch it. At these times of lessened visibility, solid, or bi-colored marabou flies, rabbit-strip leeches, and similar designs become notably effective. They are not detailed, casting a densely opaque silhouette that I find very useful when visibility is low.

Fancily detailed flies with lots of movement and simple marabous with a little movement are clearly interchangeable in like water conditions. Remember, it's the fly's powerful presence swimming across the current that's most important. However, there are times when by adhering to these philosophies I believe there's an increase in the odds of hooking a steelhead. It's also satisfying to put some thought in to fly selection whether a steelhead is hooked or not.

A Fly Box for the Seasons

I choose my flies based on fishing conditions, but thankfully an exact science isn't necessary. Those precious steelies truly are forgiving. Although I own a lot of flies and a lot of fly boxes, including my favorite hop-out-of-the-boat-and-fish-a-run box—a Ziploc sandwich bag—my year round get-the-job-done arsenal of flies could be easily carried in just two boxes.

One box would be geared toward conditions I'd encounter winter, spring and early summer, the other late summer through fall. Let's call the former box

Flies are as much for the angler as they are for the steelhead. This selection of spey flies tied by one of my sports for the day was about as pretty a box of working flies I have ever seen. The flies we choose to fish often reflect our feelings toward the sport.

NIGHT HAWK

THE NIGHT HAWK is a traditional simple-wing Atlantic salmon pattern that has always captured my interest. What can I say? I find it extremely handsome, and the fish seem to think so as well. I also tie the Night Hawk in hairwing and spey versions. I've taken steelhead (as well as Atlantic salmon) on this pattern during all seasons of the year.

the coastal box, referring to the fact that the rivers most of us fish that time of year are in close proximity to salt water. The latter box we'll simply refer to as the fall box.

Remember, the patterns, not the volume of flies, in these boxes are confidently selected to handle any river or situation I may encounter. The coastal box I carry on Washington's Skagit and Sauk rivers in March is the same box I carry on the Dean River in British Columbia in June or July, or Oregon's Sandy River in February. Keep in mind, the contents of these boxes are simply guidelines designed for this writing in hopes of giving you a better understanding of how I gear up. Specific patterns are not important; those that I name are for reference.

With that in mind, if you were to peek into the working fly boxes of, say, 25 veteran steelheaders, I can almost guarantee you wouldn't see many of the

same patterns repeated in another's box. You'd definitely see repeated sizes, styles, colors, and overall theme, but, for the most part, experienced steelheaders design and tie their own patterns.

Knowing that basic size and shape are of first importance, we are given copious amounts of freedom and latitude to mix and match colors and materials to create workable flies that we can call our own. You can even give them a fancy, frou frou name like

BLACK AND YELLOW MARABOU

THE BLACK AND YELLOW MARABOU is a color combo I turn to in spring and early summer when moss and algae begin to form on river rock, and the river is running a little high and cloudy from runoff. It has been a good producer for me, particularly on the Stilliguamish and Sauk rivers.

Starlight Wanderer Spey or Jeremy's Special Dark—but please, no matter how tempting it may seem, don't name a fly after your wife or girlfriend.

"How'd ya do today Dave?"

"Awesome, I landed an ass-kickin' 16-pound buck. Jumped five times and damn near spooled me twice. Check out the size of the line burn on my finger!"

"Wow, what fly'd he take?"

"A size 2 Precious Pamela."

BLACK AND YELLOW MARABOU

HOOK: Tiemco 7999

BODY: Rear half—yellow marabou palmered
        Front half—black marabou palmered

COLLAR: Natural guinea hackle

"Nifty, I caught one today too using my Amorous Amy. . . ."

Let's take a look at how I'd fill my basic coastal box, starting with color. We'll begin with a quick, down-and-dirty glance followed by a more in-depth look. The difference between black, purple, and dark blue to me is fairly insignificant as far as their efficiency at hooking fish is concerned. I carry all these colors

PURPLE MARABOU

I CAUGHT MY FIRST STEELHEAD on a *Purple Marabou, so I will always hold an affinity for it. Purple is simply a superb no-nonsense color for steelhead. It shows up well in a wide range of conditions, and is probably the best color for water with poor visibility. I use Purple Marabous frequently as a guide-fly during the Skagit River's catch-and-release season. I know if we can get it in the vicinity of a steelhead, it will work.*

PURPLE MARABOU

HOOK: Tiemco 7999

BODY: Rear half—purple marabou palmered
Front half—purple marabou palmered
Between halves add flash if desired

COLLAR: Natural guinea hackle

alone and in combinations though mainly for some spicy variety. I also carry bright patterns with orange, red, yellow in combinations, along with some pinks. That's it. You really don't need much more. If you want to carry more flies, be my guest, but the bulk of my box is half dark, half bright with a few neutral

toned patterns mixed in. I carry heavier-dressed spey-style flies along with marabous and prawn-style flies in sizes ranging from 1/0 to 3/0. What's more important than hook size, however, is the size and length of the fly. For these conditions my flies are in the one-and-a-half-inch to three-inch range.

Sticking to the basic size range, I carry flies varying

PURPLE AND CERISE MARABOU

THIS FLY IS JUST A REPRESENTATIVE of the multiple colors I blend with purple to give the fly a little contrast. Other common colors that work well to complement purple are: orange, yellow, kingfisher blue, and black. But you can mix and match as you wish —I truly believe the steelies love it all.

PURPLE AND CERISE MARABOU

HOOK: Tiemco 7999

BODY: Rear two-thirds—purple and cerise marabou plumes wound simultaneously. Front one-third—purple marabou palmered

COLLAR: Cerise guinea hackle

in the size of their dress. Some are slimmer and lighter, reducing buoyancy and sinking a little quicker, when I feel I need some extra depth. I also design some flies with buoyancy in mind for fishing over large boulders or a shallow stretch of water. The General Practitioner is a good example. If tied with a fairly wide shellback, the golden pheasant flank feathers tied on top of the hook will actually plane a

bit. I don't care much for changing my sink-tip in the middle of a run. By changing to a fly designed for the situation and lengthening or shortening my leader, I effectively and quickly adjust to the present conditions.

Occasionally I feel the need for a smaller fly. It's always when I have a steelhead in front of me that plucks but won't make a full grab. After covering the

RED AND HOT ORANGE MARABOU

BEFORE I STARTED FISHING the Orange and Yellow Marabou, Red and Orange was my choice when I wanted to fish a bright marabou fly. It's caught a lot of steelhead for me over the years.

RED AND HOT ORANGE MARABOU

HOOK: Tiemco 7999

BODY: Rear half—hot orange marabou palmered. Front half—red marabou palmered

COLLAR: Red guinea hackle

fish a time or two with a different pattern in the same size and no results, I try one more time with the smaller fly. Often it's just the ticket. The smaller fly I chose is roughly half the size of the original fly that found the interested fish. If the original was three inches long, my follow-up fly is one and a half inches. Consequently, the smallest fly in my box is about three-quarters of an inch to an inch long.

The fall box is geared for water conditions typical of late summer and fall: floating-line time! Wet flies are predominantly dark with purple and black taking up most of the space. A bright pattern or two ride along, as follow-up flies for a persnickety yet interested player. Light-toned, drab patterns for the same purpose take a seat; some Muddlers, a Bomber, and a Steelhead Caddis round things out. All these flies are tied on sizes 2 to 6 hooks of varying degrees of fullness and sparseness.

You can carry and fish all the patterns your heart

desires. It's part of the fun, but for all practical purposes one needs only several patterns to cover the floating-line conditions encountered in steelhead country. To drive this point home, I'll put together a fly box of minimal selection right now for you that I would be perfectly confident with on dozens of fall rivers where surface-fishing conditions exist. Remember, it's not the volume that matters here, it's the selection. Here goes:

No-Name Summer Fly (could also be a Purple Peril, Green-Butt Skunk etc.) in size 3 or 4

Natural Muddler in size 4

Black Dress tied sparsely on a size 5 or 6

Bomber in size 6

Steelhead Caddis in size 8

To really refine things, if you told me all I could take was the No-Name Summer Fly and the Muddler—that's it—for a whole season of floating-line fishing, I wouldn't feel handicapped one bit. I sincerely mean that. The good news is I don't have to. I love having lots of variety in my fly box—but it's mainly to please me.

The Magic of Marabou

I have much adulation for tying, fishing, and simply admiring the grace and beauty of classic Atlantic salmon flies and their seductive steelhead derivatives. But the simple, some may say lowly, marabou fly is a central component in my arsenal of steelhead catching flies, particularly as a workhorse, no-nonsense, "guide fly." What marabous may lack in elegance, they more than make up for in efficiency and ease of tying. What's more, a properly dressed marabou looks incredibly fishy in the water and clearly exudes that desired squid-like shape. They can be tied in every color and combinations of colors imaginable.

Flies tied with marabou are not new to steelheading. The late, great angler, Al Knudson, fished a humungous white marabou fly he designed for cold off-color water as early as the 1940s. However, marabou was not widely used and recognized as an important material until the late 1970s and early '80s. Washington river guides John Farrar and Bob Aid are often credited for being the first to fully recognize its virtues and experiment with tying techniques. Until John and Bob started experimenting at the vise, marabou was typically tied in simple clumps to serve as wings and throats. Farrar began tying spey flies using marabou as the hackle in an unconventional manner. He spun the marabou in a dubbing loop where he could adjust the length and blend colors as he wished. At once thoughtful and beautiful, the

technique is difficult and can lead to some frustration. Bob Aid, intrigued with John's resulting fly, but not wanting to deal with the complications of tying them, began wrapping the whole marabou plume on the hook like a long rooster hackle—brilliant! If Aid is the innovator of this indispensable technique, not enough credit has been given him. Thank you, Bob!

Bob's marabou flies typically utilize two marabou blood plumes of the same or contrasting colors, followed by a hackle to support the marabou. The supporting hackle is an important component as it creates a vortex that keeps the fine, soft marabou from completely collapsing in the current. Hackling can be accomplished with all sorts of feathers, but I have found duck flank and guinea hackle the best at providing support to create a good vortex. It's also extremely important not to over-dress the marabou. It's easy to apply too much. This makes the marabou so dense that it doesn't sink, and in some extreme cases, won't even penetrate water, floating down the river looking like a duck. This brings us back to the importance of the hackle and resulting vortex. The right amount of applied marabou is able to take full advantage of the vortex, creating the illusion of bulk. It allows the marabou to breathe and undulate in the current at maximum efficiency.

The marabou can be tied in either by the butt or the tip, each creating a slightly different overall appearance to the fly. The choice is yours. Typically the first plume is tied in half to two-thirds up the hook shank, followed by the second, and then the hackle. If any flash is desired it should be applied after the first plume and before the second. A method of application that, for me, creates marabou patterns with undeniably the most life-like action and movement is to wrap two plumes simultaneously up the hook shank in a palmered fashion. I start by selecting two long, wide marabou plumes usually of different colors, matching them to equal size. After the plumes are prepared by removing enough bottom fluff so only useable fibers are left on the stem, I match the feathers up and tie them in simultaneously, by their butts at a point slightly forward of the hook point. The plumes are then carefully wound up the shank, again simultaneously, spacing the wraps just as in palmering. Finish with the hackle of your choice and the fly is complete. As stated earlier, this technique creates a fly with superb movement. It also blends the colors in a variegated effect which can be achieved no other way. Obviously, color combinations one can achieve are endless, but I do have a personal favorite that has accounted for several hundred steelhead including

HOT ORANGE AND YELLOW MARABOU

THE LARGEST STEELHEAD I ever landed came on a variegated Yellow and Orange Marabou. Coincidence? More than likely, but this combination flashes and glows without looking out of place like no other. I use it confidently on overcast days, and when the river has a slight touch of color.

HOT ORANGE AND YELLOW MARABOU

HOOK: Tiemco 7999

BODY: Golden yellow and hot orange marabou plumes palmered simultaneously the length of the hook shank.

COLLAR: Barred wood duck flank feather

my largest steelhead ever, a mid-20-pound buck I caught on my beloved Sauk River in the spring of 1997. Hot orange and golden yellow combined in this fashion makes for a fly that glows like no other without looking out of place and overly garish.

Once again, for as much as I admire the detailed, intricate beauty of fancy flies, I must admit that over the years, marabou flies have been an incalculable

asset to my success on the water, particularly while guiding in winter and spring. I am 100 percent confident in them. They're inexpensive and easy to tie—when you lose one there's no remorse. And, contrary to the disparaging remarks one occasionally hears from fly-tying elitists, I find a fetchingly sleek steelhead marabou aesthetically pleasing.

DC PRAWN

ED WARD'S INTRUDER FLIES had an influence on this design. Namely, the extensive use of ostrich herl. The DC prawn caught me my first Atlantic salmon, a beautiful cock fish taken from the Dartmouth River on Quebec's Gaspé Peninsula. The "DC" stands for Dartmouth cock. Yeah, steelhead demolish it, too.

My Choice of Hooks

Hooks to dress one's flies can be selected for a multitude of reasons. The reason can be as simple as visual appeal to complement a show fly or as complex as matching hook shape to pattern with proper weight and balance—and a desired style of eye to accommodate a preferred knot. In a working steelhead fly, there are several characteristics that must be considered.

The most popular hooks for steelhead are traditional Atlantic salmon hooks. Their elegant shape and design, black finish, and turned-up loop eye lend themselves well to the form and function of steelhead dressings. Salmon hooks, unlike others, are normally not given an "x" designation as indications of diameter and length. They are given simple designations such as light or heavy. These are reasonably effective for communicating choice of hook, but personally I know what I want my hook to do.

DC PRAWN

HOOK: Alec Jackson spey

TAG: Flat gold tinsel

REAR HACKLE: Black saddle

FEELERS(TAIL): Orange ostrich, splayed in two bunches

RIBBING: Flat gold tinsel

BODY HACKLE: Black saddle

BODY: Two parts black seal, one part orange seal, one part fiery orange S.L.F. dubbing, blended.

UNDERWING: Long jungle cock

COLLAR: Several turns of picked-out orange seal followed by black saddle.

WING: Clump of black ostrich followed by orange ostrich.

Visually, it's plain to see if a hook is heavy or light, long or short. Common sense dictates that a fly designed to fish on the surface shouldn't be tied on heavy iron. Conversely, I wouldn't tie a fly meant to be fished deeply on light wire. But the hook is yours

ORANGE HERON

THIS IS THE FLY THAT STARTED the spey fly craze more than 20 years ago. The late Syd Glasso of Forks, Washington was the first steel-header to devoutly tie and fish speys for steelhead. The Orange Heron is perhaps the model spey fly— at least in the steelhead world—to which all later-comers are compared. Funny, I don't know many people who fish the Orange Heron, yet everyone enamored with spey flies seems to have tied it at one time or another. I am here to say that the Orange Heron is not only beautiful in its simple elegance, it's a damn good steelhead fly.

ORANGE HERON

HOOK:	Alec Jackson spey
BODY:	Rear two-thirds orange floss, front one-third hot orange seal fur
RIB:	Medium flat silver and oval tinsel
HACKLE:	Heron or blue-eared pheasant
THROAT:	Teal flank
WING:	Four hot orange hackle tips

to utilize in any manner you wish. It may be smart to carry some sinking flies tied on light-wire hooks, for instance. When covering a shallow, boulder-strewn run, the light-wire dressing rides higher in the water, thus keeping hang-ups to a minimum. When fishing flies with a floating line designed to fish just below the surface, a heavy-wire hook is useful to penetrate fast surface currents.

All the major hook manufacturers offer steelhead and salmon hooks. Hooks manufactured in Japan, in my opinion, are of the best quality and finish. The iron is extremely hard with chemically sharpened points that rarely need sharpening. I do NOT recom-

mend sharpening one until it is absolutely necessary. Many steelhead hooks from Partridge and Mustad need sharpening right out of the box. Not so with product from the top Japanese manufacturers. The loop-eye returns are perfectly tapered to the shank and the barbs are small and brittle. In addition, Japanese hooks are nearly flawless in their quality control. It's rare to find a defective hook in a package. It is still wise, however, to thoroughly inspect your hook before tying and fishing.

I tie the majority of my wet flies on two hooks: the Daiichi Alec Jackson spey and the Tiemco 7999. The elegant bend and length of the Alec Jackson spey hook is the aesthetic choice for many of my fancier flies such as speys, dees, and variances of both. The Jackson hook also lends itself well to sparsely tied prawn patterns. As a bonus, the hooks are available in several finishes including black, silver, gold, bronze, and blue. I typically stick with black, but I do utilize the other four finishes in several of my working patterns. The Jackson hooks come in odd sizes: 3, 5 and 7. The large sizes are $1\frac{1}{2}$ and 3/0. The odd sizing doesn't mean much other than, for example, size 3 is between a normal 2 and 4, size 5 falls between 4 and 6, etc.

The workhorse hook in my fishing and guiding arsenal is without a doubt the Tiemco 7999. The heavy-wire 7999 is comparable in size and shape to the Mustad 36890 and the Partridge M, but their quality and reliability are no match for the Tiemco. In sizes 1/0 and 2/0, it is the perfect hook for winter fishing with marabou and rabbit-strip flies as well as prawns and standard wets. The Tiemco 7999 is also an excellent hook for standard summer-run flies in sizes 2 through 8.

The sister to the stout 7999 is the light-wire 7989. It's an excellent option when a lighter hook is desired. It's a good choice for surface flies and low-water-style dressings. Be cautioned, though. The wire is very light. All but the sparsest of wet flies fished in slow, gentle water will have a tendency to skate on the surface. The 7999 is the better choice for bread-and-butter wet-fly fishing.

For tying surface flies, in addition to the Tiemco 7989, I also utilize the Partridge Wilson for certain caddisfly patterns, and the Partridge CS42 for all of my Bombers and Bomber variations. The CS42 is a down-turned loop-eye hook in a bronze finish that is a perfect complement to the Bomber design. The down-turned eye nicely accommodates a turle knot without getting in the way of the Bomber's forward-sloping wing.

Another hook I rely on is the Tiemco 700. The 700 is a heavy-wire hook with a down-turned ring

Longtime friend Scott Hagen tails a great Sauk River wild doe.

eye. It is the only hook I use for tying and fishing Muddler Minnows. I like to fish my Muddlers just below a choppy surface. The heavy TMC 700 ensures my fly doesn't skate on the surface. The down eye also helps to keep the Muddler's flared deer-hair head from riding to the surface. Because it is a ring-eye hook, I temporarily abandon routine use of the turle knot and instead use an improved clinch.

Hooks are as much of a pragmatic choice as they are given to personal appeal. They are tools or components in a work of art or both. Thoughtful consideration should be given to both.

The hook is literally our connection to the steelhead and—I can't stress this too many times—should be inspected for defects BEFORE tying and fishing. It certainly pays to occasionally inspect the hook while fishing. Far too many times, I've discovered the person I'm guiding is fishing with a broken hook point—usually the result of colliding with a hard surface during casting. Sadly, I've been witness to broken hooks resulting in broken hearts: Steelhead don't seem to stay attached very long to a blunt-ended hook.

"Ah, more pointless fishing, Bob?" is my usual unwelcome response to such a blunder.

Stay aware and alert! Inspect your hook, knots, leader, and rod ferrules continually. Steelies are too difficult to come by—take care of the things you have control over. Keep your hook sharp as well. I said earlier that quality Japanese hooks stay sharp for a long time. Eventually, though, even these fine hooks need to be sharpened. When that time comes, use a file specifically made for hooks. Note I said FILE. Leave the "diamond sharpeners" and cute little stones with built in hook groove in your trout vest. You're fishing for steelhead, with steelhead hooks, man! Use a file and be sure when you sharpen that hook you don't

B & O

B&O STANDS FOR black and orange. I fish the B&O quite frequently on Oregon's Deschutes River. It's a simple wingless fly that gets the job done.

just file a little point. You need to file in a cutting edge down to a sticky-sharp point. I file both sides and the bottom of the hook point, lightly hitting the top. Once you do sharpen your hook, check it frequently—a sharpened hook never seems to retain its sharpness as long as the initial chemical sharpening from the factory. Never assume because you haven't hung bottom that your hook doesn't need sharpening. Fine river sediment and sand is constantly eating away at that point, particularly in turgid flows. Your hook is literally being sand-blasted.

Another consideration is de-barbing. I never, under any circumstance, fish with a barbed hook. Barbed hooks are rough on fish you intend to release. And the removal of a barbed hooked from human flesh can be an easily avoidable nightmare. I remove the barb from each and every hook before I tie my fly. Although rare, I've seen hooks break while debarbing. What a bummer to have your exquisitely tied fly rendered useless before you even get a chance to fish it. A pair of smooth-surfaced, fine, or needlenose pliers handles the task well.

B & O

HOOK:	Alec Jackson spey, gold
TAG:	Flat gold tinsel
BODY:	Rear half—orange seal fur followed by two turns of black saddle. Remainder is black seal fur.
RIB:	Oval gold tinsel
HACKLE:	Black saddle

Surface Flies

Seeing the surface of the river erupt as a supercharged steelhead engulfs a surface fly is an unforgettable experience. Few anglers have the courage to fish on top, yet I know of no one who wouldn't be thrilled to experience steelhead angling's ultimate feat. Under the right circumstances, it isn't difficult. Why are so many anglers afraid to give it a fair go? I guess they simply lack confidence in the method.

We've been conditioned to fish deeply for steelhead and believe that surface fly fishing is done by other people under the most ideal of conditions. We are fearful of sacrifice. Yet we diligently fish a wet fly all day in hopes of hooking a single fish. The same people knot on a surface fly, fish it for a half an hour with no results, then give up and go back to the wet

DEC'S BOMBER

I AFFECTIONATELY CALL THIS Dec's Bomber, not because I invented it, came up with the color scheme, or anything like that. I call it this because I have fished the very same fly in this design for more than 10 years! It's my pet Bomber and has raised its share of steelhead.

DEC'S BOMBER

HOOK:	Partridge CS42
TAIL:	Natural polar bear hair or substitute
BODY:	Natural deer hair with band of orange deer hair in center, spun and trimmed.
HACKLE:	Brown neck hackle palmered through body.
WING:	Natural polar bear hair or substitute

fly. They continue to go fishless, happily.

The answer is simple: If you want to experience the exhilaration of a surface grab, you have to commit the same time and dedication to fishing the surface as you do when fishing below the surface. As for the challenge of finding ideal conditions to fish on top, they are all around.

Whenever floating-line, wet-fly opportunities abound, so do prospects for success with a surface fly. During late summer and autumn, prime floating-line conditions exist in nearly every steelhead river on the Columbia and Snake rivers system. The Deschutes, Clearwater, Grande Ronde, John Day, and Snake—to name a few—boast ideal conditions for surface techniques. Perfect fly water, fairly stable conditions, and water temperatures ranging in the low to high 50s comprise the perfect recipe afforded by these rivers this time of year. In fact, good conditions exist throughout the entire steelhead's range, from northern California through British Columbia and into Alaska, at one time or another.

Steelhead come eagerly to the surface in a variety of water types, and not just a smooth glassy surface that so many people exclusively recognize as surface-fly water. The flies we choose need to be engineered to perform in a variety of conditions. First, I want to be able to see my fly as it enticingly struggles across the current. That's the reason I'm fishing on top in the first place. I don't want to miss a thing. I basically fish on the surface with just two pattern styles. For smooth to slightly broken surfaces I favor thinly-dressed caddisfly patterns; in choppy, tumultuous flows, I employ Bombers.

If you haven't noticed by now, I haven't used the term dry fly. The reason is although the term is perfectly acceptable in describing where the fly fishes—

STEELHEAD CADDIS

WHAT CAN I ADD? Bill McMillan came up with an easily tied winner here. Fish it with a riffling hitch, keep your eyes focused on it, and hang on—good things are certain to happen.

STEELHEAD CADDIS

HOOK: Partridge Wilson
BODY: Orange fur dubbing
WING: Mottled turkey tail
COLLAR AND HEAD:
    Natural deer hair spun

on the water's surface—the term dry fly is more closely associated with dead-drifting a stiffly-hackled fly. The bulk of steelhead taken on top are done so with the fly swimming under tension and leaving a disruptive wake. There are several methods of taking steelhead on top, and I feel that surface fly is a more fitting general term to communicate at what level the fly is being fished. From there the techniques most commonly employed are waking, skating, and finally, dead-drifting. Each technique requires a different style of fly. The terms waking and skating are often interchanged, but I feel that the two terms have different meanings. Flies that wake are really fished at varying degrees in the surface. When you consider a V-hull or semi-V-hull boat as it motors along plowing water and leaving a wake, a portion of the hull is under water. The same goes for the fly. If at least part of the fly doesn't break the surface film it can't leave a wake. On the other hand, when you consider how a roller skate or ice skate functions, it rides on top of a surface, not in it. In my opinion, skating flies would fall in to the category of flies that ride on the surface.

Any miniscule wake it might leave is inconsequential.

Waking flies cover the broadest range of conditions encountered by the angler, and prominently defines the most accepted method of taking steelhead on the surface. Flies are generally built on light-wire hooks with materials applied to increase surface tension and create a visible-to-the-angler silhouette while leaving an enticing wake to attract steelhead. Wings are often applied to aid in creating a surface disturbance or to help the angler see the fly. Material components structured on top of the fly really aren't visible to the fish and can be applied in any manner or color desired to make it more visible. Hackle is sometimes incorporated to simulate life and movement rather than a primary means of floatation. Deer, elk, and moose hair are most often used as winging and tailing material and are the principal source of buoyancy. Bodies can be tied with natural or synthetic

GREASE LINER

I FISH THE GREASE LINER from time to time on a smooth surface out of respect to its originator and one of the finest steelhead fishers I have ever known, Harry Lemire.

GREASE LINER

HOOK:	Partridge Wilson
TAIL:	Deer or moose body hair
BODY:	Black dubbing or any color desired
HACKLE:	Grizzly saddle tied sparse
WING:	Deer or moose body hair

materials as the angler wishes. A slightly beefy body structure is often desired creating a chunky silhouette riding down in the surface film.

Patterns ranging from simple to complex all seem to work at tempting steelhead, providing the fly leaves some form of discernable wake. Generally the smoother and slicker the water surface the more subtle the wake should be. Harry Lemire's Grease Liner and Bill McMillan's Steelhead Caddis have both proven excellent flies for such surfaces. The Steelhead Caddis is the result of McMillan's variation on the Muddler as a waking fly for steelhead. Tied on a Partridge Wilson light-wire dry-fly salmon hook, the simplicity and sparseness of its deer hair design is the foundation of its effectiveness. The Caddis fishes beautifully when a riffling hitch is added to the leader just behind its deer hair head. The buoyant head planes above water while the remainder of the fly fishes enticingly slightly subsurface. Steelhead rarely miss this fly—takes rarely result in a missed fish. It's my pattern of choice when guiding people who want to take a steelhead on the surface. The ease at which

it stays on the surface and its low-riding profile making it difficult for steelhead to miss are ingredients for angler success. I set up my sports in a run or tailout with a smooth-as-glass, even flow, knot on a riffled Steelhead Caddis tied with a burnt orange body to match the natural insect, and turn 'em loose. In truth, nothing could be easier.

Lemire's Grease Liner is also designed to emulate the natural, large caddisflies of late summer and early autumn, typically called October Caddis. It is similar to the Elk Hair Caddis design with modifications intended to enhance its waking capabilities, notably the clipped ends of the deer or moose-hair head. The ends are trimmed much longer than they are on an Elk Hair Caddis tied for trout; they are also splayed out in order for water to break around the fly, causing a wake. A good application of flexible cement helps to stiffen the flared tips further enhancing its

MUDDLER

*IN SUMMER AND FALL, I believe the Muddler,
fished on a floating line and just under the surface,
is the most effective fly there is. Takes are nearly
always vicious and visible. Personally, I like to
ensure that my Muddlers ride under the surface by
tying them sparsely on a heavy wire Tiemco 700
hook. The pictured fly is tied in natural colors, and
accounts for the bulk of my work with the fly. I do,
however, tie and fish them in purple and black, and
with other various modifications just for fun.*

MUDDLER

HOOK: Tiemco 700

BODY: Silver or gold flat tinsel

UNDERWING:
> Squirrel tail

WING: Turkey tail

GILLS (OPTIONAL):
> Bright red dubbing

COLLAR AND HEAD:
> Spun natural deer hair

waking capability.

The Grease Liner requires a bit more skill to fish effectively than the Steelhead Caddis. It doesn't take a riffling hitch—it wasn't designed to, and tends to lie on its side. It requires a fairly precise casting angle to keep it from going under, and once under it usually stays there. Steelhead will still take the fly if it dips below the surface, but that's not the point of fishing on top. Right? Keeping a Grease Liner waking true across the surface is very satisfying. The fly's effectiveness at coaxing steelhead has been proven for decades.

For the ultimate in versatility, I believe the Bomber is the definitive surface fly. As with all steelhead flies, one can freely modify the Bomber style to meet one's own desires whether purely for function or aesthetic appeal or a combination of both. I enjoy tying Bombers with duel and multi-colored banded bodies that satisfy both. The banding may look more animated and interesting to the steelhead—possibly the difference between a look and a full take. Aesthetically, the alternating bands of color are pleasing to me, and give me an extra boost of confidence.

With thought and ingenuity the Bomber design is a superb pallet that begs modification. Bill McMillan's Air B.C. and John Hazel's Water Ouzel are two examples that have tempted me many times. The Air B.C. is basically a bright-orange Bomber without hackle and with deer hair wings jutting out at a slight upward angle from the sides of the body. The wings make the fly wobble, creating some interesting wake patterns. I experimented with the Air B.C. quite a lot through the early 1990s while guiding the Grand Ronde River. It's a highly visible pattern that's a pleasure to use on a choppy surface. The steelhead that came to the erratic wake patterns emitted by the fly usually attacked aggressively—the resulting take an exploding upheaval of water and fish. Hazel's Water Ouzel has a split wing and a long weeping spey hackle wound through the body. The adaptation of the spey hackle creates a wickedly lifelike presence on the surface of the river. Much like

I have done very little actual skating for steelhead. In the brief time I spent trying the technique, I did manage to raise a couple of fish. Flies designed to ride on hackle-tips define skating flies such as Roderick Haig-Brown's Steelhead Bee and the Bivisible. It seems to me that because skating flies don't cause much commotion on the water's surface as do waking patterns, they are better suited for clear water and being presented over known productive holding lies.

I have taken a number of steelhead on dead-drifted dry flies. It's an experience that seemingly defies all that we know and expect out of steelhead.

This perfect tidewater buck fell for a Skagit Mist, but I'm certain he would have taken any offering that was presented his way.

the Air B.C., the steelhead take the Ouzel with mettle.

I tie most of my Bombers using stiff polar bear hair for the wing and tail. The original Bomber employs calf tail, which works well and is highly visible, but I find the material to be a little soft, with a tendency to go under. The stiff polar bear hair keeps the fly waking nicely through rough water and is visible enough that keeping track of my fly is not an issue. Through countless hours of experimentation I've found that a size 6 hook is the perfect size for a general searching pattern. It's easy to cast, shows up well, and the steelhead like it.

They rise up and engulf the fly just like the large trout they are. I prefer to fish the dry fly in pocket-water that I know traditionally holds steelhead. The fly itself doesn't matter much to tell you the truth. I've caught more on Bombers than anything else. In my view, Haig-Brown's Steelhead Bee is the honorable choice.

No Other Way to Tell It

Even before I became intimate with steelhead and their behavior, I was enamored with the beautiful, colorful flies designed to seduce them. I had no

AIR B.C.

ANOTHER PATTERN POPULARIZED by Bill McMillan, the Air B.C. is a great Bomber variation that really gets down to business when fished on a choppy, broken surface.

AIR B.C.

HOOK:	Partridge CS42
TAIL:	Natural polar bear hair or substitute
BODY:	Orange deer hair spun and trimmed with untrimmed wings jutting out on both sides.
WING:	Natural polar bear hair or substitute

grasp of why steelhead took these showy creations that defied everything I had learned about Nature and how it applied to catching game fish. Maybe that's what partially intrigued me: a mysterious fish with a reputation and a name that was seemingly larger than life that took dazzling, vibrant flies resembling fantasy more than fish food. From the beginning, I fished them with confidence but hadn't a clue as to why.

Along the way I no longer needed to read in a book or have anyone explain to me about the arm-wrenching take an aggressive steelhead can deliver—I was experiencing it for myself! It was obvious to me that every steelhead that took my fly, no matter how subtle, or violently, was displaying aggressive behavior. With each new run I fished, every cast and swing I made, with each fresh steelhead hooked, I began to look at steelhead flies with a new eye. I began to see that they did look life-like. They did have a place in the river. They were like prey. The steelhead was the ultimate predator lurking behind hidden boulders amidst the liquid jade currents of my glacial river.

During those early days; I hung out and fished with Scott O'Donnell and Ed Ward. The three of us were inseparable: learning, discovering, experimenting, and sharing as a team. We all had the same ideas, passion, and convictions regarding flies: We knew most anything would work. We relished the fact. It was our secret. We loved flies! Every night at my home we tied flies in what we called a jam session. Like rock 'n rollers, we stayed up late creating, debating, feeding off one another until we were mentally spent. On winter days when the rivers were out of fishable shape, we'd hop in one of our rigs and head south to Seattle to make the fly-shop circuit in search of materials. We'd all spend way more money than was responsible—Ed usually bought a reel to go with his feathers. A bit of an addict, that Ed.

We'd come home with bags of marabou, rabbit

POMPIER

POMPIER MEANS FIREMAN IN FRENCH. Michel Beaudin of Gaspé, Quebec is a retired Montréal fireman who is the originator of this extremely effective pattern. Michel is one of the most sought-after Atlantic salmon guides on rivers of the Gaspe Peninsula. I had the pleasure of fishing with him one day on the York River, where I was fortunate to hook and land the salmon of my dreams on Beaudin's Pompier. Once back home in Washington I put the fly to good use on my steelhead rivers. I like it because it differs from all the usual patterns and colors being tossed around.

POMPIER

HOOK:	Alec Jackson spey
TAG:	Gold tinsel
TAIL:	Golden pheasant breast fibers
BODY:	Black seal fur dubbing
RIB:	Gold tinsel
WING:	Yellow polar bear or substitute
CHEEKS:	Jungle cock
COLLAR:	Bright green hackle
HEAD:	Red

strips, saddle hackles, golden pheasant and kingfisher skins, silk floss, and whatever the hot dubbing was at the time. A pack or two of hooks for each of us usually rounded things out. Then we'd head right back to my house to commence jammin'.

During these impromptu sessions at the vise, we learned much about materials and how quality mattered. I remember the first time I eagerly opened a bag of marabou dyed an appealing, vivid violet-blue only to find that there wasn't a single plume in the bag long enough or wide enough for my intended application. "That sucks!" I blurted out to my buds. From then on I have never purchased fly-tying materials without making a thorough inspection of them

right there in the store. If I pick up, say, a golden pheasant skin, I scrutinize it methodically, taking complete inventory of the length and quality of the individual feathers. Do I like the color? Are there enough long feathers, particularly the red flank feathers? Are the feathers straight or do they have some funky bend in them? Do the tippets have nice, even black barring? I also smell the skin. There's nothing worse than getting home, opening that plastic bag ,and getting thumped in the face by a stench that only a turkey vulture could love. Look through several—or all—of the skins for sale. Making sure you pick the very best one to suit your needs. It pays off immensely to

SKAGIT MIST

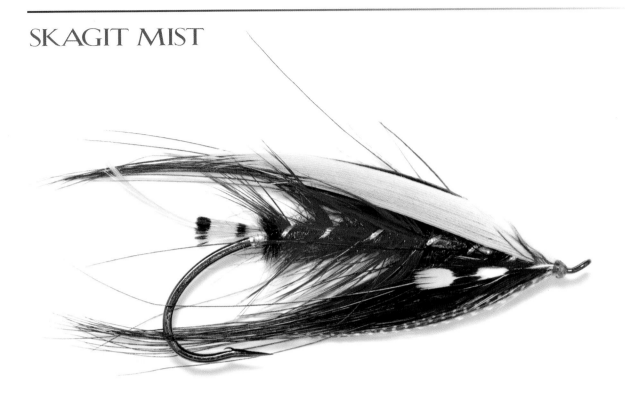

A VARIATION ON THE SCOTTISH AKROYD, my Skagit Mist has accounted for numerous steelhead on the Skagit, Sauk, and Dean rivers. It's a go-to searching pattern that shows up well under a range of water conditions. I also tie a version using black ostrich herl for the long spey hackle when I want a denser silhouette.

SKAGIT MIST

HOOK:	Alec Jackson spey
TAG:	Flat silver tinsel
TAIL:	Golden pheasant crest and tippet
BUTT:	Purple ostrich herl
BODY:	First half claret seal fur, second half black seal fur.
RIB:	Oval silver tinsel over first half, oval silver tinsel and flat blue tinsel over second half.
HACKLE:	Hot red saddle over first half, black spey hackle over second half.
THROAT:	Teal flank
WINGS:	White turkey tail
CHEEKS:	Jungle cock eyes
HEAD:	Red

tie with quality materials.

Over time, Scott, Ed and I progressively realized the importance of tying life-like flies with ample movement in their design. Ultimately it might not matter to the fish how much movement goes into the engineering of a fly, but it sure does matter to us. Finding a taking steelhead and putting your fly in position to be pelted by him is a difficult proposition. It's impossible to have any kind of control group for experimentation. You had better believe in that fly. Anything that can be done to bolster your confidence in the fly should be incorporated in its design. I'd love to tell you of both failed experiments and successful ones. But the fact is, any failed experiments I've experienced in trying out new fly patterns has nothing to do with the fish and everything to do with the fly and my feelings about it. Sure, I may have designed a fly that didn't keel properly or swam upside down, but that's engineering oversight. If I were to tough it out

mentally and fish with a poorly engineered fly, I'm certain that eventually it would catch a steelhead.

The fly patterns and designs that take steelhead are infinite. How we combine our personal aesthetics and what we, as individuals, perceive is fishy determines if we have the confidence necessary to faithfully fish that fly for many hours without a grab. Pardon me for not leading you into this smoothly but, to illustrate

THE MAHONEY

BRIGHT RED IS A HOT COLOR for steelhead. It's probably my favorite color to employ when fishing behind other anglers in late winter and spring. The Mahoney is a simple spey fly I tied in honor of Jerry Mahoney of Seattle, Washington, a fine steelhead angler who frequents the Sauk River. After the flood of 1990, the Skagit and Sauk saw many dramatic changes. One of the positive changes was on the Sauk where a beautiful and reliably productive run was formed. Jerry Mahoney was the first person I ever saw fishing it. So my immediate reference to the spot was, "Mahoney's," hence the name of this now popular run, and my red spey fly.

THE MAHONEY

HOOK:	Alec Jackson spey
BODY:	Rear third red floss; balance hot red seal fur.
RIB:	Flat pearl Mylar followed by medium oval silver tinsel.
HACKLE:	Black schlappen, one side stripped.
COLLAR:	Hot red schlappen followed by red guinea hen.
WING:	Four matching hackle tips from a hot red rooster neck.

my point, I am compelled to bombard you with some hard-won insight.

I once witnessed Ed Ward fish the same Intruder fly day in and day out for an entire winter—it was pink and white.

Bob Budd, an ophthalmologist from Pennsylvania, faithfully fished with me for four days on the Skagit, Sauk, and Skykomish rivers every April for a decade. He's an experienced, methodical angler whose success ratio while fishing with me was quite remarkable. His go-to fly (and the one that

accounted for at least 80 percent of his catch) was a purple and black Egg-Sucking Leech. My point? I don't know of a single other person from the vast number of knowledgeable local anglers who ever fishes that pattern. In Bob's confident hands it's deadly.

On a warm, sunny March day on the Skykomish, I was guiding in the good company of a man who had very little experience at winter steelheading. I've since forgotten his name, but I'll never forget the lesson he taught me. He had placed his faith in a size 6 little drab brown fly that had accounted for several steelhead for him while fishing the Wenatchee River, a high-desert stream, in autumn. First thing that March morning, I shoved a three-inch-long size 1/0

COAST ORANGE

DETAILS OF THE COAST ORANGE appear in the text of this chapter. The design of this fly lends itself well to variations. I have experimented with it extensively.

COAST ORANGE	
HOOK:	Alec Jackson spey
TAIL:	Natural golden pheasant flank feather
BODY:	Orange seal fur, thinly dubbed
RIB:	Wide flat pearl mylar and copper wire reversed wrapped.
COLLAR:	Same as tail
UNDERWING:	Orange polar bear hair or substitute
WING:	Cree hen neck hackles tied in tent style.

hot orange and red marabou in his face. It must have looked like a whole live rooster in drag to him. It did. He had no confidence in the fly whatsoever and desperately pleaded with me to fish his little no-name summer fly.

I explained to him my appreciation for his favorite pattern, but it was not fitting to our late winter conditions. Just as he needed confidence in the fly he would be fishing, as his guide, so did I. We fished all morning, carefully probing all of my favorite spots with no sign of steelhead. Periodically, he asked me if he could fish his fly. I just couldn't allow it. Fishing had already proven to be slow this morning; the last thing I felt we needed was to be fishing with a little, dingy fly. With the fruitless morning now over, we sat in my drift boat and ate lunch beside a beautiful run we had not yet fished. As we sat there eating, watching the river go by, the man turned to me and said, "This run sure reminds of one of my favorite runs on the Wenatchee." I could see his pleading eyes—please let me fish my fly. The words were just about to come out of his mouth when I told him to go ahead

and fish his fly through the run. Out in the river he looked like a completely different angler. He was poised and alert, commanding the run as if it were his. He was confident. You know the rest of the story. Yep, he hooked a Skykomish winter-run steelhead on his little, drab summer fly. Confidence is everything.

Another me and Ed story: Ward and I were on the Stilliguamish River one October day enjoying one of those magic times when the steelhead are aggressively taking and there were lots of them around. As I recall, the two of us landed 13 fish that day. Both Ed and I were changing flies after just about every fish we hooked. That's the time to experiment with flies: when you've found the mother-load, and they're biting.

Each newly knotted-on fly was sent out into the sparkling Stilly with great confidence. About two-thirds of the way through this terrific day, a young man who had been shadowing us came over and said, "Do you mind if I ask what the heck fly you guys are using?"

I could tell by the desperate look on his face and all the soaking-wet flies stuck on the fleece of his vest that he wasn't enjoying much success. I looked back at Ed, having every intention of helping the kid out, smiled and winked. Ed privately snickered back.

"Well," I said to the young angler, "We've hooked 'em on orange marabous, purple marabous, black General Practitioner, Thunder and Lightning, a funny hackle-tip thing in black and orange, a fly I call the Jungle Cock Rock . . . and whatever he's using right now!" As I pointed to Ed, he was instantly into another fish as if on queue. The kid hung his head and said, "I get it, I get it." I put my hand on his shoulder and told him that any one of those rejected flies hanging off his fleece patch would work today as long as he left it on and stopped worrying about the fly. I explained to him how and why Ed and I were changing flies after every fish—because we could— then I gave him a quick tune-up on his presentation. Within 10 minutes he was playing a steelhead of his own. He was thrilled.

I could go on and on sharing similar stories. I think I've made the point that confidence in your fly and how you present it are paramount. How you gain the confidence needed can come from many different angles and episodes.

I Prefer the Natural Look

As Scott, Ed, and I developed as steelheaders, we continued sharing many of the same opinions and convictions about steelhead fishing and flies, but now our flies were beginning to reflect our individual personalities and our evolving perceptions of what the fish wanted.

We took note of what flies other people were fishing on our rivers, particularly those whom we admired and respected as veteran steelheaders: Jerry Wintle, Charlie Gearheart, Harry Lemire, Bob Stroebel, and Jerry Mahoney to name a few. I'm always interested in what's in a person's fly box and what's attached to his leader. When it's the caliber of angler as those mentioned, I pay attention.

Harry Lemire's flies revealed to me the appeal of a buggy, natural-looking fly. Back when I first met him on the Skagit, Harry was fishing a prawn fly that looked incredibly realistic in the water. It was colorful yet neutral, brilliant yet subdued; it wasn't very large, simple yet complex in detail. The fly had a distinct life of its own. It had a powerful presence. Harry told me he had created this fly by tying with all-natural materials, in natural colors whenever possible. He used some dyed materials, he said, but never anything bold or fluorescent. Later I came to realize that all of Harry's patterns are this way. I was immediately captivated by the seductively natural look of Harry's flies and ever since have worked to incorporate this quality in my own flies.

Natural materials, for obvious reasons, look more real in the water than do synthetics. Can you picture a fox with a Mylar tail? I use synthetic material sparingly. If I use any at all, it's usually a little Mylar flash tied in a marabou or several strands mixed in a hair wing. Of course, ribbing material is synthetic or some sort of metal. There's no question that steelhead take flies and lures made with flashy, plastic-looking, synthetics, but I want my fly to appear as though it belongs in the ecosystem.

A season or two later, on a gorgeous spring day, I was sitting on a riverside log next to Lemire chatting with him about our favorite subject. Our talk turned to flies as I usually steer it when I'm with Harry—I really admire his stuff. He explained that he'd been having success with a pattern called the Usk Grub, an old Welsh salmon pattern named after the River Usk. I had seen the pattern in books but never tied one. Harry had one strung on his rod and encouraged me to go take a look at the fly in the water. I happily obliged him and discovered one of the sexiest flies I had ever seen. I swam the fly around my legs, watching it closely as the blend of orange, red, black, badger, and jungle cock could have sprung to life right out of the gravel bottom. I had to tie some. I committed Harry's version to memory:

Tag: Fine oval silver tinsel
Tail: Reddish golden pheasant breast feather
Rear body: Orange seal dubbing
Mid-hackle: Orange saddle followed by white
Front body: Black seal dubbing
Rib: Fine oval silver tinsel
Front hackle: Badger saddle hackle
Wings: Jungle cock

My well-stocked fly tying inventory didn't let me down. I had everything I needed to tie an Usk Grub. I chose an Alec Jackson spey hook in size $1^{1}/_{2}$ for its seductive shape and dove in. I chose the longest reddish golden pheasant breast feather for the tail hackle I could find. The tail of the Usk Grub represents the forelegs and feelers of a krill and is a major component.

OLIVE GARDEN

I BREAK OUT THE OLIVE GARDEN and similarly colored flies in late winter–early spring when the river has seen a lot of fishing pressure and the water is running low and clear.

I had to decide if I was going to wind the hackle in or clump it as Harry did. I was already a bit familiar with grub patterns, most of which have tails that are wound in. I could try both ways, but for the first one I decided to wind it in.

Silver tag laid in, I wound the pheasant feather by the tip, folding it as I wrapped to ensure a nice, neat hackle. I had never previously wrapped a golden pheasant breast feather, having used them many times for the shell-back on General Practitioners and for wings on spey flies. I really liked what I saw taking shape, and immediately envisioned the possibilities for other flies. I made the body as I do for most of my flies, particularly speys and dees. When I make a dubbed body, I like to spin the dubbing in a loop of split silk floss of the same color. Using floss instead of thread allows me to apply the dubbing sparingly and still achieve a neat uniform body without gaps. Silk floss is nice to work with and lies exceptionally flat. I almost exclusively use seal fur dubbing for luster and translucency; it has a crinkle that synthetic material can't duplicate. To me, the best synthetic dubbing is

OLIVE GARDEN

HOOK:	Alec Jackson spey
TAIL:	Light olive marabou from a dyed chinese pheasant.
BODY:	Olive seal fur
HACKLE:	Olive saddle
RIB:	Medium oval gold tinsel
COLLAR:	Black schlappen
WING:	Four matching hackle tips from a grizzly rooster neck dyed olive.
CHEEKS:	California quail flank feathers

SLF Dubbing by Partridge, standing for synthetic living fiber. I use SLF by itself or blended with seal. For my first Usk Grub I used straight seal.

I topped off the fly with what is perhaps its most interesting attribute: the jungle cock wing. The wing is simply two jungle cock neck feathers set on top and on both sides of the hook. I choose feathers of equal size from opposing sides of the neck taking advantage of the slight natural curve of the feather. I was extremely pleased with my finished Grub and couldn't wait to fish it.

The Usk Grub became my staple fly for the rest of that season, accounting for a number of beautiful

Beautiful, elegant flies are not just for show. All of these patterns, pulled directly from my winter fly box, have the intricate beauty and movement that cast a spell on the steelhead—and me. Fishing such patterns is extremely gratifying.

steelhead. What I learned from tying the Grub was equally exciting. I was intrigued with the wound golden pheasant hackle tail and the simplicity of the jungle cock wing and began experimenting with patterns of my own. I had recently acquired some interesting grade-3 hen necks produced by Metz that beckoned to be tied with. There was a cree neck that was vividly barred and edged in a deep, rich brown which to this day I've not been able replace. Normally when I sit down to design a new fly I may or may not have a basic idea of what I want. I just start tying and let my creative mood dictate what happens. Not this time. I actually had this entire pattern worked out in my mind in a matter of seconds starting with a tail just like the Usk Grub. The body was dubbed orange seal ribbed in pearl Mylar. Pearl Mylar breaks easily under the rigors of fishing, so I counter wrapped the rib with copper wire. I then thought the fore hackle would flow nicely with the tail if it were tied identically. So I wrapped in another long golden pheasant breast feather just as with the tail. I tied in a sparse under-wing of orange polar bear hair to support the cree hen feather wing and my fly was finished.

I had created many patterns more complex than this one over the years, but I don't remember ever being more pleased with a new creation than I was with that one. It looked so good in the water, the cree neck natural and radiating with life, the GP tail trembling in its effervescent reddish glow. I don't typically name my flies—I never stick with one pattern long enough to bother. This one, however, had staying power and spawned many variations for me. I named it the Coast Orange. The name, just like the fly, is simple yet mysteriously captivating. It's an excellent producer year around on coastal rivers when river conditions are stable.

The Intruder

I have no problem calling a fly pattern my own. Nor do I have a problem with someone else calling a pattern his own. There are established patterns that have been around for years and recognized as standards of the sport: Comet, Green-Butt Skunk, Skykomish Sunrise, Boss, Silver Hilton, Purple Peril, et al. Many "new" patterns are in fact derivatives from these old standards. Nothing fundamental changes.

A bare hook is like a painter's palette—we are free to dress it as far as our imaginations take us.

USK GRUB

AN OLD WELSH ATLANTIC SALMON pattern from the River Usk, the Usk Grub is a favorite of mine. Refer to the text for the full story on my initiation to this marvelous fly. The Usk Grub is important to me because it inspired me to tie the Coast Crange and all its variations. I fish the Grub in early spring when signs of a warming river begin to show—algae-covered rocks and newly hatched salmon fry.

USK GRUB

HOOK:	Alec Jackson spey
TAG:	Fine oval silver tinsel
TAIL:	Natural golden pheasant flank feather
BODY:	In equal halves, rear half hot orange seal fur, front half black seal fur.
RIB:	Oval silver tinsel
MIDDLE HACKLE:	Between both halves a hot orange hackle followed by a white hackle, one turn each only.
COLLAR:	Badger hackle
WING:	Jungle cock feathers

When we create our own patterns, they tend to be based on an existing style: standard wets, Speys, prawns, or spun marabous. We change the colors around, utilize a rare or unusual material and add our own personal flare. But I don't believe they are functionally original creations much beyond that. For a fly to be deemed truly original, I believe that a unique model must be developed, a style markedly different from anything we've seen before. It must then catch the attention of serious anglers and prove itself in practice on the water as viable and genuine. It must catch fish like nothing else. If you think about it, considering the decades of traditions of steelhead fly fishing combined with those borrowed from centuries of Atlantic salmon fishing, that's a tall order to fill. Well it's happened. I feel proud and honored to have witnessed it. Best of all, the originator of this completely new steelhead fly is one of my closest friends.

Ed Ward's Intruder is not just another fly born of someone's flight of fancy. Rather, the Intruder is a style that was thoughtfully and carefully engineered by one of the greatest, most inquisitive anglers ever to grace a steelhead river.

Ward migrated to the Pacific Northwest from Michigan were he grew up fanatically fishing the streams leading to Lake Huron. Ed was born an angler. He has maintained his exuberance at a fervor pitch throughout his life. He moved to Washington

State in the late 1970s for a stint in the U.S. Navy. Here he got a taste of what real steelheading was all about. After the Navy, he moved back to Michigan, but the call of the wild steelhead didn't let him remain for very long. He was back in the Northwest to carry out his mission in life: standing waist-deep in a steelhead river somewhere on the planet no fewer than 250 days a year.

I met Ed one day in 1989 while fishing for sea-run Dolly Varden in a saltwater channel near my home in Mount Vernon, Washington. We immediately hit it off and have remained close friends ever since. Fishing beside Ed is not like fishing with anyone else. The first thing I learned about him is that he's very much his own man when it comes to his approach to the river. His level of awareness and willingness to experiment is unsurpassed. He's constantly thinking, observing, and processing information. Anything he touches—from tackle to flies—is modified and improved to Ed's personal satisfaction.

About the same time I was playing with the Usk Grub and Coast Orange, Ed's mind was at work designing the soon-to-be-unveiled Intruder. Ed and I were working together in Alaska during the summer of 1993. We shared a room where we often stayed up late after the day's guiding for salmon and trout talking longingly about steelhead. One morning I was awakened as my bed shook violently. I popped up to see Ed standing over me and grinning from ear to ear.

"Check it out dude!" Ed said. A large fly hovered in front of my face dangling from a two-foot piece of monofilament in Ed's grasp. My immediate reaction upon focusing on the bouncing fly was, "Whoa . . . let me see that!" What I saw was anything but traditional. The hook exploded with long, leggy "hackle." I could tell the fibers were turkey radiating from the hook in two separate stages. There was no wing. Long, shaggy orange and pink dubbing shared space with the protruding hackles. I had never seen anything like it. It was definitely a buggy looking critter.

"Leave it to you, Eddy," I said. "That thing is awesome."

"Yeah, I think I'm on to something, Dec," he replied. "I've just been wanting something really buggy that fished in the round like a marabou but buggier." I could tell he was really excited about his new discovery. Ed went on: "I've got a bunch of other really neat ideas for it. I think it's going to be a killer."

"It looks incredible, Ed—betcha can't wait to fish it. What're you gonna call it?" I said with a sarcastic chuckle. We don't normally name our flies.

"Intruder," Ed quickly replied. Jerry French, another friend and fellow guide, had taken one look at it the night before and pronounced, "Dude that thing is an *intruder*."

That fall after the Alaska season ended, Ed went berserk with his new creation. The next time I saw him sometime during the winter of 1994 he was armed with a whole quiver of Intruders. They had grown in size to immense proportions. The original prototype hanging over my bed that morning was a couple inches in length—now Ed was showing me flies that were every bit five inches long. It wasn't so much their length that impressed me, but their overall mass. They were huge! I thought my buddy Ed had gone mad.

"Ed, have you really been fishing these?" I asked. "They look amazing, but aren't they a little big?"

"I know, they're massive, but I've been getting fish on them. The takes are incredible—they just crush it! Dec, you know how only occasionally you get a really hard take?"

"Sure, one really hard take for about every 10."

"Yeah, well, every single take with these is vicious." There was fire in Ed's eyes as he spoke.

The Intruder had Ed's special touches all over it. They were tied on straightened-out hook shanks to which he attached a tiny loop of monofilament to accommodate his leader and a separate hook, much like a tube fly, but Ward style. He had carefully filed the blunt end of the shank after he cut off the point and barb with a pair of dykes. He then painstakingly ran his leader material though the eye and, with a bodkin, cleared a path over the fly to the waiting built-in loop at the rear. A tiny sleeve made from the plastic tube that comes with a can of WD-40 was then passed over the leader prior to the hook being tied on. Once the hook was attached, the sleeve was fitted over the end of the shank to keep the fly from sliding up and down the leader. I'm sure Ed had additional reasons for this measure.

The flies were big, but Ed claimed he used a minimal amount of material, applying it in such a manner as to give the impression of size without the bulk of excessive material. This was true. No matter how you sliced it, though, they were large flies—so large that Ed resorted to attaching lead eyes at the head of his Intruders to counteract their resistance to sinking due to their mass. It was like trying to sink a parachute.

"People think I must be fishing them right on the bottom when they see the lead-eyes, but I'm lucky if they sink a foot or two," Ed told me once. "Without the lead, they'd skate on the surface!"

NO-NAME SUMMER FLY

I HAVE LEFT THIS AS A "NO NAME" because it's really just a standard wet fly with a purple body. I never tie two alike. I may change the butt, hackle, tail etc. The fact remains, a purple-bodied fly fished on a floating line has more than likely surpassed the popularity of the ubiquitous Green-Butt Skunk.

NO-NAME SUMMER FLY

HOOK:	Tiemco 7999
TAG:	Flat silver tinsel
TAIL:	Cerise golden pheasant tippets
BUTT:	Hot pink or cerise wool or floss
BODY:	Purple seal fur
COLLAR:	Purple or violet saddle hackle followed by teal flank feather.
WING:	Natural polar bear hair or substitute

That's when the lights went on for me as to why Ward consistently got such hard takes with his Intruders. Ed and I discussed it exhaustively. The extraordinary violent strikes baffled him. Was it simply because the flies were big, and the steelhead took them extra hard to make sure they were good and pummeled? That seemed logical. But when he revealed that the fly didn't fish deeply, it made sense to me that the steelhead were not only attacking something large, they were rising high in the water column to get it. What goes up must come down: When it's a large winter steelhead attacking a humungous fly, the going down part is going to pack a thunderous wallop! Ed liked my idea, but the fact was he was merely happy for the hard grabs, irrespective of the cause.

Over the years, Ed remained highly secretive of his Intruder, sharing it with only a few close friends. He believed that if everybody else was fishing it, it would lose its advantage of being something different. From time to time I tie on an Intruder but never feel I am missing out by not fishing it. Ed and a few of his other buddies swear by it; many, in fact, appear to have lost confidence in just about everything else. To me the Intruder is another valuable addition to my arsenal, an unusual and effective style to tie and fish on occasion. I enjoy all the various styles of steelhead flies. I could never commit myself to fishing one exclusively. I could no more spend the rest of my angling days fishing only dee-style flies, either, as much as I love them. I must admit that when I do fish the Intruder, I do it with utmost confidence, and something good nearly always results.

The Intruder has evolved over the years (Ed has scaled down the size a great deal) and is no longer a secret. The mysterious, intriguing Intruder has gained wide acceptance during recent seasons and has found its place in steelhead fly fishing's history and future. Kudos, Ed.

THE INTRUDER

Photo courtesty of *Fish & Fly* Magazine

TIED BY ED WARD

HOOK: The fly itself is tied on a size 2/0 Mustad 36890 salmon that has been straightened out and cut off. The trailer hook is a Daichii 2451—size 2 for steelhead that average under eight pounds, size 1 for those that run eight to 16 pounds, and size 1/0 for fish larger than 16 pounds. Sand smooth the part of the hook shank you have cut.

RIBBING: Tie in a loop of 25-pound test monofilament a quarter-inch up from the end of the shank. Tie in oval gold tinsel and take two wraps in back of the mono loop, one wrap in front.

REAR HACKLE:
Tie in a long, soft, black hackle and take three wraps.

FEELERS: Tie in nine strands of dyed-orange ostrich plume, on each side of hook shank. Tie in dyed-orange ringneck pheasant tail and take three or four turns.

BODY: Tie in a long, skinny badger hackle and leave hanging. Tie in burnt-orange chenille and wrap forward tightly to within a half-inch of the eye of the hook. Wind the badger hackle forward through chenille, ending with three successive turns at the point where the chenille terminates. Spin a small clump of black deer hair and trim butts flush with the shank. Tie in orange ringneck pheasant tail and take three or four turns.

SHELL: Tie in two cree hackles on each side of the shank for "wings." Tie in dyed-orange guinea hackle and take four or five turns.

HEAD: Tie in a small ball of black chenille. Tie in lead eyes. Whip finish. Cover head with Aquaseal thinned with Cotol.

TYING NOTE 1:
Ringneck pheasant tails are split down the stem with a single-edge razor, so they can be wrapped as a hackle. Soaking the tail for 10 minutes in warm water can aid in the splitting-and-wrapping process.

TYING NOTE 2:
Other species of pheasant produce differing appearances; Amherst is particularly striking.

Rigging the Intruder: Pass your leader through the eye of the hook, then through the monofilament loop, then through a quarter-inch-long piece of 16-gauge electrical wire from which the wire core has been removed. Tie the leader to the trailer hook with Lefty Kreh's nonslip loop knot. Push the electrical insulation up onto the end of the hook shank and pull slowly on the leader to draw the knot snugly into the other end of the insulation, making sure that everything pulls together with the hook point riding up.

Ed prefers to tie the Intruder on straightened Mustad hook shanks. He shared with me that, for the innovative anadromous tier, the pattern can also be tied on tubes or Waddington shanks; this would eliminate the need for his clever monofilament loop. One more thought Ed asked me to share with you: Please do not tie the Intruder on single hooks larger than size 1/0. Single hooks larger than this, he reminds us, can be harmful to wild steelhead, every one of which should be released alive and unharmed.

CHAPTER 3

CASTING
YOUR FLY
TO THE WATER

ONLY RIP VAN WINKLE WOULD HAVE MISSED the dynamic shift in casting methods for steelhead: During the last 15 years, two-handed rods have taken over as the serious steelheader's rod of choice. The change has been astonishingly swift and nearly total. As I write today, I recall with some amusement that had I been writing this in the not-so-distant past, I would be explaining all the wonderful merits of the two-handed rod. I would be promoting these merits convincingly by painting pictures of river scenarios with limited or no room for a back cast; explaining how great distances can be achieved with relative ease; and, most important, how the long rod is a masterful tool at presenting and controlling the fly. I'd tell you that that the two-handed rod, although seemingly large compared to a single-handed rod, doesn't overpower and make the battle with a steelhead less enjoyable—quite the opposite.

You should know that the two-handed rod originated in Scotland two centuries ago. As the technique evolved, long double-tapered lines made of braided silk were used to perform what came to be called the spey cast, after the River Spey. But these basics you

Duking it out with a Skagit River winter chromer in January.

probably already know. Staying consistent with the personal nature of this book, I wish to share with you a brief history of my own exposure to the two-handed rod. It happened just prior to the spey-casting explosion, so my experience closely parallels the events leading to where we are today. My aim is not

boastful, but I guess you could say I am a Pacific pioneer of present-day two-handed rod. The story I'm about to share with you is solely from my perspective. I have purposefully left out details that I didn't know at the time—likely some of which I'm still unaware.

As you read, please understand this. If who's who is left out or such and such was over looked as the assumed originator of a certain cast or line design, etc., sorry. Please accept my apology. This is the story as I lived it.

As I've already shared with you, I cut my teeth on the North Fork Stilliguamish River, where I spent an entire summer feverishly pursuing steelhead with my single-handed fly rod. Everyone on the river fished this way. I fished through the fall and into winter on the Stilly never seeing or even hearing of a spey rod. Eventually, I found my way to the muscular Skagit River, where I must admit, I was humbled in my casting. While the Stilly's trout-stream narrowness size gave me a false sense of casting prowess, the Skagit's broad expanse brought me back to Earth. Moreover, I was the new guy on the Skagit, still relatively new to steelheading.

I had nothing but respect for anyone I saw fly fishing the Skagit—in my mind they were all veteran steelheaders. One enviable condition we enjoyed

Father and son two-handed rod aficionados Marty and Trevor Howard casting in unison. When these two are on the river, the steelhead don't stand a chance. Never discouraged, they fish methodically non-stop from sunup to sundown.

that's markedly different from today: As good as the fishing was, surprisingly few people were on the water. There was a handful of local regulars and the occasional out-of-towner, but that's about it. I was a young stranger for only a short time. Some of the regulars, to my delight, were notable steelheaders whom I had heard about. To me, this validated the Skagit as "the place to be." Single-handed rods with sink-tips or shooting heads were the common tackle. There were, however, two seasoned veterans using extraordinary rods that took two hands to cast. I remember seeing them easily making this quick, odd-looking move that sent line all around themselves, and in the blink of an eye shot it out over the green water. It looked so fitting.

Harry Lemire and Bob Stroebel looked as though they had seized control of this enormous river. I couldn't relate. I don't remember where, when, or who told me about it, but I learned that these rods were popular in Europe for Atlantic salmon fishing. I had to have one. Other than Harry and Bob, there

were only two others that I saw using the two-hander: Mike Kinney and Pete Soverel. My pal Ed Ward ordered an Orvis spey rod from their catalog—I couldn't afford one. I believe it was a 13½-foot for a 9-weight line. Ed strung the rod with a heavy weight-forward line and went to work. Although Ward struggled with the cast, he was completely elated with the water coverage his new rod offered him. I tried it a couple times—now I really had to have one!

That season I started my guiding business: It was the only way I could responsibly satisfy my crazed obsession to be on the river. George Cook of the Sage rod company told me that Sage had six brand-new prototype two-handed fly rods ready for production; well-known caster Jim Green, working with suggestions from Harry Lemire and Al Buhr of Oregon, had designed them. George informed me that he was giving the rods to six influential guides and steelheaders in the Pacific Northwest and that I was one. I was thrilled.

"But George," I said, "I don't even know how to spey cast." Also, whatever my aspirations, I knew I was anything but an influential, well-known steelhead guide.

George's confident reply was, "You'll learn and you will be—just fish the rod." Cook went on to tell me that the two-handed rod was going to take over steelheading and that it would start with these six prototypes. I couldn't wait to fish my new rod. It was

casting. Fishing the rod was a joy—pick up the line and pop it out there. Bang, bang.

I'd never experienced this level of line control with the single-handed rod. That first day on the water, I knew I'd never go back.

It wasn't long before I hooked my first steelhead on the 9140: a fresh, rip-snortin' 10-pound Skagit chromer followed by another nearly twice the size of the first. They took my fly 20 minutes apart. It was a

The spray coming off the water in this photo is caused by the D-loop pulling on the anchored fly. This spray is often referred to as "the white mouse." Visually recognizing it greatly aids one's timing. Essentially it means that everything was done correctly up to this point and the rod is fully loaded. Ed Ward gettin' it done on a warm summer day in British Columbia.

designated model 9140-4, a 14-foot 9-weight four piece. I learned that Sage had several other two-handers in production to appeal to the European market. They were big stiff, heavy rods compared to the new lightweight, moderate-action 9140, which was specifically designed for steelheading.

I didn't have time to research what line to put on my new rod, let alone learn how to spey cast. So I threw my everyday reel with a Teeny 200 line on it and headed up the Skagit. My plan was to overhead cast until I could talk with Lemire about lines and

magical evening. All my amigos were there, and they all caught fish, too.

One spring day I got up the nerve to invite Harry Lemire on a float down the Sauk River. Nerve, you ask? I was a 26-year-old newbee, waders barely wet as a guide—Harry was a living legend in steelhead country. He graciously obliged my invite, saying in his New England accent, "I never turn down a chance to go fishing."

So there we were: me, my new pal Scott O'Donnell, and Harry Lemire floating down the Sauk

River in my new Lavro drift boat.

It was a superb day with a fitting end: Lemire caught the one and only steelhead just before the take-out. Scott and I learned a great deal from Harry that day simply by watching him fish. And I picked his brain about how to line and cast my rod.

I saw that Harry's line system and casting style were all about ease and presentation. Long-line spey traditions were replaced with comfortable, close-in efficiency. Harry's line consisted of an .040 running line looped to 17 feet of floating belly section taken from a 12-weight double taper, looped to 15 feet of high-speed high-density 10-weight sinking line. He stripped in until the 12-weight floating section was about two feet below the guides. He then made a slow, compact double-spey move and literally "slingshot" the line out, shooting several coils of running line. Once on the water, the 17 feet of thick 12-weight belly section steered the sink-tip around with exceptional control. Harry looked at me and said, smiling through his signature white goatee, "It's just like fishing a long, skinny bobber."

I was sold. If it was good enough for the great Lemire, it was good enough for me. I became proficient at casting Harry's custom line. Along the way I learned more about spey casting and its roots in northern Europe. Occasionally I ran into some river folk who looked down their noses at what I was doing claiming, "It's not true spey casting . . . it's not traditional." A bunch of my friends, including Ed Ward and Charlie Gearheart, were also learning to cast similarly. We chuckled at these elitist comments.

"Whose tradition are they talking about?" we said. "We're steelheaders! Instead of spey casting, let's call it Skagit casting."

Ignorant comments aside, as time went on I became serious about learning more about the "traditional-style" spey casting. My chance came in 1992 when I was guiding in Alaska. We had the good fortune of guiding a large group from the United Kingdom headed by Atlantic-salmon angling and spey-casting guru Arthur Olgesby, who during the early 1960s, had been taught personally by the famous Tommy Edwards, principal of the London School of Casting. Each of these British gentlemen had a spey rod to accompany their single handers. They broke out the two-handers only when they deemed necessary for distance. Their rods were much larger than ours: thick and heavy, with 16 feet the norm. They used long double-tapered lines that required a lot of rocking and body movement to cast. Their casts looked painful to execute. It seemed to

No telling what critter those two-handed rods will dredge up!

take several attempts to get the line out to a fishable distance. They swung their rods as if they were 10-pound sledgehammers trying to break concrete. Some of the more experienced casters weren't so bad—they looked as though they were using eight-pound sledges. Most of the blokes eventually tired and surrendered, retreating to the comfort of their single-handed rods. If this is what "true" spey casting was all about, Dec Hogan wanted no part of it! I did, however, remain open-minded enough to learn a thing or two from Olgesby, mainly casting motion. He had a superb single-spey stroke.

Back in the lower 48, I kept improving my basically self-taught casting technique. I certainly struggled from time to time, but I was absolutely in love with two-handed rod. Then Sage came out with a sister rod to the 9140, a 13½-foot 7-weight 4 piece. The new 7136-4 was a slim, sexy little rod designed for summer-run steelhead on floating lines and small flies. I strung a Wulff Triangle Taper 8/9 through the guides and thought I would have to learn how to cast all over again. This was due to my inexperience. I was conditioned to cast with one rod and one line. I quickly overcame my inadequacies. The change— the ability to adapt—ultimately made me a better caster.

More and more anglers were turning to the two-handed rod. It's ironic: Here I was, still relatively new to casting the two-handed rod and being hired weekly to teach the technique. People hired me to guide, sometimes when there was little chance of hooking a fish, so they could learn to cast. I taught them what I knew. The act of teaching was also a boon to my own casting. It forced me to really think about breaking down the mechanics of the cast. Watching my clients trying to execute what I was teaching them was enlightening.

It seemed, though, that for every person eager to jump on the two-handed-rod bandwagon, there were two who were skeptical—or outright hostile—about its practicality. Many were professionals in the business of fly fishing. Their resistance was, I thought,

Keith Balfourd on the Skykomish River, Washington. Notice that Keith's eyes are trained on his anchor. It's good advice. The cognizant caster is always aware of the fly's location.

motivated by ego. They felt threatened and felt comfort remaining "stuck in their ways." I can tell you now that each and every one of them hid out, practicing with a two-handed rod "behind the barn" only to emerge as The Local Authority. It was hilarious to watch. And that's fine—my own sense of self must be assuaged from time to time.

I went to work guiding on the Grande Ronde River, draining the eastern Oregon high desert, in 1991. I brought with me my affinity for the two-handed rod. My new 7-weight was ideal for this river and style of fishing. When I had time to do some personal fishing, I never was alone. Cars constantly stopped along the river road to watch me do my strange style

of casting with the odd, long rod. It got back to me. People were talking. "He doesn't need that big thing here! It's too much rod for this river," they said, among the more polite comments. The locals even confronted me personally and asked me why I chose to fish such inappropriate tackle on their river. "A single-handed rod is all you need," they told me. I felt like Rosa Parks and tried to explain to them the virtuous wonders of the two-hander. Back then, unless Ed Ward and our friend Steve Kruse came down to visit me, nobody on the Ronde fished a two-hander. Drive along the river this October—everybody fishes one.

Sometime during my four-season stint on the Grand Ronde, Jim Vincent came to visit from Idaho to teach a two-handed-rod clinic with me. Jim had been using the two-hander for several years. He had the foresight to see the direction steelhead fly fishing was heading, and had recently started a new company called Rio Products to supply the growing demand for specialty fly lines. Jim and I hit it off. We had plenty of time to get chummy—there was only one student enrolled in our three-day clinic. Jim complimented me by telling me that I was the best spey caster he had ever seen, with the exception of Simon Gawesworth. I had never heard of Simon. I was flattered but wasn't sure if I felt worthy—there was still so much room for improvement. Jim's new company was working on manufacturing several fly lines for two-handed rods, including the popular weight-forward style we were using on the Skagit. Vincent asked if I would assist in his field testing. He shipped me enough loosely coiled fly lines to fill an ice-chest. I spent a couple weeks trying out all of the various designs—some were horrible, some seemed sent from Heaven. The line I liked best became the popular Windcutter.

The Windcutter is similar to Harry Lemire's crude, yet effective, original in that it features an exceptionally heavy weight-forward taper connected to a thin running line designed for shooting. The Windcutter, however, is longer and has taper. It feels more like casting, although its design still utilizes a bit of the sling-shot concept. With the introduction of the Windcutter, interest in fishing the two-handed rod for steelhead accelerated. It was great for guides and lucrative for fly-shop owners: We could simply tell someone what line to buy rather than breaking out scratch paper and concocting a formula that required buying several lines and then learning to cut and splice them together. By this time there was a multitude of complex line recipes in circulation.

In the meantime, tackle salesman George Cook was aggressively conducting free spey-casting clinics at fly shops throughout the Pacific Northwest; Mike Maxwell of British Columbia was teaching his unique method of casting; and guide-instructor John Hazel down in Oregon was assertively converting his vast steelhead clientele to two-handed weaponry. In addition, guides such as I, John Farrar, Mike Kinney, and a growing corps of serious steelhead commandos throughout the Northwest were stoking the spey-rod fire until it was burning out of control. There was enough interest in the two-handed rod that seemingly overnight all the top rod manufacturers were cranking out their version of what they thought we wanted. Many of these early rods were hastily designed; the poor ones were later improved.

As the popularity of two-handed rods grew, casting styles evolved. There were those few who kept to the Scottish traditions of heavy, long rods and double-tapered lines; the Scandinavian style of underhand casting popularized by Swede Göran Andersson, whereby a fast-action rod is used with a short-bellied line and long leader, and casting motion is minimized by the short head and extreme use of the bottom hand during the casting stroke; the long-belly crowd that uses long, 70-plus feet of essentially weight-forward line; and the Skagit-style that was developing, which in actuality is an efficient blending of all the global styles, taking what I feel are the best

attributes of each and incorporating where they best fit.

"Style" may fall into what best describes a particular line system and rod action, this is true. However, when we speak of casting style we can't overlook the human physical element. No two people are alike in physicality, coordination, athleticism, or—just as influential—personality. Therefore, I believe there are as many casting styles out there as there are people fishing. There is one constant that makes all of us and our myriad methods of casting the fly to the fish equal: physics.

All the various approaches to spey casting are based upon the same principles of rod motion and line manipulation in order to make a cast. The physics behind this is not unlike throwing a football, hitting a golf ball, or swinging a baseball bat. Top pro-

These two characters, for some reason, caught on quickly and were easily taught how to spey cast. PGA stars Mark O'Meara and Tiger Woods.

fessionals in these sports possess unique styles, and I'm sure some have personal mechanical philosophies on how they execute their forte. But I'm also certain none would deny that the physics needed to accomplish the feat at its maximum efficiency are invariable.

So here we are in 2006: Virtually the entire steelheading community fishing the two-handed rod, displaying many different styles on the water. Even entry-level steelheaders are purchasing the two-hander as their first rod—that's how you play the game these days. I'm not suggesting the single-handed rod is out altogether, but then not many of us will be showing up on the river this season wearing rubber-lug-soled canvas waders either!

I have personally tried—I believe with an open mind—all the well-defined casting styles at one time or another in an effort to better understand each. I consider myself a true student of casting. As in the quest to hook a steelhead, no stone goes unturned. I'm not only a better caster for it—I'm a more well-rounded instructor. At the very least, I can answer my

students' questions with a breadth of solid experience to back my answers. As for my chosen casting style, if you would call it that, I have not traveled too far from my early beginnings. It's interesting. I like a 13- or 14-foot rod that's moderately fast and full flexing. I enjoy using the shorter-bellied weight-forward spey lines in the 50- to 60-foot range backed by a shooting running line such as the Rio Windcutter and the excellent new Airflo Delta Spey (the design and testing of which I was, in the interest of full disclosure, involved and influential). These lines are easy to cast, afford great mending and line control, and I like having to strip in a bit at the end of the swing. Stripping in some line keeps the fly from hanging bottom as I prepare for my next cast. It also allows me to add speed to the fly when fishing over a shallow, yet productive, latter portion of the swing by slowly stripping in some line. The 50-foot belly is long enough to require defined, necessary casting motion and all of the associated joys of casting coupled with the deliberate, powerful feeling of shooting line—all this with minimal

Steelhead maniac and superb caster Keith Balfourd launching a laser-beam over the Skagit River. Loops don't come much tighter.

body motion.

So much of what I have learned about two-handed casting, and my personal development, I owe not only to countless hours of practice, but to all of the good people I've guided and instructed. I've watched the good, the bad, the ugly, and the spectacular for more hours than I have fished myself. Watching you cast has forced me to see—to really analyze—proper physics in motion. The experience has also revealed disasters that happen when mechanical failures abound, right there for my own eyes to see. You've enabled me to watch you struggle, as I desperately and clinically tried to arrive at a diagnosis and remedy to your problem—a remedy that had to be presented in the simplest and clearest of terms so as not to exacerbate the problem to the point of no return. Sometimes it could not be avoided, forcing us as a team to work through it, even if it meant reeling in a bunch of line and starting over from the beginning. I see things while I'm watching you from my streambank vantage that I would never be able to recognize if I were the one making the casts. All of what I have learned from you, I have been able to incorporate in my own casting, along with the necessary tools to share it with others. You have taught me more than I can ever express, and I am truly grateful. Thank you.

Here's What I Have Learned

We all want to cast effortlessly, sending out consistently tight loops that travel gracefully high over the river and unfurl to a gentle kiss of the water. We want to be able to cast far if we need to with an unforced economy of motion. The ultimate in two-handed casting is the ability to work down a run and not have to think about and fear casting. When casting becomes second nature, all of one's energy can be devoted to presentation and reading the water—our heart and soul committed to feeling that steelhead lurking below. The place to begin the quest of attaining this expertise is to relax and simply slow down.

You must feel the line load the rod in order to make smooth casts. Grip the rod lightly. Move the rod slowly. Think about what you are trying to accomplish. Don't try to cast the line, let the rod do it. You paid top dollar for your equipment for a reason—let it work for you. Throughout my career I've often joked about showing up to teach a casting clinic wearing a tee-shirt and ball cap with the words SLOW DOWN printed in bold letters. They are the two most useful words and invaluable tools you'll ever use in casting.

Question: "Dec, I'm having this problem. Whenever I make my forward stroke, my fly pops out of the water and makes this loud cracking sound."

Answer: "Slow down."

Question: "When I try and place my anchor to my downstream side during a double spey cast, it always shoots past me and lands upstream—any suggestions?

Answer: "Slow down."

Slowing down is not the cure-all for every casting ailment, but it is a great place to start and words to live by. At this stage in my casting evolution, I never find myself on the river in a mechanical funk, but you can bet when things aren't going right for me it's always the same thing: I need to relax and slow down.

I NEVER cast without wearing sunglasses to protect my eyes from flying hooks and line! Dale Hightower was wearing glasses the day this picture was taken, and although he got bloodied-up, I believe the glasses may have deflected the fly from hitting and severely injuring his eye. Study the photo and you will see that the glasses are cracked. Please protect your eyes—fishing is too fun not to.

Now that we've all taken a breath and told ourselves to slow down, we can talk about casting. I like to use a wide grip because I rely heavily on using my arms in casting. Some methods teach weight transfer through the legs which means proper foot stance and body rocking. The steelhead I fish for tend to hide out in heavy structure and really don't care whether I have a smooth flat spot to set my feet for my weight transfer. I set my feet where I can as I stop to make my cast. My casting is all about fishing without missing a beat. There is definitely some body movement in the cast. It's good to face your target. And the better you get at casting and wading simultaneously, there's a tendency to make a bit of a natural weight shift. The more athletically inclined a person is, the greater the likelihood of this occurring. But for starters never think about transferring your weight—there's enough to think about already.

It has been said time and again to use both hands in concert, in a push-pull method: push with the top hand while pulling with the bottom. I disagree. Pushing is not something we do in casting. You can't push a rope; nothing happens. But you can pull a rope all day long. In casting a fly line, we are essentially pulling on a rope, stopping the rod, and watching the rope as it gets catapulted in whatever direction we pulled it. To me, the motion is *pull-pull*. Pull with the top hand, pull with the bottom. This is not just for the forward cast, but for anytime we are moving line. Every time you move line with that rod you are casting.

Spey casting is a series of motions that moves line, to set it up for a change of direction, which is followed by the final forward cast. Several small casts are made in order to make the final. Basic casting

with a certain element of the cast, it will most certainly manifest itself in the preceeding maneuver. Then your cast becomes a salvage operation. What starts bad usually stays bad—what starts well usually ends well. From the moment you begin lifting that rod to begin your chosen cast, you've set the wheels in motion as to what the end result will be.

Presented to you here are illustrations and text touching on how it's all done. I'm not going to kid you, though, and claim this will teach you how to cast. It won't. Videos, photo sequences, illustrations, and friendly written "how-to" advice can certainly add to the bank, but they are no substitute for one-on-one, hands-on instruction with a knowledgeable, skilled instructor. That said, be cautious when choosing your instructor—be sure he or she possesses the

Two-handed rods have taken over as the rod of choice on most of our western steelhead rivers, and they're here to stay.

fundamentals strictly apply to each of these casts. That is, every cast requires a smooth acceleration of the rod followed by a stopping of the rod. No stop, no cast. In the hands of an accomplished caster, some of the stops may appear indiscernible but, trust me, they are there. All the set-up moves are fluidly tied together. But when learning, it may be necessary to practice certain elements of the cast.

All moves tie together—if you are having trouble

casting style you want to emulate. There are a multitude of styles out there. If you are beginning, pick one with thought and stick with it until you are comfortably in control of your casting. Then if you want to explore other styles, rods, and lines, it won't confuse and retard the learning curve. One more warning: There are a number of instructors out there who are still saying (and believing) that their's is the only way. You and I know different. Keep an open mind and you'll go far. For now, follow my advice, and stick to one style.

Irrespective of style, remember to take it slow and, more than anything, keep foremost in mind that the D-loop—the loop of line you send behind yourself that loads the rod—is your back cast. It needs to be cast in the opposite 180-degree direction of the intended forward cast. Every time. Remember, whenever you are moving line you are casting. Forming the D-loop is no exception. You must move and stop the rod in the direction you want it to go. Where you place the anchor helps to determine where you can send the D-loop. All this we'll cover in the illustrations, but you can never hear it too much.

In this illustrated casting clinic, we'll learn the six casts that I commonly use and instruct. They are by no means the only casts I use. The two-handed rod, coupled with understanding of how the cast works, is a wonderful tool that beckons creativity and experimentation. Not every cast has a name, not every cast is technically beautiful. Sometimes I find myself in a hellacious fishing situation where I'm wading up to my chest with tree branches pushing at my back. Friends, the fish don't care and neither do I: Sometimes you simply have to find a way to muscle it out there, however ungracefully. Style points don't count when your back's against the wall. Be grateful to get your fly out there, mend your line, and fish it! Remember one of the things that attracted us to the two-handed rod in the first place: being able to cover water that is nearly impossible to cover with a single-handed rod.

Another thing to consider when you're learning to cast is that you'll have good days and bad days, good runs and bad runs. You'll be casting along in a blissful groove thinking, *Hey, I've got it down!* Then BAM, the door slams shut. Your line is in tangles. Your casts collapse. Your every move is off. You'll pull your hair out trying to figure out what went wrong when everything was going so right. Here is your answer that I sincerely hope will calm you in such times of frustration.

Spey casting is a water-dependant cast: We load the line off the water via the anchor, the same as in roll casting with a single-handed rod. Savvy? This means that all various depths we wade—from standing on dry ground to wading to our armpits—change every facet of the cast. Water speed also can play a dramatic role in the tempo, pace, and feel of things. The head of a run is fast and shallow, the mid-body is deep and slow—more changes that affect your casting. It takes a good long time under a variety of con-

Rock 'n' Roll hillbilly Charlie Gearheart kickin' out a nice little D-loop with his 7 weight. Charlie knows how to take it slow.

ditions before one is fully able to subconsciously adapt to the changing circumstances. But it's fun, fun, fun! Recognize these changes as they occur and dedicate yourself to making adjustments. It'll save you some grief. I promise.

Casting with the two-handed rod is fundamentally easy. You can fish effectively right away, not knowing much. Heck, I used to pick it up and overhead it when the fishing was good and my casting poor. There are no rules—only those you make up. The more you practice and learn, the better you'll get. Basic stuff. If you glean one nugget from this chapter that you can carry streamside for the rest of your casting life, it's to—you guessed it—SLOW DOWN.

THE DOUBLE SPEY

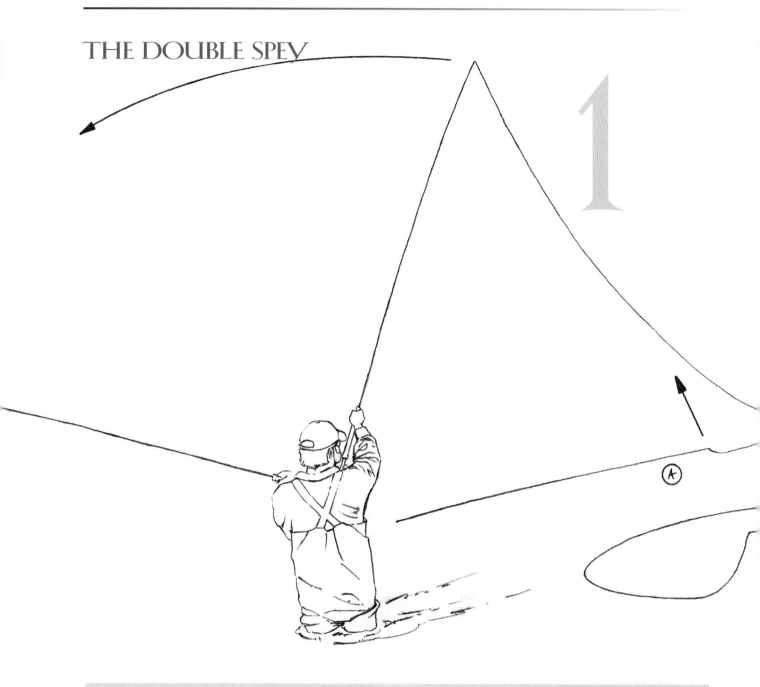

The double spey is, in my opinion, the easiest cast to learn. That's because with the double spey we're given a little forgiveness in the most difficult element of casting with a two-handed rod: timing. "Slow down and relax" are words to live by.

The double spey is my favorite cast to use when the wind is blowing downstream, or any time you desire—provided the wind is not blowing upstream. People get so comfortable with this cast I've seen anglers using it when they shouldn't. You'll get away with it for only so long before you get nailed with that hook.

For right-handed casters, it's best to begin practicing on the right side of the river looking downstream, with the current flowing from left to right. (Vice versa for left-handers.) Be sure to give yourself plenty of room. The double spey, at maximum efficiency, does require that some line go behind the caster.

Step One: At the start of the cast your line should be hanging in the current directly downstream. With your rod tip an inch or so above the water, be sure the current has pulled out all the slack—your line should be taut. Slowly lift the rod to the one o'clock position. It's critical that the rod be lifted slowly and smoothly. Your objective is to get the line and fly moving, making it easy to break the surface tension of the water. If you lift too abruptly your rod will over load; you'll lose all control. Notice in the illustration that my line is taut with very little bend in the rod.

Step Two: Once the rod has been lifted to one o'clock, sweep the rod upstream with its tip traveling over the water well in front of you (parallel to the water's surface). The rod tip gently casts a bow of line upstream, landing the fly just below you. This is where the fly is "anchored." The remainder of the cast is built around—and is vitally dependant on—this anchor. Notice the position of my arms in the illustration: crossed and close to my body.

Your fly should be anchored roughly a rod-and an arm's length away, and 45 degrees across and downstream from you. This maneuver takes some practice. If the line is cast too hard, the fly will land upstream; too soft and the fly will be too far downstream to effectively complete your cast. If the fly does land upstream, or even in front of you, DO NOT ATTEMPT A FORWARD CAST! If you do, chances are certain parts of your anatomy will hitch a ride, painfully. Always know where your fly is. Once the anchor has been placed, allow a moment for the line above you to settle on the water. Don't rush. When the line has settled, the tip of your rod should be a foot or two above the water and pointing upstream.

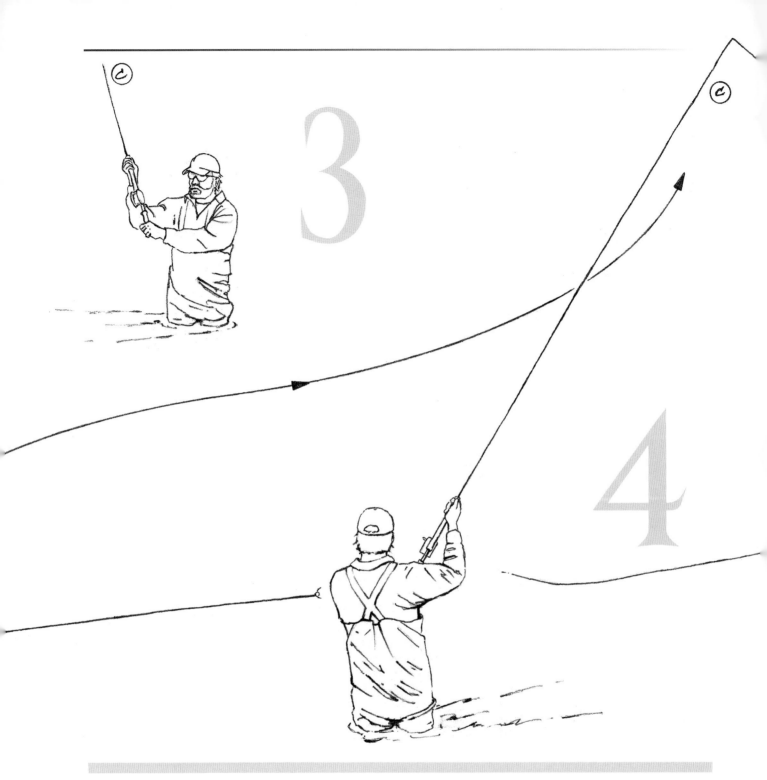

Step Three: This is where the fun begins. Anchor set downstream, begin moving your rod downstream horizontally, tearing line off the water. To accomplish this effectively, at the start of the move, rotate your top wrist and forearm until your thumbnail faces skyward. This allows you to smoothly "pull" the rod downstream.

Continue moving the rod downstream horizontally. As the rod passes in front of you begin a smooth acceleration. Now, as the rod passes downstream, it's time to start bringing it upward and behind your downstream shoulder. Continue in a smooth arc. You are in essence "casting" a belly of line that is moving around—and behind—your anchored fly.

Step Four: To form the belly or critical "D-loop" behind your downstream shoulder, the rod must be stopped at the 11 o'clock position. Remember that forming your belly is a cast in itself. All the mechanics of good casting apply: smooth acceleration, stopping the rod, and pausing long enough for the cast line to follow. The most desirable (efficient) shape of the belly is narrow and pointed. This again is accomplished by smooth, precise acceleration and a crisp stop.

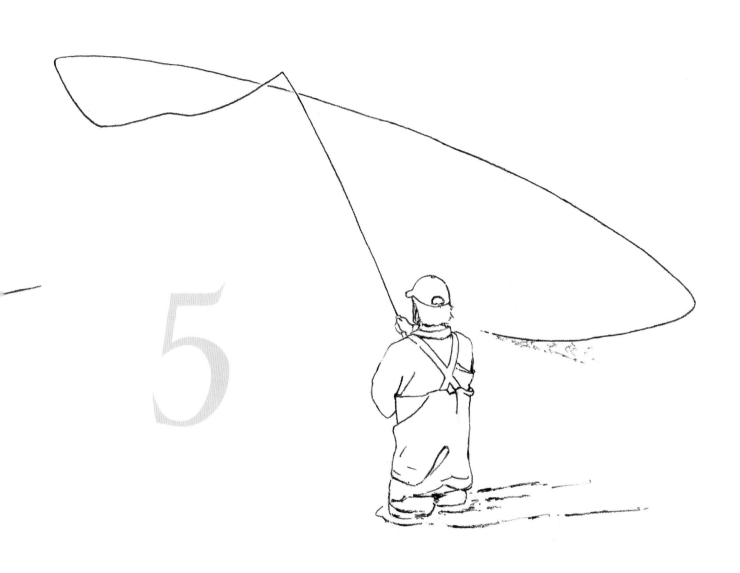

Step Five: The forward stroke. If you've successfully completed steps 1 through 4, now all you must do is stroke the rod forward and down, stopping sharply at two o'clock—out she goes in a beautiful, tight aerial loop.

THE CIRCLE SPEY A.K.A. THE SNAP-T

The double spey is a wonderfully useful cast, and perhaps the easiest to learn. No wonder it's the favorite cast of most anglers packing two-handed rods. But as with all casts, it has its limitations, specifically, when the wind is blowing upriver or when the area behind you is full of obstructions. Trying to double-spey cast with the wind blowing upriver is not only ineffective, it's hazardous to your health!

Traditionally the cast to use in the above situations is the single spey as it anchors the fly upstream of the caster. The single spey, however, is the most difficult cast to learn due to complications in proper anchor placement, timing, etc.

In an effort to avoid the dreaded single spey, casters from around the globe have come up with some pretty ingenious (even comical) methods of getting the fly out there. Chief among them is what has come to be called the snap-T, a name that I and many other instructors do not favor. A "snap" and a "T" are not good visual references when learning the cast. Circle spey or C spey seems to work better. Either way, the circle spey is a move that places the line and fly beautifully when an upstream anchor cast is needed or desired. The origin of this cast is truly Pacific Northwest, although its history is starting to get a little clouded. I'll clear that up right now, and give proper credit where it is justly due.

I was working the International Sportsmen's Exposition in Seattle at the Sage booth with tackle representative George Cook and fellow guide John Farrar. John and I were standing in front of our booth, which was located adjacent to the casting pond where Loomis rep Tom White was giving a single-handed casting clinic. Tom's show was full of insightful, basic techniques along with some crowd-pleasing trickery. With his line stretched out 70 feet Tom would pull someone from the crowd, have her stand next to him, and tell her, "Hold your arm out to your side—we need to check the fly." Tom raised his rod slowly, then suddenly snapped it downward where a tight loop of line came barreling back toward Tom and his volunteer. The line unfurled, landing the leader and yarn-fly gently over the woman's outstretched arm. Pretty cool.

John leaned over to me and said: "Dec, I'll bet that cast he's doing could somehow be useful in spey casting. See what you can come up with."

Several weeks later, while guiding Nick Gayeski of Lynnwood Washington, Nick asked if I'd seen the new cast that John Farrar had come up with. I had not, but knew exactly where this was headed. Nick, two-handed rod in hand, made the same move Tom White had at the show, with the rod tip traveling over the river and in front of Nick. Bam, the line was instantly set up and anchored to Nick's upstream side where he swung the rod around to form a D-loop and cranked out an energetic cast.

"You've got to be kidding me!" I yelled. This was a monumental moment—a cast to replace the difficult, impossible-to-teach single spey. (As a guide fishing beginning two-handed casters, the single spey can be slow and difficult.)

I immediately fell in love with the cast. But I found the violent snap that sets the anchor difficult to control and tiresome. Casting should be smooth and fluid. I couldn't see any reason why this cast should be any different. I made the initial lift of the rod higher than Farrar did, thus bringing the sink-tip closer to the surface with less resistance. This allowed me to slow down and smooth out the cast. It worked beautifully. Later George Cook named the cast the snap-T.

"Snap-T" is a seductive name for a cast: It rolls off the tongue nicely and it sounds as though it means business. For teaching purposes, however, it doesn't present a good mental picture. To the adrenaline-pumped novice, "snap" translates to: smash the rod as hard and fast as I can! And I'm still not sure where the "T" fits in. The actual snap—where line and fly are sent upriver—is a reverse cast. For sake of argument I'll call it the "cut." Because the cut is a cast, we have control over the loop. You can make a tight loop by making a sharp, narrow cut; or you can make a wide loop by making a wide, circular reverse "C." When teaching any new cast I opt to instruct a wider loop—it's easier for the student. The snap-T is much easier to teach and learn with a wide loop. By teaching the student to inscribe a large reverse letter C with the rod tip, the cast is understood and learned very easily.

So to clear some confusion among the Internet-chattering masses, the snap-T, C cast, and circle cast are all one and the same. They are all the same cast mechanically with different loop sizes. The snap-T features a tight loop; the C and circle casts, a wide loop. Once you've master the wide-looped circle cast, tightening the loop comes naturally.

Where and when the cut is made is crucial to anchor placement. Imagine the clock in front of you running parallel to the current. A cut made early in the nine to 10 o'clock zone sets up the anchor for a narrow downstream cast. The cut made at 12 o'clock sets you up to cast straight across stream. Anything after that sets up to deliver upstream. You can see that you have total control of anchor placement, as you should. If you find that your forward casts are weak and the fly is landing upstream of the line, chances are you're making the cut too late—you're anchoring for an upstream cast. This is a very common mistake made with this cast. I strongly suggest you experiment with all the possibilities of making the cut, even those of you with experience. There's always something new to discover.

Step One: At the start of the cast, the line should be hanging in the current directly downstream. With the rod tip an inch or so above the water, be sure the current has pulled out all the slack—your line should be taut. Slowly lift the rod to the 11 o'clock position and slightly out in front of you. It's critical that the rod is lifted slowly and smoothly. Your objective is to get the line and fly moving, making it easy to break the surface tension. If you lift too abruptly, the rod will over load and all control will be lost. Notice in the illustration that my line is taut with very little bend in the rod.

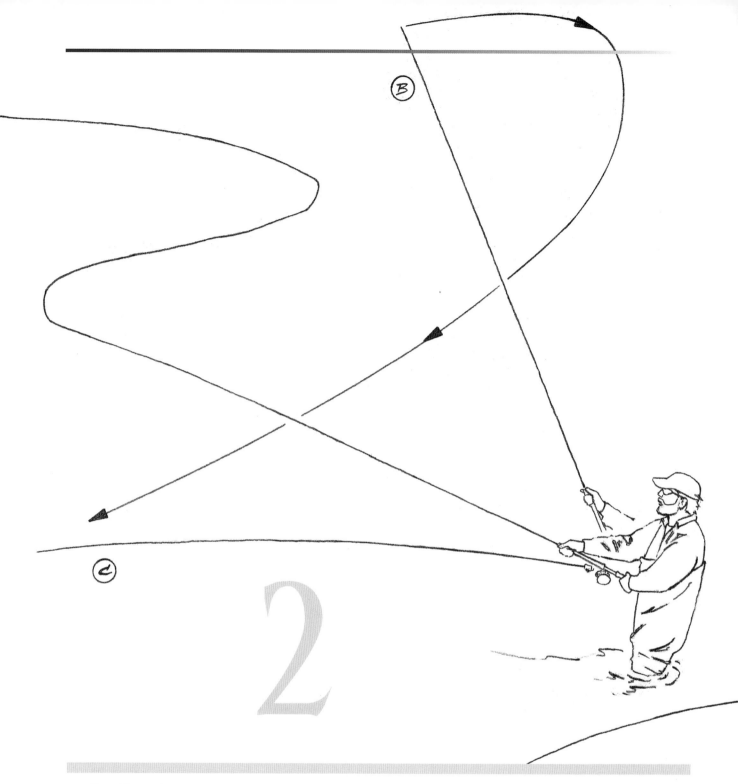

Step Two: This is it, the set up that is the namesake of the cast. You've raised the rod to 11 o'clock. Now, without pausing, draw a large half circle moving from right to left like a reverse letter C. This cast (drawing the half circle) should be made with the rod tip parallel to the plane of the current and finishing with rod pointed downstream. As the rod tip passes in front of you it is imperative that the rod keeps moving downstream out of the path of the fly moving upstream. The movement in its entirety should be fluid and graceful with smooth acceleration applied throughout. Follow the arrow in the illustration showing the path of the rod. Always remember that any time you are moving line you are casting. Making the circle is most definitely a cast.

Even when there's plenty of room to overhead cast, spey-casting techniques are still preferred and utilized for their speed and efficiency. Learning to spey cast efficiently is an enjoyable and ongoing process. Seattleite Bill Lum on the Deschutes River, Oregon.

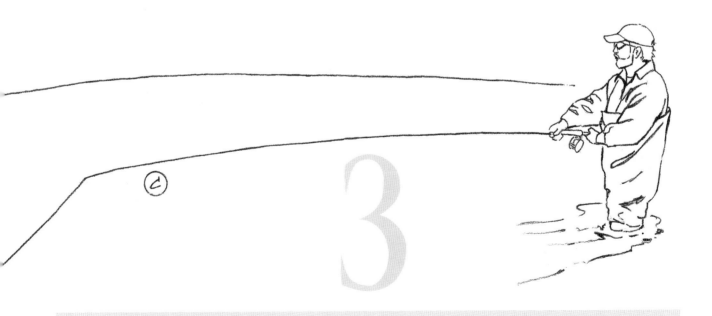

Step Three: The well-executed circle cast sets the line up beautifully. This illustration is static—the line has been set up and is resting on the water. Notice the semi-elliptical shape of the line in front of me. It's laid out perfectly. Always let your line settle on the water momentarily before forming the D-loop or belly.

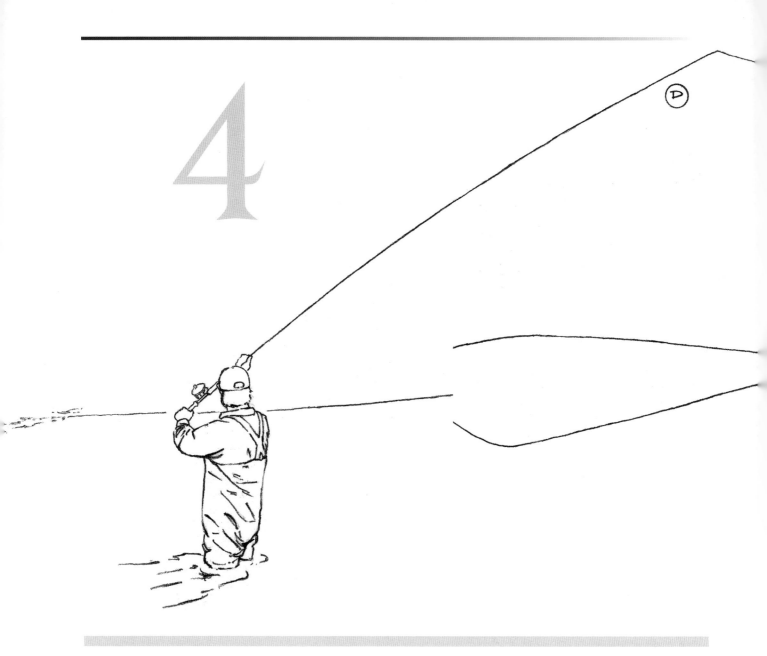

Step Four: Make the D-loop or belly just as you would with a double-spey cast, only now you are making it on your upstream side rather than downstream. Either way, proper execution must remain constant.

Step Five: Loaded and firing! The circle spey loads the rod like no other. The reason is simple: The circle set up lays the line out in front of the caster so efficiently that the rod load is naturally built in. All you have to do is swing the rod around and behind. All is super-loaded, ready to launch to the moon.

THE SINGLE SPEY

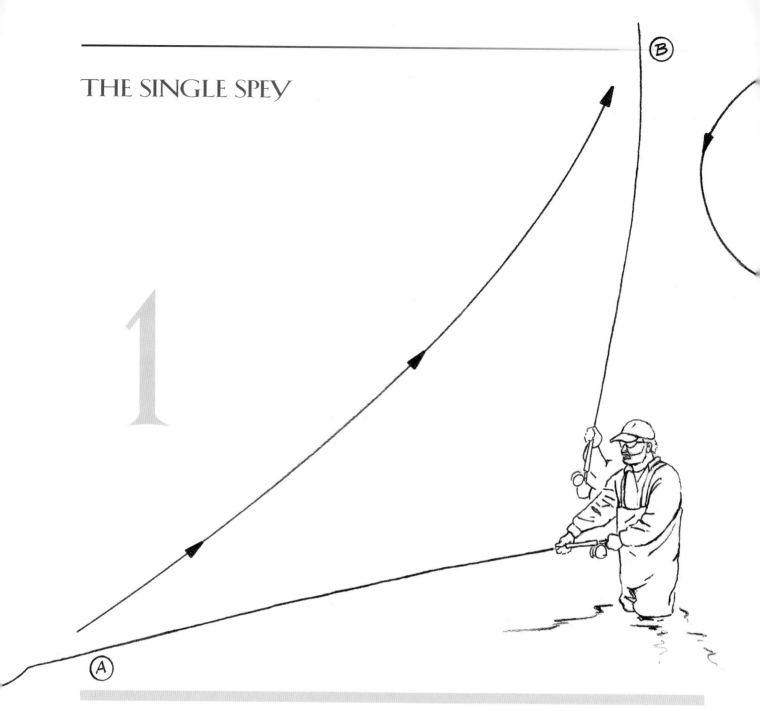

The single spey is the simplest cast mechanically, but unquestionably the most difficult for most anglers to execute successfully. Line and fly are brought from downstream to upstream of the caster, where the anchor is placed and D-loop formed, all in one continuous movement. With the double spey, we have the luxury of placing the anchor, pausing, and forming the D-loop by tearing line off the water, thus creating an easy-to-feel load. The single spey permits no such luxury, but feels oh so good when you get the hang of it.

The basic single spey is a traditional Scottish cast used when the wind is blowing upriver, or when conditions warrant. It's fast and efficient. Some skeptics of the single spey have condemned the cast to being limited to only a quartered-down angle of delivery. Another inaccuracy! The key to single-spey casting at any angle you desire is to bring the rod in to your side of the bank on the initial lift, and sweeping the rod out over the river and up to place the anchor and develop the D-loop. Follow along with the illustrations and you will get a clear picture of what I mean.

Step One: The single spey starts like every other cast: line downstream and taut, rod low to the water. But now as you slowly raise the rod to begin the cast, you need to also move the rod in slightly to your bank. How far you bring the rod in is determined by at which angle you'll be casting. For instance, if I were quartering the cast, I would move the rod only several inches in. If the cast were being presented straight across, I'd move the tip in at least two feet. You need to practice and experiment to find out what works best for you.

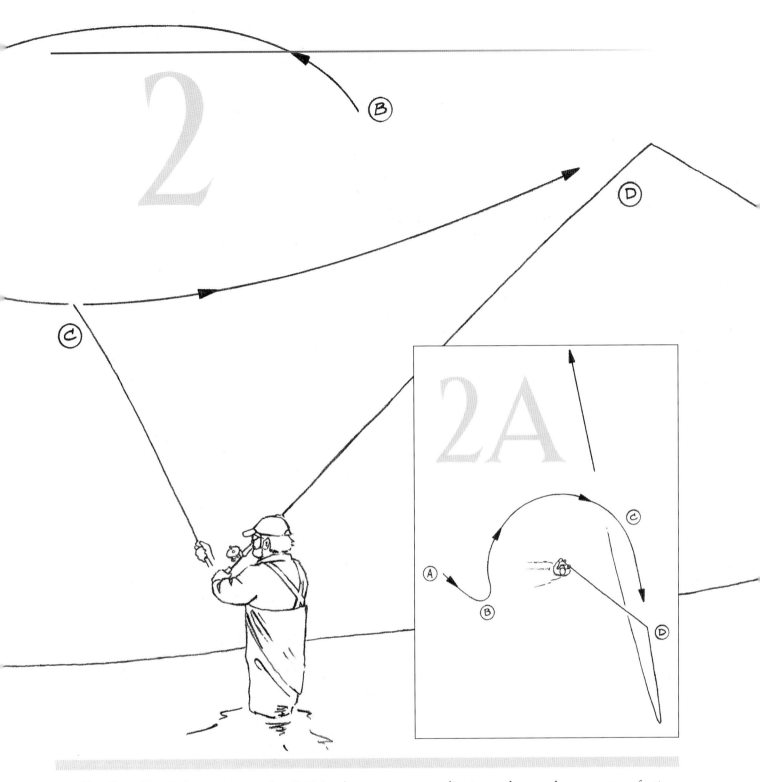

Step Two: Here's the tricky part that WILL take time to master, but is worth every hour spent perfecting. Once the rod has been lifted up as in step 1, continue without pausing, moving the rod out and over the water in front of you—out, around, and up to form the D-loop where there is finally a slight pause in order to let the D-loop develop. It may seem confusing explaining the cast in one breath. But that's really how it happens: one continuous movement from the time the rod is initially lifted to just prior to firing. Look closely at the illustration 2A. Follow the rod path from A to D. The only discernable pause is at position D. And if you've done everything correctly up to that point, the pause is for only a microsecond. The D-loop forms quickly.

Now, what the illustration doesn't depict—and is the most difficult part of the cast—is that the line and fly are aerialized from position B to C (anchor point) in illustration 2A. It would be rather simple to copy the rod movement depicted here, but it takes some getting used to doing it at the right speed and acceleration to get the line and fly to follow correctly. The first thing you must do is trust the prescribed rod path—the line and fly will follow. Practice, practice, practice. And don't give up!

3

Step Three: Fire away! Be alert, though. For some reason this cast encourages people to deliver the forward stroke out of plane of the D-loop. Remember, in whatever direction that D-loop travels, the forward stroke needs to travel in the opposite direction. Deviating from that leads to trouble.

George Cook of Sage Manufacturing deserves a lot of credit for helping to popularize two-handed casting in the West. Hundreds upon hundreds of aspiring casters and the curious have attended his free casting clinics spanning 16 years.

THE SNAKE ROLL

Funny how you learn some things. By the late 1990s, I had been fishing the two-handed rod for nearly a decade. I was obsessed with it—learning, experimenting, practicing, constantly thinking about its possibilities, sharing ideas and information with both friends and strangers. I was and still am abreast of the latest technological advances in equipment, but more important to me is the rod's river application: maximizing its potential as a fishing tool.

I was feeling pretty good that I had discovered and mastered nearly all of the creative possibilities that could be accomplished with the two-handed rod. I was by no means closed-minded at this point, but there really was no situation that I could not cast my way out of. I was content. Then one day while floating down the Deschutes River one of my clients asked me what a snake roll cast was. Puzzled, I told him I had never heard of it before. Then a week later another client asked me the same thing. I asked him where he had heard about a "snake roll." He said he had been to a Simon Gawsworth casting clinic where Simon discussed it briefly. My dude tried to describe it to me, but he wasn't making sense to me. I pulled the boat over and asked if he could show me. He was unsure of himself, but began trying to explain it while he drew a half-hearted circle with his rod at the start of the cast. Nothing happened. He was working hard to remember the move, when, as I was watching him, struggling to interpret what he was trying to do when . . . bingo! I saw it. I could see that the circle he was drawing with the rod was trying to set the line up anchored and loaded ready to fire.

"Unbelievable," I yelled out loud. "Give me that rod," I ordered. We were on river right—the double-spey side for right-handed casters. I raised the rod and made a counterclockwise circle from right to left, accelerating throughout. Sure enough, the fly popped out of the water and landed at the perfect anchor point downstream of me, with a nice D-loop behind it. I instinctively let 'er rip and made my first-ever snake roll cast. It was effortless with minimal movement of the arms and rod—a very easy, relaxing cast. I learned enough about it in the next 10 minutes of playing with it that I was able to teach my dudes. We had a ball with this new cast. I was thrilled with its potential for enhancing my arsenal of practical casts.

The snake roll is used in the same situations as the double spey, but it has several advantages: The snake roll is quicker from start to finish. It loads the rod with less line behind the angler. And it is physically far less fatiguing than the double spey. I hear it said frequently that the snake roll is good only for floating-line application. Not so. If the double and single spey were brand-new casts, the same could be said. The floating-line-only excuse is just an insecure copout to sound mechanics. When using a sink-tip, you must first slowly raise the rod to get the sink-tip near the surface. The rest is gravy, irrespective of the cast made.

Step One: The snake roll places the anchor downstream of the caster like the double spey. Start with a low rod tip, line and fly dangling below. Slowly raise the rod as usual. But now as you lift, bring the rod slightly in toward your bank. This movement is critical to the anchor and D-loop placement. The farther downstream the cast is intended to be made, the more the rod is brought in toward the bank. A word of caution: If you don't move the rod toward the bank, and simply raise the rod and begin the cast from straight downstream, the fly will land dangerously close and in front of you. If the caster is oblivious to this and makes the forward cast, chances are he or she will be wearing the fly.

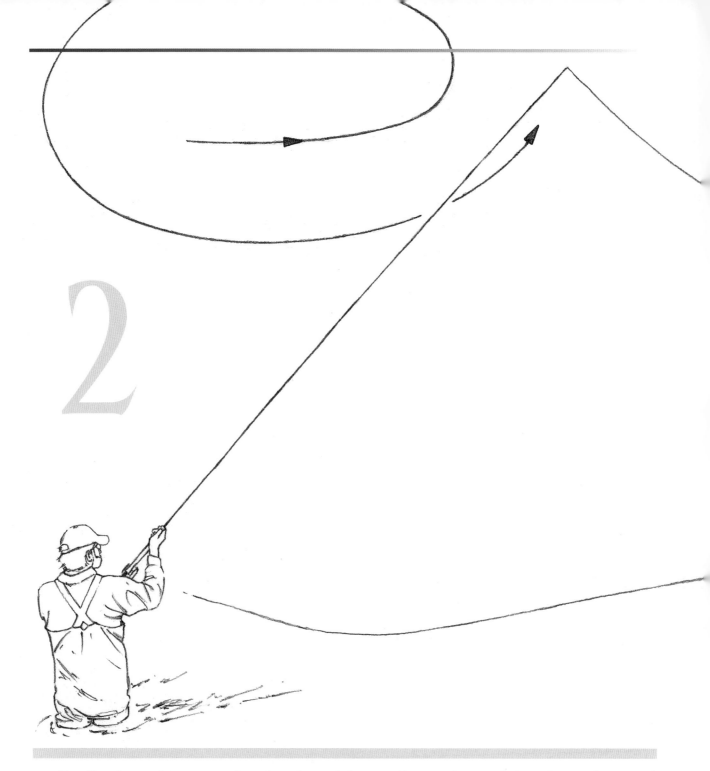

Step Two: Learn this move, and you have learned the cast. Once you've raised the rod up and in toward the bank (how far in is determined by the angle at which you're casting). Now I want you to think of your rod tip as a pencil. Stop for a minute and don't even think about casting—rather, think about drawing.

You are drawing a big, lower-case letter "e." The rod tip—the business end of your pencil—starts at the center of the "e" moving from left to right, just as you would write it on a piece of paper. In one continuous motion draw the letter "e." Practice drawing the "e" a few times until you're comfortable. Now we can turn the "e" into a cast.

The "e" is a cast—you are moving line and aerializing the fly. Now when you form the "e" you must, without stopping, smoothly accelerate the rod from the lower half of the "e" and into the firing position. Get it? Start the "e" and, once you've made the top of the "e" and are about halfway down its left side, begin your acceleration. Continue moving and accelerating through the rest of the "e" and into the firing position. It takes some practice to determine the size of the "e" and for you to see for yourself how it affects where the anchor is placed.

3

Step Three: If you've made the "e" correctly, the fly is anchored and the D-loop formed, ready for the forward stroke. Fire away!

THE REVERSE DOUBLE SPEY

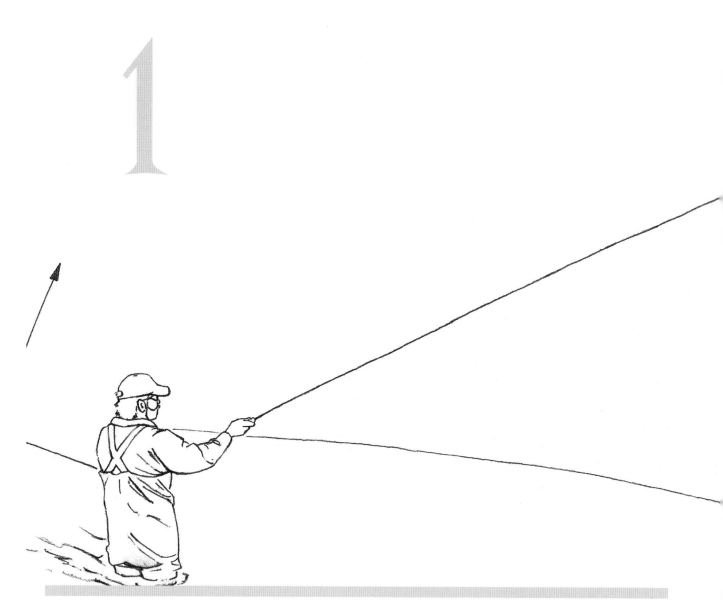

The reverse double spey is the most commonly used off-shoulder cast. It's also the cast that I've seen cause the most hook-inflicted injuries. It's an exceptionally useful cast for those of us who are not comfortable switching hands when on river left with the wind blowing downstream, etc. The reason people hook or hit themselves with this and other off-shoulder casts is just that: Forming a D-loop and stroking the rod forward on the off-shoulder is awkward to many. Casters have a tendency to take measures to protect themselves from the hook. In trying to do so, they inadvertently make the cast even more hazardous.

Here's the most common mistake I see made: When the D-loop is forming, the caster consciously or sub-consciously tries to keep the fly and line away from himself. As the rod passes in front and to the downstream side of the caster, instead of taking the rod up and back in the opposite direction of the intended forward cast—thus forming a D-loop—the rod is sent up and downstream away from the caster. Where does the D-loop go? In the direction it was cast: downstream. Now the caster executes his forward stroke slightly down and across river. Where do you think the fly is going? Yep, right back at the caster. In essence, the D-loop just formed was inadvertently set up to be cast upstream and across. Remember, remember: The D-loop is your back cast, and the back cast must be 180 degrees from the direction of the forward cast. It feels awkward when performed from the off-shoulder, but you must trust it.

All casting should be done slowly and smoothly. When we are struggling with a cast, we have a tendency to speed up. We need to do the opposite and slow down. Be aware that if you are performing a cast that you struggle with, you are probably rushing it. Even after you read this and you know what you're supposed to do, I guarantee that you still need to SLOW DOWN. I believe I have the reverse double spey reasonably mastered. Yet I still from time to time must remind myself not to rush. All it takes is for that fly to come whizzing by my ear one time to wake me up!

Step One: Start as usual, slowly raising the rod tip to get the line and fly moving. When the rod tip reaches the appropriate point (usually around 10 to 11 o'clock), it's time to set the anchor by moving the rod out in front of you and accelerating to a position upstream.

Gary Rawson of West Linn, Oregon demonstrates how to effectively fish the two-hander in close quarters. Fishing this run on the Skagit with a single-handed rod would be futile at best.

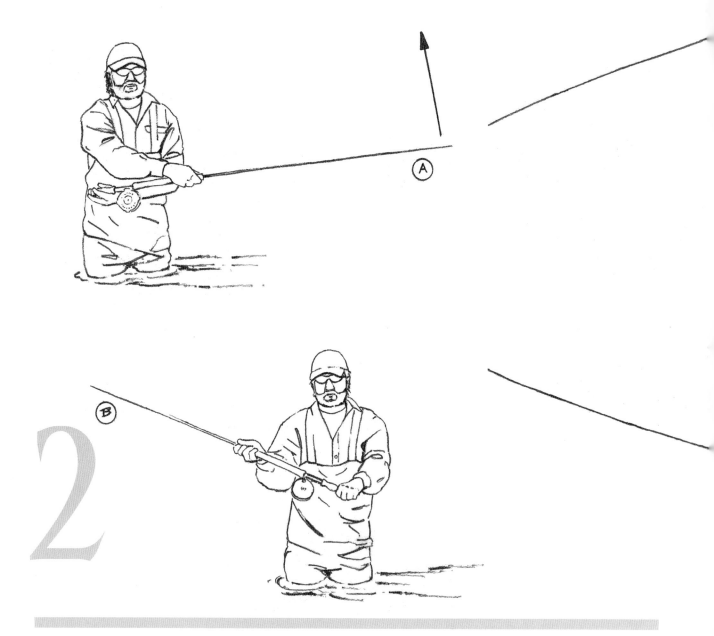

Step Two: Let the line settle on the water for a moment. Now sweep the rod slowly downstream, moving line around the anchor and up to form the D-loop. Remember, this is where you can get into trouble—the D-loop is supposed to go behind you in the opposite direction of your intended cast. Only you have the power to control where that D-loop goes. DO NOT RUSH. Don't stop the rod prematurely and send the D-loop downstream. Stay in control. (Refer to the double-spey illustrations as this cast is identical, only on the opposite side of the river.)

Step Three: Loaded and ready to fire. Note the rod position in steps 3 and 3A—straight over the top of my head slightly favoring my left shoulder (off-shoulder.) Don't be tempted to point the rod downstream and away from yourself. This is another counterproductive defense mechanism I see people doing when in fear of being struck by the fly. The line and fly follow the path of the rod tip—a basic rule of casting. So, if your anchor and D-loop are all lined up and you commit to the forward stroke as in the illustration, the line and fly won't even come close to hitting you. When all of the various casts are done properly, the reverse double spey is an extremely useful and powerful cast.

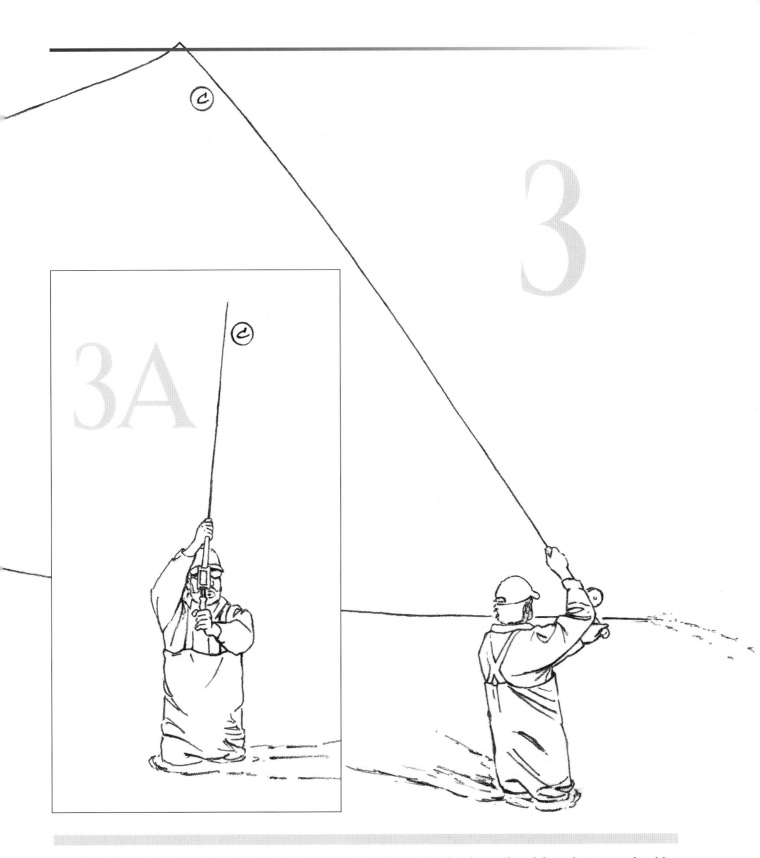

Step Three A: Shows the hand and rod position after the anchor has been placed for a dominant-shoulder double spey. Compare it to illustration B which is the off-shoulder reverse double spey.

Step Four: As with all the casts when done correctly, the reverse double spey is extremely powerful. Let 'er rip!

All good casts start with a slow lifting of the rod to get the line and fly moving before the fly breaks the surface, especially with sink-tips. Dave Olson making a reverse double spey on the Sauk River, Washington.

THE REVERSE CIRCLE SPEY (REVERSE SNAP-T)

1

While fishing one spring evening back when I had only a couple years of experience with the two-handed rod, the wind started to blow fiercely up river as it so often does on our West Coast rivers. I was fishing on river-right, enjoying making double-spey casts. The nagging upriver wind quickly put an end to my fun, killing the loading of my D-loop by blowing it behind me. I persisted, ducking to my left in order to keep from being hit by my fly that was rocketing dangerously close to my head. This lasted for a short while, though. The party was over. I knew I needed to be casting off my upstream side. A single spey would have worked, but I wasn't yet proficient at casting with my left hand on top, especially in wind. I tried to single spey reverse style, but that was futile. It's a sad fact, but I quit fishing that evening.

After I discovered and taught myself the reverse circle cast, an upriver wind while fishing river right has never been an issue. In fact, I welcome it. A little directional wind really makes for an efficient D-loop, which means a super-loaded rod and thus an extremely powerful tight-looped cast with tremendous line speed. The opening two-page photo of this chapter is me casting the reverse circle cast amidst a brisk upstream wind.

When making this cast, all the rules of a dominant-shoulder circle cast apply (see the circle cast a.k.a. the snap-T). Because it's a reverse off-shoulder cast, pay attention to the principles of the reverse double spey. As always, take it slow.

Step One: Start with a low rod tip and a taut line. Raise your rod slowly to get the line and fly moving and break the surface tension. (Refer back to the circle cast to determine how high the rod should be lifted.)

(A)

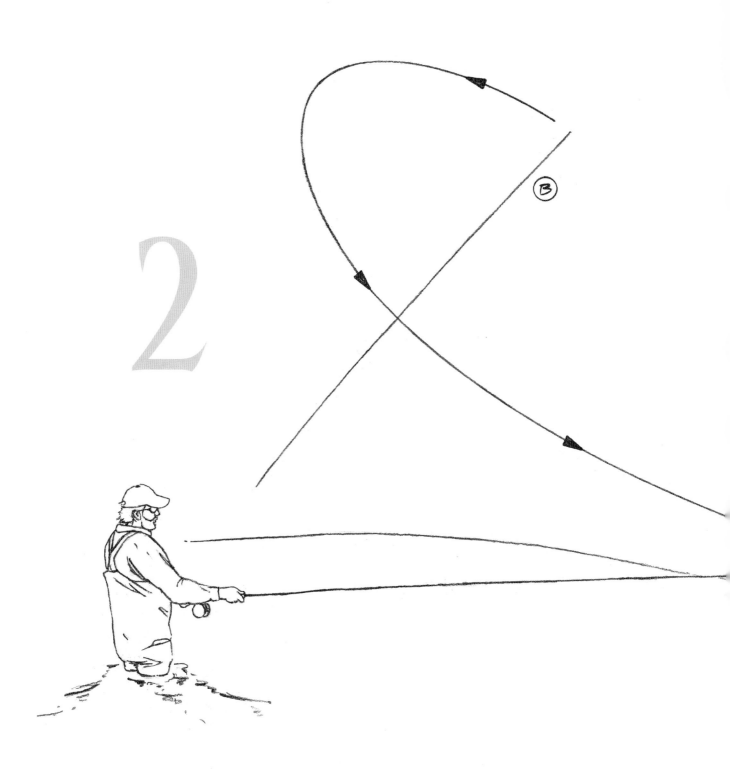

Step Two: Make the cut by drawing the letter "C" with your rod up and out over the river. The fly is anchored upstream of you, and your rod has traveled down where you pause to let the line settle momentarily on the water. Because the anchored fly is to the upstream side, many anglers feel they need to hurry to get the cast off in fear of the current's bringing the fly too close to them. Just cast at the pace you normally would; there's plenty of time. Besides, when the D-loop is being formed the fly stalls and is drug slightly back upstream.

Step Three: Sweep the rod up and around, smoothly accelerating to make the D-loop and fire away. Notice my hand and rod positioning are nearly identical to their position when doing the reverse double spey.

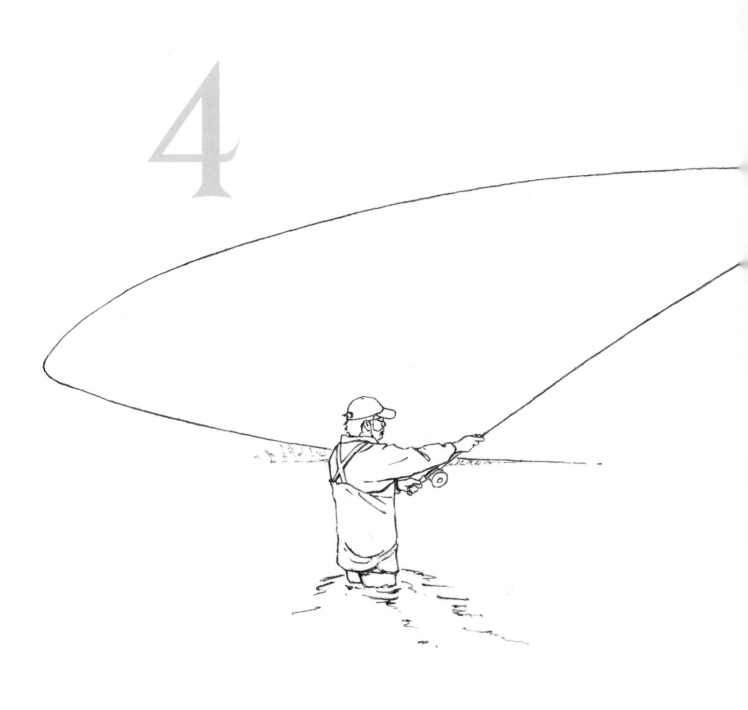

Step Four: Out she goes. When all is working well with just the right amount of upriver breeze, the reverse circle is perhaps my most powerful cast.

Reverse Single Spey and Snake Roll

I purposefully did not include illustrations of the reverse single spey and reverse snake roll. These are casts that can be executed, but both are awkward to learn. By referring to the illustrations and detailed descriptions of the single spey and snake roll—coupled with the reverse double spey and circle cast—it will be easy to apply those steps to the reverse single and snake roll. Although they are not commonly practiced, don't discount these casts. I employ both of them from time to time; I never know when I might need them. The two-handed rod is as versatile a tool as you allow it.

Casting with impeccable form, Amy Christensen is about to unleash one on the Salmon River, Idaho. Note the "white mouse."

CASTING FOR DISTANCE

Amy Christensen casting a long, crisp line on a gorgeous October day. Casting for distance is best acheived by taking it slow.

Jacking big line is just plain fun! There are, however, times and places where being able to cast 100 feet or more is vital to your success with steelhead. And if you've never had a grab at the start of the swing that was made by a 110 foot cast straight across river, I can only tell you: It's scary fun.

You must know—because I do—that no matter how much instruction you receive, a clean, powerful, honest-to-goodness 100-foot cast made while wading to your waist might not be attainable for everyone. I've had the time to practice. I've dedicated a major portion of my life to perfecting two-handed casting. I may be able to beat Phil Mickleson at arm wrestling, but I'll never drive a golf ball as far—it's his life. That said, you can add distance to your cast by understanding and learning a few key essentials.

First, before you try to rear back and cast yourself out of your Danners, you must be competent at casting at least the head portion of your line. This means all facets of the cast, particularly, a tight, crisp D-loop in line with proper anchor placement. If you have control of casting the head, you're ready to shoot some line for distance.

Rule No. 1: If you want to make a long cast, you have to make a long stroke. I accomplish this by drifting the rod up, back, and down as the D-loop is forming. Then I extend the forward stroke.

Rule No. 2: Smoothly accelerate the rod. Never try and heave the rod all at once—it never works. If you were to watch me make my longest cast, you'd be amazed at how slow the forward stroke appears.

Rule No. 3: Stop the rod high. I've never seen a quarterback throw a long bomb by releasing the ball at helmet level.

Rule No. 4: Incorporate a lot of bottom hand late in the stroke. Pulling with the bottom hand late in the stroke lengthens the stroke and influences the rod bend much like pulling on the line during a single-handed-rod double haul—it increases line speed. The bottom hand is also critical to a crisp stopping of the rod. You'll never achieve much distance without a precise, abrupt stop.

Adhere to these four elements and you'll be on your way to new horizons and private distant steelhead lies! Don't try and do it all at once, though. Practice adding several feet at a time. When the line recoils and wants to travel farther, it's time to add a little more. If you've found your limit and begin to struggle, reel in some line and back off a bit. Casting beyond your means is not beneficial.

Once things start to click for you, you'll need to manage the running line you strip in. Carrying several large loops is far better than trying to manage many small ones. Everybody controls his or her loops a little differently; that's fine. You need to decide what works best for you.

Here's how I take care of mine. (Follow the illustrations.) The length depicted is how I manage 15 feet of running line, which is about how much I need to handle for an 85-foot cast made with a 53-foot headed fly line.

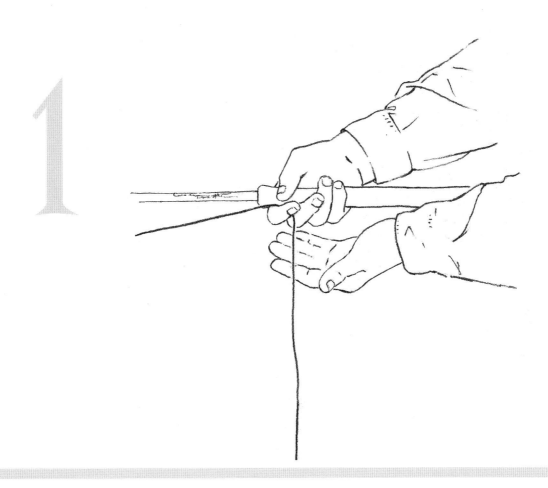

Step One: Here I've already stripped in enough fly line to lay a short length on the water. I've turned my hand palm up to pinch the line between my thumb and index finger. I grab it this way rather than palm down so I don't create a closed loop. The palm-up method lays the line between the fingers like an accordion, and tends not to tangle as easily—it's how rock climbers coil their ropes. Once you've pinched the line palm up, you can turn your hand back over to comfortably strip in the loop. Just be sure not to let go of the line you already have pinched off.

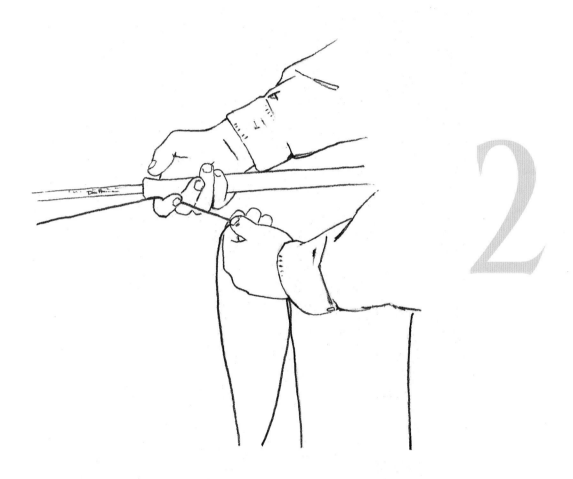

Step Two: I take just enough strips of line to touch the water but slightly smaller than the first loop. Once the second loop is made, I start making the third loop with a conventional palm down pinch. This ensures I keep consistent with my "accordion lay."

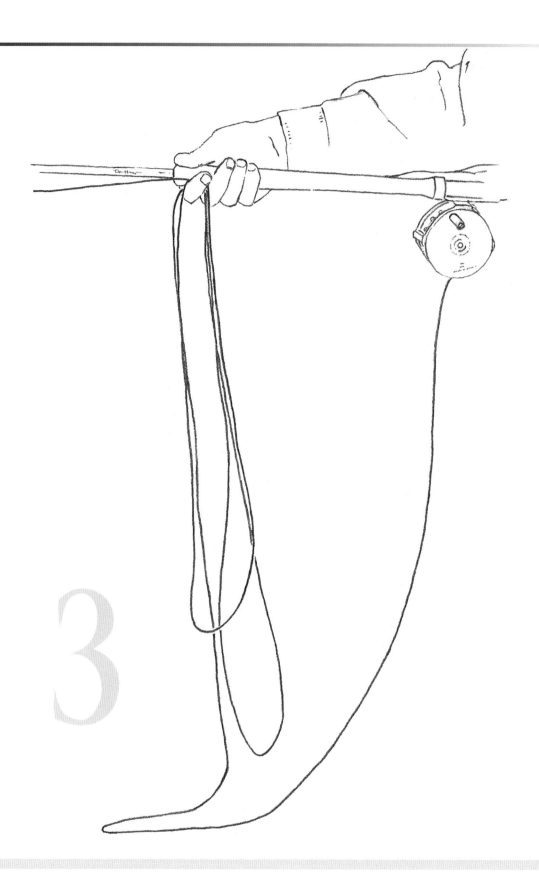

3

Step Three: The third and final loop in this case is formed smaller than the second. Large loops that progressively get smaller are the key to a smooth shooting, tangle-free cast. I then transfer the whole works to my right index finger (top hand) where I pinch it against the cork. I use my top hand (some anglers use their bottom) to hold and shoot the loops. Holding in the bottom hand is not comfortable to me, but maybe it would be for you. Try it both ways and decide.

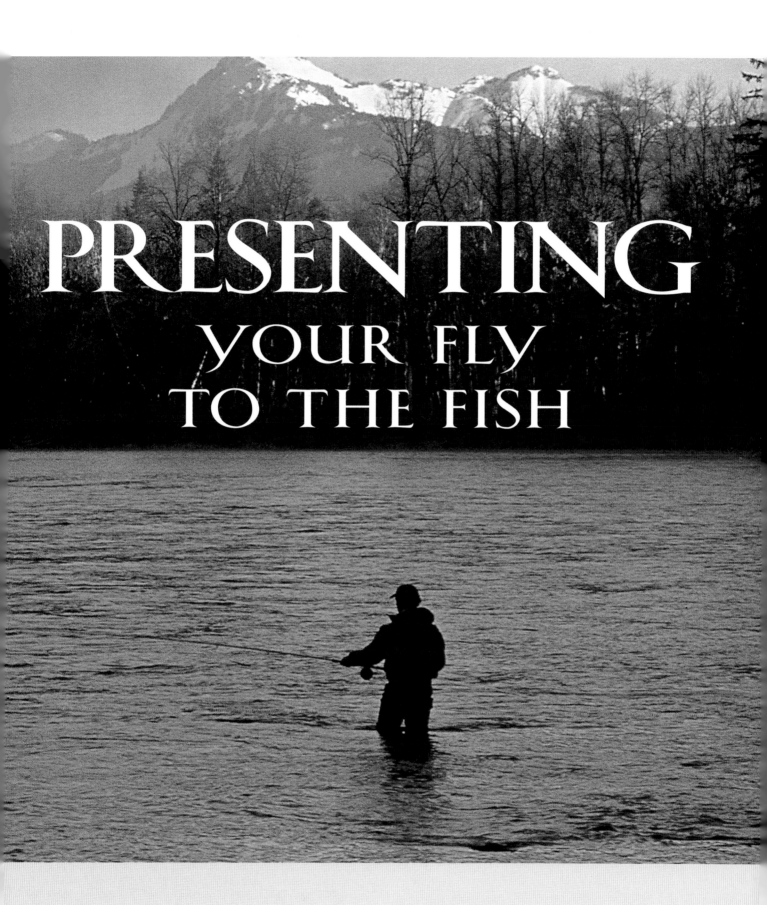

PRESENTING
YOUR FLY
TO THE FISH

PRESENTING YOUR FLY TO THE FISH is ultimately where it all comes together—the reason you're on the river. The finest tackle and wading apparel made, the fishiest fly attached with the perfect knot cast to the most promising water at prime time won't catch you a thing without fundamental understanding and solid execution of fly presentation. Sure, steelhead can be extremely aggressive at times, and lucking into one does happen occasionally. I've seen so many steelhead smash the fly in odd and unlikely situations that one of my compulsory mental mantras when guiding is, "When the fly is in the water, it's at the mercy of the fish." But chuck-and-chance fishing is not how you—or anyone serious about steelhead fishing—wants to spend your valuable time on the water.

As in most pursuits in life, the better you are and the more you learn about something, the more enjoyable it becomes. When we are first introduced to our chosen pursuit we are a clean and often clumsy slate. Strapping on snow skis for the first time feels awk-ward, dorky, and out of control. Your only real basic concept of the usage of your new six-feet-long slippery feet is gravity. As that gravity carries you and your flailing arms spastically down the hill for the first time, you are not skiing—you are fighting with every

The broad expanse of the Deschutes River's steelhead runs keeps the fly fishing beautifully throughout the swing.

inch of your being to survive. The inevitable happens. You find yourself face-planted in the snow, only to look up and see your rental feet racing down the mountain without you. Somehow, once safely back on level ground, you realize that was fun. Then you think, *Hey, with some practice I might get to like it.* You set your sights on improving your skills, and have a blast conquering the mountain. Over time you not only blossom into a good skier, but you understand the effects of climate and weather as it pertains to mountain and snow conditions. You come to recognize and appreciate the different qualities of snow. You know when the mountain will be crowded with other skiers and when you can head up and have it all to yourself. You have a thorough working knowledge of the equipment and what works best when, but mainly what works best for you. The list goes on. Learning to present flies to steelhead and all the nuance it entails is not unlike learning to ski: It takes time, patience, practice, perseverance, gobs of awareness, and, yes, falling down. The rewards are infinite.

Presentation at its most basic level is a simple wet-fly swing. Cast across and slightly downstream, mend some line up behind the fly and follow the fly's path across the current with your rod tip until the fly slows to a stop. Take a step or two downstream and do it again. That's it. As the fly swings across, it is under tension by the force of the current. Generally, the goal is to have the fly swing as slowly across the current as possible. In broad, even-flowing water this is easy to accomplish. There are no conflicting currents that need to be manipulated in order to achieve a slow, steady wing. As I tell my clients in this type of water, "Put it out there and don't mess with it!" The simple swing is the foundation of all presentation for traditional steelhead fly fishing.

All of my presentation, too, is based on the swing. There's been plenty written on the multitudes of angles at which to present a fly: butt first, fully broadside, three-quarter view, etc. I have studied and experimented with them all. But I'll let you in on my secret: I don't look at a piece of water and decide which angle is likely to work best. I let the water tell me as I feel it. Getting overly mechanical can lead to poor presentation and frustration; it retards learning the subtleties of currents and its effects on the swing.

What I mean is that once the fly is set up properly (which we'll discuss presently), the current pretty much dictates how the fly will fish. If the fly starts to swim slightly broadside to the current, that's what it needs to do and how it will fish best. Trying to keep the fly swimming butt first by constant mending is futile—you'll end up jerking the fly all around as it continuously fights to regain its broadside attitude. I typically try to exploit the fly's current-influenced behavior. If the current makes the fly swim broadside, I encourage it by leading the fly with the tip of my rod. Conversely, if the fly wants to show butt first, I may follow with my rod as the current keeps the fly swimming parallel.

My goal is for the fly to swim enticingly under tension at a slow, seductive speed. My method is to maintain continuous contact. The fly fishes smoothly and with a powerful presence, signaling to the steelhead that it is alive. This is how it feels to me,

anyway. Clumsy mending kills the pulse, rhythm and pace of the fly. Proper mending—correcting the course of your fly by careful manipulation—requires an exceptional sense of feeling and perception as to how the fly is buffeted by the current. It's not easy. It requires a light touch. And always you must swing your fly with the mindset that there is a steelhead down there that you are trying to coax on every cast. I can watch a person fish and know if he has the mojo working by reading his body language. If I'm making this sound a little Zen-like, that's because I believe it is. Don't let this intimidate you, however. You can easily build the framework of sound presentation with lots of fun practice and experimentation. The Zen Zone is likely to manifest itself with experience—if you let it.

Ed Ward swinging a fly amidst the late afternoon glow that precedes a Dean River sunset. This run typifies "the classic bar."

Learning presentation by the written word and diagrams has its merits, and it's a good place to begin, but nothing beats experience. In gaining this experience, there's a bit of an ongoing Catch-22 at work. Steelhead are not easy to come by, even for the most experienced anglers. And the best feedback you can receive as regards your proficiency at presentation is of course from the steelhead. Hooking one, two, even half a dozen steelhead will boost your confidence tremendously. No question about it. But it takes many, many grabs, and oodles of hours and runs fished before one truly has a keen working knowledge and understanding of what it takes to become a master steelheader—even a competent one. Forget about short cuts. You need river time. Maybe these are hard words for you to swallow, but there's nothing wrong with having to pay your dues; it's called life. Experience is the keystone to success. Everything you do associated with steelhead fishing adds to your experience bank, including reading this book. The more insight you can gain, on and off the river, the better.

Wading Into Position

How and where we wade is not often discussed or considered as an integral part of presenting the fly, but it most surely is. How you wade has a great effect on fly speed. Theoretically, the closer your rod tip is to the fly, the slower it will travel. It makes sense: There's simply less line on the water perpendicular to the current. Does this mean you should wade out to the top of your waders everywhere you fish? Absolutely not. It's all dependant on where in relation to the run the steelhead are likely to be holding. If the water is three feet deep, with steady flow right off the bank, then you'd better not wade out much past the bank. If the run gradually deepens from the bank, and the moderate speed water doesn't occur for 20 yards beyond shore, you'd better wade out there.

If I'm working down a run, wading to just above my knees and suddenly get a pull from a steelhead in the early stages of my swing, it's obvious to me that the fish was holding out there pretty far. When I make another cast to try and get him back, more important to me than changing flies is to fish the same fly slower. The surest way to do this is to back up a step or two and wade out a little farther. Wading out will automatically fish the fly slower over the steelhead's lie. I also help the cause by getting even closer to the fish and thus a slower swing by extending my arm and rod out over the river in the direction whence I had the pull. I want to give the fish a good, long look at the fly.

Another time to wade out for a slower swing is when covering a specific pocket or piece of structure. Here again, the closer you are the slower the fly swings, the longer it stays in the pocket.

As for the pace at which one should step down the run, I definitely have an opinion on this. Experienced steelhead anglers, guides, instructors, writers, and sharers of information always say, "Take two steps and make a cast—two steps down the run." Two steps has been pounded in to our heads. Well, suppose I'm guiding Shaquille O'Neal and Danny Devito, and I say, "Shaq, I want you to start at the top

of the run. Danny, you take the lower half and jump in by that log on the bank . . . Okay boys, two-step it downstream and catch me a steelhead!" What do you think will happen? Shaq will be casting to Danny's wader belt in a matter of a few minutes, not to mention all the water he missed by moving 10 feet between casts. I think I've made my point: The length of one man's "two steps" might equal to four or five of another's.

What about wading ability? The unsure, unstable wader might take five little steps to move one yard, while the strong, confident wader can move the same distance in one step. Here's my remedy. I tell my clients to move as far as a good-sized steelhead is long, about a yard. There are times, of course, when we may step a little less and times when we may step more. That comes when you are really intimately familiar with a piece of water. Until then a yard is good for general searching, whether you take two steps or 10.

Fishing big water is intimidating to some, in this case the Snake River, but it needn't be. You must see the stream within the river and mentally toss the rest. In the photo there's a large boulder between the anglers that's breaking the surface. The good holding water is to the inside of that boulder all the way down the run—a 60- to 70- foot cast covers the run adequately.

SET-UP AND SWING: THE PULLBACK MEND

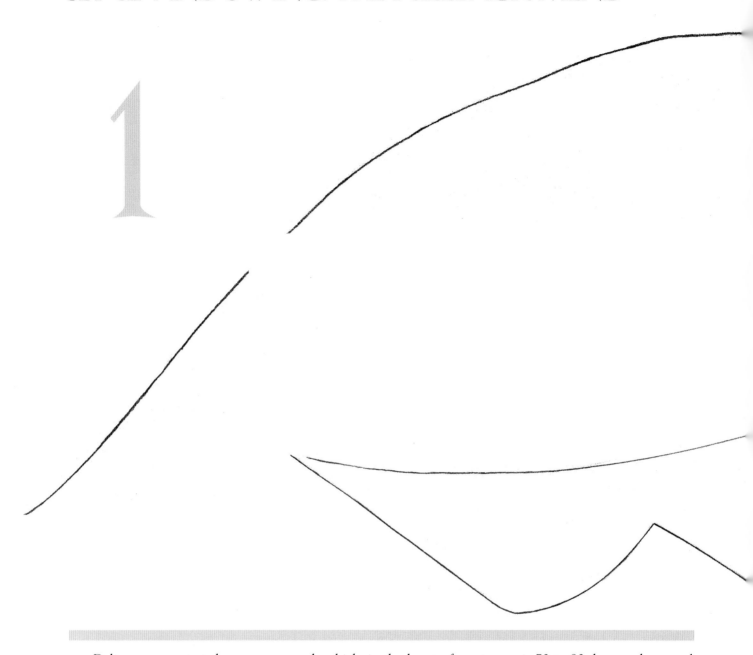

Deliver your cast at the necessary angle which, in the heart of most runs, is 70 to 80 degrees down and across—slightly less than perpendicular to the current. Make the cast long enough so it extends slightly beyond the breadth of the suspected likely water. The extra line is important to ensure proper set up. Once your fly and line touch down, give it a moment to settle on the water before making the next move. It's important that you have plenty of tension on the line from the rod to the sink-tip. Now lift the rod, literally pulling the sink-tip far enough to get lined up with the outer edge of the swath of water you are aiming to fish. I've always casually referred to this motion as the "pullback mend," so now I'll make it official: It's called the pullback mend.

It does two things: It accomplishes the aforementioned, plus slackens the line, freeing the sink-tip of tension and allowing it to begin sinking. How far you pull the tip back determines how deep the tip will be allowed to sink. So the distance you pull back on the tip will change throughout sections of the run as depth and current speeds vary.

Now you need to mend the floating portion of the line up and behind the tip. The two moves are separate from one another but are fluidly tied together. Watch an experienced angler execute this initial move and it appears to be made in one motion. But it's not. It's first a lift and pull, then a mend. The pullback mend.

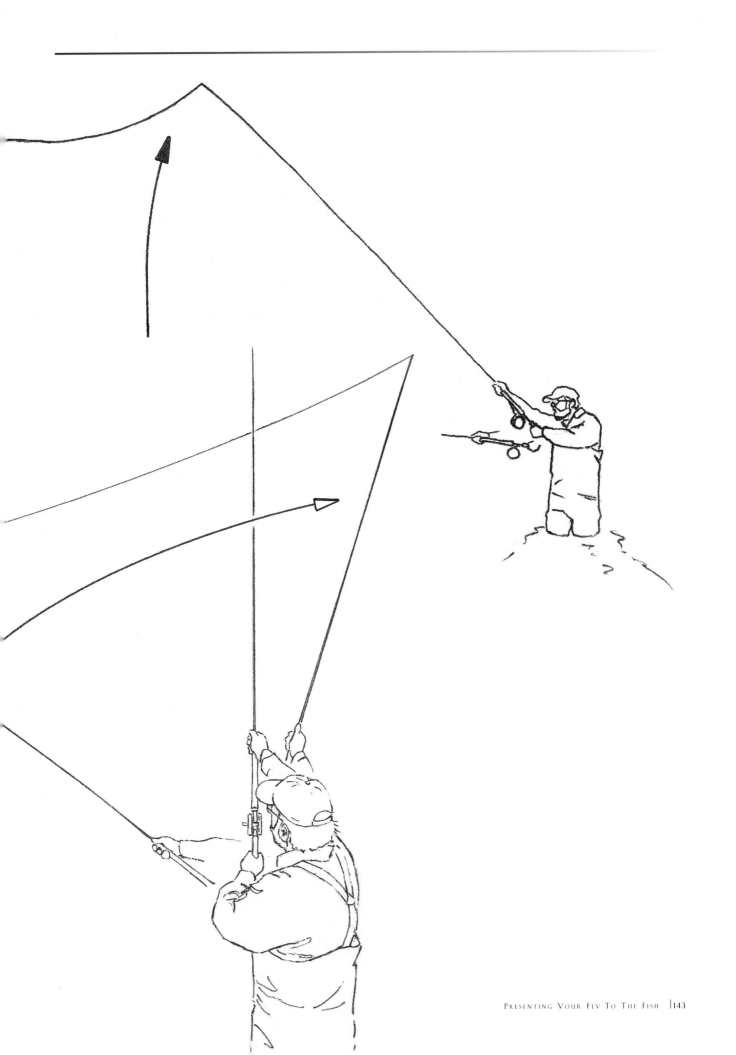

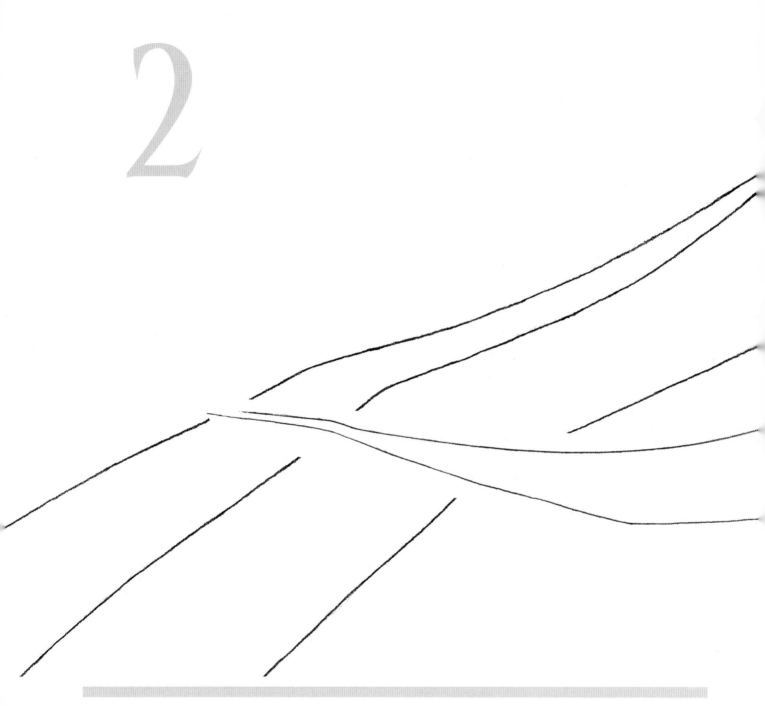

2

Now that you have executed the initial setup properly, your sink-tip and fly are freely drifting and sinking. In order to prolong this, you must lower your rod smoothly and with the pace of the current carrying the fly. Just before line begins to tighten, it is often necessary to mend some line up behind the tip and fly. Do this gently, without moving the tip and fly. The fly is at its maximum depth and just about to start swinging. You don't want to disturb it. This extra mend is essential in order to achieve the slowest swing possible. Do it carefully. Pay close attention, as very often you'll need to make another small mend. Watch the effects of the water on your line and you'll know if it's necessary.

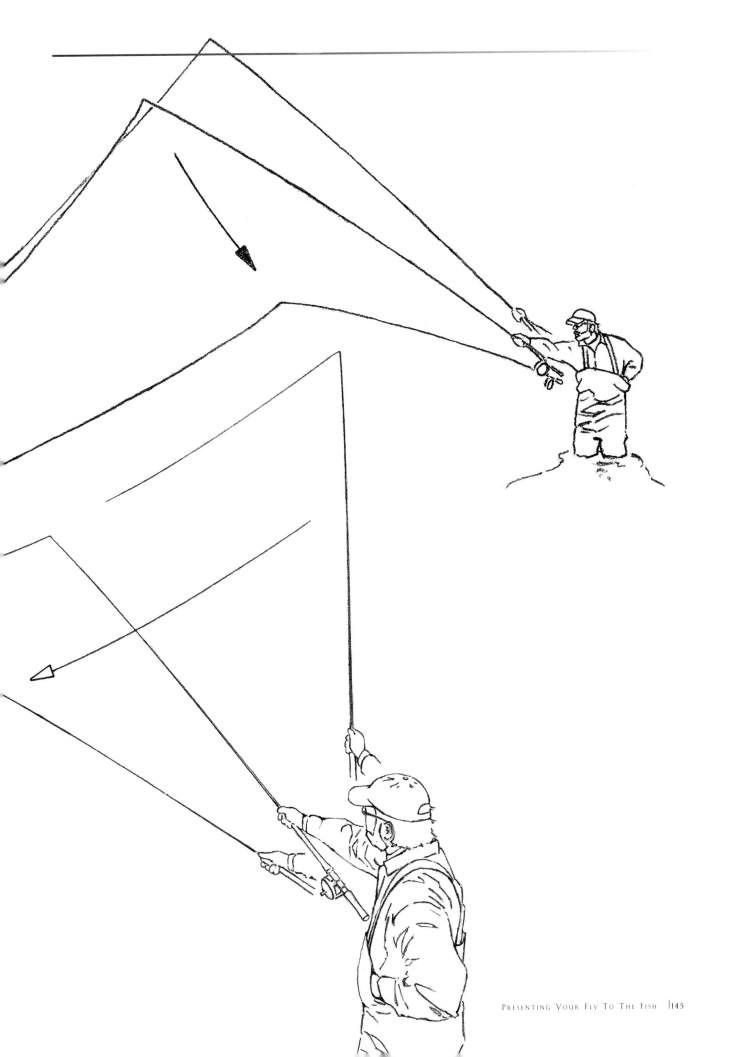

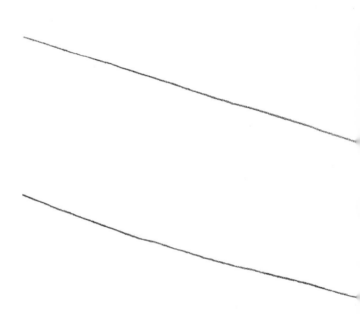

If everything has been done correctly up to this point, your fly has started swinging. Your rod tip should still be elevated slightly during the early part of the swing. While the fly is still a ways out there, the higher rod position will keep line off the water, reducing drag, and encouraging a slow swing. The rod is continuously lowered until roughly half way through the swing, which I call the heart of the swing. Here is where a great deal of takes occur. The sweet spot! Any mending or fidgeting at this point is bad, bad, bad. In fact, the whole process needs to be silky smooth and fluid.

Now follow the line with your rod tip until the fly is dangling directly below you where it's time to take the required steps and do it all again.

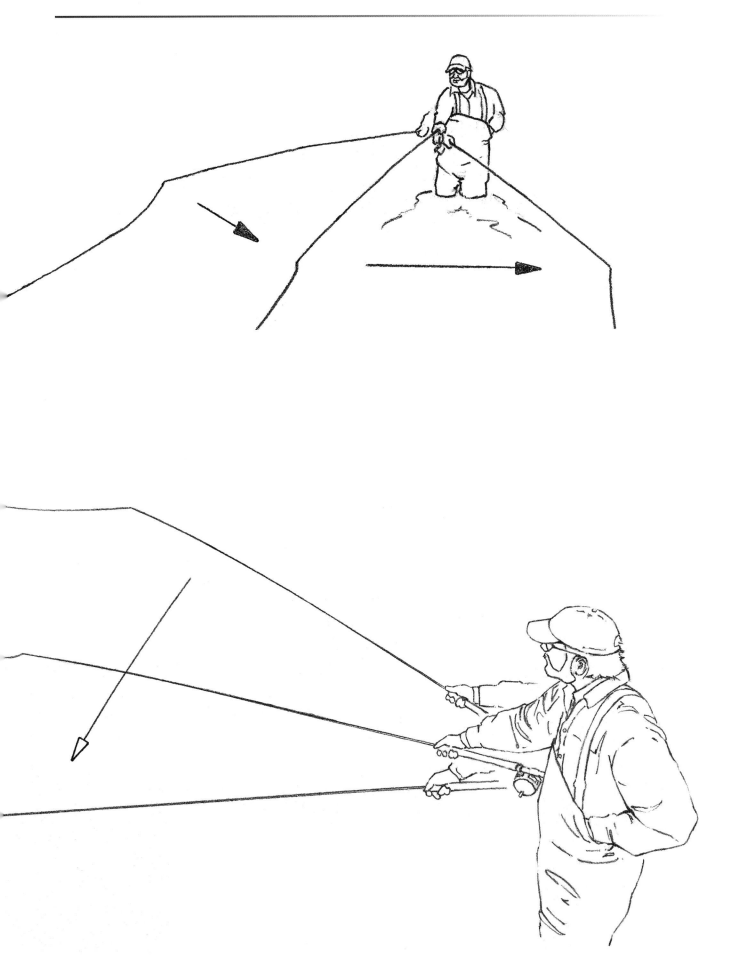

GOOD SWING VS. BAD SWING

There are situations when purposefully adding speed to the fly is desired. It's usually when you're trying to coax a "player" into taking during the game of changing flies. I would never approach my normal hunt with unnecessary speed on the fly, however. The angler has as much control of fly speed as the current will allow. If you find you can't fish the fly slowly, chances are you're fishing in the wrong type of water or that particular section of the run is just too fast.

If you look to the illustration, you will see a depiction of a fly fished overly fast and one fished just right. The fast, out-of-control, poorly presented fly is being swept fiercely across the run as the current pushes on the fly line—a result of an improper casting angle and/or poor line control. The fly and line stay near the surface throughout the racing swing. The entire anatomy of the fly is severely compressed, negating any thoughtful engineering that may have been built into its design. This is no good. Conversely, as you view the well-presented fly, it hovers enticingly just above the fish: hackles splayed and undulating in the current with the wing doing its job righting the fly while adding color, size, and shape to the overall impression of life. Take a good, long look at this illustration. Carry a mental snapshot of it when you step into the river. As you fish down a run, ask yourself what your fly is doing—or not doing.

You know what you want it to do. It's up to you to make it happen. Decide for yourself which presentation you'd rather be fishing. The speeding, out-of-control fly will, on rare occasion, be intercepted by a fired-up steelhead, but that same fired-up dude and most of his less enthusiastic buddies prefer the slow, seductive fly nearly every time. At the very least, you will have the satisfaction of enjoying everything involved in making good presentations. It just plain feels good when you're doing it right.

POOR PRESENTATION: BAD SWING

1

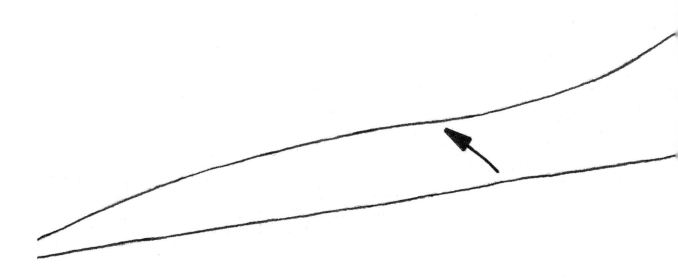

You've made your cast with not much thought or regard to angle of delivery. Then you make a half-hearted mend—for no other reason than you think you're supposed to. You fidget around with your feet attempting to find a more comfortable stance. Meanwhile, your line begins to belly. . . .

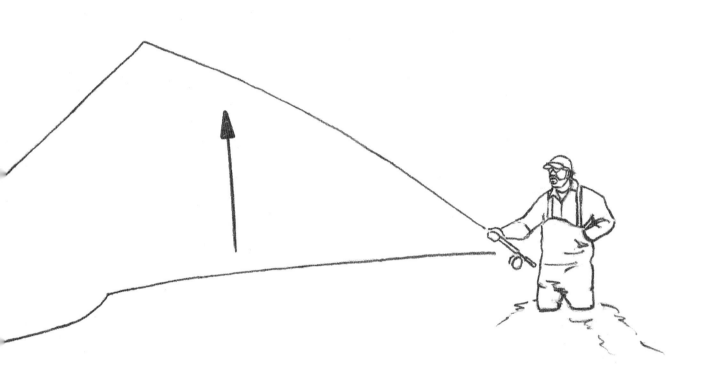

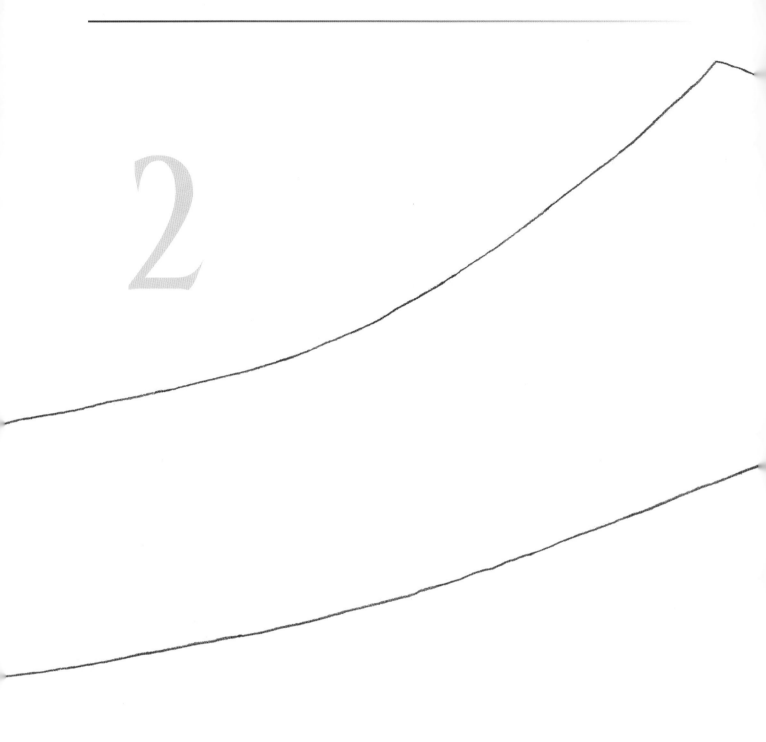

You are unconscious of your rod position—it's way ahead of the line and fly. At this point the fly is racing across the current as it chases the severely bellied line. The more the rod is pointed downstream and toward the bank, the worse the situation becomes. The purpose of these illustrations is twofold: One is to depict what happens to the fly with no regard to line and fly control; the other is to simply show what the results are when the rod tip is brought downstream and in toward the bank way ahead of the fly, instead of making good use of mending and following the fly with the rod tip. Slightly leading the fly is a good thing only after the fly has come through the heart of the swing.

HOW DEEP IS DEEP ENOUGH?

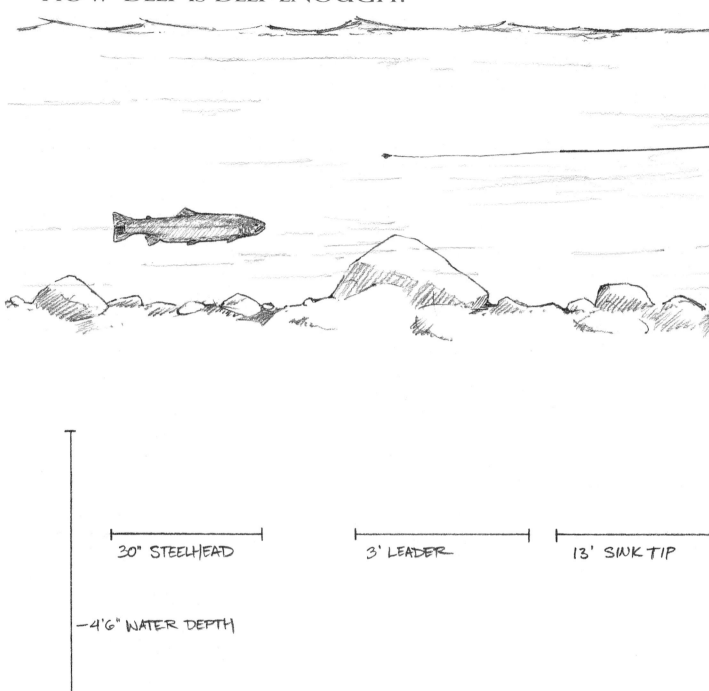

30" STEELHEAD

3' LEADER

13' SINK TIP

—4'6" WATER DEPTH

Early in my steelheading career I, like many, felt the need to fish my fly as deeply as possible. If I wasn't losing flies, I wasn't down enough. Over the years, I've experimented with every imaginable sinking line, from lead core to shooting heads and various densities of sink-tips spliced together, to lead-eyed flies, even split shot on the leader. I must confess I often kept these practices to myself. I was ashamed because I really wanted to fish for steelhead as sportingly as possible—I wanted my fly fishing to be pure. I really wanted to believe that the naturally aggressive wild steelhead I was pursuing would move for my fly.

Some things you have to find out for yourself. But here's a preview of what you, too, will eventually learn: Steelhead, even in extremely cold water, will in fact move to your fly. Not all of them, of course—a lot of them won't even bite if the fly hits them between the eyes. That's just the way it is. Finding a biting steelhead is not easy. It never will be. But I've long since abandoned the practice of going super deep. Now as a guide and instructor I find I spend a lot of time trying to convince anglers who ask that they needn't worry about fishing on or near the bottom. Think about it: If your fly is on the bottom hitting rocks and such, it's not really fishing. And certainly if you're wasting precious fishing time breaking off flies and replacing them, you're *really* not fishing! Casting heavy lines and flies is difficult, tiresome, a bit dangerous, and not much fun. Looking back, I can honestly say that I didn't hook any more steelhead with the super heavy stuff than I would have without it.

Typically, steelhead that are biters don't hold tight to the bottom. They suspend themselves, sometimes by quite a bit, allowing the hydraulics of the river to hold them comfortably in place. If you consider that good steelhead water is from three to six feet in depth, the fish is anywhere from a foot to two feet off the bottom. The fish, even if it's a small one, is two feet long and five inches wide. Because steelhead spend their lives ambushing their prey from below, you can plainly see that much of the water column is eliminated. Doing the simple math, it's evident that by scraping rock bottom, you're inadvertently placing yourself at a fishing disadvantage.

I'm satisfied in knowing that my fly is fishing at mid depth. I've read and heard it said from time to time that, "You either fish on the bottom or right on top—nothing in between." I'm certain that many misfortunate anglers have been influenced by this warped view. It's bad advice.

The more confident I became realizing that aggressive steelhead would move to the fly, the less frequently I found myself changing my sink-tip. There is a sameness to most good fly water. Runs may look different— topographically and geologically very different—but in all the diverse rivers I've fished, steelhead universally like to hold at a fairly constant water depth of steady velocity. These days I rarely change sink-tips. During steelhead season, I rely on a 150- to 160-grain type 6 10-weight tip measuring 13 to 15 feet in length. If I feel I need to go to something heavier, it's not to gain more depth, but to compensate for those few runs with heavy surface currents.

I also carry a sink-tip or two in the six- to nine-foot range, which I use in runs or sections of runs strewn with large boulders. The shorter tip is easier to manage with less potential for hang ups while negotiating a watery rock garden.

STEELHEAD LIE: SMALL STRUCTURE

The structure steelhead use is not always large and dramatic. Structure is a relative thing. In the middle of a gently-flowing run with a bottom made up of shot-glass-sized pebbles, if there's one rock mixed in the size of a dinner plate it could hold a steelhead. I've seen steelhead on numerous occasions nosed up to such rocks. This illustrates the steelhead's fondness for rocks, not just to break up the current, but also for a sense of security. It also illustrates the importance of fishing through a run systematically and thoroughly, especially on new water where you have little or no experience. Every time a steelhead is hooked in a run there's a reason that fish was there. I don't believe it's ever a random event. So, as you fish down a run hurriedly casting between the known sweet-spots, slow down. Don't be overly anxious. You may be missing out on an easy fish.

RIVER RUN 1: THE CLASSIC BAR (OVERLEAF)

This diagram takes a look at what I call the classic bar. This type of run is every steelheader's dream water: a long, open run of medium depth and perfect speed with structure in the form of boulders the size of softballs to basketballs. The run nearly always has a defined, shallow head coming in riffly and fast that gradually yet distinctly slows as the water deepens in the body of the run—a steelhead "hot zone." The body extends and continues to slow until the bottom contour begins to rise as it nears the tailout. Here the current begins to accelerate—again, another hot zone. The water continues to grow shallower and swifter until it's no longer fishable.

An aerial view would reveal that the middle to far side of the run has a more powerful current than the fish-holding side. Hence the reason the fish hold relatively close to shore: to stay out of the heavy flow. And let's not forget what makes a bar a bar. The fishing side of the run is marked by a large exposed gravel or rock bar. Wading into the run, the water deepens gradually as the riverbed gently slopes toward center river. These are easy places to fish with pleasant wading and an abundance of room to cast.

The most productive bars that are consistently attractive to steelhead always have some dramatic river feature both upstream and downstream: for instance, the famous Mixer Run on the Skagit River in Washington. Directly downstream from the Mixer is an extremely deep pool—nearly 30 feet deep. Above the Mixer is a long, shallow, fast section of water. On another great bar on the lower Skagit downstream of the run, the river divides into three distinct channels. Every great bar I've ever fished possesses something like this. Without it the run is fun and worth fishing, but just average in its productivity.

The illustrated bar is on the Sauk River. Its special downriver feature is a long fast transitioning tailout that swiftly sweeps left then spills into a long, narrow chute that accommodates the whole river in a space less than 20 feet wide. The run itself approaches 200 feet wide.

To fish this run, always start high—well into the fast water above the main body of the run. Look for the spot where the current starts to break away from the bank, and go a little higher. The first steelie in the drawing is lying right where the current breaks. Most people don't start high enough in a run—and not just this one. You need be only ankle to shin deep at this point. Start with short casts, gradually lengthening your line after each swing. Casts should be quartered downstream in this fast section. There's no need to cast too much line right now; any fish in this zone will be close to shore. Start taking steps between casts. As the river starts to slow, broaden, and deepen, now is the time to take a step or two out and add some more line. You would be about parallel with the submerged tree limb at this point.

Now you're making long casts to a fairly even current as you fish through the body of the run. You've waded out a little to stay close to the current which has moved out away from shore. You're thigh to waste deep now. Because the water is broad, long, and even casts should be made across at a 70- to 80-degree angle. Be sure to let your fly swing to a complete stop: You're wading in water deep enough for a steelhead to feel safe in. As you work down the run, resist the temptation to wade in too deeply! If the current starts to pick up pace around you, back up a bit. Fishing down into the tailout, you'll feel the current start to accelerate. As I mentioned earlier, this is a hot zone for steelhead, usually the last area you can expect to hook one in the run. Keep fishing down until the water gets too fast, too shallow, or both.

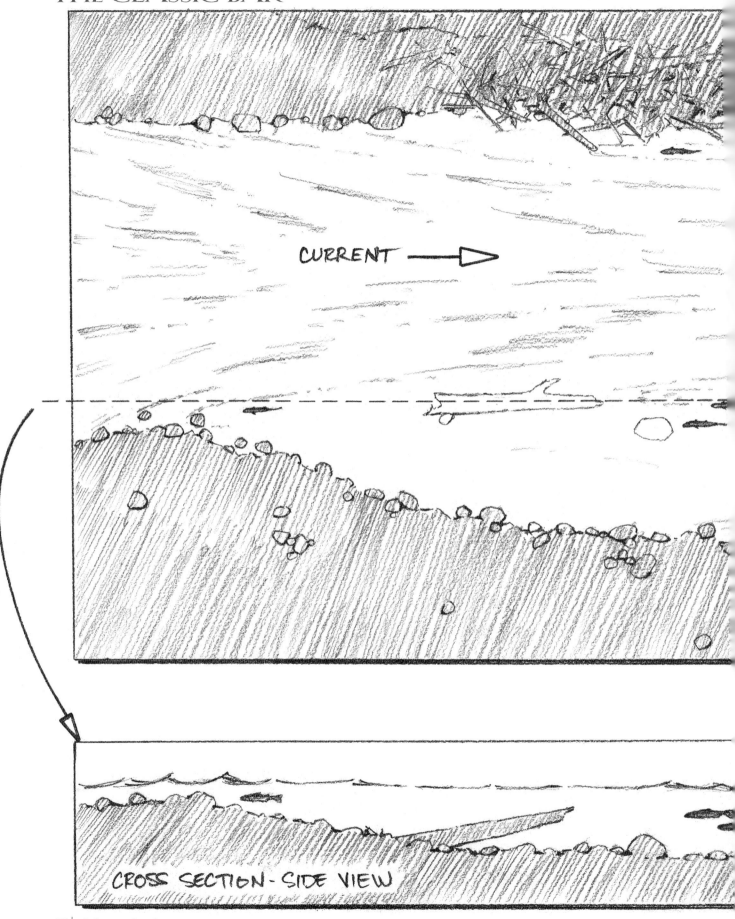

CURRENT →

CROSS SECTION - SIDE VIEW

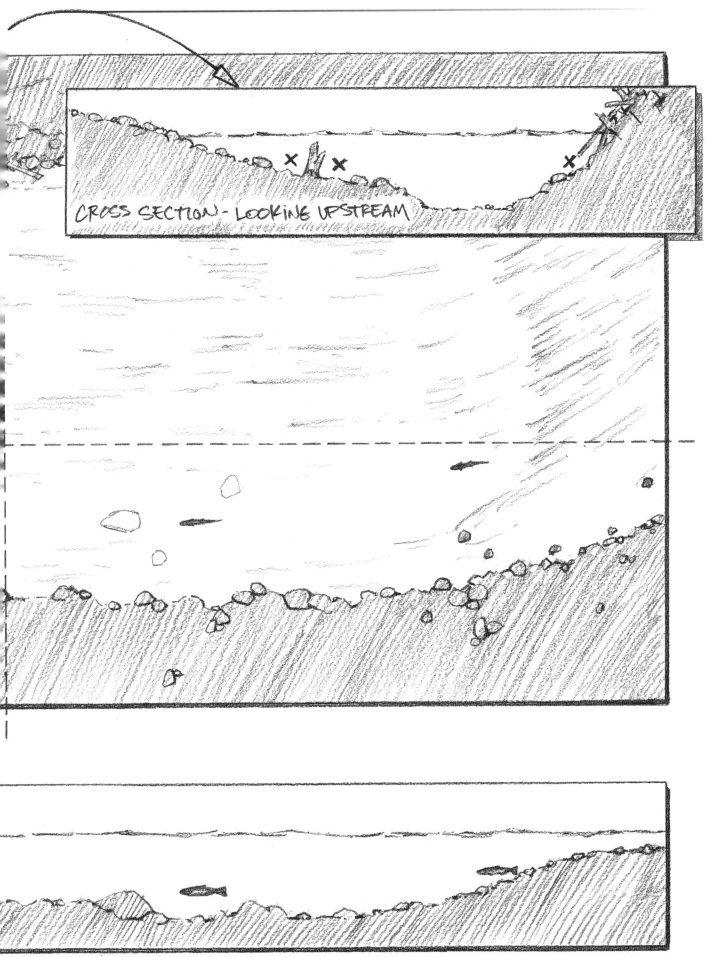

CROSS SECTION - LOOKING UPSTREAM

STEELHEAD LIE: SHALLOW RIFFLE

Most steelhead runs have defined starting points: the place that says, start fishing here. It's usually where there is a dramatic change in depth and/or hydrology. Most notably—as seen in the typical classic run—is where shallow current breaks away from the bank and starts to deepen. Every great steelhead river has an abundance of such places. Sometimes the shallow water running right up to the bank extends for a substantial distance before breaking away and deepening. The surface current is often defined by dancing water that bounces and leaps as it is forced over streambed rocks and depressions. This type of water is what we all know as a riffle.

You've heard it time and again, and those of you with experience under your wading belts diligently practice it: Start high in the run. You want to be sure to cover the highest possible smidgeon of water that a steelhead could be holding in. If the top of the run is a riffle, chances are you haven't been starting high enough.

Steelhead love to hold in shallow riffles—surprisingly shallow. Eighteen inches deep is not too thin. And I'm not speaking of spawning steelhead. I'm talking about fresh, migrating steelhead eager to grab flies. Where riffles may lack steelhead cover in the form of depth, they make up with a choppy surface. Surface currents may appear exceedingly fast, and sometimes they are, but often there are hidden soft spots. Explore these places with your eyes and your swinging fly. It's the only way to find them. To actually see the soft spot can be difficult to the untrained eye; an expanse of turbulence makes it hard for the eyes to focus in any given area. As you fish through, however, the pace of your fly and line will clearly reveal areas where the current slows. The fish will also tell you when you've found a hidden lie!

Then, visually, these places are plain as day to see. A buffer zone in a fast, shallow riffle doesn't need to be large in order to hold a fish—in the scheme of things, a good-sized steelhead doesn't take up too much space.

Riffles are not confined to the heads of runs. Sometimes they *are* the run. Seek them out and fish them. Remember that riffles are typically shallow. Do not let that be a deterrent: Steelhead love to hold and rest in shallow riffles.

Make your casts quartering down with the rod tip extended over the river in order to get a slow swing. Grabs are typically sudden and jarring. Be ready for a blistering initial run—what was once a secure place to rest is now a confined space that the steelhead needs to vacate NOW.

RIVER RUN 2: PRIME TIME (OVERLEAF)

This spectacular piece of water happens to be on the Deschutes River in Oregon. This run is one of those special places that is remarkably productive. It's difficult for me to refrain from thinking of it as a barometer for the rest of the river: If you can't catch one there during the prime times of day, there must not be any fish in the river. Yes, it's that good.

The actual run itself has it all: a fast head that slows and broadens as the current passes over perfect basalt boulders scattered nicely throughout. The current speed and constancy of flow are so ideal, making it what I call self fishing—"Put it out there and don't mess with it!" Hang on and let the current do the work. What really makes this run so steelhead friendly is, once again, the hydrology above and below.

This run at about 75 yards long is really the head of an enormously long, deep pool. The pool is slow and "froggy" for nearly a quarter mile. Above the run is another long piece of water—this one, however starts, as sizable class-2 rapids and races downstream for the length of a football field until it reaches the run. Study the illustration and it will all make sense.

Let's go fish it. Start right at the very top and well above where the current begins to slow. Start short and believe strongly in your first few, short casts—steelhead hold right off the bank in the first available pocket. (See illustration.) The top part of the run comes in fast, so angle your casts at 45 degrees, down and across. One good upstream mend usually suffices for a good swing. Through the entire run, pay close attention to the fly as it swings below you: There are holding lies wherever the water is wet!

Working your way down, you'll sense that the run begins to slow and broaden. Now it's time to angle your cast 70 to 80 degrees down and across—time to take a bigger slice of pie. From here on out the current takes care of the line, swimming your fly perfectly. If you feel you need to mend, do it early, just after the fly touches down. Any mending after that and you're asking for trouble. If you don't care to listen and you do throw in a random mend, I promise you that the fly will get jerked sharply many feet, right out of a steelhead lie. Most good fly water is this way. That's why it's good fly water. The lesson? Let the fly swing!

Keep fishing downstream; the water will begin to deepen. As the run begins to transform into the deep pool below, you'll notice a few swirls breaking the sur-

face of otherwise smooth water. The swirls are made by a cluster of large, distinct rocks that often hold a fish. Fish down until you are parallel to the rocks and you'll find that your fly doesn't swing well at all anymore. You're in the deep pool, and the run is over but not the fun. A run this good should be fished a second time.

PRIME TIME

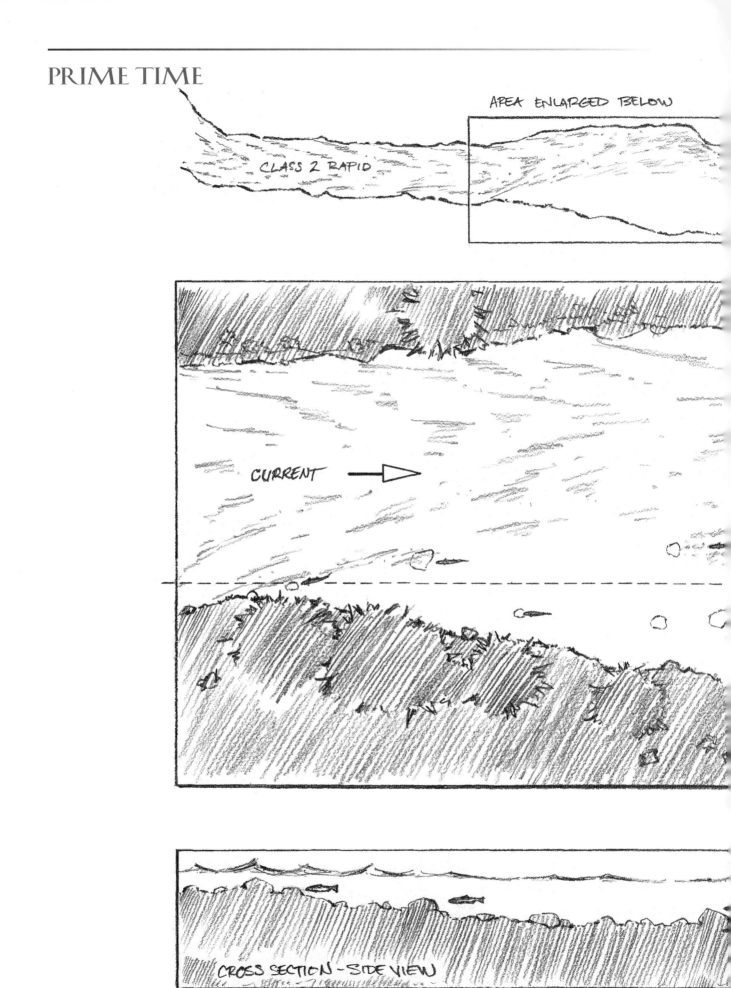

AREA ENLARGED BELOW

CLASS 2 RAPID

CURRENT

CROSS SECTION - SIDE VIEW

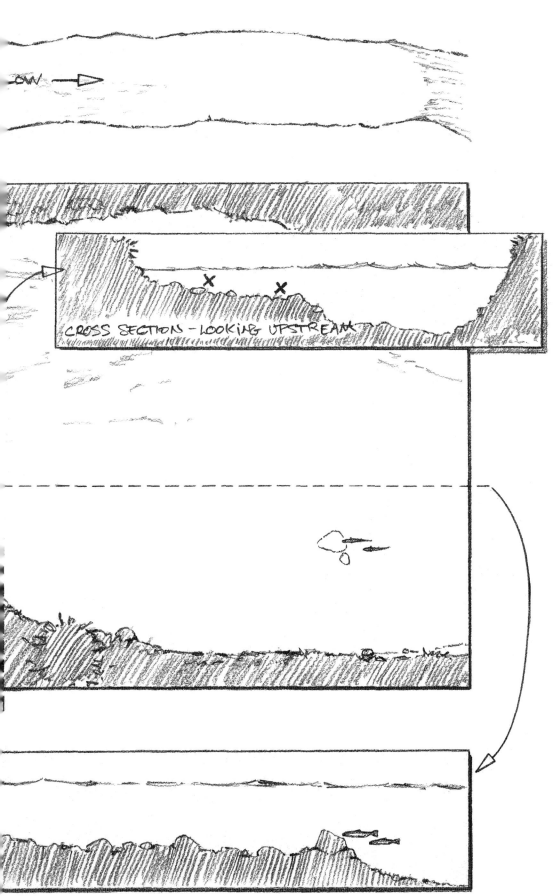

FLOW →

CROSS SECTION - LOOKING UPSTREAM

STEELHEAD LYING IN FRONT OF BOULDER

Steelhead are often imagined lying behind rocks and boulders rather then in front of them. My experience confirms this is the norm. If there is a cluster of rocks they often hold right in the middle, placing themselves between rocks. However, steelhead do hold in front of rocks and boulders. In my experience, the boulders I see steelhead in front of are somehow uniquely similar to each another. They are usually fairly large—from the size of a beach ball up to that of a trash can—and often in the lower half of a run. I'm not suggesting this is gospel. Yet it is my experience. There must be a reason steelhead hold in front of some rocks and not others. I'm convinced it has to do with hydrology. Interesting that of the boulders I know where steelhead hold in front, all do so consistently. From day to day and season to season, these same rocks hold a changing cast of different steelhead.

All this is endlessly interesting and adds to our knowledge of this fascinating species. One final point: As I fish down a run, I'm going to assume there is a steelhead in front of as well as behind every likely looking boulder. Happily, it's also my experience that if the boulder does harbor a steelie ahead of it, the fish is nearly always a taker!

RIVER RUN 3: BIG BOULDERS (OVERLEAF)

the boulders. This top section is a miniature run in itself. Look to the cross section inset of the illustration, and you will see what I mean. The miniature run shallows and tails-out, leaving you at the top of the next—and main part—of the run.

Right here you have a decision to make: You can continue down with the line you've already worked out while fishing the top portion, or you can reel up and start the main section as if it were a new piece of water. Since I'm guiding you, I want you to choose the latter. I believe that by starting over you give yourself a better (and second) chance at hooking the steelhead holding behind the submerged boulder at the top of the run. As usual, cast, swing, and lengthen progressively until you're casting a comfortable length of line. Then begin stepping.

As you fish through this middle section, you'll find the natural flow of current draws you out a bit. Be alert to what's ahead—the current subtly breaks back in toward your bank as you near the two large boulders in the tailout. You'll plainly see them breaking the surface enticingly, winking at you to come and get 'em. It's easy to get caught wading out so far that your fly could miss the fish on your initial approach. Which isn't that big a deal other than, once you realized your fly wasn't fishing over the best water, you'd have to back up and reposition yourself.

Fishing around these boulders requires tactical ingenuity. Big boulders like these will eat your fly and even have the potential of entangling and robbing you of your sink-tip. Be careful. And know where your fly is. Fish sometimes hold in front of the first boulder, but the sweet spot is in between the two. After you've covered the water behind the second boulder the run immediately shallows, speeds up, and ends.

This is one of my favorite runs on the Sauk. It's exciting to fish because of so many variations throughout, with lots good fishy-looking surface disturbances to get your heart racing as you step closer to them.

The run is roughly broken up into two sections. The top section is the head of the run and your starting point. The water breaks in quickly then is slowed by some large exposed boulders. Start just above the boulders with short casts. Work some line out so your fly lands just on the edge of the fast water outside of

BIG BOULDERS

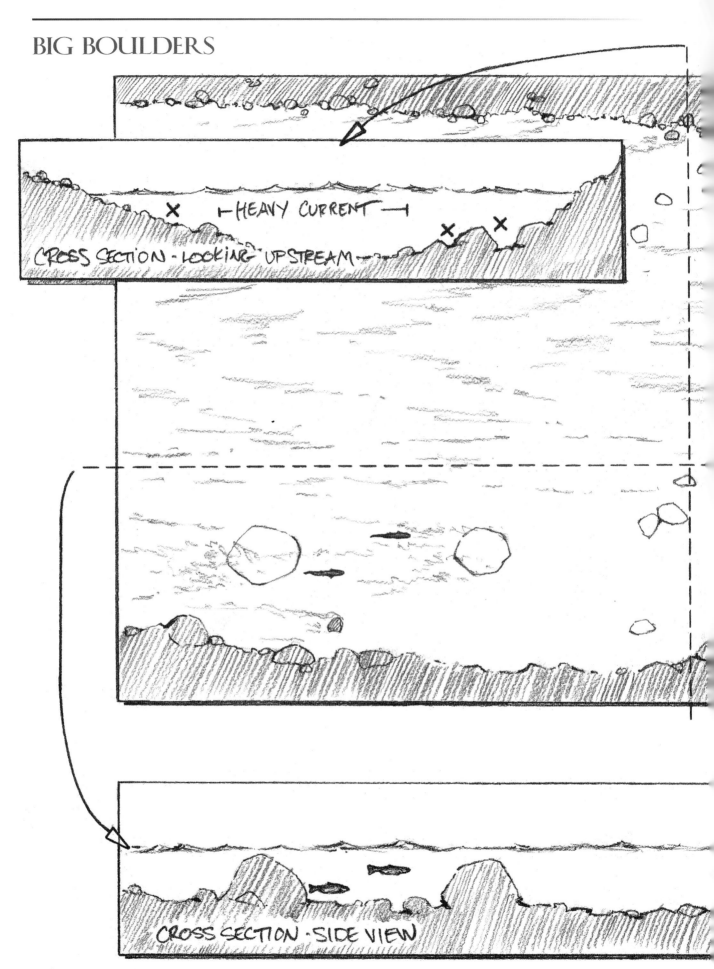

HEAVY CURRENT

CROSS SECTION - LOOKING UPSTREAM

CROSS SECTION - SIDE VIEW

CURRENT

STEELHEAD LIE: LEDGE ROCK

A whole chapter could be devoted to fishing ledge rock. That is not my objective here. My objective is to make you aware that it exists—and that steelhead love it.

Some famous rivers such as the North Umpqua in Oregon have an abundance of basalt ledge-rock river channel. Sections of river are carved out right through ancient lava flows. Other rivers throughout the steelhead's range have similar habitat or rock outcroppings, usually formed of basalt or granite. Whatever the scenario, if it's solid rock, steelhead will usually be there. Most ledges, as they are often referred to by anglers, can either be that—a simple ledge that steelhead hold against—or an intricate network of slots, channels, depressions, holes, heads, and peaks with steelhead utilizing any and all facets.

Fishing over a ledge is not markedly different from fishing a classic run: You swing the fly to get maximum coverage. Wading can be difficult, even treacherous, with each step downriver a potential sinkhole. The best scouting strategy is to view ledge runs in the middle of a well-lit day from the highest vantage possible. Through polarized glasses, you'll see clearly the potential wading hazards. Such daytime surveillance will also give you a keen understanding of where steelhead are likely to take up temporary residence. You may find that wading a run down its entire length is impossible. Conditions might require that a specific section be fished from one casting station. That is, standing in one spot and lengthening line between casts to cover the run, until the lie is covered properly or you can't cast any farther. Sometimes a stretch of river is covered by a series of these casting stations where it is necessary to enter and exit the river several times in order to safely and effectively cover all the potential lies.

RIVER RUN 4: HIDDEN BAR (OVERLEAF)

Not all great water is custom made with a defined starting point. Such is the case with upper Larson's on the Skagit. The run has changed over the years, and it continues to change. There was a time when it ran down the old channel, as per this illustration; it featured a beautiful choppy head with a distinct starting point. The old channel filled in, but left behind the run which is a channel itself. (See illustration, cross section looking upstream).

Current from the main river sweeps across a submerged bar—actually an island in growth—then spills in to the channel forming the run. From the lip of the submerged bar all the way to the tailout is good holding water, but only a portion is fishable. This is why I'm sharing this run with you. Although unique, I've stumbled across several other runs on other rivers similar to it.

As you can see, there is a lot of dead water between the mouth of the old channel and the submerged bar. Even flow near the bank doesn't occur until at least a third of the way down the run. Wading out across the old channel to get close enough to the main flow to swing a fly is not an option: It's too deep.

Here's what to do. An angler's level of skill greatly influences where one begins fishing. I wade out into the old channel parallel with the tip of the island. My aim is to get as close as I can to the flow, without going over the top of my waders. Here I strip off a bunch of line and send it out in search of some current. Don't dally here if you're using a sink-tip. If there's little or no flow, your fly will be on the bottom before you know it. Continue wading down, casting and trying to feel for a swing. Once you connect with the current and you're getting a decent swing, you've found your starting point. Start fishing as usual, keeping in mind that with each step downriver, the current is moving closer to the bank you're fishing from. You need to stay in line with that. You start the run wading as deeply as you dare and finish in the tailout, wading to your knees.

The real sweet zone in the run occurs when all the current coming over the submerged bar evens out and flows parallel to the bank. It's where the two fish are lying side by side in the illustration.

HIDDEN BAR

CROSS SECTION - LOOKING UPSTREAM

CROSS SECTION - SIDE VIEW

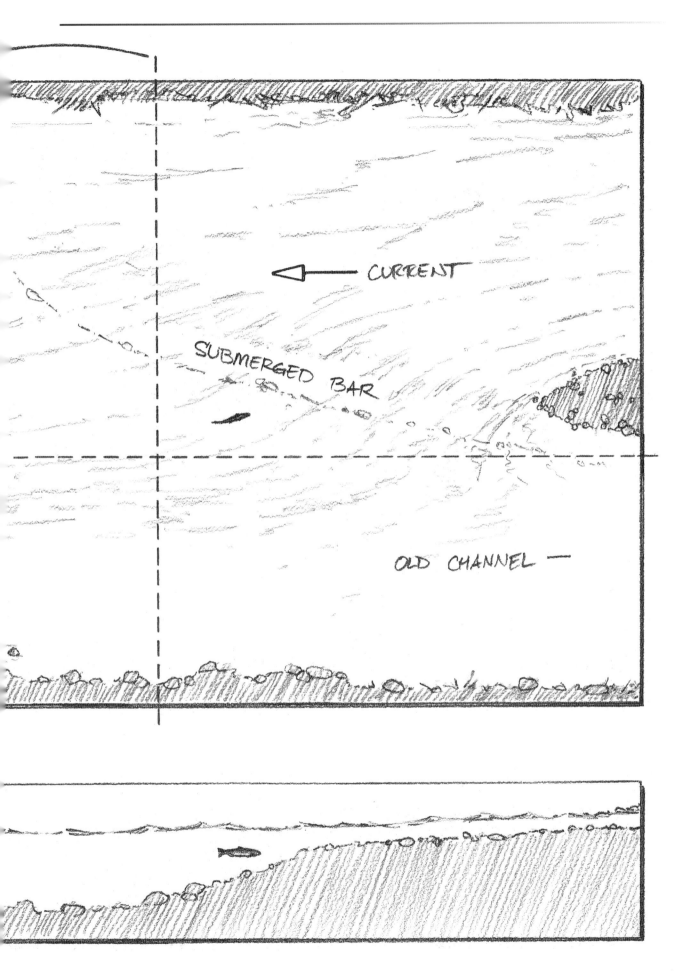

CURRENT

SUBMERGED BAR

OLD CHANNEL —

STEELHEAD LIE:
TRENCHES, HOLES, SLOTS AND DEPRESSIONS

By now you know that steelhead like to hold in and around structure: It gives them a sense of security. It's pretty rare for a steelhead to hold in a shallow, barren stretch of river. If you do find them here—and I have seen it—normally they are not biters, nor do they remain exposed for very long.

Structure takes many forms. We expect it as something protruding from the river bottom: boulders, rocks, logs. But what if there is a hole in an otherwise flat bottom? Drop in the hole and there is structure on all sides, the current is slower and, if the hole is deep enough, it is darkened. Sounds like good steelhead water to me. Truth is many of the more productive zones within a lot of the bars we fish are, in fact, holes or depressions.

Floating in my drift boat, I see them as I float over the swing zone of the run. (Only when there are no other anglers around, of course.) I clearly see the rocky bottom as I'm drifting along—it looks fishy enough—when suddenly the bottom drops out for a distance. The hair on the back of my neck stands up: "Now that's fishy!" I look to shore to see where in the run I am, exactly. Sure enough, it's the main bucket, the most productive part of the run.

How these seemingly random holes are created hydraulically, I am not sure, but I'm glad they exist. Some holes are created as water gouges out a depression around some type of structure, say, a root-wad or boulder. The hole occurs in front, behind, to the sides, or a full 360 degrees around the obstruction depending on hydrology.

Trenches and slots are really just long holes created in a variety of ways—steelhead love them. Look for a strip of water darker than the surrounding flow, and you are looking at a possible steelhead holding slot or trench. They are often found along the bank but not always. Keep your eyes and mind open when exploring the river.

RIVER RUN 5: FABULOUS (OVERLEAF)

There are three lessons to be learned in breaking down this fabulous run on the Deschutes River. Let's go fish it and learn what they are.

It's a fairly long run in its entirety. You can mentally divide it into two sections: the top half from the head down to where the run substantially broadens out and from there down to the tailout. The first thing you'll notice about the upper section—and our first lesson learned—is that upon first sight it looks horribly fast. Looks can be deceiving. You can see in the illustration that the run is relatively narrow with a strong current pushing along between the banks. But there is a seam where the current breaks away from the bank, and along that slower seam lies an abundance of football-sized rocks with a few larger ones mixed in. Those rocks slow the subsurface current considerably. Steelhead wanting to stay out of the heavy center flow suck right up to those rocks. So, yes, the swing you get is relatively narrow, but it's perfect and the steelies are in there!

Notice how close the fish are to the bank. That's where the good water is. When you step in to a run like this your butt should be touching the grass behind you. Don't wade out too far or I promise you'll miss fish. Begin high in the fast water of the head before it starts to break away from the bank starting short. As you work down the narrow swath of water, a cast quartered down slightly into the fast water aided by a small upstream mend is all it takes. Start working down, being mindful of your close-to-shore line of wading. Let your fly swing right into the bank.

Lesson No. 2 comes as you get to the large submerged boulder half way down the run. You can see the surface disturbance it's making. It sure looks enticing. *There's got to be a fish behind it*, you think to yourself. But your fly just whips through at blinding speed. It's too fast out there. The lesson here is that not all boulder pockets are good steelhead water. I'm all for experimenting, and it certainly doesn't hurt to

put a cast or two out there, but I see so many people making a career out of probing a rock like this, spending way too much time putting repeated casts on and around it. If the boulder is in the main, heavy flow, outside the seductive cushiness of the run, it's a pretty sure bet the steelhead won't use it.

As you wade down the top half, you are walking and standing on good-sized rocks. As the run broadens out, you sense that the rocks are absent beneath your footing. You are now standing on pea-sized gravel. With each step down, things are not changing. You wade out a bit hoping to find some rock and restore your confidence in this piece of water. Nothing. Everything about the run save the absence of structure looks good. It has the right depth, the fly swings perfectly—only no rocks. Most anglers, including me, get bored in this kind of water. We're inclined to give up. But consider this: There's a lot of river bottom out there. There's bound to be a boulder or two strewn somewhere. Well, there is, and they are fish magnets. Think about it. Even to the steelhead entering the pool it must to feel like home as far as speed and depth are concerned. Particularly if they've just swum up through a long, fast stretch of river, which in this case is exactly what they've been forced to do. Even the smallest bit of structure might attract a lone fish to pause for a rest. It's a treat to find water like this because such spots normally don't get much pressure.

FABULOUS

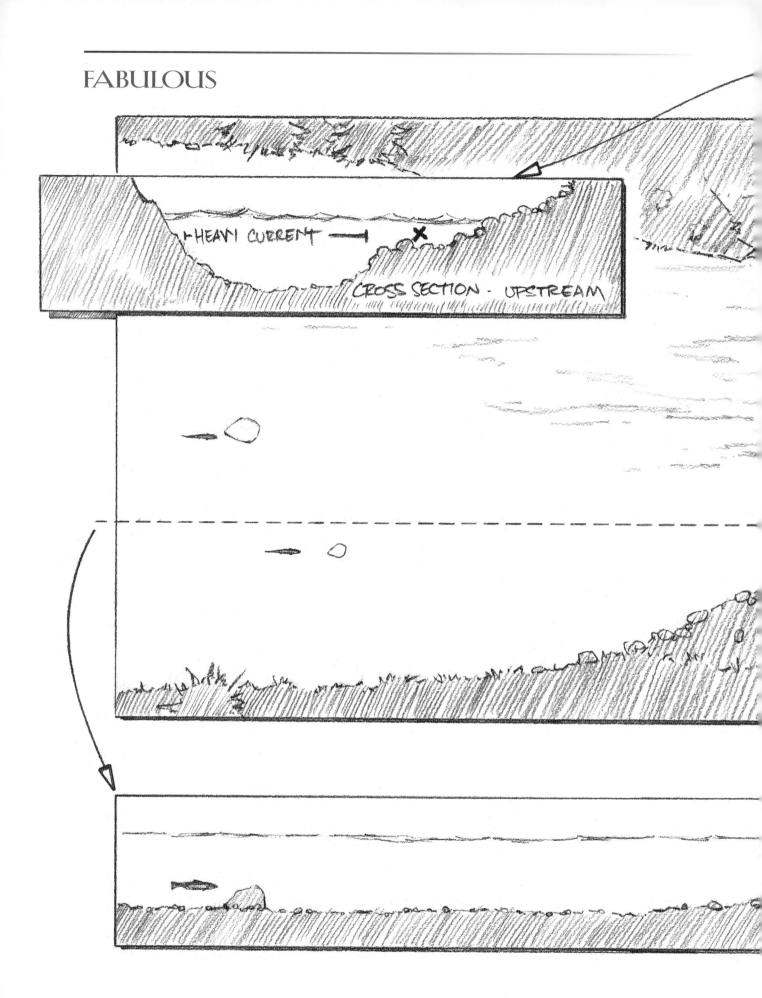

HEAVY CURRENT

CROSS SECTION - UPSTREAM

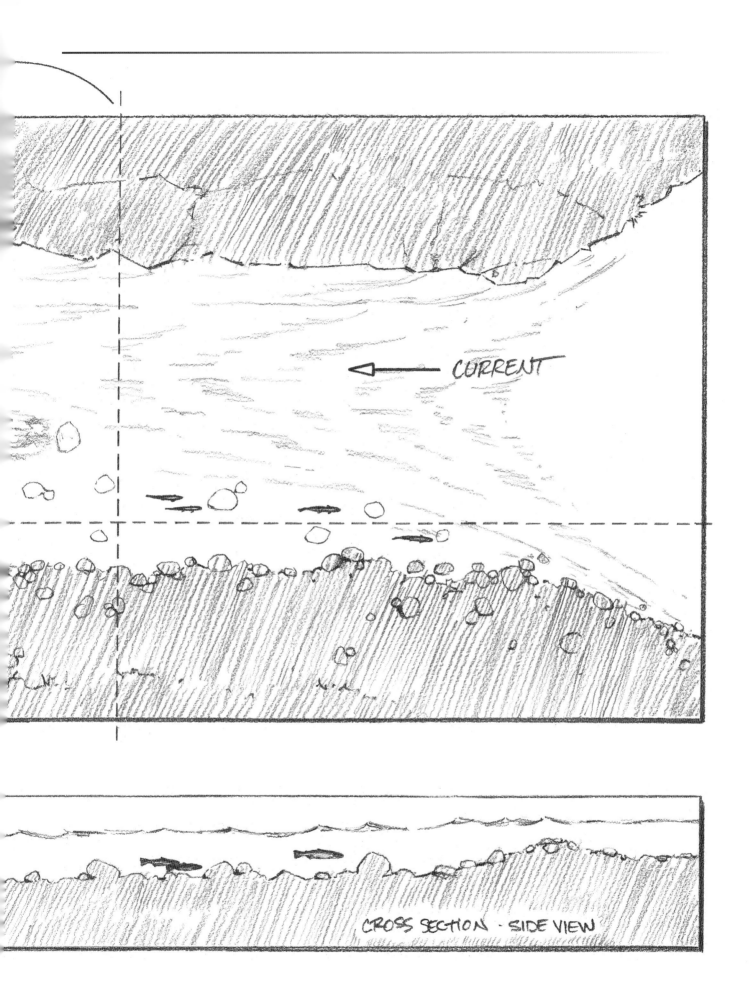

CURRENT

CROSS SECTION - SIDE VIEW

STEELHEAD LYING BEHIND BOULDER

We've learned from the beginning of this chapter that fish in rivers like to hold behind structure. While creek fishing as a little boy, I zeroed in on the pockets behind rocks, learning that some rocks were better than others and why. Rocks provide fish protection from the current, a sense of security, and their meals—drifting food is delivered directly to the rock pocket by swirling eddies: truly a micro sanctuary.

Once back in fresh water, adult steelhead are not much interested in food delivery, naturally, but instead hold behind rocks and boulders to enjoy all the other comforts the pocket offers. When fishing behind distinctly visible rocks and boulders, there are several things to consider.

There are two types of visible boulders: the boulder that breaks the surface, and you see a portion of the exposed rock, for one. The other is submerged, leaving a tell-tale swirl that lets you know something good is down there. Each will make your fly behave differently and requires modifications in how you fish them. The exposed boulder has less current behind it and a stronger eddy effect. If you cast directly behind it, close to the rock, your fly will remain stationary for a moment, then suddenly be ripped away as the current pulls your fly line downstream. Occasionally, your fly will get caught in the eddy and be pulled upstream right into the boulder, where it more than likely will remain—snagged. You need to find these things out for yourself. I would never deny you the joys of trial and error, but I can tell you steelhead won't be lying right behind the boulder. I know, every situation is different. However, steelhead will almost always be holding downstream a ways from the boulder where the two currents breaking around the structure begin to join. Although steelies are known to shield themselves from heavy flow, they do like to feel some current around them. Naturally, the smaller the rock, the smaller the pocket—the closer to the rock the steelhead will be. Likewise for the larger boulder. I've seen large boulders, both exposed and submerged, breaking the main current to such an extent that there's a 20-yard-long miniature steelhead run behind them!

The same tactics apply to fishing around a submerged boulder, only now that the current comes over the top of the boulder, steelhead could be holding fairly close to it. Keep in mind that the surface swirl left by the boulder does not reveal its precise location. The swirl is downstream of the rock. How far down depends on how deep the top of the rock is and the velocity of the current: The deeper the rock and the stronger the current, the farther down the swirl is.

RIVER RUN 6: ACE IN THE HOLE (OVERLEAF)

In our quest to learn about, understand, and locate good water, we need to sometimes think creatively: that is, look beyond the classic runs complete with head, body and tail, seeking out small unremarkable spots. One day while conducting a steelhead clinic with my buddy John Hazel, one of the students asked excitedly, "John, what's good steelhead water?" John's brash reply was, "The whole river, pal!" While John's response to the question was intended to be snap and comedic—we were lecturing on something completely off the subject of water—there's a lot of truth in his answer. I've made a habit of looking at the river in its entirety, from bank to bank, as potential resting or holding water. So in essence I'm taking a real close look at all of the possibilities. Then it's a matter of a process of elimination.

What I'm looking for are secret spots that aren't obvious: a barely perceptible break in the current, a short hidden pocket, rocky reefs hidden in otherwise barren glides—the list goes on. I've made a career guiding on some of the most popular steelhead rivers in the West collecting these ace-in-the-hole spots. Most are good for half a dozen casts. But one of those six casts can make your day. Once you suspect you've found a potential spot, you can't effectively size it up without actually fishing it. You might not hook something the first or even second time you fish it, but you'll gather more information about the water after you've stood in it and cast to it. You also might find that some of these fantasy places are really fun places to fish. I've discovered a few that seemed so perfect that I was bound and determined that someday I would find a steelhead there; if I didn't, it didn't matter, because they were so cool to fish. I'm pleased to say that in most of them I eventually found a fish—extremely satisfying. Other secret spots instantly became nearly automatic—doubly satisfying.

The illustrated water is one such place. It's a small swath of water tucked to one side of the tailout of a large, deep pool. Nothing about the pool says fishable steelhead water. Even the tailout looks deep, fast, and featureless. Except for the tiny strip of rocks nestled against the east bank of the tailout. This holding water is obvious when you are standing next to it, but if you let your eyes see only the big picture, it's easily missed. That's how the majority of these little nook-and-cranny spots are. Look carefully at the illustration, including the insets, and you'll understand why the steelhead are there.

This particular spot is on the Deschutes River and happens to be an exceptional place to fish a waking fly. It's really the only way I fish or guide there. How would you fish it?

ACE IN THE HOLE

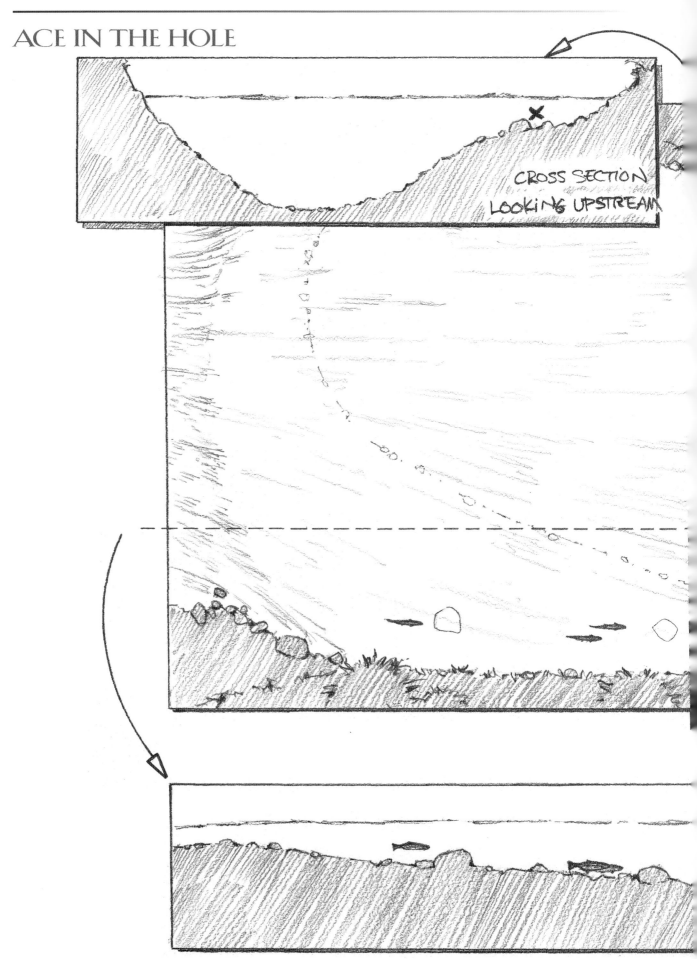

CROSS SECTION

LOOKING UPSTREAM

DEEP POOL

CURRENT

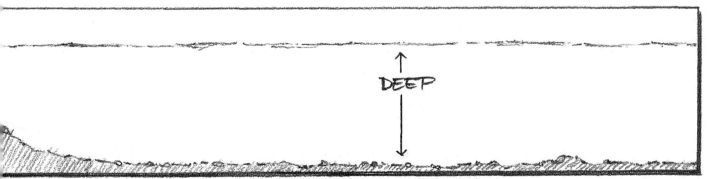

DEEP

STEELHEAD LIE: CHINOOK BEDS

   Steelhead share their rivers with Pacific salmon, notably the chinook or king salmon. Kings are the largest of the five species; they dig the largest spawning redds. The salmon return to the same areas year after year, digging new redds and freshening up old ones. The areas are comprised of many redds and each area is referred to as a bed. If you've never seen a king salmon bed, it's impressive. There are holes in the river bottom the size of cars followed by heaping mounds of rock and gravel that look as if only a bulldozer could have placed them. All this done with a fish's tail!

   Chinook beds are made in fairly deep water—three to six feet with moderate flow, not unlike that of good steelhead water. Bingo. When the aggressively spawning salmon are absent from the beds, steelhead use the holes and mounds as holding stations the way they use any other form of protective structure. That's not to say that every vacant salmon bed will be a good steelhead spot, but it's one more thing to be aware of in your search for a taking fish. As far as the steelhead is concerned, structure is structure.

RIVER RUN 7: SEAM (OVERLEAF)

in the head of a run. When fast water spills into a pool there is usually an edge created where the fast water glides past slow water near the pool's banks. This is a current seam. Most of the time the seam deteriorates as the water evens out, filling the pool. Typically this occurs one-fourth to one-third of the way down the run. So when fishing the top of a run, the seam is very important until it diminishes, where you then concentrate on fishing the even flow. In the case of the run illustrated, the seam appears the entire length of the run.

This run is a fast, narrow chute with a huge rapid below. Steep, fast water lies above. The traveling steelhead haven't much choice but to stay in the small seam running along the bank. It just happens that the seam runs right over the top of a nice rocky shelf. The fish have just come through the rapid and have found a safe place to take a rest before advancing up and through the next obstacle.

Start working this run as you have most of the others: high and short. Remember you are really only fishing the seam—ankle-deep wading and short casts. Casts placed well into the fast water equate to down time. They could also quite possibly leave your fly short of entering the fish-holding seam: It'll just dangle in the fast water if it's on too long a line. Fish the run down until your fly swings right to the lip of the tail just before spilling into the rapid.

At some point, the beginning steelheader learns about fishing current "seams" and the steelhead's propensity for lying in them. A seam is a place where fast and slow waters meet—simple as that. Steelhead travel the path of least resistance, yet stay relatively close to it, because the resistance or strong flow is what's drawing them upstream. Seams are often found

SEAM

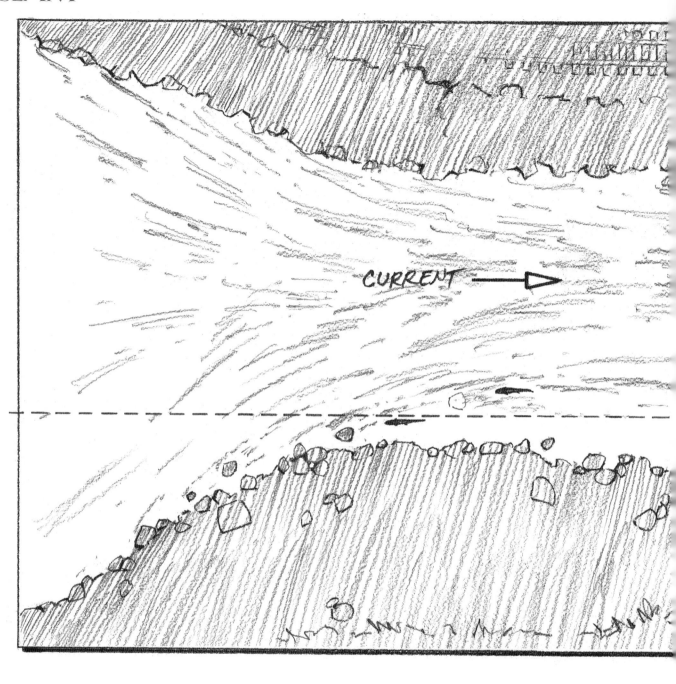

CURRENT →

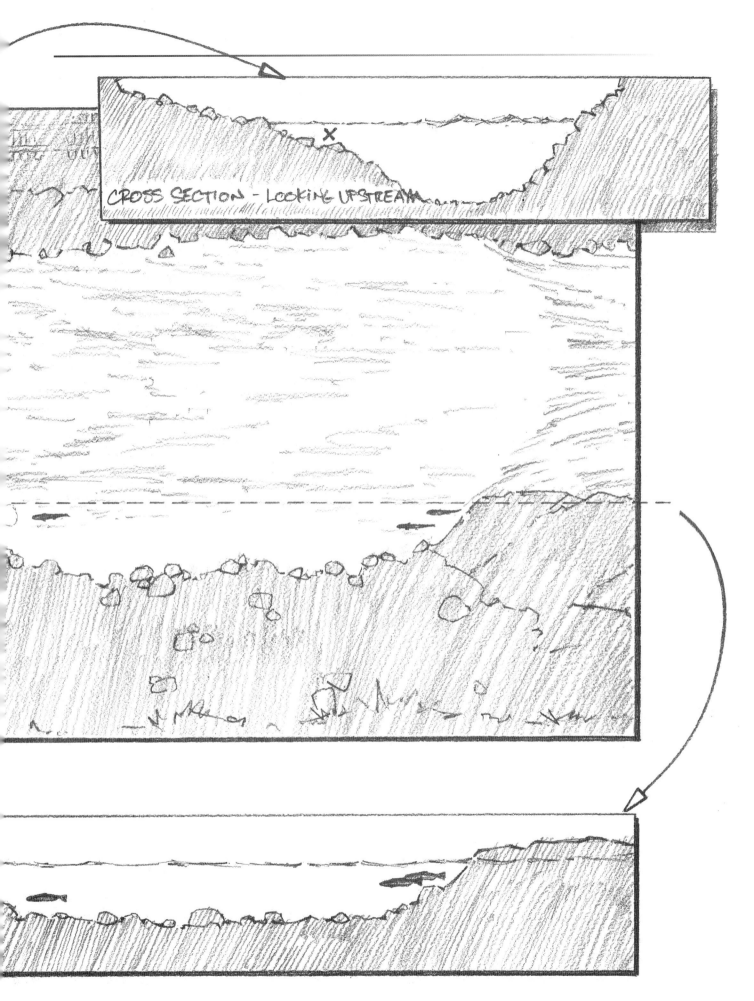

CROSS SECTION - LOOKING UPSTREAM

FLOATING LINE SET-UP AND SWING

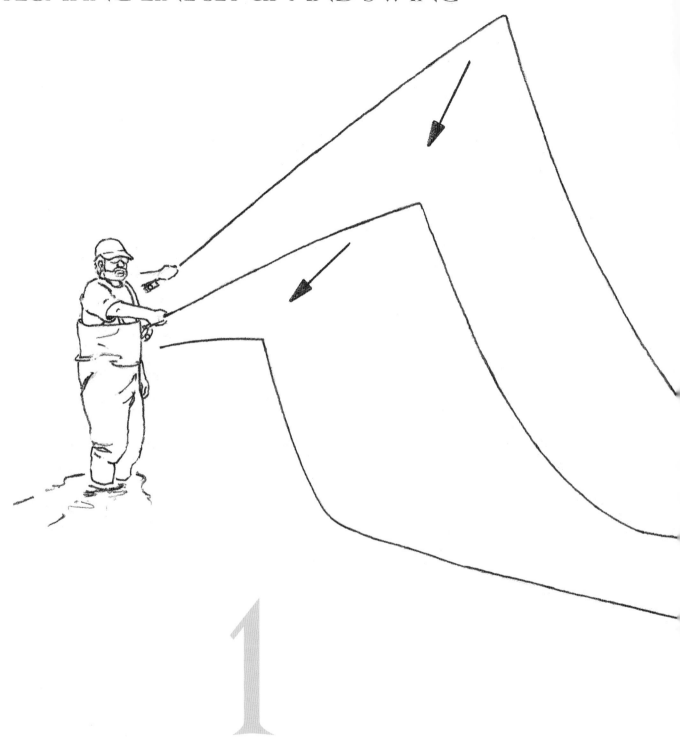

Swinging a fly in water with complex currents often means fishing with a high rod-tip. The less line on the water the easier it is to keep the fly riding slowly. Steve Kruse is on the stick.

Fishing a floating line either using a wet or a dry fly is different from fishing a sink-tip line in several ways. Mainly in the setup. You are not trying to gain depth, so any sort of pullback mend is of no use. Cast to the target area, letting the line settle for a moment, then place the necessary mend if any at all. I try to get the fly fishing as soon as possible, mending only if it's necessary. When fishing a dry or surface fly, an ill-placed mend frequently pulls the fly under, defeating the purpose of fishing on top. Usually the fly stays under. Trying to mend your way out of it, as so many of us do, only exacerbates the problem.

Early in the fly's swing, your rod tip should be fairly high, keeping as much line off the water as possible to help facilitate a slow swing. As the fly comes across, the rod is lowered in pace with the current. This keeps the fly's speed constant.

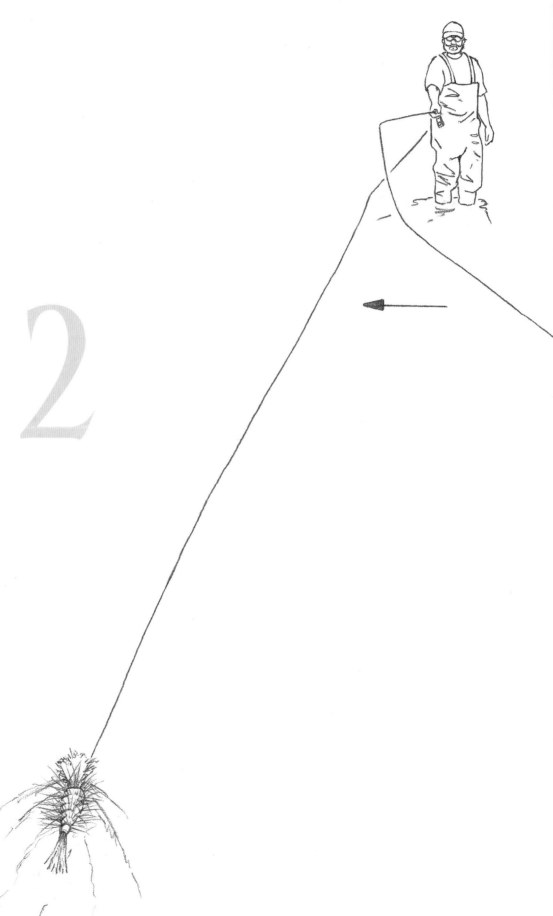

2

The rod tip is continuously lowered until it reaches the heart of the swing. By then, it should be hovering just above the surface. I like to fish this way. It keeps a lot of tension directly on my line finger, which allows me to feel acutely in touch with my fly. I feel how the fly is swimming. And should a steelhead even breath on it, I instantly sense it. Keep in mind that every piece of water is different; a low rod tip might not always be practical, particularly if the water surrounding you is faster than the water where your fly is fishing. If this is the case, you'll want to do whatever it takes to keep your line off that fast water. Usually this means fishing with your rod held high above your head and out over the river. Be alert. Recognize when it's time to adjust and adapt.

As the fly is swinging, normally you are following the fly's path with the rod tip. As the fly passes through the heart of the swing, the water typically slows in relation to where you are standing and the fly's pace. Now you need to slightly lead the fly using the current to help it along. Don't be in a hurry to overdo this—give the fly a chance to swing on its own. Leading too much and too fast will pull the fly many feet upstream and look extremely unnatural. Be patient. Let things happen.

Incidentally, I highly encourage you to fish a surface waking pattern as often as possible. The waking fly is an invaluable tool in helping to create a clear understanding of what happens when fishing a wet fly. You can see the effects on the fly by currents, mending, not mending, bad mending, casting angle, fidgeting, leading, leading too much, etc. You'll be surprised and educated with what you learn. The surface fly never lies. See for yourself.

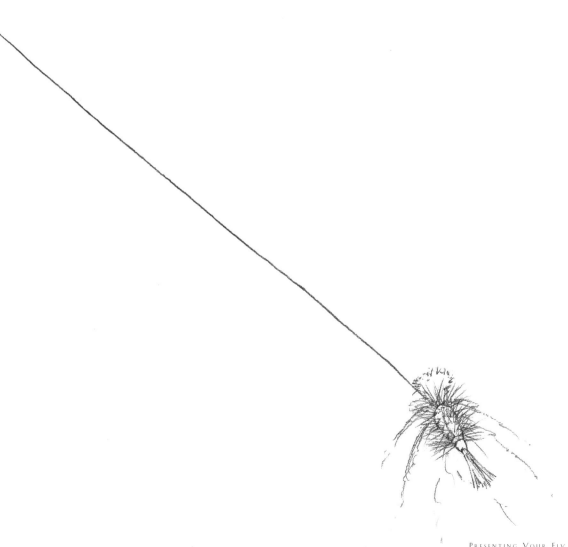

SWING ZONE: FLOATING LINE

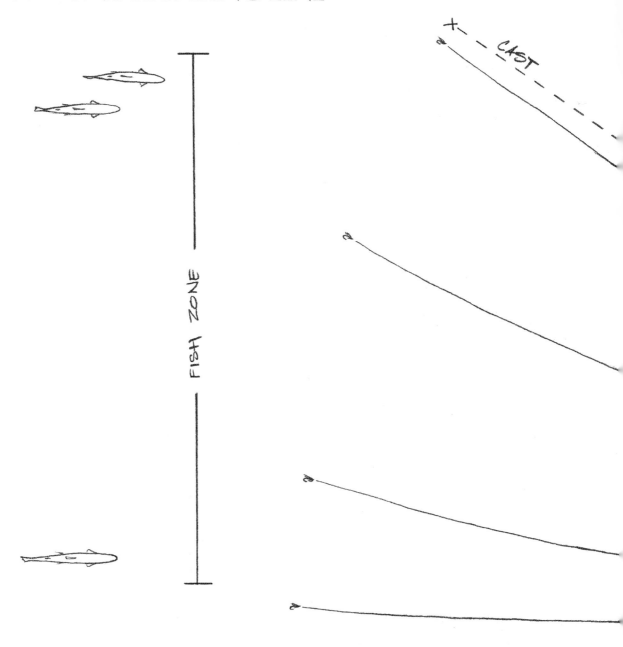

The physiology of the swing whether fishing a sink-tip or floating line, wet fly or dry fly is essentially the same. The only real difference is where the fly fishes in the water column. What happens before the swing is where there is a marked difference between fishing the two. Simply put, when fishing a floating line, the pull-back mend is entirely unnecessary and equates only to meaningless down time. When fishing a sink-tip you must cast beyond the potential water and set up the line and fly, wait for it all to sink, and eventually the fly will enter the steelhead zone. With the floating line, you want to cast ever so slightly beyond the productive zone and get your fly fishing as quickly as possible. You can see that you don't need as long a cast as you would fishing a tip, and the time it takes to set up and sink is eliminated. Therefore, you need to look at the water a little differently when fishing a floating line. Again, any casting outside the productive water is time wasted as your fly swims through no man's (fish) land.

Look at the illustrations on the next three pages for a better understanding of how a fly on a sink-tip sets up before entering the fishy zone, and how a floating line can be cast right to the edge of the zone. I find myself

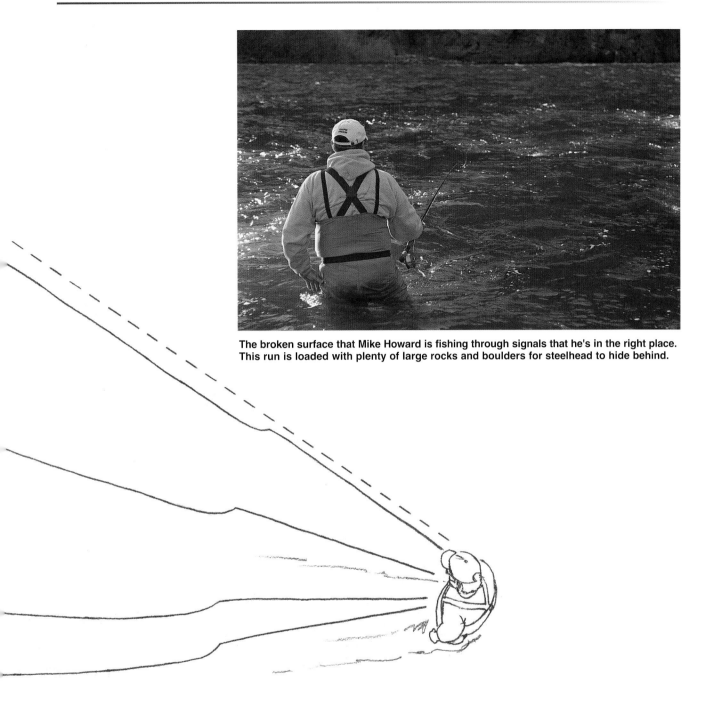

The broken surface that Mike Howard is fishing through signals that he's in the right place. This run is loaded with plenty of large rocks and boulders for steelhead to hide behind.

explaining and demonstrating this constantly to my clients on the river. Judging by their enlightened reactions (unless they've been humoring me), most of them had never given it much thought but were glad to have gained the insight and knowledge.

As you can see, the fish zone is the same irrespective of your choice of line. Bottom line: Cut to the chase when fishing a floating line. Remember, there's no need for much of a set up. Once again, cast the fly right to the edge, or slightly beyond the fish zone and get her fishing. With the tip you can cast across the zone, set up, and by the time the fly is fishing it will be in the same location to which you would cast your floating line. Good stuff.

SWING ZONE: SINK-TIP

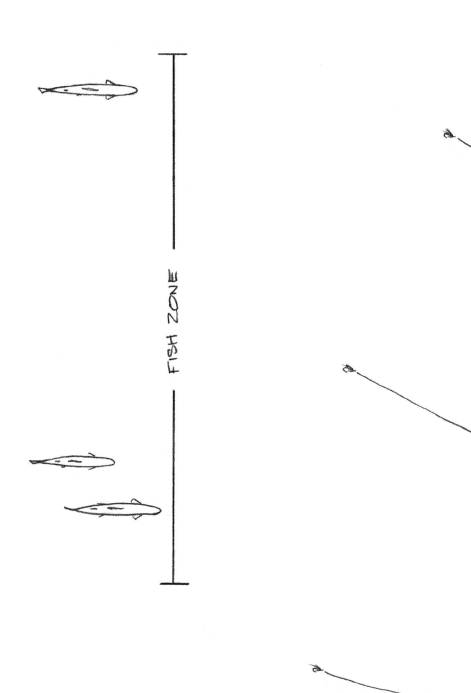

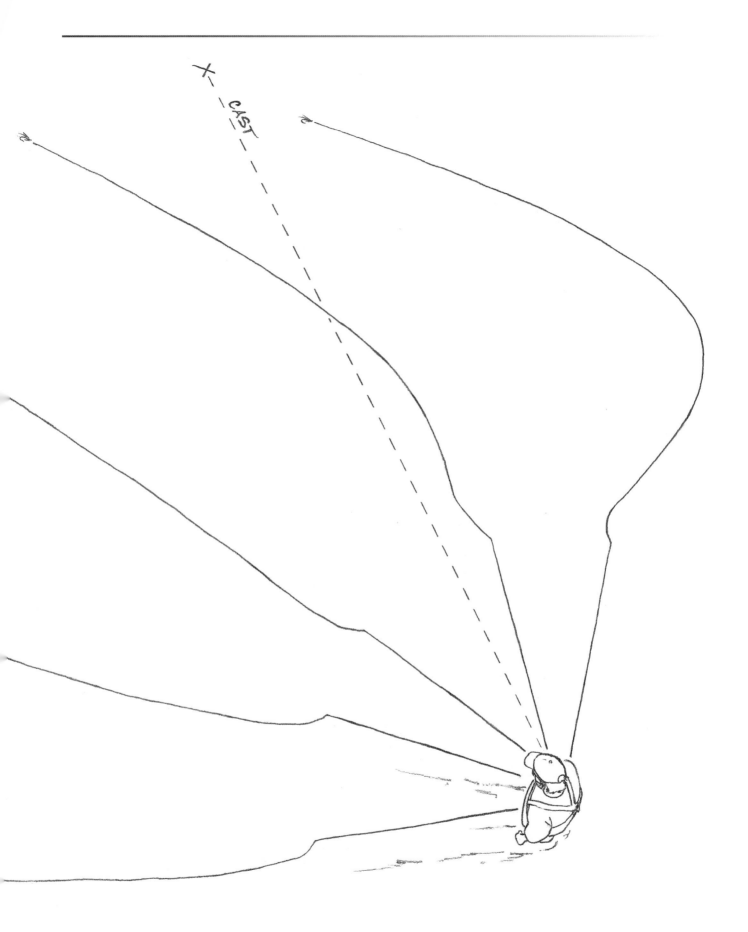

X - CAST

STRIKING THE FISH

The budding, enthusiastic steelheader, if he or she is truly passionate about the sport, will be all ears and eyes when in the presence of more-experienced anglers. If it's in his nature he'll read anything and everything he can get his hands on pertaining to steelhead. Inevitably, the beginner will soon be subjected to and haunted by steelheading cliche: "The fish hit me like a freight train!" "I mean, he just took the fly like a bolt of lightning!" "She took like a ton of bricks!" "Oh man, that fish absolutely crushed my fly!" And on it goes—the many superlative descriptions of how a steelhead takes a fly. It gets my blood boiling just thinking about it. These kinds of takes do occur, and there's nothing more exciting than swinging your fly after hours of fruitless casting when you are violently blindsided by a crushing blow from a freight train that was shot out of a cannon and hit you like a ton of bricks. Yeah, baby!

Reality, however, is that far fewer than half the steelhead takes encountered are flamboyant. The greater half of the steelhead-grabbing phraseology often sounds like this: "I felt this dull pull." "My fly just sort of stopped." "I don't know, I just felt some weight, and then my line started moving." "I felt a little tick, and he was on." Wait—it gets better: "Damn, I missed him!" "He took it so hard, I don't know how I could've lost him so quickly" "I shoulda' had him!" And the one that is near and dear to my steelhead guide's heart, *"Dec, what the hell am I doing wrong?"*

The fact is, yes, sometimes the steelhead climbs all over the fly and hooks itself, but more often the fish needs time to turn with your fly and swim away with it, thus allowing the hook to make purchase. The steelhead is not aware that the fly is tethered to an anchored string—all its life, when it inhaled or mouthed food, the stuff goes right in. No problem. We as anglers need to be aware of the physics behind this and let the steelhead take the fly. I'll say it again: LET THE STEELHEAD TAKE THE FLY. A hair-trigger strike response is the nemesis of many a good steelheader. As Bill McMillan told me long ago, imagine dangling a fly tied to a piece of monofilament in a toilet bowl. Make sure there's tension on the fly—no slack. Now flush the toilet. As the toilet is flushing simultaneously pull up and back on the fly. What happens? Your fly pops out of the toilet as the water goes down. Do it again. This time, as the toilet flushes,

drop your arm a bit. Don't pull back. The fly disappears. The same thing needs to be practiced with steelhead. Not only should you wait for the steelhead to make its turn with your fly, you need to incorporate some slack or loose line in order for the fish to turn freely, taking the fly with it. This delayed reaction to a take is especially necessary when fishing a floating line.

The floating line rides in the upper current which is usually faster than subcurrents. Your fly, whether riding right on top or barely subsurface, usually stays in line with your line within inches. You can see there's little or no slack in the system to allow the steelhead to pick up your offering and turn before you see it. There are several methods experienced steelheaders use to allow the steelhead a free turn with the fly. One is simply allowing the steelhead to take the fly without lifting the rod too soon, which in my opinion leaves too much room for error. Another is to fish with a raised rod tip, which creates slack line as the line from the rod drapes and sags to the water. This affords the steelhead plenty of slack to turn, but I prefer to fish with my rod tip as close to the water as possible—it helps me feel what the fly is doing. Some anglers fish with a high rod tip and actually drop it to the water when they see or feel a take, lifting once they feel the fish a second time, confident he's made his turn. I've met others who fish with a very loose drag and simply let the steelhead peel some line off the reel before lifting.

I have experimented with all of these techniques plus a few more. For me and the hundreds of anglers I have guided—some of enviable experience who have taught me a thing two—carrying a loop of line between the reel and rod hand, and allowing the steelhead to pull it out until it comes tight to the reel is the most efficient, fail-safe method there is. Follow along with the illustrations, and I'll tell you all about it.

THE RIGHT LOOP

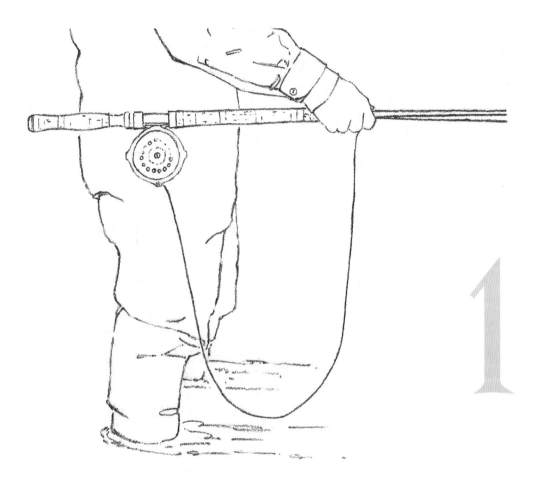

1

The first thing is you need to carry a substantial loop, not just several useless inches as I see a lot of people fishing with. You want the loop to be at least the length of a fair-sized steelhead, say, 30 to 36 inches. Cut this in half and you get a loop hanging 15 to 18 inches below your reel. That length is usually sufficient, but I sometimes use more. If the water I'm fishing is a little deeper than average, I've found that the steelhead needs a little more line to take down with him. Also, if you're fishing a river where the average steelhead is large—say, the Thompson or Babine in British Columbia—a larger loop is an advantage.

I recommend getting in the habit of forming the loop before your fly is doing its fishing business. Form it early, immediately after your initial mend. You want this loop to be secured and ready to be snatched up through the entire course of the swing. Pull the loop in from the cast line, not the reel, for two reasons. One is you want the loop to be free of kinks from memory. The other is if you pull 30 inches of line from your reel, by the time you're half way down the run you'll have way too much line out. Common sense, I know, but I've seen it happen many times.

The index finger of my rod hand controls the loop. It's what I pull the line through to form the loop, and it's how the loop is pressed lightly against the rod to keep it secured while fishing. Notice I said lightly pressed against the rod—you want it loose enough so a steelhead can pull it out. Practice this with a friend. On dry ground, form a loop and have your buddy pull it out at varying degrees of slow and fast. This will help you get a feel for it. It should go without saying that while the loop is being pulled out, whether it by a steelhead or your buddy, DO NOT TRY TO SET THE HOOK! You will be defeating the purpose of the loop, and you'll pull it away from your fish nearly every time.

LOOP GOING OUT

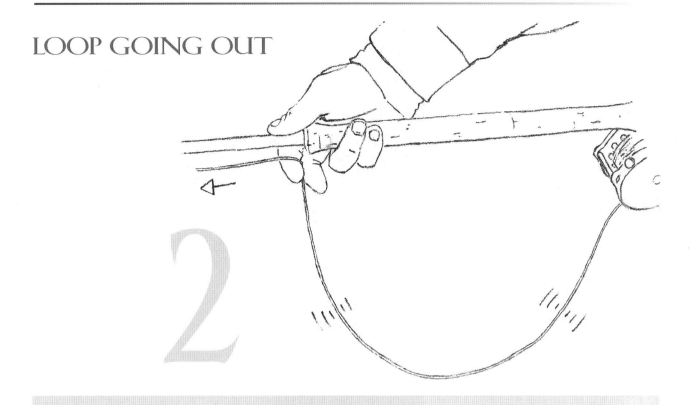

DO NOT TRY AND SET THE HOOK! You really need to pound this into your head. One of my guide sayings in trying to convey this message to my clients is, "I've never missed a steelhead by waiting too long." It's true, but I've missed plenty trying to set the hook too quickly. The impulse to clamp down and rear back is strong. It's entirely up to you how you handle it: Lift the rod, and your chances of missing the steelhead dramatically increase, or let him take the loop out nearly guaranteeing a solid hook-up.

Be prepared for the loop to go out so fast you don't even have time to mess it up, to so slow it seems like it will never go out. No matter how slow it seems, the right thing to do is NOT SET THE HOOK. Every time.

TIGHT TO THE REEL

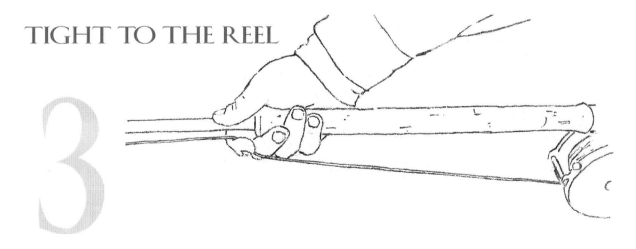

The loop goes out, and the line comes tight to the reel. Awesome. At this point you still shouldn't be in a hurry. Try to remain calm. I know, the house is on fire and the tsunami's on its way. Remain calm. Yeah, right. Just remember: The more you are in control of your actions, the greater the likelihood of a successful hook-up. Once she's good and tight, maybe even the reel clicking a bit, pinch the line against the rod.

RAISING THE ROD

Line pinched against the cork, raise the rod up and toward your bank to drive the hook home. You don't need to give it a gorilla set. Lift the rod with some smooth authority, but there's no need to overdo it. Each encounter is different, with some steelhead taking hard and fast, others slow and subtle. You need to raise the rod accordingly.

When Mr. Steelie hits with an electrifying jolt, he pretty much sets the hook himself. Heaving the rod tip up as if setting up on a halibut will usually result in a break-off. Bad. A simple lift does the trick; the fish will probably be off to the races anyway. A slow take usually requires a sharper lift.

If you have the presence of mind to do it, it's good to lift the rod toward the bank you are fishing from. Steelhead typically take the fly from the inside out, resulting in the fly finding purchase in the corner of the jaw closest to your bank as he swims with it back toward center river. It makes sense to pull the hook in the opposite direction the steelhead is going.

OFF TO THE RACES

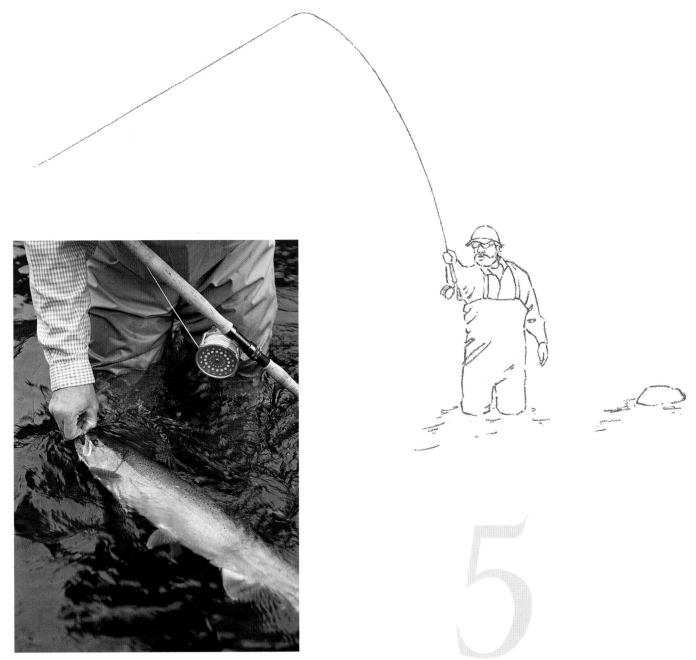

Desert doe caught by the two-handed rod of Beau Purvis.

Okay you've got him! Get your finger off that line, and let'm run, let'm run, *let'm run*. Wish I had a buck for every time I yelled that out.

Most steelhead take off on a strong, long, screaming run as soon as the rod is raised, and they realize they're in trouble. Hang on, and let it go. If the fish doesn't run, you need to get reeling fast in order to keep the line tight and the hook from falling out. This often spurs the fish into a panic that makes it run. The main thing is to be ready. Once you raise the rod, something *will* happen.

HOW A STEELHEAD TAKES YOUR FLY

FOR NEARLY A DECADE I HAD THE BEST SEAT IN THE HOUSE. From 1995 to 2003, I watched more than 1,000 summer-run steelhead move to the fly. Watching a steelhead suddenly, without warning, appear out of nowhere to take a fly fished just below the surface is without a doubt the most incredible event I've experienced in Nature. Each time I see it—whether the steelhead takes the fly or not—I get a huge flush of adrenaline. My knees get weak, and I usually let out some form of involuntary moan. I want to yell out, "DID YOU SEE THAT?"

Watching all these little dramas, I've learned a great deal about how a steelhead responds to the fly. I've seen some popular myths deflated. And I've had beliefs and opinions I've formed over the years confirmed. It's revealing what a pluck, pull, and big grab really look like.

Watching the fly swing has also been a boon to angler hook-up success in my guiding. Ever wonder how many fish move to your fly without taking it? A lot. You have no idea a steelie just came so close to your fly it could have counted the fibers in the tail. You take your two steps and cast again, oblivious to the interested fish you almost hooked. Then 20 minutes later, your buddy who's been following you down the run is screaming "Fish on!" He gets bragging rights for hooking a fish behind you; you question yourself why you missed it.

Watching the fly swing has allowed me to take advantage of opportunities that may have otherwise gone undetected while fishing completely blind. One memorable day in October 1995 while guiding three anglers we hooked 11 steelhead. I watched each one take the fly, but saw 24 separate movements. Not all the steelhead I saw that day were hooked, while some of the hooked fish were caught on their second or third rush at the fly. Had I not been watching we still would have had a superb day—but we wouldn't have hooked 11 fish.

I can't take original credit for my steelhead-watching habit. That goes to my close friend and fellow steelhead guide John Hazel of Maupin, Oregon. When I showed up to work with John in 1995 on Oregon's spectacular Deschutes River, he had already been dean among guides there for 15 years or so. He asked me in almost a hushed tone, "Dec, you ever watch the fly swing . . . do you ever see the steelhead take?"

I paused for a moment. I could tell his question had some depth. Before going to work with John on the Deschutes, I'd been spending my fall seasons guiding on the Grande Ronde River. "Well, yeah," I said. "I watch when we're fishing dry flies."

John smiled and said, "I thought so, but you haven't seen 'em take a wet fly." The rest of that first night John got me totally jazzed as he talked for hours about things he had seen watching his anglers' flies swing through the currents of this broad, deep-canyon stream.

The Deschutes River runs fairly clear with a slight blue-green tint. The bottom is very dark, mostly made up of algae-covered basalt, so to spot holding steelhead is extremely rare. Most of the runs and pools in the section we guide, however, don't have gravel bars and usually run along a high bank. Most of the best steelhead lies are very close to shore, making it easy to see the fly swing from my high vantage point on the bank. As long as the fly has a white wing, with maybe a little flash in it, I can see even a size 8 plain as day. I stay even with the fly as the angler works down the run. If he makes a good cast and the fly turns over nicely, I can usually pick it up as soon as it touches down. This is a great way to guide. I'm fishing as intently as my angler—with my eyes.

As I watch the fly swing, several things become apparent. The first is near and dear to my heart. Mending the fly line while the fly is in the heart of the swing is BAD. Just let it swing. Even the tiniest of mends is counter-productive. Simply put, the fly jerks—sometimes several feet. This alone is worth watching. I can't say it too many times: *Let your fly swing.* Another mistake people make, revealed while watching the fly swing, is fidgeting. Nervous hands and feet have the rod tip bouncing all around. Guess what the fly's doing? Yep, bouncing all around.

Have your feet set before you cast. Stay put. And fish like a heron.

The grab and first blistering run is the drug that keeps us coming back for more and the mystical allure that ties it all together.

Another no-no that is plain to see is picking the fly up too early in the swing. I've been watching the fly countless times, completely focused, waiting for a shark to appear, when all of a sudden the fly is rudely ripped from the water. AAAGGHH! What's going on? It's like watching a climactic scene in a movie when suddenly the power goes out. Be patient, and let the current carry your fly until it stops. To hook a steelhead is the primary reason we're out here, and, if I remember correctly, the fish are in the water.

The fly itself is a fascinating study. Irrespective of the pattern being fished, the swinging fly exudes tremendous power and movement as it fights the current. Nothing else I've seen in the river has the same appearance. As I watch, it's evident that power and movement are the most important functions of the fly. All you fly pattern junkies are not going to like this, but I truly believe that the actual pattern is the least important link to the steelhead. That said, don't change a thing, baby. I too love steelhead flies, and have built tremendous faith in a multitude of styles and patterns. Faith and confidence go a long way in

this game.

Once you get your favorite pattern swinging properly, you'll see that a steelhead's rise from the depths to meet it looks completely reflexive on the fish's part. It's not a conscious decision; the steelhead can't help itself. I've always thought that steelhead move to the fly due to a conditioned response: Fly in the water, fly in the water! There it goes! Gotta have it, *gotta have it*! That's exactly what it looks like. They just can't help themselves. At least that's how it appears to me.

Over the years, I've seen steelhead react to the fly in many different ways. And yes, some of them are quite comical to me. (I love those little fish). The accompanying beautiful illustrations drawn by artist and steelheading friend, Greg Pearson, depict the behavior that I most commonly see. Photographs would be near impossible to take because of low-light fishing conditions, and the unexpected suddenness of the steelhead's reaction. Greg's stunning work has accurately captured what I've seen.

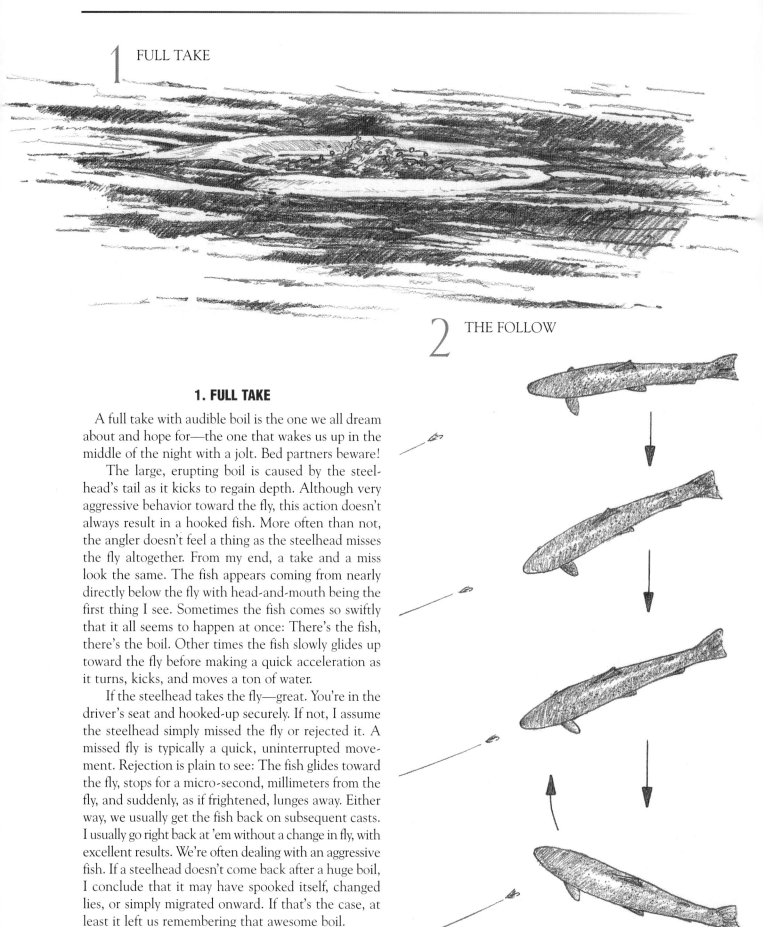

1 FULL TAKE

2 THE FOLLOW

1. FULL TAKE

A full take with audible boil is the one we all dream about and hope for—the one that wakes us up in the middle of the night with a jolt. Bed partners beware!

The large, erupting boil is caused by the steelhead's tail as it kicks to regain depth. Although very aggressive behavior toward the fly, this action doesn't always result in a hooked fish. More often than not, the angler doesn't feel a thing as the steelhead misses the fly altogether. From my end, a take and a miss look the same. The fish appears coming from nearly directly below the fly with head-and-mouth being the first thing I see. Sometimes the fish comes so swiftly that it all seems to happen at once: There's the fish, there's the boil. Other times the fish slowly glides up toward the fly before making a quick acceleration as it turns, kicks, and moves a ton of water.

If the steelhead takes the fly—great. You're in the driver's seat and hooked-up securely. If not, I assume the steelhead simply missed the fly or rejected it. A missed fly is typically a quick, uninterrupted move-ment. Rejection is plain to see: The fish glides toward the fly, stops for a micro-second, millimeters from the fly, and suddenly, as if frightened, lunges away. Either way, we usually get the fish back on subsequent casts. I usually go right back at 'em without a change in fly, with excellent results. We're often dealing with an aggressive fish. If a steelhead doesn't come back after a huge boil, I conclude that it may have spooked itself, changed lies, or simply migrated onward. If that's the case, at least it left us remembering that awesome boil.

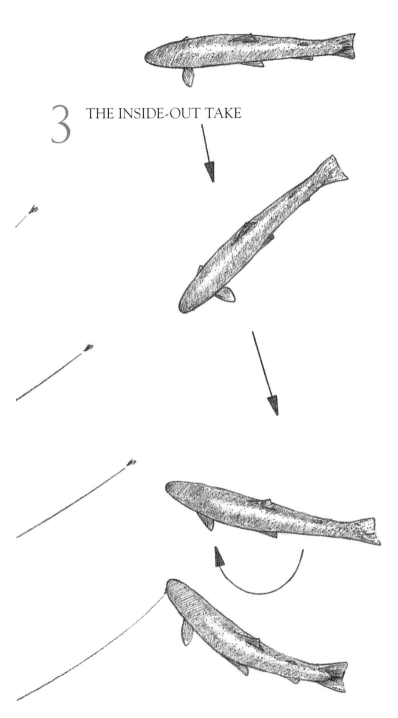

3 THE INSIDE-OUT TAKE

2. THE FOLLOW

The fly has passed over the suspected lie and is heading toward shore. I am still attentive, but have lost a little interest when in my periphery I see a fish following the fly. Sometimes the fish makes a quick acceleration and takes; mostly it disappears as suddenly as it appeared. My feeling toward this one is that the fly was traveling too fast as it came over the

The song sparrow almost always shares the bank with me.

resting fish. Without changing flies, I give the fish a moment or two to return to its lie, and then have the angler make a slower presentation. This is done by wading out a little farther if possible, or by holding the rod tip out over the river as the fly passes over the general area. Either way, the closer you are to the lie, the slower the fly swims. This fish usually comes back with the first slowed presentation. *Yee-haw.*

3. THE INSIDE-OUT TAKE

A steelhead that has followed the fly as in sequence 2 and commits to taking the fly usually does so from the inside out. Passing the fly up, heading relatively close to shore (and me), the steelhead takes the fly as it turns back out to the main river. This one has really confirmed my belief that you should fish your fly until it is directly downstream of your position or has stopped swinging altogether. Unfortunately, when a steelhead follows close to shore and either misses or doesn't take the fly, I have found them very difficult to get back. I believe they may have spooked themselves. I've seen steelhead so focused on the fly they nearly beach themselves.

4. INHALING THE FLY

With or without a boil, a full, aggressive inhaling of the fly leaves me with the most intense rush of adrenaline. I'm calmly and intently watching the fly swing when suddenly there appears a huge, gaping white mouth and flared gills all over the fly. The attacking steelhead quickly turns . . . fish on! The steelhead has inhaled the fly. As with every move a steelhead makes to a fly, however, it doesn't always result in a hook-up.

Witnessing this "miss" was perhaps my most exciting speculative belief come true. You know how you can get an incredible pull from a steelhead without hooking it? You're standing there shaking in disbelief, *How in the world could I have missed that fish?*

I often thought that possibly the pulling jolt I felt was the fish violently inhaling the fly, but coming up empty—the vacuum effect created by the steelhead's inhalation pulls the fly without the fish ever touching it. The steelhead doesn't know the fly is tethered. In his oceanic world he sucks in food, and it goes into his mouth freely.

So what to do? When you feel a good pull, let the fly continue swinging. Remember, the fish didn't feel the fly on the first attempt. I've watched them come back a second time and pummel the fly. How dare you get away from me—I'm a bad-ass steelhead!

5 THE NIPPER

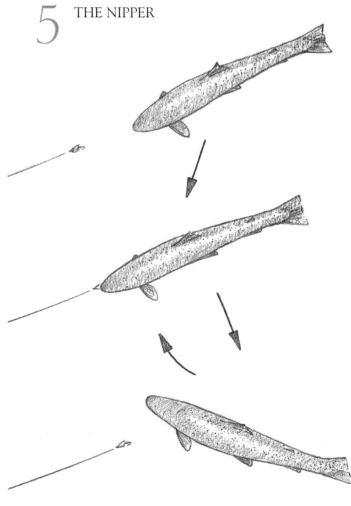

Many steelhead may move to the fly without the angler ever knowing it. It pays to fish a good piece of water a second time.

5. THE NIPPER

Another beautiful sight. Although in truth, this one is bittersweet. A steelhead that gives a little nip at the fly rarely does anything more than that—gives a little nip that the angler rarely feels. If something is felt, it's usually a little pluck. A change of fly will often bring the nipping steelhead back . . . for just

another nip. I've spent enough time over the years failing to make one of these guys take the fly that I'm confident to try 'em once or twice and move on in search of a more aggressive fish. I've seen several of these nippers come to my anglers fly in a day's fishing—sometimes they are all that come to his fly. He may feel or see nothing, but in actuality move three or more steelhead in a day's effort. I see them all. That's why I like being the steelhead-watcher.

6. REJECTION

Rejection is, oddly enough, a lot of fun to watch. Simply, it's another legitimate reaction to the fly that I feel honored and fortunate to witness. The beautiful thing to see during rejection is the steelhead almost always stopping close to the fly for a quick study. So there's the anticipatory moment when I don't know what the fish is going to do. Are we going to fight a steelhead, or aren't we? Then it's over, the hair on the back of my neck standing on end as I explain to my angler what I just saw.

"Damn, I wish you could have seen it!" is what usually bellows from my mouth. About half the time you can get the rejecting steelhead back by going through the fly-change drill. The eventual take is typically slow, yet deliberate.

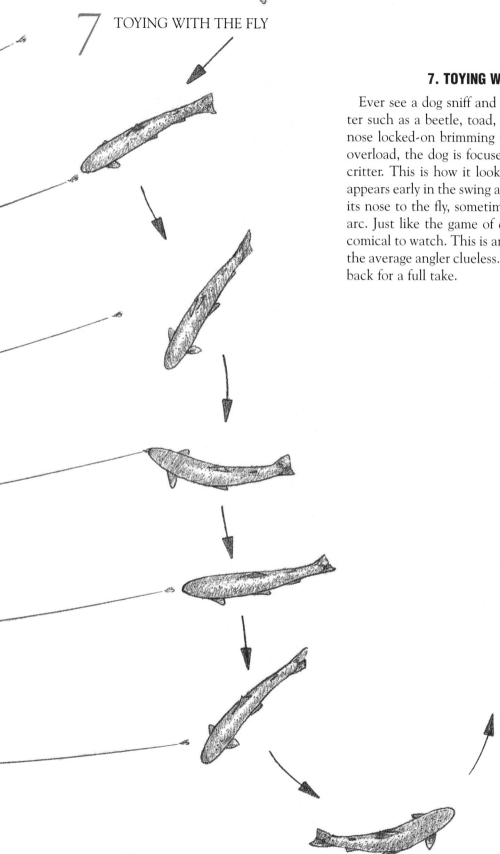

7 TOYING WITH THE FLY

7. TOYING WITH THE FLY

Ever see a dog sniff and follow a hapless little critter such as a beetle, toad, or baby bird? Head down,
nose locked-on brimming with curiosity and sensory
overload, the dog is focused on nothing else but the
critter. This is how it looks to me when a steelhead
appears early in the swing and follows but never takes,
its nose to the fly, sometimes nipping at it for its full
arc. Just like the game of dog-and-critter, it's almost
comical to watch. This is another scenario that leaves
the average angler clueless. The fish rarely ever comes
back for a full take.

8. HEAD-AND-SHOULDER TAKE

My Favorite: a solid take with the steelhead turning on side. Man, do I love this one! The depiction in the illustration is usually all I see: a side profile of head and shoulders, quickly gone, followed by a screamin' reel and a screamin' angler. Although it happens fast, I often get a clear enough view that I can sex the steelhead by the shape of its jaw. The majority of the steelhead I see fought and landed by anglers of all experience levels usually starts with this kind of take. The hook is nearly always deeply embedded in the corner of the steelhead's jaw. Right where you want it to be.

. . .

There's an infinite number of ways a steelhead responds to and moves to a fly. I've shown you eight of the most common. There are many more that I see routinely. Often an aggressive fish swims away from its lie toward the fly for a viscious interception. This is exceptionally aggressive behavior; each time I see it I'm grateful that steelhead don't carry guns. Sometimes, all I see is a peek-a-boo head and mouth, never to be seen again. I get the chills and sometimes ask myself if I really saw it. Of course, I did. Other times, with the speed of a camera flash, I see the whole fish. There and gone. The momentary feeling I get is the strength of 10 men. Oh, I can't get enough.

Occasionally I see ghostly a movement eerily coasting well below the fly as a steelhead follows along without rising. Although very interesting to watch, I've never been able to hook one of these fish. Getting the fly closer to the fish by switching to a sink-tip might work, but I'd rather spend the time it would take changing lines looking for a free-rising steelie. It's nice to know the fish was there, though.

Once in a while a steelhead appears several feet from the fly and swims in zany circles, out of control, like Daffy Duck, zigging and zagging, backward and forward until eventually crushing the fly. Many times I've seen a steelhead rise, pick up the fly, and literally drop back downriver. The fly pops out and the angler is left having experienced, a "good pull." The list goes on.

If the opportunity presents itself, I strongly encourage you to lay the rod down and check it out for yourself. Seeing a steelhead move to the fly—particularly a blind fish—is not only enlightening, it's an incredible sight. I encourage you to participate, and not only in hopes of seeing a fish move. I'd like you to see how the fly swims and reacts to mending and not mending, the effects of variances in current, etc. The ardent student of the sport should savor this.

. . .

There is another experience that had a profound influence on my understanding of steelhead behavior that I'd like to pass on to you. This one only took a couple hours rather than 10 years.

A guide buddy of mine and I found ourselves visiting a well-known steelhead hatchery along a tributary of the Columbia River system. The name of the hatchery will remain nameless in order to protect the guilty. I'm not sure if what we did was against the rules—but it sure was fun.

There we were on a warm October day standing next to a large concrete holding tank teeming with adult steelhead of all sizes. It was a majestic sight. The tank was probably four to five feet in depth, with the whole wad of steelhead suspended well off the bottom at about mid-depth. We watched quietly. I casually reached in my pocket and pulled out a shiny penny. You know what happened next: I pitched it in. I was hoping, of course, to get some kind of reaction from the fish. I wasn't expecting much to happen. That penny hit the water and damn near every steelhead in the tank came to life.

They came from every part of the tank, racing to the penny—*whoosh*, the penny was inhaled. Cool! In an instant my friend and I were frantically digging in our pockets looking for change. We had enough to entertain us for a while longer. Every piece of metal currency was swiftly sucked up by the aggressive tank-bound steelhead. It seemed, though, that with each toss of a coin, fewer steelhead went for it. We also saw that the fish were progressively holding deeper. Then we ran out of coins. Since hatcheries are not equipped with change machines, it was off to the local bank where we got a dollar's worth of pennies, a roll for each of us.

Upon our return—we were gone for about 30 minutes—all of the steelhead were again stratified at mid-depth. The first penny we tossed in was met with the same fervor as the original one I threw in an hour earlier. Nearly every fish in the tank came rushing for the penny. We kept tossing; they kept coming. After a while, though, instead of steaming at the fly in a competitive groups of five or more, they came in pairs and singles. Their reaction was more delayed with each toss. The school began to sulk near the bottom until we could no longer get a rise out of a single one. I guess you could say we put them down.

We decided to "rest the pool" and see what would happen. We walked away from the tank for 10 minutes. We chose 10 minutes because that's the length of time I have found works best to rest a pool when actually fishing.

8 HEAD-AND-SHOULDER TAKE

To our surprise, after exactly 10 minutes, every fish in the tank was back at mid-depth. Their reaction to the onslaught of penny-pitching was every bit as aggressive as our earlier barrage. With the whole process repeating itself until once again, the school was put down. We had enough pennies left to rest 'em one more time. Ten more minutes and it was déjá vu all over again.

Eventually, we bankrupted ourselves. The game was over. But man, what a great experience! In addition to watching the steelhead gradually becoming despondent and eventually cowering on the bottom, then before a repeat performance, a few other questions were answered.

What happened to the pennies (flies) after they were inhaled? The vast majority were ejected from the steelheads' gills—where they were often picked up by another steelhead when they were still fresh and rested. I assume the pennies that I didn't see expelled from their gills were ingested.

I also always wanted to know if a steelhead would react to something presented behind them. The answer, at least with the pennies, is yes. I took great care to drop many pennies behind individual steelhead; quite a few of them turned completely around to engulf the coin. I also saw several steelhead swim downward in order to snatch a penny, including one that actually made an attempt to grab a penny that had settled to the bottom. When they're hot they're hot.

If I've learned anything from all these experiences, it's to fish a run a second time if it's known as a productive piece of water, and particularly even more if fish were hooked or moved on the first pass.

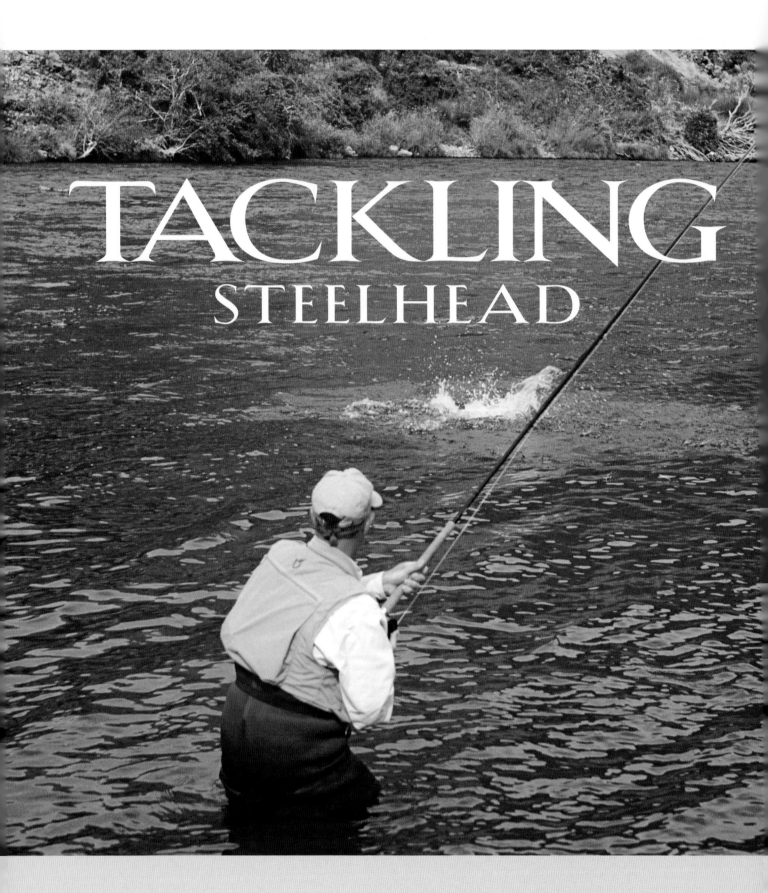

CHAPTER 6

TACKLING
STEELHEAD

CONSIDERING THE COUNTLESS HOURS we crazy steelheaders spend: wading; casting and swinging flies; driving, hiking, or floating to and from the runs; tying flies; messing with tackle; reading and daydreaming; planning, the actual pinnacle of it all—the hooking, playing, and landing of a steelhead—is an infrequent event. This is another area where experience is the best teacher. But because it doesn't happen often, preparedness is paramount. Steelhead aren't just big. They're blistering fast; they jump, cartwheel, greyhound, sulk, nose into heavy cover, suddenly change directions, twist, spin, and turn. They rapidly go where they want to go—which might be the last place we hope they'll go. Like through the tailout, out of the pool, and into the rapids below. All of this in less than a minute after hooking one!

I've seen the manliest of men who are CEOs, corporate high rollers, and distinguished icons in their professional worlds instantly become terrified and panic-stricken creampuffs when confronted with the fury of a hooked steelhead.

"Dec!" echoes through the river valley or off the canyon walls, followed by, "What do I do? *What do I do?* DEEEECCC!"

I come clambering over to my epileptic sport and say, "Calm down." "You're a lot bigger than the fish is, Dave." But more often I yell, as spastically as him, "Let'm run, let'm run, *let'm run!*"

Yes, let him run—no truer words were ever spoken about how to tackle a hooked steelhead.

The initial few seconds of a meeting with a startled steelhead can be very terrifying. (Isn't that what we love about them?) Trying to stop a fish on its first blistering run is futile. And why would you want to stop it anyway? When all your efforts come together and a hard-won chromer is melting line off your reel while the backing knot blasts through the snake guides like a small-caliber bullet, your reel screaming at a pitch you didn't know existed and your rod is a flattened-out, useless stick. At this time everything in the Universe is right.

Let him run.

Eventually your fish will stop—it may be in the next county, but it will stop. Until this time, the angler's task is to watch and enjoy the show. I've always maintained that the first half of a fight with a steelhead is a spectator sport. Within these heart-stopping early rounds the steelhead may not only go on a long scorching run. He may frantically jump and cartwheel end-over-end in an effort to throw the hook. He may be doing this so fast and out of control that four jumps, two multi-cartwheels with a change of direction, and a few corkscrews feel to the angler like one continuous run. The fly line is bookin' straight downriver when out of the corner of your eye you see a steelhead violently leaping directly across the river—maybe even upstream from you. *Huh, what?* Pause as your brain tries to process information *Holy shit, that's my fish!* Yeah, they're crazy, crazy, crazy! And I love 'em, love 'em, love 'em!

Let him run.

Reel drag-tension should be set just heavy enough to avoid over-running of the line. It should never be set with the intention of making the fish have to work against it—save that for deep-sea fishing. I set my drag and leave it. When I feel a fish is running so fast I might get an overrun, I palm the reel a bit. But only a bit. I touch the spool with only enough pressure to avoid a disastrous overrun. Just as monumental a disaster can occur if too much pressure is applied. Something will give, and it won't be the steelhead. At least not on its first few powerful runs. I'm also a firm believer in standing your ground when a steelhead is racing away. I see so many anglers get the grab and immediately start running downriver chasing the fish. *Where is this guy going?* I wonder.

Usually it's blindly into harm's way. We ultimately don't want the steelhead to leave the pool if it can be avoided. If the steelhead is red-hot and running downstream and you're chasing, you've just put yourself physically closer to the danger zone. Now, the rest of the battle will be done down in the tailout and close to that area of no return. If you are chasing a fish that's 50 yards down from you and still running, guess how far you will remain from that fish? Probably about 50 yards. All you have accomplished is to move the fight downstream—that's it. Most hooked steelhead don't want to leave the pool. Typically they run to the tailout and pull out of the run and face upstream. I still stand my ground here. If you just keep very little tension on the line and exercise some patience the fish will usually start swimming back upriver. Once he's a safe distance from the lip of the pool, you can put on some pressure and get him moving again. Now if he runs again—and he will—he has room to use his energy running back to the bottom of the pool. Had we run down there in the first place, his second run would have more than likely seen him leaving the pool.

So if the first half of the encounter is a spectator sport, the second half is a fight. And I do mean fight. This is where experience and skill distinguish that fine line of what is a fight with a steelhead and what is horsing a fish.

When your fish is slowed and not on a power-run, you should be pumping and reeling like a wild man, always ready for him to take off running. If he does, let him go. The second he slows, get back on him. I reel every chance I get. Every pump made with the rod should be followed by frenetic reeling. If I can get only two cranks on the reel I take 'em. *Every time.* Keep the rod low and to the side for a better cushion and leverage. As the fish gets closer and begins to tire, counter his every move with the rod. If he moves left, sweep the rod to the right; if he darts right, counter to the left. Always maintain tension when doing this. A well-fought battle is synchronized choreography. I'm countering left and the steelhead responds with a sudden resurgent run—I instinctively raise the rod parallel to the river's surface and guide my rod in the direction the fish is running. This keeps tension and allows the fish to run freely. The rod as a fish-fighting tool is in your hands for leverage when fighting, but I believe when a fish is running the rod should be out of the way. Once the fish stops, *now* get all over him with the rod, making him work and fight. If he is stopped and can't be budged, the worst thing to do is be content with this stalemate. Change the

angle the pressure is coming from—walk downstream, get below him and pull. Try to get him moving. I even wade out and get closer to him, hoping he sees me and is spurred to run. Bottom line: If he's just sitting there, he's resting and regaining strength that will prolong the fight. It's our responsibility to land a steelhead as quickly as possible. Besides, it's more fun when the steelie is active due to our aggressive fighting strategy.

Eventually the steelhead begins to show signs of fatigue; its maneuvers for freeing itself become dampened. If you've made it this far, you've had your fun. You've played a steelhead. If possible, get a good look at your fish now. Landing a steelhead—actually getting him in your hands—is not easy. Many are lost at this stage in the game. The water is shallow and the true weight of the fish is not buffered by depth any more. In the shallows, rocks and other streamside debris can be a hindrance and the culprit to a lost fish. Although fatigued, "beaten" steelhead still possess incredible stamina and determination.

They play cat-and-mouse with you over and over. You think the game is over and he's sufficiently tired enough to attempt a grab at his tail when he suddenly he bolts back out to mid-river. You get him back. Now you know you've got him. *Zoom*, he races out again. This happens several times or more. Eventually it's time for the angler to just say "no!" and put the brakes on him. This should over-end the fish followed by rolling on his side. Find a safe spot in the shallows and lead the fish there. Walk down and firmly grasp his tail. If you are fishing with a friend, let him or her do it. It's easier on the fish, you, and potentially your tackle. And it engages your pal in the experience at a higher level.

You've got him! The world is right.

Now it's marvel-at-the-fish time and the compulsory photo shoot. It's easy to lose sight of what's really the most important aspect of this scenario: the safety and recovery of this precious steelhead. It would be a shame to inadvertently kill such a magnificent animal as a steelhead for the personal glory of a photograph. If you intend to photograph your prize, have your camera on you *before* you step foot in that river. If your camera is 100 yards upriver in the boat or in your tackle bag somewhere up on the bank, forget it—there will be no picture. Retrieving the camera is not an option. If you have your camera, great. I hope your partner knows how to operate it. Fumbling around, giving instructions on how to use a camera while a hypoxic steelhead is fighting for its life, is criminal. A little preplanning is mandatory, and you'll probably get a better photo for it. Hold the fish gently underwater with its head facing upstream while the photographer gets prepared to take the shot. Once ready—which means the photo is framed and pre-focused—the photographer gives the command to lift the fish. Fire one or two frames and *get the steelhead back in the water*. You've got your photograph. (Of course this is done over the water, NEVER over dry land.)

Now it's time to turn your attention to getting the steelhead recovered and released. Gently cradle the fish under its belly with one hand while grasping the wrist of the tail with the other. Hold him in slow-moving current with sufficient depth for easy passage to refuge once released. Make sure there is plenty of current passing over his gills. If it means walking him out a few paces, do so. Hold him steady, there's no need to move him back and forth—fish don't breathe this way. Hold onto him for as long as it takes for him to show a sign of strength. Usually he'll make an attempt to kick away. Don't let him go yet. He needs to show you he's really ready by doing this several times; each time he'll feel a little stronger. When you feel he's strong enough, let go of your grasp. Once released he'll either glide away like a transparent ghost, or baptize you with a face full of river as he revs up his powerful tail and heads home. There is no more endearing sight.

Another way to land steelhead solo, avoiding the uncertainty of cat-and-mouse, is to land your fish in deep water. This method requires care and skill. Extensive experience fighting and landing big fish in moving water is a mandatory prerequisite before attempting this. The primary advantage of this method is that the steelhead is landed quicker with less stress. The secondary advantage is that the potential for losing the fish during landing is dramatically decreased. You aren't dealing with all the hazards of shallow water. The exhausting back-and-forth game is, for the most part, eliminated because the steelhead isn't constantly being spooked by this large potential predator (you) towering over him, or the fear of being beached. Out in waist-deep water our profile is significantly reduced and the steelhead, although in trouble, probably feels safer in the deeper flow.

Play the fish normally. As he begins to tire, rather than backing into shore, stay deep and continue to tire him. When you feel he's ready, lead him upstream of your position. Then ease off a bit with the rod tension, and literally swim him down to you. He should fall right in your lap where you can grab hold of the wrist of his tail. Be ready for him to bolt away—some-

There are few things in life that elicit total satisfaction and complete contentment. Releasing a steelhead is one. Be sure she's good and ready before returning her to sanctuary. Adam Tavender releases a beautiful tidewater doe in June.

times he will, sometimes he won't. Just be ready. Once you have a secure grasp, strip some line off your reel to relieve tension from the rod to avoid breaking it. This is tricky. Remember, I said it requires skill and experience. You can shove the rod in your armpit freeing up your hand to strip off some line then cradle the fish. Or you can first pull some line off by securing it against the steelhead with one of your fingers holding her tail and pull the rod away. Then tuck the rod under your arm and hold the fish. (The photo sequence of Ed Ward throughout the pages of the presentation chapter in this book illustrate this method of landing a steelhead nicely.) Today, at this point in my evolution as an angler, I land about 90 percent of my steelhead standing in deep water. Even the big boys.

Encountering the Devil Fish

By nature steelhead are hot, fast-running, aerobatic animals. But with a little experience and the right equipment they are certainly manageable. Mind-blowing, yes, but manageable. However, every now and then one encounters a steelhead that takes things to the next level, a fish so possessed as to leave even the most seasoned veterans with a feeling of helplessness. It's a steelhead that makes the big play right out of the chute and either never stops running or leaves you in a volatile predicament. These are the "unlandables" or as I like to call them, Devil Fish.

Sometimes they'll clean your clock so fast you just have to clamp down on the reel and break them off. It's that or lose your fly line and all your backing. This is a case where I *will* run after a fish in hopes of stopping him before I lose him, and my fly line. Three times during my guiding career I had no other choice but to hop in my boat and give chase. Two of three were landed: 18- to 22-pound mean-ass bucks. The third was never seen.

If you don't have a boat in which to chase the leviathan—and you survive being spooled—you have a couple of proven options to turn a seemingly hopeless situation into a triumphant one. The steelhead is 100-plus yards downstream, and you have nowhere to go. Immediately ease tension off the line and wait. If you continue to pull, the steelhead senses the direction in which the danger is coming and will instinctively go the opposite way. You don't want that. Back off, give it a minute, and see what happens. I even slowly strip some line from the reel allowing the current to take some line behind the fish. Now the line is pulling from below the steelhead and he usually starts swimming upstream away from it. When you sense that the fish is moving back

upstream, it's important not to reel too quickly—you want to keep the tension light so as not to alarm him into running back down. Stay one step behind him as you reel. Once you get your line back on the reel and you feel he's well back into a safe area to rekindle his spirit, put the wood to him and get him fighting again.

Another trick to bring a long-distance runner back is to stick your rod tip well down in the water and start reeling. I'm not sure why this works, but it does. As you are reeling be sure to stop if you feel great resistance. It usually passes quickly and you can commence reeling again. I've never had a fish take off on a run while doing this. Come to think of it, this technique has never failed me.

The Devil Fish doesn't have to be a monster to unleash its wrath, it only has to be a steelhead. Ah, steelhead!

Gearing Up

RODS: Several years ago I took an informal survey of the bulk of my clientele's tackle inventory, namely, their rods. My findings didn't surprise me, although I was impressed with the volume. My dudes

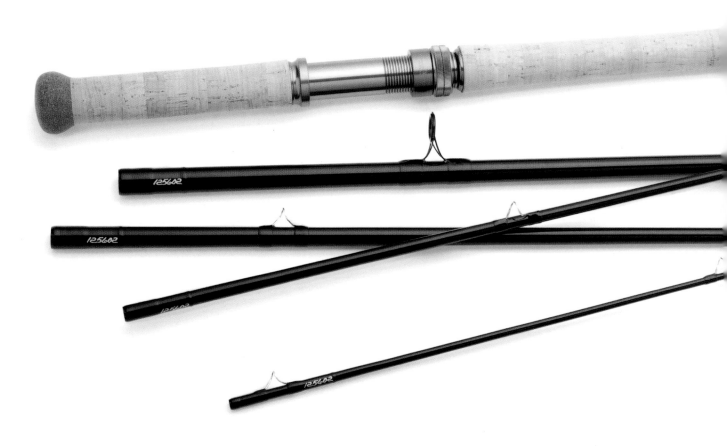

Increasing demand for high-end saltwater fly-fishing tackle benefits steelheaders. The superb Tibor Gulfstream makes an excellent reel for your best spey rod.

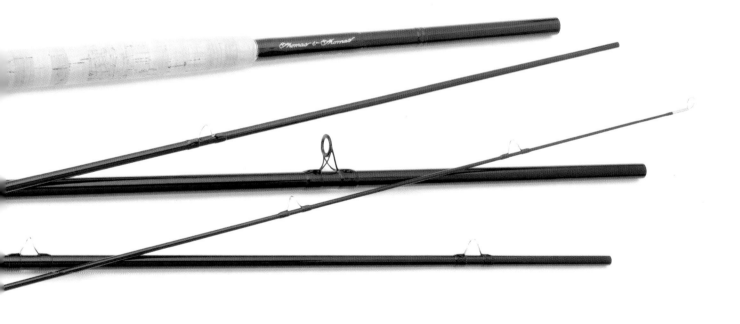

Using superior technology and the innovation of rolled graphite sheeting, American manufacturers of fly rods have transformed the traditional European slow, heavy salmon rod and produced a new generation of two-handed rods for steelhead that are lighter and more responsive. This Thomas & Thomas five-piece model is ideal for traveling by air to distant rivers.

own an average of four and a quarter two-handed rods per man. Most have a single-handed rod or two in steelhead sizes that get their play on the occasional bonefishing trip. Some of my guys who are solely devoted to steelhead don't even know how to cast a single-handed rod, let alone own one!

Of the four-plus spey rods in their possession, nearly all of my anglers own at least one 14-foot 9-weight, a 15-foot 10-weight purchased in the early 1990s and now collecting dust, and a smaller, slimmer 6- or 7-weight rod in the 12- to 13½-foot range. The balance of their rods are duplicates or similar models of various manufacturers in their quest for the "right fit." (Personally, I think it's an obsessive need to have more toys.)

My clientele represents a good cross section of the tackle in use today from the casual weekend angler to the perpetual addict. And the fact is two-handed rods more than dominate as the rod of choice. Single-handed rods I'm sure play an important role with steelheaders who frequent smaller creeks and streams, but that's not the focus of this book. For sake of thoroughness, however, a sturdy 8-weight nine and a half to 10 feet in length is an excellent choice—it's what I and many others used before making the permanent switch to the two-handed rod. On occasion I still enjoy waking a surface fly with a single-hander where a medium-length cast is all that's needed. My 10-foot 7-weight Sage RPL with floating double-taper line usually gets the nod. I often end up spey casting it single-handed with my line hand giving a haul where I normally would pull with

Do you bow the rod when a steelhead jumps? I've hooked about a dozen tarpon and the same number of Atlantic salmon—both great jumping fish that require bowing the rod when they are aerialized. When I was connected to each of these two dozen fish. I could sense when and where they were going to jump. Bowing the rod came easily and instinctively to me. Of the 1,000-plus steelhead I've fought, I've never felt the building pressure of one that's about to become airborne: Usually they unexpectadly come flying out of the river in an area I wasn't even focused on. I would bow to them if they gave me some warning.

the bottom hand on a spey rod. It works. It's slick. Spey casting is by no means limited to a two-handed rod.

My client's rods cover the gamut of all the top rod manufacturers: Sage, G.Loomis, Thomas & Thomas, Scott, and Winston. FlyLogic, Redington, and St. Croix round things out as do the beautiful, finely crafted rods of independent rod maker CF Burkheimer. All have similar histories in research, development, and marketing.

By the mid-1980s, Sage, G.Loomis, and Scott were manufacturing a limited number of two-handed rods designed specifically for the European market. Scott rod designer Jim Bartschi describes their early model G series as "slow and heavy." Loomis's first Euro-model was a 15-footer made from IM6 graphite and labeled the Atlantic Salmon Fly Rod, as told to me by rod designer and world-champion caster Steve Rajeff. Sage had a 16-foot 10-weight rod that was most sought-after by Scandinavian anglers along with a 14- and 15-footer.

With these few rods manufactured in the United States, it didn't take long before the resourceful steelhead crowd became interested (see Casting Your Fly to the Water.) Sage became aware of the growing interest and began developing a two-handed rod tailored to meet the demands of the Northwest steelheader. It needed to be lighter with an action that would cast weight-forward lines and a range of fly sizes. The rod was Sage's legendary 9140-4, a 14-foot 9-weight four piece. It was considerably lighter and trimmer than its European predecessor—an instant hit over the Green Monster. Master rod designer and caster Jim Green designed and built the very first 9140 as early as 1982. It's a little-known fact shared with me by Sage's longtime director of marketing, Marc Bale: "Jimmy made an annual Atlantic salmon trip to eastern Canada—he loved the Moise River. He began tinkering with a light two-handed rod just for that trip. That was really the first 9140-4." Sage built and sold fewer than 10 of these rods to a few interested individuals during the coming years. Then, by 1989 with design suggestions from Al Buhr and Harry Lemire, the first generation of production rods was born. They hit the market by storm in 1990.

Sage has stayed at the forefront of two-handed rod design as it pertains to global demand and interest. "It's difficult to try and please everyone, but we're constantly chasing the end of the design curve," Marc said. "That's our greatest challenge."

Loomis immediately produced a similar line of rods in their inherently light, crisp GL3 technology. Scott and Thomas & Thomas jumped on the band-wagon producing similar light rods designed for the growing interest among the steelhead angling community.

A late-comer to the boom was Winston. Today, Joe Begin of Winston admits that their early rods were merely extended versions of their highly regarded single-handers. Unfortunately, this made for a poor-casting two-hander. Winston has corrected the problem and now offers a fine, easy-casting rod made of boron and graphite marketed under the name Boron 2X.

Among the efforts of these "big-hitting" fly-rod companies was a one-man shop operating in quiet seclusion along the banks of Washington State's Washougal River. Kerry Burkheimer is a rod designer and builder who rolls his own graphite blanks with painstaking care and attention to detail. He turns out the most beautifully, ergonomically designed cork handles. His finished products are not only superb casting tools, they are stunning works of art. The same is true with his two-handed rods. I have nothing personal to gain when I say that, in my opinion, the two-handed rods manufactured by CF Burkheimer Rod Company are the finest ever made. To give you a better idea of what goes into designing a rod—and better yet, what goes on in the mind of a rod designer—I'll let Kerry tell you, in his own words, about the evolution of his two-handed rods:

My designing spey rods started about 1988. John Hazel, a good friend and fellow guide, came to me with a wish list to make a two-handed rod 15 feet in length. At the time I thought he was crazier than hell, but he seemed quite passionate about the whole thing, so I committed to making one. I remember "fishing around" for a starting point. I had been very successful at designing trout and saltwater sticks, but never had attempted a two-handed rod. We did not even have lines to try on these things, so we came up with an altered double-taper 10-weight with a front taper made from a double-taper 8 looped on. This seemed to work well, and we were off and running.

My first few attempted rod designs were quite fast. I had decided to error on the stiff side, but eventually John and I started to get a feel for what we thought would make a good casting spey rod. I spent hours test-casting different combinations—tips with different butts, with different mid sections, many made out of different materials—trying to understand just what it I was I was trying to achieve. Then one day it just kind of hit me. I started to get a sense of how the rod needed to load. The more I fished these prototypes the more lengthy the list of tasks we wanted the rod to perform.

I gradually realized that a two-handed rod for steelhead needs to be powerful while casting smoothly. It must load easily. It should lift sink-tips easily, change

For more than a century, British-made Hardy reels have been a fly-fishing tradition. Old and new models alike are ruggedly constructed with a vintage look. The beautiful "S"-handled Cascapedia Mark II and the handsome Bougle Mark V are replicas of early Hardy classics. Both are perfectly suited to the rigors—and aesthetics—of contemporary steelhead angling.

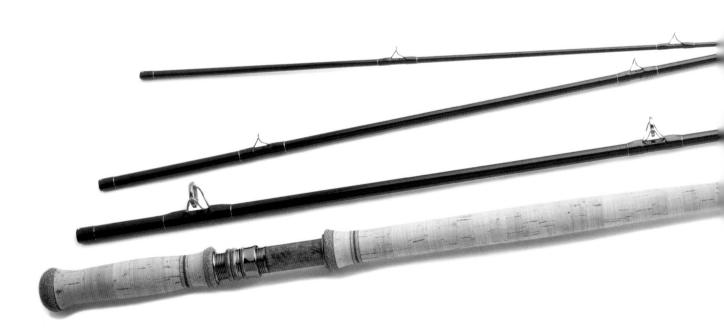

Compared with only a decade ago, today's steelheader can choose from dozens of well-built commercial two-handed rods. For those who want to cast something extraordinary, there are custom-made creations such as this beauty by CF Burkheimer.

direction on a whim, change over from tips to floating-line setups without losing performance. Through trial and error, I managed to come up with a blend of materials and different tapers that made the rod perform well. When presented the prototype to my friend John, he took one cast and nodded with approval: The first CF Burkheimer spey rod was made—15 feet for a 10-weight in three pieces. John's final test on the Dean River consecrated the design. Other anglers tried my rod and decided they too liked it. Orders have been coming in ever since.

I wanted my second spey rod to be shorter and lighter. I set out to make a 13-foot 8-weight. Remarkably, the taper was similar to the 15-foot model; so was the blend of materials. I finally decided to change a pattern cut using a different butt-taper to enhance the responsiveness. I made a mistake and cut the pattern two inches too long. After the parts were made, I had discovered my mistake but ferruled the blank any way to see what I had. It trimmed out at 13 feet three inches, and to my amazement cast unbelievably well. I ran a few more combinations to refine what I had started. This rod became known as the 8133-3 which still sells to this day. Like the 15-foot rod, it has a wonderful full-length loading quality that helps the angler relax and change direction from the

moment the cast starts until the moment the fly is delivered. I've design all these rods to have very strong tips. By blending various materials and selecting specific tapers, I've found a way for the rod to store the kinetic energy generated. I also design my rods to flex or load deeply and then rapidly unload or straighten quickly—generating very high line-speed and distance. It also helps in picking up sink-tips out of the water or casting larger flies.

The next rod would be the in-between model: 14 feet for 9-weight. I spent a fair amount of time trying to figure out what was making the other two rods work. So back to the design board I went, making several prototype sections, and decided to try a slightly different approach with a new material–mandrel combination. The end result was a rod that came out more like the 8133-3 than the 15-footer. It cycled deeply and had huge power but was quite light in hand for the amount of power it generated making it an easy rod to fish all day. It had incredible power to pick up heavy tips and still handled the floating line superbly. The original model came out 14 feet one inch but the rod just felt better at 14 foot three inches, and so the 9143-3 was born and is still considered one of the best 14-foot rods made.

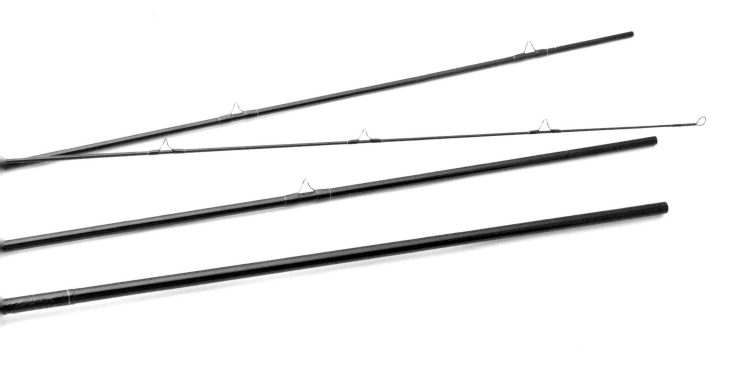

Finding a large reel that didn't weigh a ton used to be a challenge. No longer—never has the spey aficionado had so many models to choose from. This elegant, smooth-as-silk fly reel by Nautilus is as light as a feather and is priced right for the angler on a budget.

It can be argued that Sage—innovative maker of graphite rods on Bainbridge Island, Washington since the 1970s—is responsible for igniting the two-handed rod conflagration that spread rapidly during the 1990s. For years the 14-foot 9140 four-piece for 9-weight has been the spey rod of choice throughout steelhead country. Sage remains at the forefront of fly-rod technology and design.

In 2006, as I write this, there has never been so many two-handed rods available to the steelheader. Loomis alone offers 24 models—half of which are price-point models appealing to the budget-conscious among us. Most rod companies have similarly priced models available.

As for action, length, and weight, I still find something in the 13- to 14-feet range with moderately fast, yet full-flexing action and an 8- or 9-weight line designation the perfect choice for all-around practical application. I have three pet rods that fit this description: Sage 9140-4, FlyLogic 1308-4, and CF Burkheimer 8133-3. I cast all of them with either a

9/10 Airflo Delta Spey or Rio Windcutter 9/10/11.

To best find the rod suiting your style of casting, I suggest you try as many as you can, and settle on the one that feels best. An excellent way to sample many of the rods and lines available—as well as gain great insight from many of today's most accomplished casters and instructors—is to attend a so-called "speyclave." These gatherings are becoming more and more popular around the West and Great Lakes regions. Usually sponsored by a fly shop or fishing club, a speyclave is typically a two-day event with an extensive lineup of demonstrations and clinics. The demonstrators are all happy to answer your questions and talk

The Waterworks Lamson ULA Force 4 is a good example of a machined, large-capacity reel with a high rate of retrieve and a lightweight, open-frame spool. It carries a thick spey line and more than a football field of backing.

Airflo offers unique technology and tapers in their excellent-performing specialty spey lines. I am privileged to have been personally involved in their design and development.

two-handed casting. Manufacturers' representatives are present, and eager for you to try their rods, reels, and lines. Check the Internet for dates, times, and locations. Maybe I'll see you there.

REELS: A common phrase among fly-shop personnel and fly-fishing instructors is, "Buy the best reel you can afford." Although I've said it myself out of habit, I don't necessarily agree with such a general statement. First of all, what constitutes best? There are so many high-tech reels today that, in my opinion, are so grossly over-engineered their full potential

One of the most significant advances in recent years is Rio's development of interchangeable-tip fly lines for spey casting.

can never be matched by even the meanest of thoroughbred steelhead. As for durability, yes, it's important, but we're not using our reels for rock-climbing expeditions. Besides, fly reels are another piece of equipment subject to personal appeal. Better to modify the phrase: Buy a reel that's pleasing to you within a price range you can justify.

There is a multitude of reels suitable for steelhead on the market—more with the large capacity we require for large lines and lots of backing than ever before. A reel for steelhead should obviously be of sound construction, which isn't much an issue considering that any reputable tackle dealer doesn't deal in junk. It needs to be large enough to accommodate a minimum of 150 yards of 30-pound backing and the appropriate fly line to match your rod. Reels with at least a four-inch diameter are the norm with two-handed rods. For single-handers, three and a half to four inches is the reasonable choice. The rest is up to your personal preference. I admire high-tech, smooth-as-silk-drag systems that could stop a train, but I don't believe they are necessary. The choice is yours. A large to medium arbor is a nice feature that is popular these days. The large arbor makes for faster line pick-up on a fly reel's one-to-one retrieve ratio. The majority of modern reels are very quiet with only a slight, smooth clicking sound when line is pulled out. Personally, when I'm connected to the elusive steelhead, I prefer that all of my senses are engaged. I like a loud, audible click that when revved up to the RPMs that only a steelhead can attain—screams, wails, and whines. A little music if you will. That's why I still like British-made reels by Hardy. The total fish-fighting experience is a tad more *mano y mano* with their simple click-pawl drag systems. They have a classic, somewhat industrial look to them that appeals to me. Taking the sensory overload concept further, I really enjoy fishing my Hardy Bougle. There is no counterbalance on the spool—that little weight that sits across from the handle to smooth things out when a fish is on a fast, long run. Without it my Bougle, spinning at maximum RPMs, wobbles like a jackhammer, its shrill voice pulsating with high-pitched vibrato. I love it!

Whatever you desire in a reel, I can assure you it's available. If you can afford to spend $500 to $1,000, enjoy. The choices are many. Take your pick from these highly regarded manufacturers of elegant reels: Abel, Loop, Peerless, Sage, Tibor, and Hardy's new Cascapedia. In the $275 to $500 range, Bauer, Hardy, Nautilus, Ross, and Waterworks-Lamson all make excellent reels. For the steelheader on a budget,

From 3M Scientific Anglers, a superb line of spey lines is available for their loyal followers. 3M's floating steelhead taper is notably smooth-handing on single-handed rods when fishing on or just below the surface in summertime.

there are functioning reels for under $200 by FlyLogic, G.Loomis, Sage, Solitude, Temple Fork Outfitters, and Tioga. Any of these reels, in a broad range of prices, are perfectly suited to the rigors of steelheading—the rest is up to your personal preference and wallet.

KNOTS: Back in my Navy days, I was stationed on an island surrounded by the salmon-rich waters of the Puget Sound. One of the chiefs under whom I worked was a crusty, dyed-in-the-wool Pacific salmon angler. He and I saw the natural world with somewhat opposing views, but when he invited me for a morning's fishing my curiosity got the best of me and I accepted.

Trolling along as the sun was still tucked under the horizon, the chief tossed me a large plastic diving lure and barked, "Here, throw this on." I instinctively attached the lure to the 30-pound test monofilament using an improved clinch knot. Looking for his approval, I asked the chief if the knot looked acceptable. His reply was, "If you have to ask, it's probably not." Those words have never left me.

Of the boundless proven knots available to the steelheader, one needs only to choose and learn several. What's most important is to tie them properly. If any knot in the system is tied poorly, with even the slightest imperfection, you can be sure that Mr. Steelhead will find a way to capitalize on it. *Fish off!*

Practice tying your knots before you step into the river. Learn to tie them at home, expeditiously, and with your eyes closed. Tying the perfect knot should become second nature. It's not difficult, but it does require repetition and care to become proficient and consistent. If it sounds like I'm making a big deal over

this, that's because it is. Losing a hard-won steelhead due to a poorly tied knot is the sin of sins. You'll get no sympathy from me.

I use five basic knots on the terminal end of things, from the end of the fly line to the fly: nail knot, perfection loop, blood knot, triple surgeon, and double turle. I'm not much of a gadget guy, but I find the Tie-Fast nail knot tool very useful for attaching leader-butt to fly line. For the floating line, I use a straightforward nail knot with five or six wraps. For sink-tips, however, I use a slight modification. Occasionally my fly gets hopelessly hung on the bottom. After I tactfully attempt to free it to no avail and finally surrender, I want my connection to part at the fly. Far too many times I've broken off only to find the conventional nail knot had slipped off the small-diameter sink-tip. To remedy the problem I double the end of the sink-tip, then tie the nail knot over the doubled portion as normal. Before tightening the knot down I pass the standing end of mono through the loop that's been created by doubling the fly line. This knot has never let me down.

The butt end that I attach to the tip is a 12- to 15-inch piece of 30-pound Maxima brown (I like its stiffness). I then tie a small perfection loop to the end of the butt. From here I attach my tippet, which for the majority of my sink-tip work is 10-

To successfully manage a hard-bodied, sizable steelhead such as this, quality equipment and sound fish-fighting skills are a must. Bob Shoemaker hooked, fought, and landed this gorgeous doe using a CF Burkheimer 8133-3 rod and Abel 3 reel.

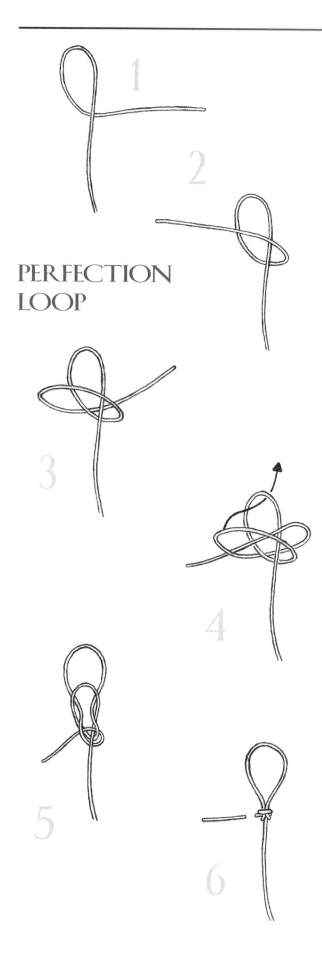

PERFECTION
LOOP

pound Maxima Chameleon, 25 to 30 inches long. I tie a perfection loop in one end of the tippet and join it with the butt section to establish the leader. It's a simple system that is easily adjusted in length. A tapered leader isn't necessary until leaders go beyond four feet in length. I never have found the need to fish a leader longer than four feet when using a sink-tip. Anything longer and the fly rides higher than the tip.

I attach the fly with a double turle knot. It's a good knot for me both practically and aesthetically. I like the way it harnesses the fly becoming one with the hook shank. The knot stays put and doesn't slide around on the hook eye and it's really easy to tie in dim light—I truly can tie this one with my eyes closed. As far as knot strength, the double turle has proven to be plenty strong.

Whenever I need to add length to my tippet, I do it quickly and efficiently with a triple surgeon knot. The triple is stronger than the commonly used double and it joins the two ends much straighter.

The last knot I employ is the simple blood knot. I use the blood when I'm building leaders with taper for floating-line work. The blood knot looses its integrity if the two pieces of adjoining monofilament have a disparity greater than .002 of an inch. Look at the diagram and learn to tie the blood knot correctly. Many people are guilty of not tightening and seating this knot correctly. It's called a blood knot for a reason—you need to tighten it down so hard that it sometimes cuts your fingers and hands. The finished knot can't have any gaps or abnormalities. Make it look like the illustration, nothing less.

PERFECTION LOOP

1. Make a small loop with tag end behind standing end.

2. Now form another loop around, and smaller than the first loop.

3. The second loop has been formed. You should be pinching both loops and the standing end leaving both loops exposed.

4. Simply lay the tag end between the two loops and secure it by pinching.

5. Pull the small second loop through the first big loop.

6. Tighten and seat knot. If you've tied the knot correctly, the tag end will be jutting out 90 degrees perpendicular to the loop.

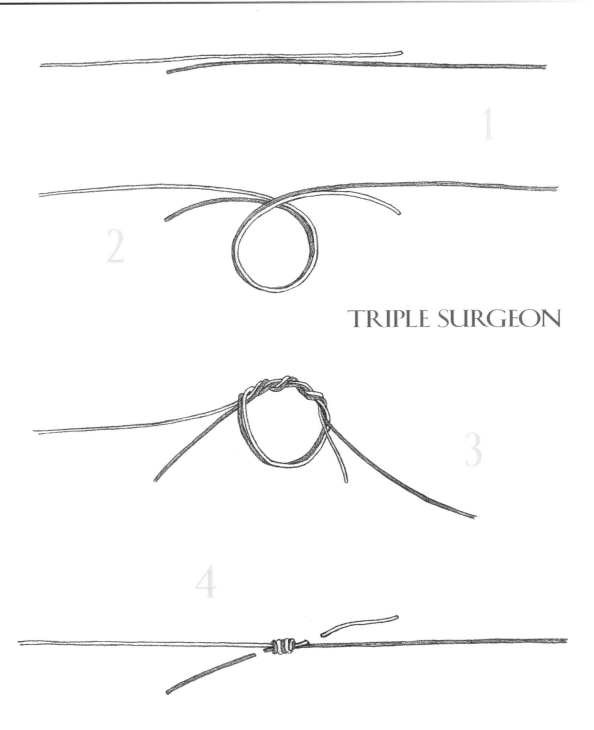

TRIPLE SURGEON

TRIPLE SURGEON

1. Lay the two ends to be tied side by side with ends opposing.

2. Form a single loop using both ends.

3. Overhand wrap both standing ends through the loop three times.

4. Lubricate and cinch down all four ends simultaneously to seat the knot.

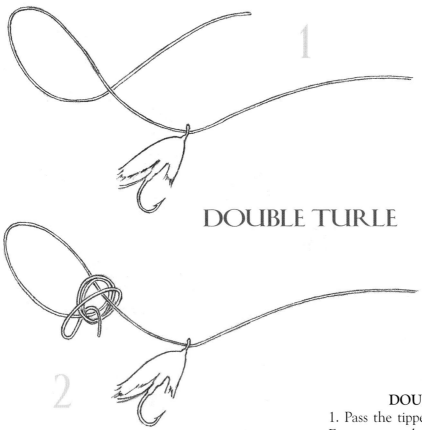

DOUBLE TURLE

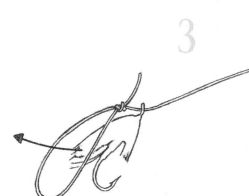

DOUBLE TURLE KNOT

1. Pass the tippet through the eye of the hook. For an up-eye hook come up through the underside of the eye, down eye through the top. Slide the fly up the leader, and let go of it.

2. To form the knot start as you would if you were tying a perfection loop: Make the first loop, followed by an encircling second loop. To this point it's just like a perfection loop. Now make a third loop around the same size as the second. In essence you should be pinching three loops—two small loops around one larger loop. Now take the tag end completely around all three loops and up through them. Pinching all three loops and the tag end in one hand, pass the big loop through the two small loops. Tighten the knot by maintaining tension on the tag end and standing line with one hand while spreading the big loop open by spreading your fingers of the other.

3. Pass the fly through the loop as shown in illustration.

4. Tighten the knot by slowly pulling on the standing tippet. Be sure to lubricate the untightened knot. The knot should be resting on the top side of the hook eye with the loop portion snuggly harnessed around the base of the eye. Clip the tag end and the double turle knot is complete.

Having a friend assist in landing your steelhead makes the process much easier on the fish, you, and your equipment. Communication and patience are two requirements for success. To the assistant: A verbal waiver of liability wouldn't hurt!

BLOOD KNOT

BLOOD KNOT

1. Lay the two ends to be tied side by side with ends opposing. Give yourself plenty of line to work with.

2. With one of the tag ends make five wraps around the other. Pass the tag end in the "v" created at first wrap. Pinch at this point leaving the "v" and five wraps exposed.

3. Now make five wraps on the opposing side. The "v" has now become an opening or hole. Pass the tag end through the hole. It needs to go through the hole in the opposite direction that the first tag end went through. If the first end is up, then the second needs to go down or vice versa.

4. Lubricate as always before tightening. To tighten, it's important that you never pull on the tag ends. This is true of all knots, not just the blood

What's wrong with this picture? I underestimated the hefty bulk of this foxy lady and was a little too aggressive with the rod when landing her. There's a fine line between fighting them aggressively and horsing them. I tend to straddle that line at times.

knot. Simply pull slowly and evenly on both ends of standing line. When you feel the knot is tightened—pull harder! Be sure that the knot is seated all the way—no gaps. Remember it's called a "blood" knot for a reason. Trim the tag ends leaving a slight nub as a safeguard to compensate for slippage. Slippage only occurs if the knot is not fully seated—a common problem. Get bloody!

NAIL KNOT
(modified for sink-tip application)

I like to tie the nail knot using a Tie-Fast knot tool, but for illustration purposes we thought we'd show the conventional tool: a nail or small dowel of some sort. Either way, the knot is tied the same. Refer to the illustration and tie the knot as you normally would, but loop the end of the sink-tip. Before tightening the knot, pass the

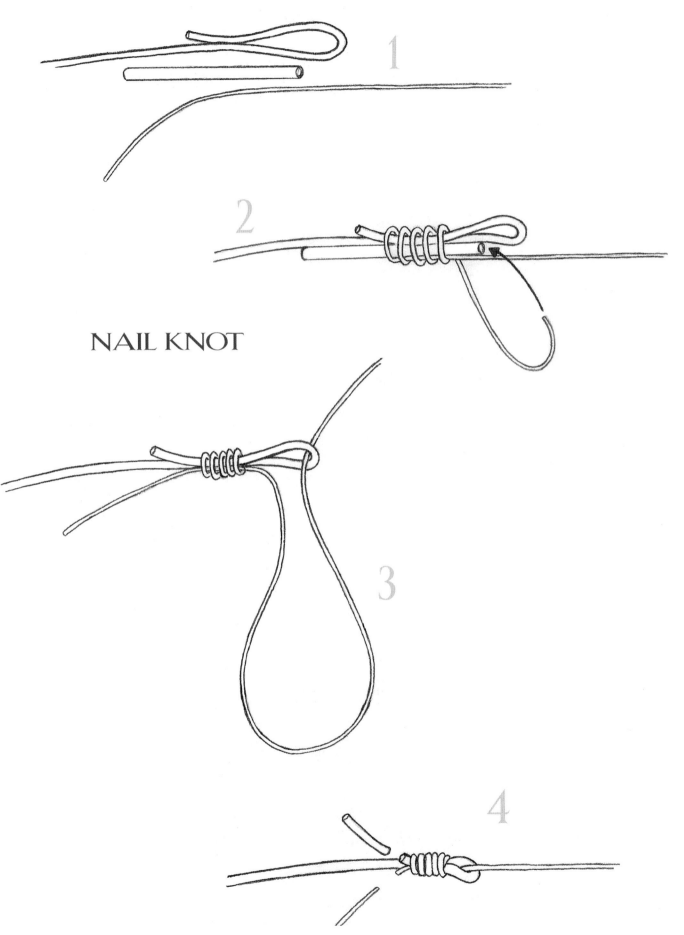

NAIL KNOT

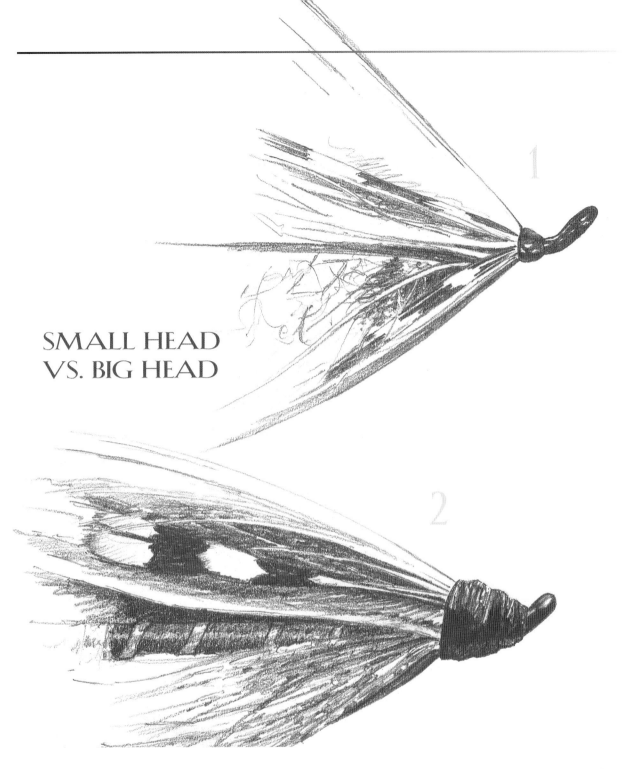

SMALL HEAD VS. BIG HEAD

standing end through the loop of sink-tip. Follow the illustration, and it will make sense.

SMALL HEAD VS. BIG HEAD

I don't believe that anyone will argue that a fly tied with a small head is the more aesthetically pleasing than one with a big head. A small head looks cleaner and doesn't detract from the fly itself. It's also the mark of an experienced fly tier—small heads don't just happen. The fly needs to be tied neatly and concisely in order to not have a big, crowded mess at the hook eye that needs to be hidden by excessive amounts of thread.

Overly large heads can also negatively affect the functionality of a fly, namely when knotted on to a floating line. Big heads tend to make the fly plane on the surface. I've seen it many, many times. The person I'm guiding informs me that his fly keeps waking and won't go under. He'll ask me if the water is too fast. Since I know the water is perfect, I say, "Let me see your fly." He pulls it in, and sure enough the fly looks as though it has a big black afro. We change to a smaller headed fly and all is well. It looks better too.

THE
FOUR
SEASONS

SUMMER
AND FALL

S O MANY RIVERS TO FISH—from the famous to the lesser known, from northern California up through Oregon, Washington, into rock 'n roll British Columbia and on over to the big bad water of Idaho. A generous three- to four-month window of opportunity provides enough variety in water types, scenery, and conditions to satisfy and challenge any steelhead junkie's soul.

Fall is the cornucopia season for the steelhead fly fisher. It's payoff time for the year-round hardcore steelhead bum who sticks it out through winter's frigid stranglehold and plays dawn-patrol to secure that golden first hour of opportunity during the dog-days of summer. It's when the ophthalmologist from Pennsylvania schedules his annual week-long sojourn to ensure his fix by vacationing to steelhead Mecca: British Columbia. Fall is when most guides make their bread and butter, and fly shop owners watch Green-Butt Skunks and spey rods fly out the door like candy canes and spiced fruit cakes at Christmas time. It's the season when most rookies loose their steelhead virginity and become addicts who can never get enough. Yeah, autumn is steelhead season.

It was mid-season on the Grande Ronde River, steelhead were plentiful and fishing was superb. I was guiding nearly every day for a strain of steelhead that swim more than 400 river miles, portaging via fish ladders at eight massive hydroelectric dams on the Columbia and Snake rivers. They must evade heavy predation by sea lions at the mouth of the Columbia, negotiating their way around countless gill nets set by tribal fisheries—not to mention the constant barrage of sport fishers' offerings of doom. But here these beautiful fish are, resting comfortably in the sanctity of the Ronde's lively riffled pools and runs nestled beneath majestic canyon walls of ancient basalt and a plethora of high-desert flora and fauna.

The majority of Grande Ronde steelhead are four to six pounds, one-salt hatchery fish with a modest count of one- and two-salt wild fish making up the remainder. The fish that inhabit the river's high-desert pools in September and October likely begin entering the Columbia River as early as May and

June—thus "summer-run" steelhead. These fish mature in fresh water. Spawning is many months in the future. (Ocean-maturing races enter their rivers, often shorter and coastal, close to spawning.)

Steelhead don't typically enter water markedly warmer than their current environment, so it's not so much the miles that takes them so long to arrive on the Ronde, but water temperature disparities between the dams along the way. Then they wait until their chosen river is of comfortable temperature before entering. To you and me, 60-degree water is frigid enough to cause hypothermia if exposed for too long. For steelhead the opposite is true: Warmwater lethargy starts to set in and really slows them down. At the very least, if the water below, say, Bonneville Dam is 54 degrees Fahrenheit, and the water coming out of the reservoir above is 61, the steelhead stay put until conditions change. The phenomenon is often referred to as a thermal-block. Anyone who has spent any length of time fishing the many tributaries of the

Columbia and Snake rivers system understands—and lives with—this term.

In the case of this particular season, conditions were good, the Ronde's water temperature hovering in the mid-50s, morning readings a few degrees cooler—perfect conditions for floating-line techniques, including fishing on top with waking patterns. In fact, for some reason, the Ronde fish relish a waking fly and can predictably be taken with dead-drifted dries. I'm a believer that given the right conditions, all fall steelhead rivers offer good surface-fly opportunity, but I must admit that the Ronde fish do show a little extra gusto for surface offerings over a wide range of water temperatures.

Steelhead, like most wildlife, are more active in low light and during the mild parts of the day. In the case of a typical fall day, in September and at least the first two weeks of October, east of the Cascade Mountain range, this is mornings and evenings. We humans should regard ourselves as wildlife (some wilder than others) and answer for ourselves, "Why is fishing best in mornings and evenings and on cool, cloudy days?" In the middle of a hot, sunny day we seek shade, and try and plan outdoor activities for mornings and evenings. It's more comfortable.

In low light, steelhead feel safe and secure. They move to shallow lies throughout a pool. Morning is an excellent time to take fish that have dropped back into the tailouts. As the sun gets high, and the steelhead feels exposed and vulnerable, they retreat back to the deeper parts of the pool or areas of heavy cover.

Consequently, when I'm guiding in early to mid-fall, we fish hard in the morning, take a midday siesta, and then hit it hard again for the last couple hours of fading light. Later in fall, the days begin to shorten as the

There is so much to do in the sparkling days of autumn. For several years in the early 1990s I spent these days along the banks of the Grand Ronde River guiding, fishing, and enjoying the spectacular scenery. No regrets, just good times.

sun sets further to the south. Shadows are deep and long and fishing can be good all day.

As I stated earlier, fishing was good that season. I knew my section of river in and around the Washington–Oregon border exceptionally well. When I say I knew it well, I knew not only which runs to fish, when to fish them, and where there was a likely looking boulder or pocket—I knew precisely where in the runs the steelhead would take and where they wouldn't. It's nice to have plenty of fish around to give feedback!

The Grande Ronde is certainly not the only steelhead water on which I have experienced this kind of intimacy. Everywhere I've guided—the Deschutes, Skagit, Sauk, Skykomish, and Stilliguamish—my rivers have all become part of the fabric of my being over the seasons. But it takes fish in the rivers. No fish, no feedback. No true intimacy. Fortunately I've experienced marvelous returns on all my rivers at one time or another. So here's a guide's dilemma when fishing is great (a good one at that): If I know that in run X the fish will consistently come out of two places in the run . . . and run Y is a beautiful, long pool with excellent flow and structure throughout, but 90 percent of the steelhead have been coming out of the first 15 yards of riffly head, and so on with all the other runs I fish . . . why do I make my clients fish the runs in their entirety and not just cherry pick? If we fish six pools in the course of the day and hook four steelhead, why not move quickly, hitting 12 pools and hooking eight or nine fish? I'll give you my answer in a minute, but first I must tell you about the first time I went cherry-pickin' when all the trees were ripe.

It was that very season on the Ronde in 1992 when I asked the same question. I had a morning off from guiding. I formulated a plan to attack the river to see how many steelhead I could hook before noon. I picked five different pieces of water, all accessible by foot, and each with a bucket or two that had been producing well. I had backup runs in mind if any of my primary spots were occupied by other anglers—crowds were far fewer then but just in case.

My fly of choice was a size 4 natural Muddler because it's a deadly no-questions-asked pattern for summer-run steelhead. None of this touchy-feely stuff. Steelhead hammer the Muddler.

Up bright and early, a cup of coffee to start my motor, and the game was on. I pulled up to the first spot, grabbed my rod and scrambled to the river. I walked right up to the primary bucket, made three casts and was into my first fish. I landed her, let her go, reeled up and drove the short distance to the next stop. Out of the truck followed by a quick jaunt to the run's first bucket and in minutes I was into another fish. One more prime boulder to cover 50 yards down from the first—fish on! The rest of the morning went this way. In short, I fished all five spots, hooking a total of seven steelhead. What's more, I beat my deadline by more than an hour: I was loaded up heading back to camp by 11 a.m. Pretty doggone cool, I sure got 'em this morning! But at what expense? I had a great time, and am glad I did it, but it's not reality. Now I'll explain why I don't do this guiding, even if it might mean more steelhead hooked.

Steelhead fishing is a total experience, not a race to see how many fish can be tallied up. When I was walking at a blistering pace down the trail I had one thing on my mind: *Find the bucket, hook the fish.* That's it. I didn't notice the dew-laced spider webs elegantly strung to the wild sunflowers along the trail. I missed out on the first glimpse of the run in its entirety, viewing it as a living entity that I am fortunate enough to become a part of, if only for a moment. I failed to notice the bighorn sheep defying the laws of physics as they majestically graze on small bits of lichen clinging to moisture darkened basalt cliffs 500 hundred feet above my pool. The rock-perched American dipper singing melodiously not 15 feet from where I stood casting frantically fell on deaf ears. I really cheated myself out of the rhythmic dance of step, cast swing, anticipate. . . .

And I have to be honest and say that every time I reeled up in search of my next conquest, I was left wondering what sort of opportunity did I leave behind. Was this the day that the run was chock full of steelhead? Every fall I experience what I call "the loaded run." The run is teeming with aggressive steelhead. I've had lucky clients hook well in to the double digits—in one run. Who knows? Maybe I would have hooked only one more fish in a pool, but it may have been a 12-pound wild fish that came from an unexpected part of the run, tearing up the entire pool, running, jumping, and thrashing the water to a froth. I'll never know.

Fishing in such a hurry is not relaxing. There is a certain element of hard work that comes with steelheading, for sure, but overall I see it as a mentally relaxing form of recreation. Go, go, go can be fun at times, but I feel the experience is much more enjoyable if we slow down and let it unfold. I have no regrets whatsoever for fishing this way that morning. It was a blast. I might even do it again someday. In the meantime, I'll fish the runs from top to bottom and anticipate the known sweet spots as they come.

So how does my little story about cherry-picking the runs pertain to fall and summer steelheading? Because these are the seasons when you are likely to encounter the conditions to conduct such an experiment. I was able to fish quickly under ideal water temperatures using a floating line with an abundance of steelhead present.

A brightly colored fall buck being released by Beau Purvis.

As we've learned, there are generally two races of steelhead: those that return in summer and those that return in winter. Winter-run steelhead spawn during the immediate spring of their arrival; summer-run steelhead winter-over in the river and spawn the following spring. Many coastal tributaries have returns of summer steelhead in late spring and early summer. Good fishing opportunities can be enjoyed during high-summer months—June through August. These are rivers such as the Stilliguamish and

Skykomish in Washington, which flow directly into the Puget Sound; Oregon's North Umpqua that joins the South Umpqua and empties directly into the Pacific Ocean; or the Dean River in British Columbia that spills into the Dean Channel. Tributaries that experience summer-run steelhead returning in the fall months are those that drain into massive river systems. Namely the Columbia–Snake stretching from Oregon and Washington to Idaho and all of its many fabulous tributaries of which there are too many to list; the Skeena in British Columbia with its storied tributaries—Bulkley, Babine, Kispiox, and Sustut; and the Fraser with its principal fall steelhead tributary, the Thompson.

Just as in the coastal rivers, steelhead begin ascending the parent rivers in early summer. The closer the tributary is to the mouth of the parent river, the earlier steelhead will show up. The little Kalama is a tributary of the Columbia River close to the Columbia's mouth, and you can find fresh steelhead there in May. Six hundred miles east, Idaho's Salmon River is virtually devoid of adult steelhead until the middle of October.

There's no magic formula for fishing for fall steelhead. As I've stated repeatedly throughout this book, conditions are what dictate how we approach the river. At least it's a baseline by which to work—we are certainly free to fish any way we choose, as long as it's enjoyable. I once saw Bill McMillan fishing the Grande Ronde with a waking fly in November when the water temperature was 40 degrees. Everyone else, including me, had put the floaters away. We were fishing sink-tips. Bill knew he'd probably hook more fish had he gone deep, but merely hooking a steelhead was not Bill's objective. He was fishing on his own terms—a personal standard he set for himself. Bill did in fact land a steelhead on his waker that day. I'm certain it was a most satisfying feeling to know he beat the odds. Choice in methodology is first and foremost subjective to personal preference.

Unfortunately, most of us have precious little time on the water. We want to optimize our chances of hooking a steelhead. Playing to the prevailing conditions is the logical approach. Fall and summer at various times see water temperatures that fall into the 50s. This is the perfect opportunity to use a floating line. My philosophy is that, if the opportunity is there, why not jump on it? Yet I still see and meet so many anglers who feel they always need to be fishing deep, even when conditions are ideal for the floater.

Do you know why steelhead are such a great fly-rod

The splendid sights, smells, and sounds of the ever-changing mood of the river are as infectious as the steelhead themselves.

fish? Because they are aggressive and MOVE to the fly.

Besides, the floating line allows the angler to cover more water with far less fuss in setting up and mending. Fishing shallow runs heavily laden with rocks and boulders is a cinch with the floating line. And fishing pocket water is fast and easy—you know exactly where the fly is and what it's doing. What's more, by fishing a floating line there is often the exciting element of a visual take, which adds tremendously to the experience. A huge swirling upheaval of water instantly followed by the big grab—c'mon, give me some of that! Sometimes the swirl happens but you feel nothing: The steelhead missed the fly. Are you going to take two steps down and make another cast like nothing happened? Hell, no! You've found a steelie, and he told you all about it. Chances are you'll get him back by firing right back out there. If the same fish missed the fly when using a sink-tip, you'd never know and the lucky dude fishing behind you, the guy you beat to the run, will soon be showing you what you missed.

I don't live and die by water temperature, but I do like to have a general idea of what's going on. As autumn nights begin to lengthen and cool, morning water temperatures are significantly lower then afternoon and evenings. During my seasons spent guiding on the Grande Ronde, this often came into play sometime toward mid-October. Water temperatures could fluctuate as many as seven degrees from morning to evening. Morning temperatures dipped into the mid-40s, which makes the typical cold-blooded steelhead less apt to move near the surface to take a fly. So we fished sink-tips. Evenings would be up into the low-50s, and we'd go back to fishing floaters. There are times in the hot, long days of late summer and early fall when the same phenomenon occurs. This time, however, morning temperatures *start* in the mid to high-50s and become warm enough in the afternoons to render steelhead lethargic. When evening water temperatures jump to 60 degrees and above, it's best to concentrate on fishing the early morning hours. Not only is it difficult to move a fish in hot water, but a hooked steelhead can become taxed by over-exhaustion to the point of death. We all need to be aware of and respectful of this.

Floating-line fishing in summer and fall is popular and fairly well practiced by the steelhead-fishing population, but sink-tip fishing probably still dominates throughout the range and season. I have friends who regularly fish the Bulkley, Kispiox and Skeena rivers in British Columbia when conditions are ideal for the floating line. They opt to fish sink-tips, claiming

that by gaining some depth they tend to hook larger steelhead that don't rise as freely to the surface as the smaller ones do. They also believe they hook more fish this way. It's all probably true, so this puts us back to fishing on our own terms—what we want to experience and gain.

I have not had a lot of experience fishing in Skeena country. I'm too too busy guiding when rivers there are at their peak. So I can't in fairness speak from much experience. I have hooked and seen hooked plenty of steelhead that qualify as big (13 pounds plus) hooked on a floating line. I have seen countless multiple-fish days fishing near the surface. But I also know that truly large steelhead tend to stay put in heavy cover, with deep refuge close by. Although individual large steelhead can show the same aggressive behavior as a smaller fish, the very nature of their holding lies may make them less vulnerable to floating-line techniques. Just as a small steelhead doesn't know he's small, I don't think a large one really knows he's big. There are no rules, only tendencies. I like it this way. We are free to draw lessons from our own experiences and fish how we please.

You've Found A Player

The swinging fly any time of year—but mostly in the fall for a variety of reasons—is subject to being struck at by a steelhead without making a connection. In other words, "He missed it!" But in your heart of hearts you know it was a steelhead. You've got adrenal tremors and the hair on the back of your neck is standing on end. You may have even seen a boil on the surface, which really confirms your belief. Either way it's time to take action. You've found a player.

The first thing I do after I've had a good pull is let the fly keep swinging. A steelhead sometimes swims it down and grabs it more securely just after they've missed it. They don't know it's not real. If that fails to work, I make the exact same cast. If that doesn't make things happen, it's time to back up a few steps and change flies. I like to change to something a size smaller and of similar color. That is to say, if I'm fishing a dark fly, I stay with a dark fly, only smaller. With the new fly, I fish a cast on each of the several steps I took upriver back to where the pull was felt. This should get him back. If not, or if you feel another pull, it's now time to change to something completely different, back up again and start over.

The new fly can be anything you want, provided it's small and markedly different in color from the original. If the first fly was a size 4 Purple Peril, and the second a size 6 Green-Butt Skunk, then the third fly should be a 6 or even an 8, something bright or drab and neutral.

If all this still doesn't work, I tie on the original fly, back up, and fish through again. I can't tell you how many times going back to the original, after all this, inevitably gets the steelhead. When going through this drill, with each new fly, it's wise to fish a step or two past the point of contact with the fish. Just because he grabbed where he did doesn't mean that's exactly where he is lying—he may have been holding several feet downstream and swam forward to slash at the fly. I think that could be why the original gets them back so often: When we tie on the original, we tend to have given up on the fish and proceed down in search of another and end up relocating our player.

That's pretty much how I do it. Each scenario tends to be a little different. Being acutely aware of what's happening on each cast often dictates what modifications may be necessary. (See Chapter 5, "How A Steelhead Takes Your Fly," to gain more insight.)

There comes a time when we have to accept that we may not get a fish to come back. You can waste a lot of time on a non-taking fish that gave you all he had on his first attempt at the fly. He might not even be there any longer, having swam on his merry way after he checked out your fly. If it happens to be that the angler missed the fish by pulling back on the rod too early, you can almost guarantee that this fish won't be coming back for more. But not always—try him again a time or two. You may be given a second chance and a huge break.

If it's a surface waking pattern that the fish missed, I go right back at it with the same fly. But this time I make a special effort to slow down the fly in the heart of the swing. This is best accomplished by wading out a step or two farther if possible. If not, extend the rod and your arm out over the water as far as you can to help slow the fly. If I feel I need to change flies, I switch to a small, size 10 Steelhead Caddis tied on with a riffling hitch. I've made the commitment to fish on top, and my steelhead showed on top, so I like to stay on top. I don't ever immediately put on a wet fly—I know it works, but I want him on top. The small floater usually gets the job done.

The Riffling Hitch

The riffling hitch is a means of placing two half hitches from the leader over the fly and behind the head in order to facilitate waking. This makes the fly

plane as it rides slightly crossways to the current. It keeps the fly riding on the surface with ease. And you can adjust the size of the wake by moving the hitch closer to—or farther away from—the head of the fly.

I tend to use a riffling hitch only with the Steelhead Caddis. Bombers and similar bulky flies if tied correctly shouldn't need it. It's important that the second half hitch be placed over the first: This is what locks the hitches in place. The hitch should be placed so the leader comes off the fly toward the bank you are fishing from. Hold the fly over the river with its head facing upstream. The side facing you is the side to apply the hitch. I like to tie my riffling hitch slightly under the fly, but favoring the proper side. It gives the fly a little lift, and rides a bit more naturally than it would with a severe 90-degree hitch. Experiment. You'll discover what you like.

Summer and fall make up half of the steelheader's angling calendar with fall getting the most play from the masses. Opportunity abounds as at no other time of year. Conditions run the gamut of extremes starting with warm, low water in late summer, and usually ending with high, cold, colored flows brought on by the first storms of winter. Fall steelhead are in the river for the duration. Any change in conditions can have a positive, or adverse, effect on their behavior. The stale pools of late summer and early fall are brought to life at the arrival of a fall freshet. Once-dour steelhead are revitalized, have found new holding lies throughout the pools, and are ready to pounce on anything that swims by. The same freshet could have cooled the river enough to bring in a new batch of fish as well. Newly arriving steelhead are usually very grabby.

After a rain, water with low to moderate visibility can be a good thing. Steelhead break free from the security of hidden lies of the gin-clear flow of a drought stricken fall river and hold very close to shore. They feel a new sense of security, once again lashing out at most any fly.

That's the story. I don't feel I need to say much more about fall or summer steelheading. If you think about it, this book is about steelhead fishing under a range of conditions that can occur anytime of year. Fall and summer ring throughout the book, intermingled with winter and spring, and viceversa. Be ready for anything.

WINTER
AND SPRING

WINTER STEELHEADING. The words alone conjure images of a cold, dark, lifeless river. Of standing waist-deep in this potential liquid death casting, hands stiff with chill for an unseen phantom that rarely ever materializes, accept for in our minds.

It's 38 degrees with a wind-driven upriver rain. Casting is difficult, but you manage to get the line "out there" somewhere. A stiff upstream mend aided by the nagging wind cures the poorly delivered cast. Hood cinched up tight and hat brim pulled down low, you are aware of the elements that enshroud you but remain impervious to their hostile attempts at sending you home.

Your fly confidently swims the viscous flow, hoping to stir an attack. Nothing. You cast again. Still nothing. It's been this way for five consecutive outings.

You can't wait until tomorrow.

This is often the case during the cold, wet months of a Pacific Northwest winter. For those in the know, there is no more peaceful yet exhilarating sport at a given time of year. It could also be deemed the most challenging form of fishing—one to several hooked steelhead a season is considered a success. With such low odds stacked against the angler, it pays to have a good game plan, and stick with it.

To the neophyte steelheader observing a veteran winter angler plying a snow-fed winter drift, it may appear to be chuck-and-chance fishing, as the angler sends out an enormous amount of line then seemingly "hangs on" as his line and fly are swept by the current. He takes a step or two, and does it again . . . and again, repeating the process until a fish is hooked or the angler completes the run. This is traditional steelheading. But as you already know, there's a lot more going on at the hands of the angler. If there wasn't, there'd be no real value to this book, other than "show and tell" by Dec.

Winter fishing conditions normally allow the angler the narrowest range of angling methods, water temperature being the most important factor in steelhead behavior. Winter water temperatures typically fall below 43 degrees Fahrenheit, which makes the steelhead lethargic and less likely to move very far to intercept a fly. By and large, the most advantageous angling approach is to fish slow and deep. I still believe—even in cold water—that we don't need to dredge the bottom. But now is the time when I might fish with lead-eye flies and a heavier sink-tip line. (If I start hanging bottom frequently, off they come.) Fishing the fly as slowly as possible is the central tactic.

Because the water is cold and the steelhead less active, they tend to hold in the slowest parts of the runs. It's less work for them. We still must cover the run in its entirety, however. I've taken many winter fish from the riffles in heads of pools. The take of a steelhead smitten with dulled senses transmits to the angler as nothing more than a slight hesitation in the swing with a barely perceptible tug. The steelhead merely closes its mouth around the fly. I am certain many steelhead takes go undetected by the winter angler—including me. If the steelhead turns with the fly, a yank and pull are sure to follow, and all is well.

A remedy to the subtle missed take? I have none: It's all part of the game. If you are so inclined, swing the rod at anything that feels different. But then you run the risk of pulling the fly away from a fish that was about to turn with it, thus ruining the chances of what was possibly a secure hook-up.

In my early days of winter steelheading, I was so eager to be where the action was, I found myself driving all over the state chasing rivers reported to have the "hot bite." It seemed that by the time I arrived the report was old news. "You should have been here yesterday" is the phrase that haunted me up and down the gravel bars. Funny, but whatever river was afflicted with poor fishing on the day of my tardiness, I would hear of another river that was producing well. And off I'd go.

It never once panned out for me. So I decided to stay home and fish the Skagit and Skykomish on a regular basis, confident that when a wave of fish showed up, I'd be there—not driving off to some unfamiliar territory. My new plan was a success; I

started hooking fish. It was nice finally to be the news maker, not the news chaser. Not only is it a smart strategy to stick to one river during the winter season, but during the short, cold days it pays to become intimate with several pieces of water. Frequent them often. Multiple passes through two or three runs seems to put the angler at better odds of finding a taker than shotgunning a bunch of runs through the day.

Cold winter flows demand a large, brightly colored fly to activate the feeding response of a lethargic steelhead. I turn to simple dressings tied of marabou, or rabbit-strip patterns. Hot orange, reds, blends of pink and white are all proven colors. When the river is running turgid, the color purple stands out well. Purple patterns have accounted for more than my share of steelhead when visibility is less than desirable. As always, there is no magic pattern, only guidelines as the fly relates to prevalent conditions. Big and bright is my choice in winter. No matter the choice in flies, it is paramount that you believe in

This thick-sided buck is the epitome of what one can hope to expect when the cottonwood trees are budding along the river.

your fly and fish it faithfully.

In winter I'm not inclined to be on the water at first light. My reason is simple: Normally the best opportunities seem to appear from midday through nightfall. As the day progresses, surface currents may warm a degree or two and help activate steelhead. Besides, it's more comfortable for me as well. I can stand in frigid water with stinging toes and fingers while combating ice-clogged snake guides with the best of them. But the fact is the best fishing comes during the mildest part of the day, and in winter that happens to be the latter half of the day. Morning is a glorious time to be on the river; I wouldn't miss it. But walking the river trail in the darkness of predawn is not part of my wintertime regime.

There is beauty all along the rivers that's often overlooked. Take time to see and appreciate—you'll be a better angler for it.

GLORIOUS SPRINGTIME

The American robin and varied thrush belong to a long list of thrush-like songbirds who are members of the family Muscicapidae. Both are perching birds. They feed on open, bare areas of ground, feasting on resplendent morsels such as raw and tasty earthworms and all sorts of insects in various stages of sexual maturity—the younger and more tender the better.

While the culinary customs of robins and thrushes may go undetected by the river's visiting steelhead angler, their melodious and haunting song does not.

The clear and happy cheer-up, cheer-up, cheerily of the American Robin, and the fading call of the varied thrush echoing through the darkness of silent forests mean only one thing: SPRING STEELHEAD.

Ascending rivers of the Pacific Northwest from March through May, spring steelhead are categorically winter-run fish. They arrive from the ocean sexually mature, filled with eggs and milt, and spawn during the season of their return. Rock-hard and chrome bright, spring steelhead are nearly always wild fish. Their average size is large. Thickly built, heavy with ripening spawn, it is not uncommon for a fish of 30 inches to weigh as much as 12 pounds. Then there are the true monsters of spring: bucks and does 36 to 40 inches or longer weighing in the high teens and 20s. A friend of mine calls them egg-wagons. Most are main-river spawners. They don't have to travel great distances as some of their summer-run cousins do. This enables them to ferry a heavy load the short distance to the spawning grounds, where they use their massive tails to excavate river rock and build their redds. Whatever the theory for their potential great size, spring steelhead and the rivers they inhabit provide some of the greatest—often terrifying—sport in all of angling.

It's difficult to describe in the written word, but for me and many others, spring steelhead hold a mystique and intrigue like no other race of steelhead. Possibly it's the culmination of many factors that make this so.

Northwest winters are long. Water temperatures stay low, which in turn makes a difficult proposition that much more challenging. To make fishing even harder, most of the steelhead returning to the rivers during the heart of winter are of hatchery origin, genetically diluted nearly to the point of being entirely unresponsive to the fly. But you persist in fishing during these short, dank days because you are a steelheader. Then slowly but noticeably the days get a little longer; the air and water begin to warm a degree or two. Before you know it, the half-hearted pluck from a small, lethargic hatchery fish is now a deliberate and heavy yank. Your steelhead turns and heads violently downriver, cartwheeling in an effort to free itself from your sizzling line.

The instant you catch a glimpse of the airborne fish you can't believe your eyes. You're not sure what's so different about this fish from the few you've hooked during the last couple of months, but it's definitely different. Bigger, maybe? Brighter? All you can see is black and chrome, twisting and turning in

Here my pal Scott O'Donnell prepares to release a magnificent Sauk River doe that clearly defines the term "egg-wagon."

a wash of spray. Then you see the steelhead up close and it all makes sense. Yes, this fish is brighter than most you can remember. And although this steelhead isn't necessarily longer than some of your previous winter catches, its girth is substantially greater.

Then you notice the fins. Not just the presence of the adipose fin—commonly removed from hatchery steelhead—but all eight beautiful, translucent fins, each one full and straight-rayed as Nature had intended, not left to stunt and deform in an unnaturally crowded hatchery rearing pond.

Once the first wild steelhead of the year is released, you know more will follow in the days and weeks to come. The intensity of your mental approach to the river—as well as your excitement level—is kicked up a few dozen notches as winter gradually turns to spring. Visions of large, chrome steelhead fresh from the ocean holding in shallow riffles under dark, cloudy skies consume you 24 hours a day. And the scent of budding cottonwood trees filling the air makes your neck swell and your tongue hang out as if you're in steelhead rut.

The joy of fishing for steelhead in springtime is half the fun. The object, however, is to catch one. For that you need a river. The choices are many. Throughout the steelhead's natural range, just about

any winter-run river will have a run of late-returning natives. Sounds simple: This leaves southeast Alaska, British Columbia, Washington, Oregon, and northern California for exploration. Easy enough. Let's go.

Not so fast—first you must decide how you want to fish. Not all rivers attracting spring steelhead are conducive to the swung fly, or what I like to call the classic approach.

Many coastal streams are short, narrow, and quick. These places are better left for nymphing techniques. I would rather spend my time on a river with quality fly water where I can make moderate-to-long casts and swing my fly in wait of the big grab.

When seeking your river, you must take special care to check your state or province's angling regulations. Many rivers and streams have special closures and restrictions. Look for the rivers with catch-and-release or fly-only seasons beginning in February, March, or April. This is usually a good indicator of a quality fishery during prime time.

Once you have settled on a river or two, it's time to get busy. I happen to live in a Mecca for spring steelhead. I have a choice of world-class Puget Sound rivers such as the Skagit, Sauk, Skykomish, Stilliguamish, and Nooksack. Not far out of range are the storied waters of the Olympic Peninsula such as

the Hoh, Sol Duc, and Queets rivers. With all this water, it would be easy to waste enormous amounts of time driving and exploring in a heated rush looking for a pot of gold. I've done it. Although it was exciting, I never found what I was looking for. Not, that is, until I settled on one or two rivers close to home where I could fish often and at my leisure, allowing me to learn their subtle moods and intricacies.

Spring steelhead don't waste a lot of time lingering in the estuaries; spawning time is here. Like cows ready for milking, they need to get to the barn. Hang around the barn long enough and you'll get cows.

Contrary to what some people believe, the steelhead we are fishing for in spring are neither sitting on the redds, nor dark and spawned-out. They are fresh, silvery fish, often with sea lice. They are holding in short-term resting water as they make their way to the spawning grounds. True, you might occasionally stumble too far in to a tail-out during low-light conditions and have your fly attacked as it trespasses through an active spawning redd. You might even hook a steelhead nearing sexual maturity and has lost some of its ocean bulk and brightness. But these occasions are surprisingly rare. If you do happen upon a visible pair of actively spawning steelhead, hold your fly and enjoy the marvel with your eyes. It is unfair and unsporting to deliberately harass them at this point. I have, on more than several occasions, witnessed some egotistical cheat practicing this unethical behavior. It sickens me, and I wonder how he can feel good about himself and his so-called sport.

Short-term resting or holding water comes in many forms but is always where the current slows from the main flow. Sometimes it is only a five-foot area hidden in a fast drop or chute, barely distinguishable amidst the froth of white water. Other times it may come in the form of a 100-yard-long glide as a soft flow of current sweeps gently over deeply anchored boulders and subtle bottom contours. Slots, depressions, edges—any structure that somehow disrupts the main flow—and of course the ever-fishy choppy riffle are used by migrating steelhead for temporary resting.

Picture yourself forced to walk three miles in a heavy windstorm. A cold, stinging rain is smacking you straight in the face. You are in an open field with small, undulating knolls spaced unevenly throughout. Several stands of trees are present, as are a couple of tractors and a barn. You are heading east to the barn with the wind howling straight at you from the east. Do you trudge forth for the barn walking in the wide open, fighting the wind and rain? Probably not. The easiest, most comfortable—not to mention instinctive—way would be to follow behind the knolls as best you can. You would take a direct path behind the trees, duck in behind a tractor for a break, then head for the barn as it breaks the wind until you safely reach it. Understanding this analogy makes it simple to see why steelhead swim and hold where they do in a swift-flowing river.

Because we are fly fishing and can send our flies only so deep in flowing water, we must also edit out water that is too deep and/or heavy. It's possible we might locate a slowing of the flow only to find that it's 12 feet deep out there. Steelhead may be holding there, but we would be hard-pressed to get our flies close enough to them. A general rule of thumb is that good steelhead fly water is from three to six feet deep. This makes sense when you consider the hydrology of a river when looking for prime resting water. The deepest water in the river is usually in the main channel, where the flow is heaviest and all but the largest of boulders have been scoured away. Luckily for us, this means that the majority of steelhead are holding relatively close to shore.

Well-rested spring steelhead often hold so close to shore that they are easily overfished or spooked off their lies without the angler even knowing. Wading deep and casting far has its virtues, but sound work ethics and attention to minute details in presentation are essential if you seek success consistently.

When preparing to fish a piece of water, slow down and take a look at the big picture. It's so easy to get caught up in the chuck-and-chance mentality: barging into the river up to your waist and heaving as much line as you can. (As much line as you think you can that is!) The best casts are those that turn over completely, landing with a relatively tight line. This gives you instant control. If you are trying to cast 80 feet of line only to leave it in a heap of disarray at 60, you might as well be fishing with a piece of cedar bark. The fly never gets a chance to fish. Back off and cast a comfortable length that you can control while fishing down a run. We all want to be able to cast farther, I know. But I guarantee you that by not struggling to gain those extra few feet, you will hook more steelhead through improved presentation. And in time your casting will improve automatically.

Fly selected and knotted to your tippet, heart beating at a slightly accelerated clip, you step into the water. Where do you think the very first potential resting lie is? Once you think you have an idea, take a few steps upstream before you start casting with a short line—a very short line. Your mission is to fish methodically toward the lie. I'm no longer surprised at how many fish are hooked on these first few, short casts before the fly has entered what I thought was the bucket. Conversely, it's advisable to fish your fly several more paces after you think you've passed through the hot-zone. Take a tailout for example. The water seems to pick up excessive speed and doesn't feel good anymore. Make a few more casts. I call this "feathering" the run. These added measures take only a few minutes and can sometimes mean the difference between going home fishless and going home with a healthy dose of steelhead euphoria.

Another area of presentation that is easily overlooked or hurried comes at the very end of the fly's swing. Too often we are in such a rush to get the fly back out there that our offering is pulled from the water long before it has completed its productive path. Remember that a resting, undisturbed steelhead will hold very close to shore. These are the ones we like—fish for them! Steelhead also love to follow the fly before committing to a full take. I've seen them practically beach themselves while so intent on chasing the feathery illusion that just invaded and passed through their domain. Give them a chance to take the fly by fishing it until it hangs below you or is no longer swinging. Imagine that on every cast you make there is a—no, make that two—steelhead in hot pursuit of your fly.

In order to fish your fly to a position directly downriver from you, select the right line. This is where heavy sinking lines that so many people think they need do more harm than good. I want a line that fishes at efficient depth in the heart of the swing, yet is not so long and heavy that it hangs the bottom before it sweeps into the equally productive shallows. Have my cake and eat it too? You bet.

Typical spring water temperatures in the Pacific Northwest range from low to high 40 degrees Fahrenheit. Plenty warm to activate the aggressive behavior inherent in wild steelhead. In other words, your fly doesn't have to hit 'em upside the head; they will come to it. This doesn't mean we can get away with the use of full-floating lines, but bottom dredging is far from necessary. A fly swimming just a couple of feet below the surface at a nice slow speed is enough to stir an attack from an aggressive spring steelhead holding in six feet of water. Sink-tips ranging from 10 to 15 feet long and weighing from 120 to 160 grains per foot do the job nicely on most good fly water. I use a 13-foot 160-grain type 6 tip for nearly all my spring steelheading. If I feel I need to make an adjustment in depth, I change my casting angle, lengthen or shorten my leader, or change to a fly of compensating weight or design—long before I change my sink-tip.

If you are not already using a two-handed rod, I strongly suggest you think about it. Not just for spring steelheading, but during every season. With the exception of the smallest of creeks, the advantages of a two-hander over a single hander is easily tenfold wherever steelhead swim. The two-handed rod enables you to:

- Cast adequate distances with ease.
- Fish with obstacles behind you.
- Cover a piece of water nearly twice as fast.
- Mend to great distances.
- Control your fly's speed with precision throughout its entire drift.
- Save wear and tear on your casting arm thus allowing you to fish comfortably all day.

Most of all, two-handed spey casting is a ton of fun. The only disadvantage in using a two-handed rod—and one easily fixed with some conscious effort—is in the short game: covering those oh-so-important steelhead holding close to shore. We have a tendency to want to cast the two-handed rod way too far. I am guilty of this. Hell, it's a blast. But it makes no sense to cast 90 feet when the productive water is only 30 feet wide. By the time the long cast has swung into the productive water, you have wasted valuable time. That piece of cedar bark could have fished it just as well. Once the fly has reached the good water, it's not uncommon for the fly to stop swinging precisely where it should have started. At least it appears that way, inclining us not to fish our cast out to the very end. Cast the distance that the water dictates and you should be in good shape. It's rare that steelhead appear magically in the middle of the river simply because we can reach it.

I guide steelhead fly anglers on Northwest rivers somewhere in the neighborhood of 120 to 150 days a year under a myriad of conditions. From the blistering sun and heat of a high-desert river on a mid-September day, to the cool sanctity of a chill mist permeating through hemlock boughs and moss-covered maples of a west side glacial-fed stream. These varied conditions are the heart and soul of life in and on the river. Like symphony conductors, Nature's climactic conditions orchestrate the river's every note and mood. As steelhead anglers, we must play first chair and adapt to the ever-changing rhythms.

Variances in conditions are never as great as they are in early spring. Winter can be reluctant to let go as the northerly sun is not yet in position for a full display of spring. The river may run low and frigid. Days later, clear warm skies bring the river's temperature up several degrees and slightly raises its level with newly melted snow. Then a heavy, warm rain comes that lasts several days and overfills the river with

has already proven itself well under these conditions, so you can't go wrong there. When the river gets low and has seen a lot of angling pressure, try something smaller in somber tones—I rely heavily on my own Olive Garden and Jungle Cock Rock. Make adjustments and experiment. Steelhead survive on instinct with a brain no larger than a pea. A little human cognizance of our natural surroundings can go a long way.

The late Monty Howard, a gem of a man, honored both the Skagit River and me with his companionship this foggy April morning. The steelhead, in turn, honored Monty. There's nothing like time on the river to bond friendships and create everlasting memories.

brown, turbid water—only to become low, cold, and clear again as winter rears back for another go.

In order for the steelhead angler to keep up with spring's topsy-turvy conditions, it pays to show up with a well-stocked fly box. Fly selection is not as complicated as we sometimes make it. Some basic guidelines, a bit of common sense, and a whole lot of faith will have you fishing the right fly every time.

As a starting point, remember that spring steelhead are fresh from the sea where they have been feeding on remarkably large marine life forms such as other fishes and squid. The rivers are still on the cool side. They are flowing at robust levels. It makes sense to use a substantial fly in any of the proven colors: orange, purple, red, and black. Squid have long, undulating appendages; so should your flies. If the river becomes high and dirty switch to something larger yet and experiment with various colors. Purple

In spring I am confident enough to fish all day. Low-light conditions are always the preferred times, but the glare of midday spring sunshine should not be a deterrent. Fish places that have some form of cover whether it's shade, choppy water, heavy structure, or a deep, green slot. I've even taken spring steelhead on clear, shallow flats in full direct sunlight. There's an old saying that "steelhead are where you find them." This is never more true than in springtime. Fish all day if you desire. Fish the runs from top to bottom. Count on spring steelhead showing up unexpectedly anywhere in the run, not only in the sweet spots. Allow no stone to go unfished.

This spring, when you hear the song of the robin and varied thrush as you walk along the gravel bar, know that the steelhead will not be far away. Nor will I for that matter.

ASKED
AND ANSWERED

HENEVER I GIVE A SLIDE-SHOW PRESENTATION or teach a formal clinic, one of my favorite aspects of the event is answering all the enthusiastic questions. For one, it keeps me on my toes—I never know what concern will be tossed my way. And two, I have a sincere interest in what's on the minds of other anglers concerning my very own favorite pastime.

There are some interesting dynamics that take place during a question-and-answer session. There's always "the front-row guy" present. Notebook in hand, he invariably ends up following me to my car still asking questions long after the show is over. Then there's the guy who doesn't really have a question but takes the floor nonetheless to share in his own experiences. The majority of the eager attendees voice a single pertinent question that most, if not all, in attendance have a keen interest in.

This book would not be complete without a solid question-and-answer session. With a tip of the hat to Jock Scott's "Asked and Answered" in his classic *Greased Line Fishing for Salmon* (1935), I wholeheartedly thank all those who participated by submitting a thoughtful question or comment—I'm sure you are all present and accounted for: The front-row guy, the storyteller, the pertinent-question asker, and of course an interested audience.

Switching From Floater to Sink-Tip

Dear Dec:

What are your criteria for switching from a floating line to a sink-tip line? Do you use a different style of steelhead fly when using a sink-tip?

DALE WASHBURN
Richland, Washington

Dear Dale:

Water temperature and clarity play key roles in determining at what level I present my flies. I'm comfortable fishing on or near the surface when water temperatures reach 48 degrees Fahrenheit. I like at least three feet of visibility as well. In winter and spring I stick with a sink-tip line and large flies irrespective of water temperature. Winter fish are difficult enough to come by; I don't want to leave anything to chance. There are several styles of flies that don't seem to fit well when fishing a floating line. Although they would probably work, marabous, rabbit strip flies, and similar styles are better suited to plying the depths with a sink-tip. Other than that, any pattern is suitable to fish with a floating line in the right sizes.

What a Player—What Did I Do Wrong?

Dateline July 27, 2005 somewhere on the Manistee River:

Anchor–D–Flick–Swing. Anchor–D–Flick–Swing, Step. Anchor–D–Flick–Swing. It feels good as the 100-foot cast sails over the seam toward the opposite bank. It must be cast number 999. It's getting kind of late now, about 9 p.m. There go a few olives and caddisflies. There goes my friend the kingfisher. Then KERPLUSH!! The water explodes. I am jarred out of my doldrums, keenly aware. I have instinctively dropped the 18-inch loop of line that I hold, but reflexively strike to the side: nothing—*nothing*. Now I am starting to shake. Frustrated, I yell out—I have just blown my chance. Calm down cast again. No, No slow down. So I step back about six feet. I check my fly, check my knot. It looks a little frayed right by the fly. Could it be wear? Could it be tooth marks? Cut it off and retie, then calm down. Once again it's

Anchor–D–Flick–Swing, Step. Now I'm back to about the same spot. SWOOSH, a toilet flushes right under my fly. This time I let it sit still. I even twitch the skating size 4 Bomber a few times. Nothing happens so I cast again and again. Now I'm totally rattled so I step back and switch to a dark sinking fly, a Green-Butt Black Bear on a size 6 double. Once again cast, swing, step, through the spot: Once again, nothing. I try a smaller surface skater, a size 6 Waller Waker. Where is it? It's getting too dark now to see the fly, as it crosses the seam. Nuts! I have to leave the river while there is still a trace of light. Whew! What a day—what a player! Steelhead 1, Angler 0. But a good time was had by all. Okay, Dec, what did I do wrong? How do you hook a player, especially on top?

Thanks,
TERRY TATARCHUK
Cadillac, Michigan

Dear Terry:

Terry, my friend, I commend you for fishing on top with your Bomber. You're a man after my own heart. When you fish a surface fly, however, you must realize that you are going to see things that you'd never see fishing subsurface—namely, the steelhead that will move to but not take the fly. I've seen it hundreds of times. There is nothing that says when a steelhead reacts to the fly it means a positive take will follow. Savor in the awesome two boils you witnessed. Sounds like you did everything correctly in your explanation of the event. If I were to be critical of one thing it would be that you tried to set the hook, as you put it, "reflexively." Don't do it pal! And don't "drop" the loop; let the fish pull it out. When a fish misses a buoyant fly such as a Bomber, I first change to a Steelhead Caddis. I was fishing on the surface in the first place, so I give the fish (and me) another shot at the surface. The Caddis is less buoyant and rides in the surface film rather than on it. It stands less of a chance of being pushed away by the water that is displaced by the fish's mass—which could have been a factor in your situation. There's lots more to be said: Refer to Striking the Fish at the close of my Presenting Your Fly to the Fish Chapter and So You've Found a Player? in the Four Seasons Chapter.

The Perils of Fishing Too Deeply
Dec:

In a magazine article you warned about fishing too deeply—about hanging up and losing fishing time, which I completely agree with. What do you consider not deep enough and what are some of the

key points to look for in the swing that would tell us the fly is not fishing in the correct depth zone? Thanks in advance and tight lines!

PAUL PETERSON
Thunder Bay, Ontario

Dear Paul:

When I choose to fish a sink-tip, as I explained in my chapter on presentation, I want my fly to fish at least mid-depth. Anything less and I lose confidence. I wish there were a hard fast way to know if your fly is running at the correct depth. There is a certain feel to the pull of the line that let's me know I'm in the right zone that comes from experience. I also know that the majority of good steelhead fly water has a certain sameness to it, and my 13 feet of 150-grain type 6 10-weight tip handles just about everything I encounter—hint, hint. When you have some downtime on the river, experiment by deliberately trying to touch bottom with your fly. Make repeated casts at increasingly steeper angles upstream; mend appropriately until you find the one that gets the fly to touch bottom. Try it in a few different runs. Make a mental note as to where you consistently find bottom—if it's just before the fly comes tight and begins to swing, you've found the perfect line that you can fish confidently without hanging bottom on a normal fishing cast. If you can't find bottom until your casts are made severely upriver, or you never find the bottom, I think you need a heavier tip. I've experimented with this extensively, and it truly has given me an understanding of what various sink-tips are capable of.

Becoming a Steelheader
Dec:

What skills are required to become a complete steelhead angler and how does one go about learning them?

Sincerely,
CHRIS CORNELIUS
Spokane, Washington

Dear Chris:

As for physical skills to become a complete steelheader, you need to have a pulse and be able to walk. The rest is desire, burning passion, and a willingness to devote a lot of time to the pursuit. A keen sense of awareness and an open mind are also paramount if one wishes to be successful. Your river time needs to be varied—fish in any and all conditions at all times of year. Embrace the fact that steelhead fishing is not about numbers and who catches the most fish. The "complete steelheader" is at one with himself and Nature. I've tried my best to teach you everything you need to know about how to catch a steelhead in this book; read anything you can find by Roderick Haig-Brown about why we are out there in the chase.

Searching for a Dry-Fly River

Dec:

What's your choice for the most productive dry-fly river?

JIM BRANNAN
Costa Mesa, California

Dear Jim:

At various times and under the right conditions, all the great summer and fall rivers can be productive with surface flies—the Dean River and all the important Skeena tributaries in British Columbia are high on the list. In my experience, Grande Ronde River steelhead in the fall respond consistently to dry flies under a wide range of river conditions.

What Conditions Inhibit a Steelhead From Taking?

Hi Dec:

My question as a beginning steelheader is what environmental factor is the most influential to the steelhead in the way of inhibiting their drive to take a fly? In other words, is it water temperature, level, clarity, barometric pressure, etc.? Not that it would keep me from fishing but solving the mysteries is part of the fun and learning about these amazing animals is a treat.

Thank you,
RYON McHURON
Albany, Oregon

Ryon:

In my observations, the most inhibiting factor is water temperature. The cold-blooded steelhead is susceptible to both cold- and warm-water lethargy. Barometric pressure and lunar phases can also influence a steelhead's disposition. But I'm like you—these things are not going to be an "inhibiting factor" to me. Consequently, I have not made a direct study on how the moon affects the bite, but I have noticed a decline in productivity during a full-moon phase. Steelhead definitely turn on as the barometer is falling and tend to be a bit zip-lipped at the onset of high pressure. After high pressure has stabilized for a couple of days, things get back to normal. Clarity and river level may be factors in the ability to find willing takers, but I've seen no evidence that supports that these things put them off. Steelhead are mysterious, Ryon. I'm glad they can't talk—it might ruin the mystique.

How Much Does Color Matter?

Dear Dec:

1. I have been fly fishing for steelhead in the Skeena system for a number of years. I recently ran across a book of the record steelhead landed for about a 50-year period and noticed an interesting piece of data. Something like 80 percent of the record steelhead had been landed on an orange or yellowish orange fly: Fall Favorite, Skykomish Sunrise, et al. In your experience, how much does color matter? By the way, most of my British Columbia fish have been on black (a black leech-type fly with red Flashabou that I tie and call the Red October) but several have been on Bob Clay yellow-and-black patterns. What colors work best in your experience?

2. What turns the steelhead on to the aggressive behavior they display when taking flies on the swing? Home water for me is the Deschutes River. One day the steelhead seem to attack the fly, and the very next day they are passive and ignore it. Same river, same runs, same weather but very different behavior—I can't figure it out.

Thanks,
MIKE ELLSWORTH
Camp Sherman, Oregon

Dear Mike:

1. I can't, in good faith, tell you that color in a steelhead fly matters to a significant degree. I honestly believe that the last steelhead I hooked would have taken any of a number of different colors. Yellow-and-orange is a time-tested color scheme—one I use myself quite often. I caught my largest steelhead ever on a yellow-and-orange marabou, but I can't believe he wouldn't have taken a black General Practitioner on the same cast. If the majority of anglers on a specific river are fishing a Green-Butt Skunk, then the majority of steelhead (even the big ones) will be caught on a Green-Butt Skunk.

2. Regarding the passive-aggressive behavior you describe, steelhead are noticeably affected by barometric pressure. There are some biologists who dismiss this theory as myth, but I've spent far too many days on the water witnessing a direct correlation in pressure changes and steelhead activity—or lack thereof. Steelhead possess a gas-filled sac in their dorsal cavity called a swim bladder. It controls the steelhead's buoyancy. A change in barometric pressure could have an effect on the swim bladder thus temporarily turning the steelhead off or on. This could be one of many determining factors that alter the mood of your Deschutes steelhead. I've witnessed this same Jekyl-and-Hyde behavior many times myself on the Deschutes—probably more than any other river I've spent

On-stream clinics conducted by knowledgable, experienced instructors are an invaluable investment. Steelhead fishing is not rocket science. That's the real value—learning, confirming, and believing that it's all pretty simple stuff.

time on. Subtle changes in the dam-controlled nature of the Deschutes's water level could also be a culprit.

Migration could be a factor as well. Steelhead bite best once they have stopped for a rest. I've gotten all kinds of plucks, pulls, and boils with no hook-ups on days that I knew the steelhead were just motoring by. The following day, if I'm in the right place, can be phenomenal fishing with many solid hook-ups. I'm not exactly sure how it all ties in, but I'm acutely aware that on the best days ALL the river's natural life is up and happy. Birds are actively singing, insect life is noticeably prevalent, I usually see porcupines and skunks in the morning's darkness, and deer are always present somewhere close by actively grazing. I too feel great on those days with or without steelhead. On those bleak days when you know there are fish in the river but not biting, I scarcely hear a bird or see wildlife activity all day. Let's chalk it up to another of Nature's splendid mysteries.

Ridiculous Questions on the Water
Hi Dec:

Time to add some humor. Tell us about some of the ridiculous questions your anglers have asked over the years. Example: "Wow! That is a huge rock! Does it go all the way to the bottom?" Or how about that guy who never believed you about how deep the runs are?

BEAU PURVIS
Silverdale, Washington

Beau:
Every winter and spring throughout the 1990s a man named Scott from Seattle employed my services as a guide for several days. He was definitely a regular. As with all my regulars, we became good friends. Scott obviously respected my opinion and ideas concerning steelhead fishing, but he often responded to some of my answers to his questions with an incredulous, "Mmmm, I don't know about that." Sometimes it would admittedly strike a nerve in me. One day he asked how deep is the run we were fishing. I responded very caring and professionally by explaining to him that good steelhead fly water is three to

six feet deep etc. I told him that the water he inquired about fell within that range. His reply? "Mmmm, I don't know; I think it's deeper than that." I remained quiet—on the outside. On another day he asked the same question, with a repeat of the previous scenario. After several years of this I couldn't stand it any longer when he asked the same question as we were pulling out of the run we just fished.

"Dec, how deep was that run?" he asked

"Five feet at most, Scott," I said matter of factly.

"Mmmm, I don't know; it has to be at least eight."

Okay, that's it! I fumed to myself. I dropped my oars and stood up in my boat.

"Scott, buddy, you've been fishing with me all these years—don't you trust me?" I shouted. "Steelhead water is three to six feet deep! Do you honestly think I would fish you in shit water?"

Scott then calmly said: "I have a hand-held depth finder that I use on lakes. I'll bring it next time."

"You're damn right you'll bring it," I said with a friendly yet reserved chuckle.

Scott's next scheduled trip with me was in two weeks. I would have to wait for a little poetic justice. Two weeks later Scott showed up with his depth finder. Being the professional that I am, I waited until after we fished the first run of the morning to reveal the facts. (I must admit, the childish part of me had the urge to forgo the first piece of water to show Scott I was right.)

I anchored the boat at the top of the run, so that when we were done fishing we'd be in position to float down and check the depth of its entirety. All systems go. I positioned the boat over what would be the heart of the swing. Scott plunged the depth finder over the side and was silent.

"What's it say, amigo?" I asked

"Well, it's reading three feet," Scott answered hesitantly. "Okay, now it says four feet, now five, back to four."

We continued floating. Scott kept barking numbers as we floated: "Four, four, six, three, two, five, five, three, three, four…" I was impressed and keenly interested in the fluctuating numbers. The bottom contour of the run was much more dramatically structured than I thought. Cool.

"Okay, Scott, did I prove my point?" I proudly exclaimed.

"Mmmm, we'd better check some others," he said.

We did. During the next several seasons, Scott and I checked the depths of at least 50 prime steelhead runs on four different rivers in Oregon and Washington. Every single one of them was three to six feet deep with the same undulating bottom contour. Between having fun fishing

and checking the depth of the runs, Scott nevertheless remained doubtful of my knowledge.

"Hey Scott, check out the mule deer up on that hill."

"Mmmm, I don't know, I think they're blacktails."

Reluctant Takers on the Dangle and More

Dec:

Greetings from the Skagit Valley. Your invitation to participate in a steelhead discussion and contribute to your new book, *A Passion For Steelhead*, is impossible to turn down.

Your magazine articles have always been educational and exciting reads. In particular, sharing your experience of visualizing summer steelhead approaching and taking the fly was very much appreciated and I look forward to reading more in the book. I wish to comment on and ask your opinion about the behavior of both summer and winter from the standpoint of the angler. The perspective I'm referring to is not visual—standing on the bank—but one of feeling and intuition. The tactile sensing of the tension in the fly line during the wet-fly swing is the means for understanding and imagining what is happening below the water surface. It has become for me one of the pleasurable and interesting aspects of steelhead fishing. Tension in the fly line during the swing is determined by many factors: current speed, position of the line in relation to the rod tip, debris on the fly, size and weight of the line, and, ultimately, a steelhead picking up the fly.

Let's look at the possible scenarios through the angler's feel of the line:

The Non-Take: The fly is swinging in the current and the steelhead approaches, opens its mouth, and closes upon the fly and continues to swim with the current. The angler has no sensation through the line. The fish opens its mouth, drops the fly, and goes about its business. Nymphing for rainbow trout produces this scenario frequently—I assume the same is so with steelhead even though they are not actively feeding. It probably happens more times than we would like to think. Have you witnessed this behavior?

Yes, I've seen it many times. The steelhead picks up the fly as it is swimming with the pace of the fly, stays with it for a second or two, and drops it—all the while the angler is oblivious.

I can think of two times when I sensed this happening and got lucky. While fishing a Grande Ronde River seam, the line tension decreased as if the fly had moved into slower water, but was still in the fast current. All of a sudden a fish was on. I speculated that the fish picked up the fly and swam faster than the current before it turned and brought the line tight. To confirm this I made repeated casts into the seam and could not reproduce the same decrease in line tension as the fly swung through the fast water. The other time occurred while fishing the Sauk River. The deeply sunken fly moved into slack water and dangled there for three or four seconds. The first retrieving strip produced a solid hook up. The fly was imbedded deep inside the mouth of the steelhead. The fish could have easily opened its mouth, dropped the fly and continued resting. I guess it is better to be lucky than good.

The Pluck: The angler feels "plucks" and "nips" that start the imagination spinning—is it a steelhead? Experienced steelhead fishers can distinguish the rapid pecking of a rainbow or bull trout and white-fish, but let the fly swing to completion while thinking of their options. I usually make a few more casts with the same length of line. If no more plucks are felt, I fish on through. On several occasions, a steel-head has taken the fly a few feet below where the first pluck occurred. One speculates that the fish dropped back a few paces or that there was more than one fish. If I suspect a steelhead, I return to that area after it is rested with a new color fly. This often results in a take and makes me feel very smart! You have advised a similar change.

The Increased Line-Tension Take: The astute angler experiences line tension as the line and fly swings through the water. A fish picks up the fly and slightly increases or decreases the tension depending upon its mood or behavior. The ability to recognize this difference enhances the fishing experience. This occurs with both summer and winter fish, creating a wonderful rush of adrenaline and anticipation. The fish picks up the fly and holds it in its mouth. The tension is not enough to take line or be called a "pull." I imagine the point of the hook is lightly imbedded in the skin of the fish's jaw—as if the fish is on a halter rope. This occurs anywhere in the swing but most often on the dangle. A solid hook up in this situation is very difficult and most attempts to set the hook results in the pulling of the fly away from the fish. This reminds me of the time I fished the Deschutes River several years ago. After many casts the line came taut with tension. A summer-run had picked up the fly half way through the swing and stayed with it all the way to the dangle. It rested there

for a few seconds and then settled three or four feet to the bottom of the river. This is when I raised the rod with great hope. The fish was released after removing the size four fly from its upper lip, right where you would expect it. Thankfully, you coached me through the whole episode. Often the results are not as positive as waiting for the fish to make the next move; engaging the hook is difficult. A steelhead has more patience than anglers. An interesting option for the angler when a fish has picked up the fly on the dangle is to keep light tension on the line and walk down stream and away from the water to a point per-pendicular to the fish. When the fish sees you, it will swim towards the middle of the river and give some line, and when the fish is straight away set the hook. This technique may seem excessive, but often the fish will wait you out and stay downstream in this difficult to hook position until you do something stupid. Dec, have your tried this technique?

Yeah, Richard, it does seem a bit excessive! But hey, you're fishing on your own terms, and that's what counts.

The Double Pump without Significant Line Tension: You feel a slight increase in tension and a pumping sensation. There is no pull or feeling of being connected to the fish. I imagine the fish has picked up the fly and is swimming with the current, shaking its head or rolling. This is the most frustrat-ing take for me. It seems logical that the steelhead has definitely taken the fly and a solid hook up would be expected. Quite often when I swing the rod towards the bank to set the hook I am disappointed. Or if I do nothing the fish drops the fly. Dec, do you have any comments? Could the steelhead be "toying" with the fly? Maybe it felt the point and is shaking its head? Or the hook has lightly engaged in the skin outside of the mouth, and the movement of the fish or the angler simply disengages the fly.

In my experience, the steelhead is, as you mentioned, trying to shake the hook. He's not doing it merely by shak-ing his head—he's furiously twisting his whole body. I'd love to say we could, but we can't hook 'em all. There are other laws at work here that are sometimes out of our control.

The Pull: I define a pull as definite tension in the line. The fish is moving away from you and you feel connected to the fish. The rod tip bends, and line is pulled from the reel or the angler's loop. The poten-tial for a hook-up is greatest if the angler waits for the line to become tight before applying added pressure and if the take is early in the swing.

The False Pull or Take: The fly and fly line contacts obstacles such as rocks or sticks, and the angler feels a change in tension. These false pickups and take sensations confront the angler with a decision. The learning curve is slow. The beginner steelhead angler often meets frustration: "Just a rock" or "I had a take." After one has fished for a while, you learn to relax and let the line tension tell you what is happening. If the sensation is a slight increase in tension and then relaxes and the line continues to swing, it could be a rock or a steelhead. I recheck the drift with another cast with the same line length. If I can repeat the same sensation with subsequent casts I assume it is a rock and move on. However, if I cannot duplicate the line tension and know I am getting the fly just as deep, I consider it a steelhead and spend more time trying for the fish. When stripping in line after the swing, there are often plucks, pulls, and stops of the fly. These are usually obstacles. One out of 1,000 may have been a fish, but I never add these sensations to my list of possible "takes" for the day. Nor do I reattempt the cast just to make sure.

The Stop: The fly is swinging through the drift, the line is straight, and suddenly the fly stops. It is not a slow stop. Rather, the line abruptly STOPS. A most memorable "stop take" occurred while fishing the Skagit River in February. The current was swift, and I was wading in waist deep water. I should not have been that deep, but there I was. The line and fly was swinging into the dangle, and the line stopped. There was enough increase in tension in the line to feel, but not enough to take line from my Hardy click-and-pawl reel. Was it a steelhead or rock? I waited. Then there were six clicks from the reel. This is getting interesting! The current is strong, but not enough to take line. Another 20 seconds and there were eight clicks. Another 30 seconds and there were 15 clicks. Moments later the clicks continued, and I went for the hookup. The fish was on for five minutes directly below me as I worked my way to shore but eventually departed. Most likely the hook was embedded in the skin of the jaw. At that time, I was using Alec Jackson spey hooks, and it seems like the fish you land with these hooks are captured in the angle of the jaw. The point I want to make is that there seems to be a difference in a stop by a steelhead and a stop by a rock. The steelhead stop is quick and definite while the rock stop is slower. Dec, any comments?

I generally agree with you, Richard, although I've had a few "rocks" suddenly transform into steelhead, and I've seen Jackson hooks imbedded just about anywhere and everywhere in steelhead mouths.

The Full Take: The steelhead has aggressively picked up the fly and self engaged the hook. The line is tight, the line is spinning off the real, the rod is bent, and I feel the fish running or shaking its head. This is the one I'm waiting for. You've described several behavior patterns of the steelhead—the inside-outside take, the full take, head- and-shoulder take— all of which must occur during this style of take.

You can tell by the length of this letter that I have thought about this subject many times. One has to do something between casts! Please comment on your experiences while holding the rod.

RICHARD RAISLER
La Conner, Washington

Dear Richard:
Sounds like you're enjoying your retirement. We've spent only a couple of days on the river together, but in that time I recognized and admired your keen sense of awareness, true love, and devotion to the sport. As for my experiences holding the rod, I think I can speak for all steelheaders with tenure, that your experiences, thoughts and observations mirror ours. Although I'm sure that you own the rights to walking downriver and spooking a steelhead into a secure hook-hold. Nice one, Richard!

Smaller Fly or Subsurface Fly?
Dear Dec:
When fishing a skating pattern and the steelhead keeps missing the fly, do you go to a smaller pattern or to a subsurface fly?
Respectfully,
LOU DUNCAN
Sisters, Oregon

Lou, you've asked a great question that deserves an in-depth answer —an answer found in several places throughout this book. To answer it briefly and to the point: Before switching to a wet fly I always first try a smaller surface fly that leaves a more subtle wake.

Views on the Great Lakes Experience
Dec:
We were fishing together the day you caught a spectacular 18-pound Great Lakes steelie on the Genesee River in Rochester, New York. What was

your impression of the Great Lakes fishery, and are there any words of West Coast wisdom you can impart upon steelhead fans living throughout the entire Great Lakes region

JERRY KUSTICH
Twin Bridges, Montana

Dear Jerry:

That was quite a memorable experience for me—thanks again. Great doughnuts, too! It would be easy to have a preconceived idea planted in one's head that Great Lakes fish aren't real steelhead. They are lake-run rainbow trout that were introduced to the area—not native

chrome beauty without a blemish (see photo). At that moment what did I care whether he fed and grew in the ocean or a lake? The whole experience was thrilling and legitimate. I've fished a few other rivers around the Great Lakes and never did I feel as though I wasn't steelhead fishing. I don't think I would go so far as to plan a fishing vacation there in lieu of a western river trip, but if I lived in the Great Lakes region I would still be a steelhead maniac.

As for words of wisdom, I don't know if they are wise, but I did make a couple observations that may be of interest to some. The first thing I noticed is that everyone was lined up fishing the heads of the runs—the riffle

This buck came from New York's Genesee River the day I fished with Jerry Kustich. How could I not have been impressed?

steelhead. Real steelhead live in the enigmatic and perilous Pacific Ocean. But there I was, spey rod in hand, swinging my fly through some likely looking water that swam the fly beautifully. Moss-covered rocks and fluorescent maple trees lined the banks of our canyon pool. A song sparrow flitted merrily from rock to bush behind me as I stepped down the run. With each cast I made, I fell further and further into my steelhead trance—I lost my sense of time and place. I could feel it was going to happen. Bam! Fish on. The great fish did everything it was supposed to do: run, jump, shake, rattle, and roll. He was a

water. Below the heads I saw beautiful, long bodies that merged in to gorgeous tailouts with nobody fishing them. I remember asking a young angler on the Salmon River in New York why nobody was fishing the rest of the pool. He said, "The steelhead are only in the tops of the runs." I ran my eyes over the inviting looking run we were standing next to and asked, "Well, how did they get there?" When I caught the big fish on the Genesee that day, as you may recall, I was by myself in the lower half of the pool while everyone else was staying put in the top. Yes, I'm sure the heads are full of steelhead, and everybody nymphs with Glo-bugs for them. If you choose to put catching numbers mentality to rest, I believe excellent, classic steelhead fly fishing is there for whomever wants it. Here at home there are methods of steelheading that are far more effective than swinging flies. I prefer to catch them on swung flies. I catch my one or two fish a day and am perfectly happy. I think many Great Lakes would-be proponents of swinging flies are not willing to sacrifice numbers for methodology. At least that's an impression I got.

Advice on the Way to Hook a Steelhead

Hello Dec:

Your DVD, "Modern Spey Casting and More," has been a tremendous learning tool for me. My casting and fishing have improved dramatically after applying your casting and fishing principles. Thank you! I await your new book with great anticipation— best of luck with the project. My question: Ideas abound when it comes to setting the hook on steelhead. Some say setting the hook is unnecessary, others advocate a sweeping motion towards the near bank; dropping line the moment of the take and setting when the weight of the fish is felt is another common method. Others simply lift the rod when they sense a take. I know there are many factors at work here, but, all things considered, from your experience which method have you found most successful in hooking steelhead?

Sincerely,
COREY TEDESCO
Cary, Illinois

Dear Corey:

Thanks for your kind words and an excellent question. I don't want to ignore you since you've taken the time to write me with a concern that weighs heavily on the minds of thousands of steelhead anglers. I'm going to leave this one to the text, however. Please head to Striking the Fish at the close of my chapter on presentation for my detailed answer to your question. Thanks, Corey. Good luck on the water.

Should I Take a Second Pass?

Dear Dec:

I'm new to steelhead fishing. When do I fish through a run for a second or third pass.

Thanks,
SCOTT GREER
Missoula, Montana

Dear Scott:

You've posed a key question. My advice to you, par-

ticularly as a newcomer to the sport, is to fish every spot a second time. You are still developing your presentation skills, so a second pass may cover any misgivings and blunders you experienced on the first. You'll get a better feel for the hydrology and subtle nuances of the run as well. After that, if you move a fish on the first pass, you'd better fish it again. It's rare that steelhead are ever alone. As long as you are moving fish, keep fishing. I've experienced many days when I never left the run. Those dang steelies wouldn't let me go! Last, if it's a known productive piece of water, fishing it a second time is not a bad idea, particularly if the river is crowded. You may leave only to find all the other good runs occupied. Besides, remember that steelhead are migratory fish—they are on the move. A run that is void of fish one minute could be filled with chrome bodies the next.

Cause for a Tip of Whisky

Dear Dec:

In my estimation, each steelhead hooked on a swinging fly is a gift and cause for a tip of whisky. If the fish slips the hook, I don't sweat it. It's better for the fish, and I'm only in it for the grab, I tell myself. I don't howl at the sky or jump up and down. I don't stare beseechingly at the river, and I don't swear a blue streak—well, not usually. But this past year the Klamath–Trinity saw an early fall run of bigger and stronger-than-average wild fish, with which I had my share of exciting and exasperating encounters. In short, I was reduced to asylum laughter after hooking 12 consecutive without a single snapshot to show for my efforts—this over the course of two months. Sadly, these are really photogenic fish. So with a handful of devoted steelheaders in my circle the debate rages: when to strike, when to drop line, when to bow to the fish—literally and figuratively—and when to set down on the bank and cry like a baby? I have my own developing theories on the matter revolving around line type, drag settings, water temperature, and hook style. But this is your forum and I'd love to hear your views. Yes, I carry a hook hone.

Yours truly,
JEFF BRIGHT
San Francisco, California

Jeff:

I like your attitude—you're welcome in my boat any time. Sounds to me like you know what you're doing. You just lost your confidence during your losing streak. I've seen it before: After you lost so many in a row you increasingly, with each newly hooked steelhead, believed you were going to lose it. You started playing the fish not to lose it, rather than fighting to win. We've all been there, buddy. All losing streaks eventually come to an end, and I'd bet that by the time this is in print you've landed a bunch of chrome beauties with pictures to prove it.

Setting With Sink-Tips
Hello Dec:

Okay, I'm going to admit that I need some help here. At first I thought I was just asleep at the wheel. Maybe I am, but this fall I had at least three fish that hit on the dangle. (Today I had the fly dangling for about 10 to 15 seconds and I felt the tug, tug.) For whatever reason I seem to not sweep the rod tip to the near shore, but I have pulled straight back. Needless to say, no hook set. I need electric shock therapy to get over this reaction. How do you implant the near-shore sweep into your sub-consciousness? How do you set the hook on the dangle? I am mostly concerned with sink-tips but is it different for skaters?

Thanks,
GARY
Grand Rapids, Michigan

Hi Gary,

Getting a secure hook-hold on the dangle-take has been, and will continue to be, the nemeses to all of us who play the game. You answered your own question—yes, at the very least you need to sweep the rod to the side. You should really be mentally prepared for this if you already know you have a good chance at hooking one on the dangle. If you're letting the fly hang for 10 or 15 seconds as you stated, you know you're asking for it. Only you have the control of what you do with that rod, my friend. My advice to you is borrowed from the old Nike slogan: Just do it.

Spey Casting With Heavily Weighted Flies
Dec:

1. When spey casting, which cast do you prefer when using heavy sinking lines and/or heavily weighted flies? 2. Same question for intermediate sinking line and medium weighted flies. 3. Same question for floating lines and dry flies. 4. I have found that a weighted fly is easier to pick off the water than a weighted line. The lack of action in the fly can often be compensated by twitching the rod. What are your thoughts and preferences between spey casting with a weighted fly or a weighted line? 5. I have read how in slow water, unweighted flies tend to sink unnaturally from back first due to the weight at the bend of the hook. Would it make sense to add weight to most flies so that the sink rate is uniform

from the front of the hook?
Thanks,
ALBERTO REY
Fredonia, New York

Alberto:

Good to hear from you Great lakes guys! To answer your first three casting questions, generally the line and fly don't dictate what cast I use. I feel that all the various cast are equally suited to sinking and floating lines, weighted or unweighted flies. A sink-tip does require that it is brought to the surface by slowly lifting the rod before any cast is made. Once the line is relieved from the tension of being deep, any cast can be executed with relative ease.

Casting weighted flies is made easier by incorporating a little extra bottom hand in the forward stroke. Pulling on the bottom hand late in the stroke will give the line and fly lift. Aim high. Personally, I would much rather cast and fish a sink-tip than a weighted fly. I think you simply need to practice casting and handling a sink-tip. Take it slow and remember that you need to raise the rod slowly in an effort to get the sunk line to the surface before the cast is made.

If I add weight to my fly, I do so with dumbbell eyes. Yes, it compensates for the weight in the bend of the hook and the effects of currents. But I rarely see the need to fish a weighted fly. My sink tip, careful line and fly manipulation, and the comforting belief that the steelhead will move to take my fly keeps the lead out.

Great Lakes Fish on the Surface?
Dear Dec:

1. As a fly fisher in the Midwest I've been successfully employing spey-rod and swung-fly techniques for steelhead on larger rivers, especially with our fall run of fish. While some of these fish have come to the fly close to the surface (and sometimes even followed the fly) I have yet to find a way to take them consistently on top. Question: Is this just a matter of fishing exclusively on top all day for that one special fish or do you think there is something inherent in the rivers we fish (temperatures/structure/gene pool?) out here that makes this a practical impossibility?

2. With the many environmental and fishing pressures facing wild steelhead in the western U.S. and Canada, what is your personal strategy for pursuing this and other near-endangered species on a fly while not feeling like you're contributing to the problem?

3. I have an opportunity to fish the Kispiox this coming September for a week. I know this is a great

time for big fish on dry flies, but also we stand the chance to be blown out. What are the best options if we do and what effect, if any, do you think the increased pressure here has on the fish and fishing?

Thanks for the opportunity to participate in this unique event.

Regards,
Robert S. Tomes
Chicago, Illinois

Dear Robert,

1. I have very little experience fishing Great Lakes steelhead, none of which was with a surface fly. In West Coast terms, yes, you need to make a commitment if you want to take one on top—the same kind of dedication you put into fishing subsurface. You spoke of seeing steelhead come to the fly and/or following it. Lucky you—the same thing happens routinely when fishing subsurface, but you never see it. I'd stick it out and see what happens. Try fishing a fly that leaves a wake but rides in the surface rather than on it, a Steelhead Caddis or similar design. 2. There's no question about it, fishing—even catch-and-release with fly tackle—is a blood sport. If it meant that it would save steelhead as a species I would be the first to

lay down my rod. But without recreational anglers I believe steelhead wouldn't stand a chance. No one would care, and all would be lost.

3. If the Kispiox blows out usually all of the surrounding rivers are experiencing the same condition. Cocktails and poker, maybe a little fly tying will help pass the time. Plan your trip for as many days as possible—the rivers don't typically stay unfishable for very long. To answer the second part of your third question, check out the comments by Mike Wallden of Prince Rupert, British Columbia, found right in this very chapter. Tight lines, amigo.

How About Jigging the Fly?
Hi Dec:

You're swinging a big wet fly on a tip, in the Skagit in spring or Skeena in the fall—big-river environment. A fish plucks, licks, or chews on (call it want you want) the fly without really taking it. You hold off and don't strike. Fly swings to the hang down . . . . nobody home. What now? Fly size? Fly color? Fly weight? If you do change your fly—how many times? Tip length? Do you go right back after the fish or wait? If so, for how long? Step upriver and work back

I don't mind sharing hard-won information. In fact, I relish it. So many steelheaders are tight-lipped regarding most every aspect of the sport. I am not necessarily going to tell you the exact spot to fish—that knowledge needs to be earned. But giving other anglers the tools and confidence is common, sportsman's courtesy. There is still a lot to be figured out through personal trial and error.

to the fish, or stay in the exact same spot? How many cast before you move? What about swing speed: speed it up or slow it down? How about "jigging" the fly?

VERN OLSON
Camano Island, Washington

Hey Vern:
The first thing I do is exactly what you prescribe—I let the fly continue swinging. Many times the fish stays in pursuit and makes the connection. If that doesn't happen, I go right back at him and try to slow the fly in the vicinity of the lick (I like that, "lick"). If that doesn't pay off, I then take several big steps back upriver and change flies, taking my time doing it. The fly I change to is usually a contrasting color to the original in the same relative size— orange replacing purple, black replacing pink, etc. I hope this works as I fish back through. If not, and I really want to persist with this fish, I back up and change flies again, this time to a large black marabou with a colorful aft section (hot-pink and yellow) and heavy lead dumbbell eyes. I hate to admit it, but this almost never fails me. The last and very important aspect of working a steelhead in the environment you describe is to expect the steelhead to take well below where he originally licked your fly. I believe, and I know many of the best steelheaders concur, that the fish in question will drop back sometimes a great distance as it takes up a new lie after their initial interest. Some of my pals also believe that the steelhead will keep dropping back with the fly as you step down the run and eventually take. I believe this occurs occasionally. As for jigging, I suppose when all else fails it couldn't hurt— steelhead are predators.

Hi Dec:
A *Passion for Steelhead* sounds like a great book; I'll have to order a copy. I'm actually starting on a book myself. I've lived on the Skeena River most of my life and have spent more than 15 years fishing it so I should have lots of material. I actually spoke with you about a year ago regarding a couple of spey rods you were selling. I seem to recall your saying you were moving or had moved to Arizona . . . guess that's why you have time to write the book.

Anyway, here goes.

My fishing buddies and I have noticed that when fish are getting heavily worked over on river like the Kispiox they are reluctant to take a fly, especially a swung fly. They may have been in the system for a while and have probably seen every fly ever designed. What do you do? You know they're in the run because you've had a couple of light takes. We've come up with a system that seems to work. We use a light sink-tip and cast the fly as usual, swinging it across where you think the fish are sitting. The difference is that during the swing or toward the end of it, the fisher leaves the fly in the water, usually in the range of 18 inches to three feet. Simply shake your rod tip or simply let it hang and let the current work your fly! Of course, this works best on a fly with a lot of movement; thin cut rabbit-strip patterns and rhea seem to work well. The large bucks really seem to like it. The strike is usually quite explosive and you rarely get one that spits the hook. It must really aggravate them.

This is not something new, but it is the opposite thinking of most anglers. Most fly fishers I know start out with a large fly and work toward a smaller closing fly if they get a hesitant take. The method seems to work on all fish. Of course, black and pink patterns work well. The idea is to imitate a juvenile Pacific lamprey that is either on the feed or has been washed downstream by heavy current.

Can't wait to read the book. Wish I could afford the limited copy. I'm sure the hardcover will do fine, though.
MIKE WALLDEN
Prince Rupert, British Columbia

Dear Mike:
You've just let your secret out! I'm sure that now there'll be hordes of people standing in the Kispiox's Potato Patch dangling rhea flies for minutes on end. I've never purposefully fished this way for steelhead, but I've had some vicious grabs as I let me fly hang in the current while having a conversation with a passer-by up on the bank. These are fish that probably would never have struck my fly had it not been dangling there for so long. When I worked in Alaska, some of the biggest trout I saw were caught by hanging a sculpin pattern in a fast seam for as long as it took to get a take—the method rarely failed. Thanks for sharing your experience. Living full-time in Skeena country is an enviable position to be in, my friend. Good luck.

Do Steelhead Eat in the River?
Dec:
Do steelhead eat while in a river—if so, what do they eat? Are steelhead a salmon or a sea-run strain of rainbow trout? Are they at all related to Atlantic salmon? When are steelhead most apt to take a dead-drifted dry fly? Is the major influence on the above water depth, water flow, water temperature, high or low air pressure, air temperature, time of year or other? Same questions for a waking fly. . . .

Tight lines,
HOWARD M. ROSSBACH
Seattle, Washington

Dear Mr. Rossbach:
Steelhead have evolved to live off stored fat and protein while in fresh water. It's another of the phenomenal characteristic of the magnificent steelhead, a.k.a. Oncorhynchus mykiss. Some steelhead do feed while in fresh water, but not with enough consistency to warrant a scientific approach in angling methodology. I've seen them rhythmically rising to Baetis mayflies—had I been prepared for the phenomenon, I'm certain I could have caught them. The steelhead is, in fact, a sea-run rainbow trout that has adapted to find food in the ocean where sources in rivers are scarce. Unlike the Pacific salmon, steelhead don't automatically die after spawning. They can return to spawn and return to sea several times during the course of their lives. The Atlantic salmon falls under the same family, Salmonidae, as the steelhead, but is more closely related to the brown trout. The two do, however, share similar life histories. The Atlantic salmon too is capable of repeat spawning.

The atmospheric and river conditions that make for good dead-drifted dry fly opportunities are identical to those required for effective waking fly conditions with water temperature being the most important factor. I start getting interested in on-surface techniques when the water reaches 48 degrees Fahrenheit. Anything in the 50s is perfect. Water running fairly clear at moderate to low flows is favored. Low-pressure fronts are always good for activating steelhead with mornings and evenings on high-pressure days choice times. These conditions are most prevalent in late summer and fall.

I inquired about your business, Firesteed Corporation—sounds like the makings for a good life: surface steelhead and fine wine! Hope these brief answers are of help.

Anorexic Winter Appetites
Dec:
Olympic Peninsula wild steelhead are known for their anorexic appetite for flies during the coldwater winter months. Please tell us what patterns, sizes and colors—and what presentation techniques— you would use during these slim pickin' months.
Cheers,
DICK BURGE
Quilicene, Washington

Dick:
Well put: But the coldwater winter months and anorexic steelhead are not exclusive to Olympic Peninsula rivers. Winter fishing with the fly is difficult. I admire you, and any hearty soul, who persists in pursuing those several grabs per long winter season. There is no magic formula. Tenacity, a desire to beat the odds, and the love of being there is the best flies and tackle I can recommend.

Fishing the Fly Slowly is Best
Dec:
Thanks for the opportunity to offer a question or two about steelhead.
1. We often talk of "getting line behind the fly" when making a presentation through a good-looking run. This of course slows down the fly and we hope makes it more interesting to a curious steelhead. Only the rear end of the fly may be apparent to the fish, however. For other fly fishing situations, it sometimes is better to present a fly in a fashion that the fly is presented "broadside" to the fish, presenting a fuller silhouette. Which is more important—slow it down or maybe present the fly a bit faster with a small amount of line in front to give a better view to the fish?
2. What is the funniest event to happen during one of your days on the river? 3. What is the most amazing thing you have ever seen a steelhead do? 4. Have you tried the new Diet Coke with lime?
Sincerely,
ROBERT BUDD, M.D.
Hollidaysburg, Pennsylvania

Dear Bob:
1. These days I let the water dictate whether the fly fishes broadside or butt first. If the current naturally pulls the fly broadside, I encourage it to do so by slightly leading with the rod. If the fly fishes butt first, I let it. Either way, I've found that for general searching, slow is best. If I'm working a player and all else has failed or if I'm fishing behind other anglers, I sometimes purposefully fish the fly broadside and with a little extra speed to show the steelhead something different. Steelhead have keen vision—realistically the fly is only showing butt first when it's directly over and in front of them. They see a much greater portion of the fly as it approaches their lie and after it has passed. Many of the steelhead that take our flies do so both before and after it presents in front of them.
2. I could devote the pages of an entire book to the funny events that have happened on the river. Many supplied by my awesome dudes: "So what do you do for a living, Dec?" I was asked that very question one morning while guiding a chap through a run. Once while eating lunch at

a picnic table at a favorite burger joint on the north bank of the Skagit River, I was entertaining my sport by telling him "funny client" stories. Every year he visits me, at some point during his stay he'll ask me if I have some new ones. I usually do, along with repeating some old favorites. He'd be rolling, laughing, as tears streamed down his cheeks and say, "I hope I haven't done anything to make your story list." As usual, I'd assure him he hadn't—to this point. On this day, just as he was making his standard statement, a little rufous hummingbird landed on the branch of a salmonberry bush right next to our table. I immediately pointed the bird out. My dude looked at the bird, then at me with big, surprised eyes and exclaimed, "I didn't know hummingbird had feet!" I stared back at him, trying not to laugh as I could tell by the look on his face that he knew he just been placed on the "funny client" story list. Sound familiar, Bobby?

3. I was fishing the broad, burly flow of the Dean River just above tidewater one evening and hooked into a screamer of average size. He was blazing back to the Dean Channel as all Dean River fish do, but this one wasn't showing any signs of slowing. Just about the time I realized my reel was nearly void of backing, way across the river, I saw a jumping steelhead. It looked tiny at such a great distance. My line was heading straight downriver, but I knew it was my steelhead that was separated by what is perhaps the widest stretch on the entire river. I watched him jumping and flopping like crazy, but no water was being splashed around. He had beached himself and was frantically squirming on dry ground! He eventually fought his way back to the river and for the next 15 minutes never let up. When I finally beached him, I was sure he'd be all dinged up from his tangle with the rocks. There wasn't a blemish to be found for his entire platinum length.

4. You know I love my Diet Coke, Bob. If I choose to imbibe a full-strength DC with lime, I prefer a twist.

How Do I Pull a Speedy Bank Job?

Dec:

In many rivers I fish, fish normally hold from the fast-slower current seam in toward shore. What is your technique for fishing deep enough to attract those out in the seam but still be able to swing the fly near the bank for fish holding there without hanging up before reaching them?

Russell W. Fisher

Russ:

As I've stated numerous times throughout this book, I rarely change sink-tips. The situation you describe is a fairly common one and you pose a valid question. The sink-tip that does the majority of my work is 13 feet of 150-grain type 6 10-weight and really allows me to cover all aspects of a run, from the seam on into shore. If I was certain (and I'm not) that steelhead within a particular piece of water held only on the seam, I would more than likely use a heavier tip. But that's not reality—covering all the potential taking-steelhead on a single cast is. I rely more on fly speed than depth when covering a narrow fish-holding seam. I set up my line outside of the seam so my fly is at its deepest point as it enters the seam, then I do my best to hold it there for as long is possible. Wade as close to the seam as you can and extend your arm and rod out even closer.

To add time and depth in the seam, I slowly walk the fly down. This is done fluidly—at a crawl. I normally don't encourage my clients to walk while their fly is swinging unless I trust they have a feel for it and are competent waders. You don't want the fly bouncing around. It's really fishing with your legs. Watch most any experienced steelheader fish a sink-tip and you'll notice that he is almost always creeping along as his fly swings. This slows the fly while maintaining depth.

Once the fly passes through the seam, I usually stand my ground and let the fly continue swinging into the shallows. So to answer your question in just a few words: Fish the fly slowly through the seam.

Do They Behave More Like Trout?

Hi Dec:

1. Do steelhead hold in the same type of water when a river is low and clear as they do when a river is high and off-color? 2. Do steelhead behave more like trout the farther they migrate from the ocean—specifically, do they feed on insects and take on trout-like behavior—and should we vary our techniques accordingly? 3. How do you suggest explaining to my wife that steelhead fishing is an addiction which requires specific equipment and significant time away from home? Thanks in advance for your response to my questions.

Happy Holidays,
Casey Capparelli
Newbury Park, California

Dear Casey:

1. When the river is low and clear, steelhead are drawn to deeper parts of a pool. They seek shelter in and under heavy cover such as rock shelves and log jams. Conversely, when the water is high and off-color, many of these deep places are running swiftly and aren't attractive holding places. High, colored water pushes steelhead into

shallow holding lies often very close to shore where the current is calmer.

2. Yes, steelhead do behave more trout-like the longer they are in the river. It's not necessarily the distance they migrate, but the length of time they spend in fresh water. Steelhead are not genetically predisposed to life-sustaining foraging activity while in fresh water, but many do actively feed. I have witnessed steelhead rhythmically rising to Baetis mayflies on many occasions during autumn. As for changing tactics, I still employ the swing, step, and search method. I use smaller flies than those for high, off-color water; surface flies become important. I still fish them like steelhead, not trout. Dead-drifting nymphs now becomes effective, but is a tactic I choose not to practice.

3. Sorry, but a "note" from your river-guide has proven an unsuccessful remedy to such a quandary. You have my sympathy. Try telling her: "Steelhead fishing cleanses the soul and frees the mind. And when I'm fresh and rejuvenated it allows all of my energy to be devoted to loving, pampering, and taking care of you, babe." Good luck, Casey. You are not alone.

The Tug's the Drug

Dear Dec:

I'm sorry to say that I am writing to you at a very dire time in my life. My doctor just diagnosed me with a terminal illness. This illness doesn't actually cause death, but it stays with you until death. I believe he called it "a passion for steelhead." This diagnosis has been a fear of my friends and family for years. The only treatment known to medicine at this time is a minimum of 20 hours per week on the water. I am writing to you because I am worried about you. After reading some of your work, I realized that there is a good chance that you are also afflicted with this medical condition.

Answer these questions to see:

1. Do you often leave the house before daylight?

2. Do you often return home after dark?

3. Do you spend many of your days in fleece pajamas?

4. Are your feet constantly numb?

5. Do you stand in the water for hours waving a long stick?

6. Do you sit at home and play with thread and feathers?

7. Do you obsessively check river levels?

8. Do you do any of these things in the company of other crazed individuals?

If you answered yes to:

One to two of these symptoms you may, or may not be in the beginning stages of this illness.

Three to four, the illness has a hold and only if you're very lucky is there any hope of returning to a normal life.

Five to six there is no return—embrace it.

Seven to eight, oh wow, you're in trouble.

My guess is that you must be in the later stages. I am truly sorry, my friend. However, I want you to know that you are not alone—I and hundreds of others are also afflicted with this illness. Together we can make it through these tough times and with luck help return our native adversary to its once-great abundance.

Everyone can't wait to see what lives in the fly boxes.

Last November I had fallen prey to "the passion" and found myself knee-deep in the waters of the Deschutes. Daybreak had come and gone, bringing the deep cold of a clear early morning in central Oregon, a cold that coated my line and guides with ice. Enveloped in thought, I cut my way through a long run; a hitched Skunk tipped my blade. My trance was broken as Elliott (also infected) approached from behind, grabbing a chance to wake his hands, asleep with cold. Three-quarters of the way through my next pass a fish grabbed. The combination of a tight line and rowdy buck left me with a problem. Upon grabbing the fly, the fish back spun my reel creating a rat's nest. Unable to give him the line he wanted, I broke it with an adrenalin-powered jerk. I was left with one hand on the rod the other holding the broken line—not a good place to be. Luckily, Elliott was still behind me. He quickly replaced me and I began digging for the other end of the line. Practiced hands were quick to throw together a blood knot, which reunited the fluorescent friends. The knot was trimmed just in time to see it head back for the Columbia. After the tug-of-war we landed our prize, a nine-pound hatchery buck. Unlike those fat fishing guys on TV, we salvaged the predicament.

My name is Marshall Cooley and I grew up in Prineville Oregon. I now reside in Corvallis (go Beavers!). I was infected with the passion about six years ago when my dad took me to the "D" for my first steelhead trip. Beginner's luck, I guess, because I hooked two fish my first day fly-fishing for O. mykiss and never looked back (I would soon realize that this was far from normal). I get back to the "D" every fall, but most the time you will find me haunting the waters of Oregon's central coast. Last month I graduated from OSU with a bachelors of science in fisheries and wildlife. Need any help, Dec? I understand you fight fire: wildland or structure? I spent my last five summers fighting wildland fires for the Forest Service. Hope this letter finds you well.

The Tug's the Drug,
MARSHALL COOLEY
Corvallis, Oregon

C'mon and join the party, Marshall! Sounds as if you have the disease real bad—or is that reel good? Thanks for sharing your incredible experience with us. The steelies have it! Recently, after lots of schooling and with the same determination and passion it took to be a steelheader, I landed a job as a structural firefighter. But as you probably already know, the bulk of my work as a firefighter is responding to emergency medical calls. I'm lovin' every minute of it. Best of all, my new job will allow me the time to actually fish more myself. And I'm looking forward to it. See you on the river, dude!

Are Steelhead Color-Blind?
Dec:
Do steelhead see color or are they color-blind? If they are color-blind why do different colors appear to work better at various times of the year?
DAN SCHOENBERG
Moscow, Idaho

Dan:
Steelhead, as well as all species of salmonids, can most definitely see color. In fact, the rods and cones—light receptors in the eye's retina—are arranged very similar to the human eye. Fresh-run steelhead react more aggressively to bright fly patterns; steelhead that have settled in the river (on your beautiful Clearwater River, for instance) are more likely to respond to darker, subtler offerings.

Should I Move to Steelhead Country?
Dec:
I am completely addicted to fishing steelhead with the spey rod and am feeling the pull to head to the West Coast. If you could live in one place on the West Coast to fish for steelhead year round, where would it be? The location would have to be close enough to some sort of population center so that employment would be attainable, yet close enough to steelheading for when one only has a few hours to fish. I'm already thinking Portland or Seattle, but I would love to know your take on it. I'm a firefighter, too, so I'm trying to test with those two departments. Where else should I consider? I'm hoping to find that balance of being able to make a living doing something I love but still live in a beautiful place with rivers where steelhead swim. Is there such a place? Thank you for your time.
P. S. I can't wait for the book.
BRIAN KOLL
Milwaukee, Wisconsin

Dear Brian:
Sounds like an exciting time in your life. For year-round steelheading opportunities with gainful employment in close proximity, you've picked the right two cities. Living for nearly 20 years an hour's drive north of Seattle and surrounded by rivers, I've hooked fresh, bright steelhead every month of the year. The same can be done living in the Portland area. As for beauty, parts of the Pacific Northwest are experiencing tremendous population growth, but its breathtaking beauty will forever remain.

A Winter's Tale
Dec:
Here on Vancouver Island, recent rains have colored and raised water levels to a point that makes fly fishing questionable. Although there are slicks, runs and pools that can be fished in virtually any water conditions, these places are usually rocky bluffs with open spaces and plenty of room to cast the relative

short distances needed to locate fish. The down side of fishing rising or high water is the unseen number of obstacles along the banks and in those areas not normally targeted.

The other day, I chose a pool with house-sized rocks on both sides, creating a funnel for incoming fish. As the water roars through this crevice it forms a barrier of sorts before relaxing into a wider boulder-endowed tailout with a distinct slick right down the middle. Hidden beneath all this water are undercut ledges carved by thousands of years of river currents and floods. These undercuts have little water current in moderate water flows and are excellent places for steelhead to hold up. I knew this and made my way to this hidden treasure only to find three pontoon boats fishing the tailout. These fellows were actually fishing in the wrong spot, where the water flow is too fast, and the old "think lazy" saying really applies in these conditions.

Putting together my Thomas & Thomas 14-footer drew some attention and a few smirks in my direction. For those more informed fishers, a fly line provides much greater versatility in presentations. My line of choice was a Scientific Anglers 12-weight tri-tip spey line, Rio's 9/10 compensator tip connected to AirFlo's 20-foot type-8 sink-tip. This graduated-line combination provides many of the assets needed to effectively fish high, murky water with the utmost control. My fly of choice was one of my patterns called Winter's Dream, a multi-colored bunny leech pattern with a marabou collar and bead head—very effective in off-color water conditions. I was about to make my first cast when I heard the roar of a jet boat coming through the crevice. The fellows on the pontoon boats left immediately as the jet boat took up root in the middle of the tailout. On seeing this I decided to get closer to the beginning of the slack water nearest the exit of the canyon. This is where the shelves begin and a good place for fish to wait. None of the previous fishers recognized this as a possibility in these conditions and left the pool without a fish.

On my third cast of about 75 feet, a small swirl of current grabbed my line and washed it beneath the ledge, carrying the floating line section in a snake-like pattern. Suddenly, the floating line formed a distinct "U" shape and a fish erupted on the surface away from where I thought end of my line was. The bright steelhead was into the tailout and on her way back to the ocean. I've discovered that by releasing the drag, a hot fish will sometimes re-enter the pool it just vacated. In this case I was lucky. She came back. After an extended battle of wills she came to

her side and I brought her into a quiet piece of water: a beautiful 14-pound hen with a few sea lice and too silver for easy photography.

Working this pool for the next couple of hours rewarded me with some impressive trout and one more small steelhead. Adjust your lines to the water you know and success is around the corner. These days are what dreams are made of.

COURTNEY OGILVIE
Qualicum Beach, British Columbia

Dear Courtney:
Thanks for sharing the interesting story. Your experience illustrates the value of being observant with the ability to adapt.

Landing a Steelhead By Yourself
Dec:

I love your idea of the question-and-answer chapter in your new book. Here's a familiar problem that I don't know that I've seen addressed very well: What's the best way to land a steelhead by yourself with a 15-foot rod while wading without beaching it? We all know there are times when beaching is simply out of the question. Although it's a little difficult, hand-tailing a steelhead or Atlantic salmon with a single-handed rod (I generally use a 10-foot rod) is something I've always had a relatively high degree of success in doing. But the 15-foot rod becomes a bit problematic.

The best solution we've used that a friend came up with is this: When the fish looks like it's ready, swing the rod over your head and behind you—effectively using your body to shorten the rod. If you intend to tail or net the fish with your left hand, the reel and butt of the rod is on the right side of your body, the tip of the rod on your left. You avoid putting an extreme (and dangerous) bend in the rod and are suddenly using a shorter rod.

Any ideas or comments? I'd love to know how you land fish in this situation. Many thanks.
Best,
BILL KESSLER
Corning, New York

Dear Bill:
I agree, long rods make a difficult proposition that much more problematic. The method you speak of is exactly what I do—check out the photo on the cover of this book. Look familiar? The most important thing to do to save your rod is release line tension as quickly as you can once the steelhead is in your hands. All the informa-

Be a responsible catch-and-release angler—fight every fish quickly. When your steelhead is on its side, sliding across the surface like this beautiful little doe, it has been defeated. Get her in your hands, revived, and released as soon as possible.

tion you are looking for can be found in the chapter *Tackling Steelhead*.

Are Steelhead Leader Shy?

Dear Dec:

Do steelhead show signs of being leader shy, or should we all be using 15-pound test tippet?

ROBERT WRAY
Washington D.C.

Robert:

To clear things up, I can tell you that one of my compulsary sayings on the river after a good fight with a steelhead is, "He would have taken that fly if it was knotted to the end of the fly line!" In general, steelhead are not leader shy. You must also consider that by using the "step-swing" method, the fly always presents before the tippet. So it's not as if a large diameter leader is passing over the steelhead alerting it to the fly's inauthenticity.

I use Maxima leader material exclusively for my leaders and tippets. My tippet size varies according to fly size, which is pretty simple. For flies in the size 6 to 10 range, I use eight-pound, size 2 to 4 gets 10-pound, and anything larger is knotted to 12-pound material. Fifteen would be fine, but I want the weakest link in my terminal tackle to be close to the fly. When I'm snagged on the bottom and need to break off, I've found 15-pound Maxima is sometimes stronger than my fly line, sink-tip, or the loop connections holding it all together—I could winch my drift boat out of the river with 15-pound Maxima.

As with anything, there are exceptions to the rule. In small, crystal-clear pools, usually in late summer, steelhead can be a bit shy of anything and everything that comes near them, including flies. But in general, they are not leader shy at all.

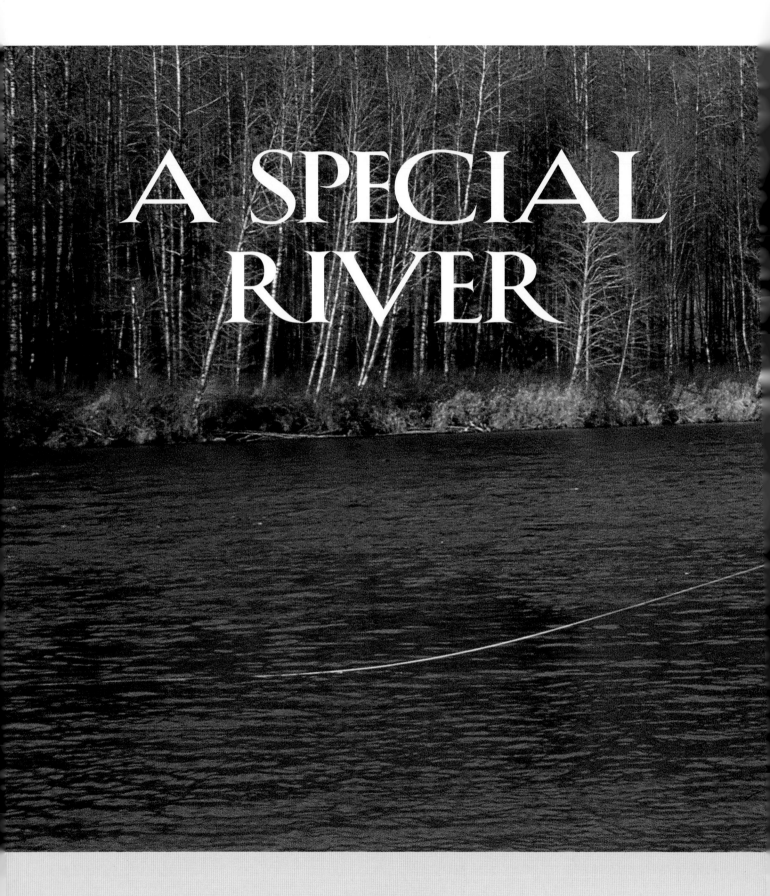

A SPECIAL RIVER

AS A FULL-TIME STEELHEAD FLY-FISHING GUIDE and well-traveled angler, I am often asked what is the best steelhead river, or where would I fish if I had only one week left to do so. Before I can answer the first question, I need to establish, with the asker, the definition of "best." Too often best translates to most fish hooked in a day—an unrealistic criteria, in my experience, when one considers the immensity of the steelhead's natural range and the hundreds of rivers they return to within that range

What I look for in my definition of "best" is a river, or river system, that first has aesthetic appeal in the form of its natural setting. I like mountains, lots of mountains, rising swiftly, and precipitously from the river valley. A valley that is thick with a heavy riparian growth of willow, alder, and sweet smelling cottonwood trees. Just beyond the riparian zone, there is a dense forest comprised mostly of cedar, fir, and hemlock trees thriving in a dank maritime climate.

Next I look to the water. I want a surplus of quality fly water. But it must be varied in its form and flow. Every run and pool should be different in its hydrology, from easily fished to very challenging. If the river has a sizable tributary of a different character yet equally alluring, then all the better.

Fishing the Skagit is always a remarkable, memorable experience irrespective of weather. Be prepared for anything.

The next challenge I like to consider is that of the fish themselves: I don't want them to be too easy. Working hard to maybe hook one steelhead in a day holds lasting appeal. This single fish is wild and stream born, fresh from the Pacific Ocean.

Lastly, my best river is fairly large. I like to cast long and feel my fly swim through a broad drift, lengthening the time of anticipation. If the river has a management plan to protect its wild stocks of steelhead—and yet allows me to fish for them under catch-and-release, artificial-lure only regulations—I've found the perfect river.

There is only one answer to both questions: the Skagit.

An Immense Watershed

The Skagit is the third largest river system on the West Coast of the contiguous United States. Centered in northwest Washington State, the 125-mile-long Skagit and her many tributaries drain 3,130 square miles starting in Manning Provincial Park in British Columbia. This immense watershed is home to a diverse list of sea-run salmonids that include all five species of Pacific salmon: winter, spring, and summer steelhead; sea-run cutthroat trout; and Dolly Varden char. As in most if not all watersheds these days, the Skagit River and her fish are not without their perils. More than 70 years of logging, urbanization, commercial and tribal net fishing, over-harvest and poaching by sport fishers, and strangled by five hydroelectric dams on the system, the Skagit has been reduced to a shadow of her historical, glorious self.

However, all is not lost. While Skagit chinook salmon are listed under the federal Endangered Species Act, and its steelhead—along with all Puget Sound wild steelhead—in 2004 were petitioned for listing due to depleted spawning returns, her natural beauty remains stunning, except for visible scars of

Spring's renewal of life emanates the full spectrum of the color green: the famous Mixer run on the Skagit where dreams come true.

clearcutting. Birds and wildlife flourish along her banks, as does one the largest populations of wintering bald eagles in the world. Some years more than 600 bald eagles congregate along gravel bars to feed on dead and dying chum salmon November through February.

The recreational value of the Skagit River system is priceless, but it is her beautiful, thickly built, wild winter-run steelhead that tug at the hearts and souls of steelhead fly anglers from around the nation.

The Skagit and her principal tributary, the Sauk, are two of a handful of winter steelhead rivers recognized as household names among serious steelheaders. Summer and fall returns of steelhead are far more attractive to fly anglers for good reason: The rivers are generally warmer, thus making the cold-blooded steelhead more active, and in turn more receptive to fly-tackle methods.

So what makes the Skagit a particularly outstanding winter fly-rod fishery? The answer is simple:

The majority of the Skagit's special race of winter-run steelhead returns to the river in late winter and early spring when water temperatures are typically in the mid to high 40s. That the steelhead returning this time of year are wild and aggressive by nature also adds to the mix. Then throw in miles and miles of shallow, broad gravel bars that afford a long, slow presentation of the fly, thus allowing plenty of time and ease for a steelhead to see and react to it. These ingredients, blended together, make for a unique winter fly fishery.

The Skagit and Sauk will always be my home waters; the more intimate I become with them, the more mysterious they are. I have a wealth of experience on other rivers, but for some reason my adrenaline surges at a higher level, and my anticipation greater when fishing at home. Maybe it's because I never know what it is that's going to grab my fly. There is nothing clone-like about these fish—each one is different and distinct. With every grab, there's this moment where I'm overwhelmed with the surging thought of, who's it gonna be — are you huge and gonna kick my butt, or are you just gonna kick my butt? Perhaps it's the mystery that comes with the vastness of the river, and the feeling that hooking a steelhead is really against all odds. There's also the fact that these are winter steelhead—anyone can catch steelhead in summer and fall. I don't know, but the fact remains, all combined, these fish hold a mystique over me like no other.

On other rivers when someone tells me they had success, I smile and am happy for them. On the Skagit, I get goose bumps and want to know details, details. I'm not so much looking to process information that may be useful to me (although you can bet I log it in my gray matter!), rather, I want to share in the experience and get as close as I can to another of the Skagit's glorious steelhead. Throughout this writing, I must make it clear that when I speak of the Skagit, I am also speaking of the Sauk. The two are synonymous to my sentiment and angling approach.

Winter steelhead enter the Skagit as early as late November. The first fish to arrive from December through January are primarily hatchery-reared steelhead, heading for various places throughout the system where they were released as juveniles. They offer little sport for fly anglers, as they ascend upon the river like a swift-moving motorcycle gang, all huddled together rarely stopping until they reach their final destination. They are better fished using conventional-tackle methods from a boat—they rarely pause long enough on the gravel bars for us to have an honest shot at them. At the very least, knowing that they are in the river lends us viable cause to spend a day fishing.

Winter Jewels

Then, sometime in late January, about the same time the hatchery fish start to dwindle in number, the true jewels of the Skagit start to show up: wild steelhead.

During this transition time, the wild push of fish starts out as a trickle—a few here, a few there. As January turns to February, and February to March, little by little, the trickle grows stronger, peaking in numbers by the middle of April. Fresh fish continue entering the system well into May, destined for

This sturdy buck, held by my friend Steve Kruse, took the fly at the very bottom of the swing in two feet of water. I was just beginning to strip some line in for a new cast when he grabbed hold. Skagit fish can hold very close to shore. Be ready.

spawning grounds throughout the system. Some steelhead are main-stem spawners, while a large portion head for the Skagit's many tributaries. Roughly half the Skagit's wild steelhead make their way to the Sauk which enters the Skagit near the town of Rockport.

The majority of Skagit–Sauk steelhead spawn later than most other rivers hosting runs of late-returning steelhead. The Skagit drains such a vast, precipitous area that spring runoff makes water conditions inhospitable for a newly hatched steelhead coming out of the gravel April through June. Steelhead are a product of their river, and Skagit steelhead have evolved to spawn so their offspring emerge when the river is more fry friendly. Spawning in late April, May, and June, by the time the eggs have hatched, runoff has subsided; conditions are safe and comfortable for the newly hatched steelhead fry. There is evidence of Skagit winter-run steelhead spawning in July. Because of this, Skagit steelhead remain fresh and bright until the angling season closes on the last day of April.

Skagit steelhead are large with the potential to be enormous. The possibility of hooking a steelhead of 20 pounds or better is within the realm of possibility. There are numerous accounts of fly anglers hooking the steelhead of their dreams on the Skagit and Sauk. Unfortunately, many anglers come to the Skagit with expectations of hooking one of these leviathans. This is too bad. Sure, the possibility exists, but it should not be the reason to fish the Skagit. Believe me, it's difficult enough to come in contact with a 10-pounder, let alone one twice that size! I'm on the Skagit and Sauk, either guiding or fishing steelhead, between 70 and 80 days throughout the winter—spring season; I hook fewer than two legitimate 20-pounders in this time each year—some years I don't hook any. My personal largest steelhead landed was taken in April of 1997 from a broad, shallow run on the Sauk. I guessed the brute to weigh in the mid-20s. What was great about this mammoth, colored-up buck was that he fought like a 12-pound mint bright doe—running, jumping, and literally cart wheeling across the pool.

Ten pounds is by no means a small steelhead; it's about the average you can expect to see if you are lucky enough to find one. According to Curt Kramer, area fisheries biologist with the Washington State Department of Fish and Wildlife, 55 percent of the Skagit's run of steelhead spends two years as juveniles in fresh water and then two years growing and maturing at sea (2/2 or two-salt fish). This makes for a fish of eight to 11 pounds. Thirty percent of the run is

made up of 2/3 steelhead: three-salt fish. These are the prized 12- to 22-pound fish, with fast-growing males returning as 16- to 22-pounders. Three-salt females typically weigh 14 to 16 pounds. Repeat spawners comprise roughly 13 percent of the run and are extremely important to the long-term health of the population: A typical two-salt steelhead carries approximately 5,000 eggs; the same fish on its second spawning run carries as many as 8,000!

For a repeat spawner, the additional year at sea does not make for a larger steelhead. It takes the fish the whole year just to replenish the weight it lost during spawning. It's the initial sea term—and how well it fed during this time—that determines the size of a returning adult steelhead. Any age class is capable of repeat spawning. If you've done your math, you will know that there are still a few percentage points I haven't accounted for. Wanna know? I'll warn you, it's really scary.

Every year the Skagit is host to a small number of four- and five-salt natives—fish that can weigh as much as 40 pounds. Can you imagine fishing happily down a run, groovin' on your casting, hoping to get a pull, when . . . along comes one of these things? I'd probably pass out, stone-cold right there in the river!

In truth, I probably don't have to worry about such a cardiac episode happening any time soon. As I said before, it's difficult enough to hook even normal two-salt fish. Between 4,000 and 6,000 winter steelhead return to the Skagit system each year over a six- to seven-month period. The river system covers many miles. Although it is graced with a lot of primo fly water, there is so much more good steelhead water that is not conducive to fly fishing. The odds of hooking anything are clearly stacked against us. Yes, it is a quality fishery, but just because the Skagit has experienced a rise in popularity among fly fishers in recent years—"hit the map," if you will—don't come here expecting to beach a bunch of bright steelhead. One grab every three days is realistic. And that's if you are familiar with the rivers and know what you're doing. The charm and mystical grandeur of the Skagit and Sauk alone should keep your spirit overflowing between meetings with their magnificent steelhead.

A Rich History

The Skagit has a rich and important history of both fish and fishers. Pioneering steelheaders such as Ralph Wahl, Wes Drain, and Al Knudson were among the first to ply the Skagit's cold flows in search of winter steelhead with a fly. Their exploits are now legendary. Wahl was probably the first to land a

Skagit winter steelhead; 1939 was the year. Efficient tackle was hard to come by. Sinking lines were not yet available and nothing was known about the sport.

These men hashed it out for themselves and came up with some impressive catches.

Wes Drain recorded Washington's first-ever, 20-pound fly-caught steelhead. Ralph Wahl later beat the record by besting Wes's fish by one ounce. Ralph, now deceased, describes these early days of winter steelheading the Skagit River in his delightful book, *One Man's Steelhead Shangri La* (1989).

Today that pioneering spirit still prevails in those who fish the Skagit. A list of names that reads like a who's who of well-known and innovative steelhead-

with the plan anyway.

From the early 1960s to the early '70s, the program flourished. The Skagit ranked as the No. 1 steelhead producer in the state for more than a decade. Dozens of guides worked the river, often running two trips a day, sending both shifts home with limits. Impact on the river's foundation of wild steelhead was devastating. By the end of January, the artificial run of hatchery fish was about over. Unfortunately, this is precisely when late-run wild fish begin to show up. Steelhead-hungry anglers attracted by the hatchery build-up began fishing later and later into the season, encountering the vulnerable wild fish.

Gary Rawson starting high in the run. Sauk river steelhead can be found anywhere. Fish thoroughly.

Sometime during the early 1970s, a severe case of botulism broke out at Barnaby Slough. Without the aid of concrete pens (steelhead were reared to smolts over a natural stream bottom) that could be cleaned and disinfected, the Barnaby Slough era was over. The skeptics were right: doomed to failure.

Meanwhile, in 1974 the federal court Boldt decision came into effect, awarding Native Americans treaty rights to harvest half the annual run of steelhead on many western Washington rivers. All of this combined rendered the Skagit's run of steelhead, once numbering in the tens of thousands, to a mere 2,000 returning adults.

ers frequent the Skagit and Sauk each season.

Back when Ralph, Wes, and Al were fishing, a good year welcomed a return of more than 25,000 winter steelhead to the Skagit system from late November to May. Summer steelhead filled tributary creeks the remainder of the year, including the Sauk, but have now dwindled to near nothing due to gross destruction of habitat caused by logging. Fishing for the Skagit's few remaining summer steelhead today is mostly a waste of time.

Early-returning winter steelhead flooded the river December and January. These small (four to six pounds) steelhead were great biters. With a generous three-fish-a-day limit, mortality was high. Runs began to dwindle. In response to the diminishing returns, the then-state Department of Game decided to start a hatchery program. Some biologists at the time pleaded that the chosen hatchery site (Barnaby Slough) was doomed to failure. The state went ahead

In 1980, Washington State Department of Wildlife biologists Curt Kramer and Chuck Phillips proposed a new management plan that would forbid the killing of wild steelhead on the Sauk and Skagit in March and April. They also secured agreements with the tribes to refrain the netting of wild winter stocks. The steelhead responded immediately to the new plan: The run quadrupled after the first spawning cycle. The new plan was a success, and thus the present day catch-and-release fishery on the Skagit and Sauk was born.

Today, catch-and-release, no-bait, single-barb-less-hook regulations are in effect on the Sauk River from March 1 to April 30, from Darrington downstream to its mouth. The Sauk is closed the month of May. Special regulations take effect on the Skagit on March 16 and run through April 30. The river is open from Bacon Creek downstream to the Dalles Bridge near Concrete. The remainder of the river is closed to all angling. Always consult official state fishing regulations. Rules and regulations are subject to change.

If you plan on fishing the Skagit and Sauk, there is no finer time than during this special season. Steelhead are in the air, as are the glorious sights and smells of a budding spring.

Miles Of River To Explore

The fly-fishable stretch of the Skagit parallels state Highway 20 on the north side and the South Skagit Highway on the south for some 60 miles, from the town of Newhalem, downstream to Sedro-Woolley. From Sedro-Woolley to the mouth, where the Skagit joins the Puget Sound, is approximately another 20 miles. However, it is extremely deep and wide with little or no fly water.

Heading back upriver, the Sauk River joins the Skagit at the town of Rockport. State Highway 530 parallels most of the fishable stretch for about 16 miles to the town of Darrington. All along both the Sauk and Skagit are a number of boat ramps conveniently and evenly spaced. Well, convenient on the Skagit anyway—Sauk launch sites are primitive at best.

If you are new to the Skagit and Sauk, floating by drift boat or raft is certainly the best way to explore the many miles of pools, riffles, and runs. It takes much time and exploration to learn the limited number of walk-in spots, particularly on the Skagit. Roads leave the river, there is dense riparian growth and many private dwellings are along the flood plain. The Sauk is a bit easier to find foot access, mainly because it's not so wide, and Highway 530 runs fairly close to her banks. With a little ingenuity and pioneering spirit, access can be found on either stream.

Should you decide to float, the choices are many: Steelhead can be found on any of these floats on any given day throughout the season.

The Sauk River from Darrington to the mouth of the Suiattle River is a full-day float. It is relatively small water with many braided channels and potential boating hazards. Even experienced boatmen need to be alert. From the Suiattle to the Native Hole, the braids have joined and the river widens. The quality fly water in this five-mile stretch of river is unsurpassed. Novice boaters, however, should exercise caution. I've even been caught sleeping at the oars a

time or two myself: Pucker city!

If you decide to float the lower Sauk, plan on a full day. Once you put in at the Native Hole, you're not getting out until you reach Faber's Landing on the Skagit (ramps on both sides of river), several miles west of Rockport. Again, use caution any time you are on the Sauk.

There are several floats you can make on the Skagit, each one distinct in character. From Marblemount, eight miles to Rockport where you take out at Howard Miller Steelhead Park, is one of the most beautiful stretches of river anywhere. The river runs clear most of the time due to the settling effects of three dams upstream and the 24-mile-long impoundment called Ross Lake. Mountains rise abruptly from the valley floor as every bend of the river reveals another gorgeous run or pool that cries for you to send a fly through. Floating this stretch is easy class-1 water, but you can get into trouble if you are not careful. The river is more powerful than it looks through this stretch.

From Howard Miller to Concrete (boat launch located on the east side of the Baker River), the river dramatically changes character once it is joined by the Sauk. The Sauk has no dams and is glacially fed.

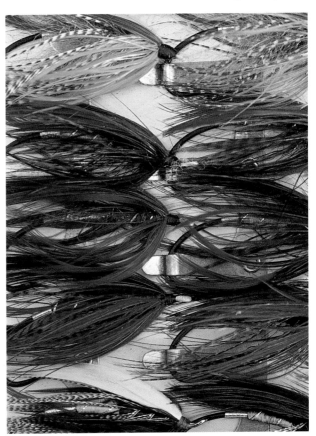

Well-traveled steelhead angler Marty Howard whipped up some perfect flies to grace the clear runs of the Skagit.

It adds color and silt to the otherwise clear Skagit. It also adds an additional 3,000 to 5,000 cubic feet per second of flow to the Skagit. This is where the Skagit starts to get big. There's plenty of fly water to fish, it just isn't as obvious. Look for big, gently sloping gravel bars and any seam or edge—no matter how insignificant it may appear. What might look like a little crease that could be covered in a few short casts often turns out to be a short, yet promising piece of water demanding the attention of 20 or more casts.

On this big river, we are looking for short-term resting water: places where a steelhead might pull over out of the heavy flow for a break. Any spot that is two to six feet deep with a gentle speed and rocky bottom deserves your attention.

From Rockport half way to Concrete is Faber's Landing should you want to take a shorter float. There is also a launch site at Sutter Creek, several miles east of Rockport. A wonderful float that combines the Skagit above and below the Sauk is Sutter Creek to Faber's.

From Concrete to Birdsveiw is another excellent float, but the river downstream from Concrete closes March 16. If you decide to take this float, plan on a full day. The runs are long and the floating slow. Downriver from Birdsveiw there are still some nice bars to fish, but I don't advise floating. The river is wide and slow here with the fishable runs spread out great distances from one another. You will spend more time rowing on a short winter day than you will fishing.

Fishing The Skagit

Fishing the Skagit is best accomplished using the wet-fly-swing presentation, with most takes from steelhead coming during the last half of the swing. Nothing new. If a fish doesn't grab, the angler takes a couple of steps downriver, makes another cast, and tries again. This process is repeated until either a steelhead is hooked or the run is completed. There is no better way to effectively cover big water with a fly.

The big water of the Skagit and Sauk is best covered using a two-handed rod. Just about everybody who fishes the Skagit and Sauk these days is using the two-hander. Single-handed rods still work, but the two-hander makes the required 70- to 80-foot casts with ease all day. Once the fly is in the water, the added length of the two-hander enables the angler to swim the fly slowly across the entire breadth of the suspected lie. Whichever rod you choose, I highly recommend a 9- or 10-weight. Remember those four-salt fish?

Sink-tips 10 to 15 feet in length, ranging from 130 to 190 grains in type 6, are the bread-and-butter

A splendid Sauk River buck taken on a cool April morning.

lines for covering the Skagit's broad runs. Going deep with a super-heavy line is not required. In fact, it can hurt you more than help. Skagit steelhead hold in remarkably shallow water, particularly during low light or in a well-rested piece of water. In addition, they are naturally aggressive, moving great distances to a swimming fly. If you are constantly hung on the bottom, you are not fishing effectively. I rarely change sink-tips and have settled on a 13-foot 150-grain type 6 tip that does most all my work nicely. If I feel my fly needs to be deeper, I might cast at a steeper angle upstream, allowing my fly more time to sink; I do just the opposite if I need my fly to run shallower. Most important is to rely on a fly line that fishes over and across the bars without hanging bottom.

What fly to use? I consider the fly to be the "least important most important" part of our tackle. Important because it is what connects us to the fish. Least important because the steelhead will take any number of patterns from a small Green-Butt Skunk to a four-inch-long hot-pink bunny fly, as long as it's moving slowly across the current. I'll make this simple: Skagit steelhead fresh from the ocean have been making their living by feeding on large, colorful marine organisms. Large (two to four inches) flies with lots of life-like action seem to work best: marabous, spey flies, rabbit-strip leeches, General Practitioners, etc. Colors? Orange, purple, black, and all the proven steelhead colors work fine. If I am fishing behind someone using orange, I try something black or purple. If water clarity is poor, something big and purple has proven itself effective. If the water is low, clear, and has seen much angling pressure I switch to something smaller and in earth tones like olive and brown. Keep it simple, but what's more important is to keep the faith and keep it in the water!

Flies should be knotted to no less than 10-pound Maxima tippet material. Keep your leader short— three to four feet. I am often amazed at how many anglers I see using the proper sinking line only to knot their fly to a 12-foot foot tapered leader. The sink-tip goes down, but the fly stays up. Keep it short; Skagit steelhead are far from leader shy.

If you are lucky enough to hook a Skagit beauty, hang on. You're in for a ride. They rarely let you down, and often leave you feeling helpless as they take blistering runs back toward the ocean. Don't step foot on the Skagit or Sauk without a minimum of 150 yards of backing—I like 200. If I need it, it's there. As mentioned before, a 9-weight rod is the weapon of choice. And I do mean weapon: It's our responsibility to fight and land these fish as quickly as possible. If you don't put the wood to 'em and fight back, they can easily be misplayed to fatal exhaustion. Never, ever, drag one of these precious wild steelhead (any fish intended to be released for that matter) onto exposed rocks or sand. Land them in the water. If you want a picture that's fine, but do it quickly and always over the water. Don't get so engrossed in getting the shot that you keep the fish out of the water for too long. How long is too long? Put your head under water, and you will get a quick sense. Handle them as you would a baby and everything should be all right.

Let's Get Along

River etiquette is vital. Our rapidly increasing, fast-paced society and an accelerating "I want it NOW!" mentality has come to our rivers. Fly fishers are not exempt. By following a few simple rules, we can fish harmoniously and everyone can enjoy an equal chance at hooking a steelhead.

First and foremost never, under any circumstance, start fishing downstream from another angler. The run "belongs" temporarily to the angler or anglers who are there when you arrive. Some drifts on the Skagit are several hundred yards long, yet this bedrock rule still applies as far as I'm concerned. Start fishing at the top of the run behind those already fishing, leaving plenty of room so as not to crowd the person in front of you. If the person already there is just starting to fish, he or she may invite you to jump in below as a courtesy. But I highly advise against asking permission to do this. The angler in front of you may feel awkward, say yes, but not really mean it. It just makes things needlessly tense. We're supposed to be having fun—right?

If you find yourself in a lineup, make sure you move steadily down the run, taking several steps between casts. Hope everyone else does the same. If you hang bottom don't wade out to recover your fly. Just break it off. The folks behind you won't appreciate your wading over the top of their fish. In addition, there is a courtesy that I often see overlooked: If you break off and have to re-rig, do it quickly. If you find that you are making a career out of knotting on a new fly, keep stepping down the run at about the same pace you had been fishing. This way you won't be holding up the show.

If you hook and land a steelhead, I believe that forfeiting your spot and starting back at the top of the run is the right thing to do. A bit of common sense and courtesy go a long way when sharing the river with other anglers. Let's each do our part to help perpetuate the tradition of good river etiquette.

On the flip side, if you come to fish the Skagit and Sauk, be prepared to share the rivers with people who fish a variety of different methods from boondoggling and drift fishing to plug pulling and plunking. Most of these people play by a different set of rules than we fly fishers. Generally they have none. They'll fish in front of you, behind you, and on top of you. Do they do this maliciously? Some do, but most simply are not aware of how fly anglers work a run or how much room we need. I used to get in screaming matches all the time over water rights. All it ever

catch-and-release, education, donations to conservation organizations, and an occasional letter or e-mail to state legislators explaining to them how much we love and want to keep our fisheries whole.

Unfortunately, there is a politically powerful fishing club in Washington State which, under the guise of altruistic motives, is fighting to close down the catch-and-release fishery on the Skagit. They say that mortality of catch-and-release fishing is too high—that closing this season will help reduce poaching and bring the runs back to historical numbers. In truth, these folks resent catch-and-release: "If I can't catch

The Skagit River is big water in big country with steelhead to match. Big flies and big rods are a bonus. It pays to be prepared.

accomplished was to ruin my day and probably theirs as well. Now I just wave hello and work around them. I still catch my steelhead.

A Precious Resource

The Skagit certainly ranks highly as one of the most beautiful and naturally diverse anadromous rivers and in the world. It would be a tragedy to lose such a valuable resource.

Measures are slowly but surely being taken to protect runs of native species from the ocean and hillsides to the river itself. We should all do our part in protecting our wonderful watersheds through

'n kill 'em—have my fun—then nobody else should be allowed to have fun." This group would love nothing more than to close the river for a couple of years, get rid of the fly anglers, see the run size increase, and reopen it to 100 percent kill.

Closing the river this time of year is ludicrous and, in the long run, would certainly do more harm than good for a number of reasons. Please write to Washington State senators, legislators, and U.S. congressmen and tell them how you feel about this issue. If we, as anglers, lose touch with steelhead, all will be lost. I guarantee it.

AFTERWORD

THE FUTURE OF OUR SPORT

AS WITH DEC, THE NAVY PLAYED A KEY ROLE in my love affair with steelhead. I fell for steelhead when I was stationed in—of all places—Vietnam. In 1967 and 1968, I was second in command of a river assault squadron of the Army–Navy Mobile Riverine Force in the Mekong Delta. Our job was to ferry battalions of U.S. Army infantry around the Delta's complex waterways in small, heavily armed and armored boats, and to provide fire and medical support for the troops on their combat sweeps.

The oppressive heat, swarming bugs, strange jungle sounds mixed with frequent contact with the enemy quickly stripped away my simplistic stateside illusions. The adventure I had sought so eagerly was not going to be fun. Life on the pointy end consisted of eight to 10 days in the field sweating like a pig, eating WW II-era C-rations, calling in air strikes or artillery, trading fire at 15 to 20 yards with an enemy we rarely saw, loading shipmates onto Dust-Off medevac helicopters— we hoped alive. Many were not.

In this improbable setting, shortly after Christmas 1967 and just a few weeks in advance of the 1968 Tet Offensive, I received a Christmas package from my mother. I eagerly opened it to find A.J. McClane's *Standard Fishing Encyclopedia*. It was inscribed, "A Merry Christmas, Peter: Moms." I didn't feel too merry.

The book changed the trajectory of my life. I had grown up on various naval stations on the East Coast and Europe and, although I was an avid striped bass fly fisher, I had scarcely heard of steelhead before opening my Christmas present. There, at the top of page 709, under the topic of rainbow trout, was a breathtakingly beautiful watercolor: "Rainbow Trout (Steelhead Form) 12-pound Female, Klamath River, California." I was smitten. And I resolved, then and there, if I survived my tour, I was going to meet one of these creatures. Survive I did, without so much as a scratch excepting some permanent hearing loss from machine gun and cannon fire.

As my tour wound down, I was selected for Navy-funded graduate school: Tufts University in Boston, Georgetown University in Washington, D.C., or the University of Washington in Seattle. The choice was a no-brainer—only the University of Washington offered the chance to meet the object of my fantasies. The rest, as they say, is history. The differences in angling opportunity between then and now, only 36 years, are shocking as well as illuminating.

On arrival in the Pacific Northwest from the East Coast, I did not know where to find a steelhead. And I didn't know anybody who could show me the ropes. But, as I soon discovered, I had many choices of where to go. In 1969, Washington State alone had 162 listed steelhead rivers. All of them had reasonably strong runs of wild fish, at least compared to present populations, but I knew nothing about the technique, the fish, or their home waters.

Right off, I made two lucky strikes. I met Wayne Gibbs and Earl Youngblood. Earl worked for Eddie Bauer downtown when Bauer had an authentic outdoor and fishing department. Earl, a recently retired naval officer, became my tackle guru. I started with my striper outfit: an Orvis nine-foot for a 9-weight impregnated bamboo rod, Pflueger Medalist 1495, Wet Cel shooting head, Cobra oval-mono shooting line, and a homemade shooting basket. I could cast adequately, but I did not have a clue what flies might work best. Earl gave me half a dozen General Practitioners. "I heard these are pretty good for steelhead," he said. "Give 'em a try."

I did and they were. The fly produced my first steelhead to the beach: a 13-pound chrome hen from the Pilchuck River. With Sean Gallagher's modifications called Sean's Prawn, I still rate the orange General Practitioner in various sizes as *the* fly I would use if I could use only one pattern: summer, fall, winter and spring. When fished by Sean, I refer to this fly simply as "bait."

Learning to be an effective steelhead fly fisher requires, above all else, live fish that reward the angler for proper presentation. Fortunately, for my learning experience, there were in those days lots of steelhead in scores of local rivers. All I needed was someone to show where and when to find steelhead. That's where Wayne came in.

Wayne was not a fly fisher. He knew, however, where the fish were. He generously showed me. We became fast friends and fishing and hunting buddies. Prior to the 1980s, there were so few winter steelhead fly fishers, at least in Washington where I fished, that you might go years between encountering another fly fisher on the river. The common, incredulous question from gear anglers was, "Do you ever *catch anything* on flies?" Wayne smiled. I clenched my teeth.

Wayne's solution to my determination to become a competent fly fisher was that I fished each run first. He followed up with bait. Yes, he caught way more steelhead than I, but I caught some, enough to see that it could be done. Enough to encourage persistence; enough to understand the basics of steelhead fly fishing. Slowly, I learned what steelhead wanted—the right kind of flies, depth, and presentation.

I figured I had arrived one February morning in 1971 on the Tolt River fishing with Wayne under our special agreement. I hooked three, landed two. Wayne got none, but he informed me that our deal was now off—we would rotate fishing first from now on.

One of the things I have come to most value about steelhead fishing is the accumulation of gifts that helped us become steelheaders, ranging from tips and advice to equipment to companionship. A quick inventory of my current equipment is illustrative of these special pleasures that, like fine wine, get better with age:

- A wading staff from a rare straight piece of vine maple retrieved from a Dean River beaver pond by my daughter and fishing companion, Chris Soverel;
- My first two-handed rod made for me by Don Fraser who also made me a beautiful reel to accompany the rod;
- Special fly patterns gracing my fly box inspired by Sean Gallagher and Ed Ward;
- Thirty years (and counting) of steelhead fly fishing with my children—Christine, Greg and Camille;
- Three decades of wonderful memories stretching from the California coast to western Kamchatka and most of the best rivers in between;
- And, above all, special friendships cemented by our shared bond with steelhead, especially my wilderness partner Greg McDonald.

...

I suspect that many steelhead fly fishers today neither appreciate the technological advances in equipment that have made fly fishing so effective, nor the alarming rate at which the fish are disappearing. Those new to our sport mistakenly take the present to be the norm, failing to recognize that the present, in reality, is but a pathetic echo of what was and what should be. We are fast becoming a generation of anglers perversely accustomed to rivers without steelhead.

As recently as the late 1960s, fly fishing for steelhead was confined largely to angling for summer-run and fall-run fish. There were a few pioneering fly fishers chasing winter steelhead. Haig-Brown wrote about winter fly fishing, but the practitioners were few and far between, especially north of California. The combination of cold water, heavy flows, and lack of modern, fast-sinking lines prevented anglers from getting flies down to depths where winter steelhead would bite them.

To compensate for these slow-sink rates, some anglers, such as Syd Glasso, made their own sinking lines by dressing Dacron fishing line with redlead. Others tied heavily weighted flies or added split shot. Some of us experimented with homemade lines, splicing 20 to 25 feet of level 10- to 12-weight floating line to a dozen feet of vinyl-covered leadcore trolling line. These were the first sink-tips. This vinyl-coated leadcore trolling line should not be confused with leadcore fly line which is now widely available and used extensively by do-it-yourself line makers today. The vinyl-coated leadcore trolling line was stiff and difficult to cast without risk to life and limb. Although this contraption got the fly down, casting with single-handed rods wasn't much fun. The line sank so fast that it often snagged on boulders. Not many anglers stuck with the experiment.

Of course, given the abundance of fish we enjoyed in the 1960s and '70s (compared to today's diminished runs but not levels of historic abundance), even inefficient methodologies and slow-sinking shooting heads worked sometimes. The inexperienced angler was rewarded often enough that he could learn through experience.

Two events changed the situation dramatically. First, in the mid-1970s, Scientific Anglers and Cortland Line Company developed sinking lines with much higher sinking rates—not as high as leadcore, but sufficiently fast to sink flies two to three feet in fairly heavy flows. This, in turn, made fly fishing for winter steelhead much more feasible. It opened productive lies in deeper and swifter water such as typically found on large rivers with cobble bottom structure. As a result, anglers had a wide variety of very fast-sinking lines from several commercial sources, including leadcore fly lines, that were much more efficient for winter fishing. The dedicated aficionados still prefer to use their own formulas combining differing lengths and weights of floating and sinking lines to make sweet casting and effective fishing lines.

At almost the same time, Federal Judge George Boldt ruled (July 12, 1974) that certain Indian tribes were co-managers of Washington's salmon and steelhead stocks, and those tribes were entitled to half of the harvestable salmon and steelhead. Actually, the court held the tribes had the rights to all the fish but had, by treaty, ceded their rights to half of the salmon and steelhead to the American settlers. Non-tribal commercial and sport anglers were apoplectic—as if, based upon the most recent 100-year record, the Indians could possibly do a worse job of managing salmon and steelhead stocks. The court required the state and tribes to establish joint, river-specific management plans. This immediately exposed the state—it did not have a clue as to the actual abundance of steelhead in the more than 160 steelhead rivers it had been managing for the preceding 90 years.

Absent reliable spawning-escapement data, the state closed most rivers to angling during March and April to protect wild steelhead. Paradoxically, Boldt's ruling led by steps to special catch-and-release seasons in March and April for late-running winter steelhead on three river systems ideally suited to coldwater fly fishing with the newly developed sinking lines: Skykomish, Skagit and Sauk, and North Fork Stillaguamish. Gear and bait anglers, at least initially, shunned the catch-and-release seasons, believing that angling recreation required killing the prey.

These rivers reopened to perfect fly-fishing conditions: fishable numbers of fresh-run steelhead undisturbed by other anglers. Although the run sizes were not large in comparison to historic

Step 1. Pete Soverel, founder of the Kamchatka Steelhead Project, momentarily capturing a wild steelhead from Russia's Kvachina River. The scientific research project is a 20-year effort of angler volunteers and international fishery agencies.

spawning returns, there were sufficient numbers of wild fish to provide superb angling, especially when combined with the technical improvements in fly tackle. The timing coincided perfectly with Dec's arrival to the sport. Through the mid-1990s, these fisheries produced the best winter steelhead fly fishing ever, and contributed directly to the explosion of interest in fly fishing for steelhead. Experienced fly fishers (there were only a few such anglers: Harry Lemire, Bob Stroebel, Walter Johnson, Jerry Wintle, Dick Goin, Bill McMillan to name a few of the most devout) enjoyed angling almost unimaginable today. Five to 10 hookups per day, if not the norm, were common. I recall one eight-day stretch while home on leave from Navy duty in Europe when I landed 42 wild steelhead—the most memorable week of springtime fishing I have experienced in North America.

On the positive side, as more and more gear anglers observed or heard of the excellent fly fishing for wild winter steelhead, our sport attracted many more adherents. The number of steelhead fly fishers has increased even as the overall number of steelhead anglers has declined.

I recall one afternoon in the late 1980s. I was about half way down a good run where I had already hooked three or four steelhead when an angler approached walking up the bar. After an exchange of pleasantries which included the admission that he had never cast a fly to a fish, he asked where he should start and what fly might be effective. I selected a Green-Butt Skunk from his box and told him to start in the broken water at the top of the run. I watched him as he started. His casting confirmed his admission—he didn't have a clue. On about his third cast, he hooked and promptly broke off a nice steelhead. He repeated the exercise three more times and, in the process, became a dedicated steelhead fly fisher answering the basic question in the affirmative—

Step 2. Placing the specimen in shallow depression to begin collection of information for research. Interestingly, if handled carefully, steelhead will generally lie quietly, making data collection easy.

yes, steelhead would bite flies.

That's the good news. Where fly anglers were once an oddity, now we are commonplace. We have wonderful two-handed rods, versatile fly lines, large-capacity reels, and comfortable clothing. Counterbalancing these favorable trends, however, are fewer and fewer wild steelhead—and even fewer rivers open to fishing.

In 1970, there were more steelhead anglers in British Columbia than there are now. Nonetheless, there are now loud complaints about "crowding" on popular B.C. rivers. How is this possible— fewer anglers but crowded rivers? First, there are far fewer rivers open now to angling. In 1970, virtually all B.C. systems were open to angling. In 2006, much of British Columbia is closed, including almost all Vancouver Island rivers. Thus, while the overall number of steelhead anglers and total number of angling days had declined rather dramatically in spite of a large increase in the total human population, almost all these anglers are now forced to fish on a handful of rivers with all others closed or devoid of steelhead—a pattern repeated up and down the coast.

The diversity of riverine systems is an essential element to quality steelheading and a fundamental feature of the appellation "steelhead fly fisher." Not only did each of the river systems present specific angling challenges, the fish themselves were different and behaved differently. This combination of different places and unique fish provided a rich set of choices about where to angle, and when. The hundreds of rivers and thousands of miles of productive steelhead water also dispersed anglers.

What is the future of our sport? This is an interesting proposition. On the technical side, we can build on the incredible progress realized over the past 30 to 40 years. Equipment advances have facilitated the rapid expansion of fly fishing by dramatically improving our effectiveness, especially for winter steelhead. Yet we are confronted by a cruel paradox: As we acquire the tackle to successfully catch steelhead across the full spectrum of their habitats and run timing, opportunities to encounter wild steelhead returning from the ocean continue to decline precipitously. There are still places where one can cast for hatchery steelhead in the Northwest, but increasingly few places where one can seek the real ones.

I should make clear that, when I talk about steelhead, I am talking about wild, naturally spawned and reared *Parasalmo mykiss* (I prefer the Russian taxonomy), not their distant hatchery outlaws. Wild steelhead are the genuine article; hatchery fish are not. The scientific literature is resplendent with the reasons why. Anglers know, or at least should know, from personal observation and experience that hatchery steelhead:

- Are not native, not wild, and do not behave as wild fish.
- Are much less responsive to the fly.
- Enter the rivers over an extremely compressed period. Wild steelhead exhibit wide diversity in run and spawn timing and thus provide year-round angling opportunity with at least some wild steelhead entering rivers on virtually every tide.
- Migrate rapidly to their release location.
- Are known to be harmful to native populations.

Perhaps the most basic question concerns the future of the fish themselves. Without robust wild populations, we will not have a sport. Ask any experienced steelheader whether his fishing is better now than in the past. Invariably, he will note that his angling and angling options are, at best, faint echoes of what was available just a few decades ago. If this downward trend continues for even a short period beyond the present, then the prospects for steelhead and steelhead angling are—to put it mildly—less than hopeful.

Curiously, anglers rarely confront the reality that, more than anything else, our sport depends upon the existence of abundant, diverse, widely distributed wild steelhead across the full diversity of habitats. These conditions are disappearing before our eyes. Equally astonishing, anglers accept these declines without complaint as if a diminished future were the inevitable outcome. In the span of a single human lifetime, we have largely eliminated wild steelhead from vast areas of their native range, from the immense Central Valley systems in California to the Columbia and Fraser watersheds of the north.

···

Consider what we have lost. I expect that you have never imagined wading deep into the junction pool where the Wenatchee River joins the Columbia. Here, as it had for tens of thousands of years, the enormous Columbia surged over a bouldery run curving to the right. Strip out all the line you can cast, perhaps 100 feet, and launch your pathetic cast into the half-mile-wide river: 150,000 cubic feet per second (1.2 million gallons a second) of cold, clear water courses over the large cobble bottom towards the sea hundreds of miles distant. The Columbia here was constrained between the towering, sage-covered basalt cliffs that channel both the water and wind. Scores, probably hundreds, of wild steelhead would have been holding in the current deciding whether to ascend the Wenatchee or continue to the Methow, Chelan, Okanogan, or a host of other streams and rivers across the Canadian border almost to Montana. These shoals of steelhead were part of the unimaginably huge run of steelhead that ascended the incredibly prolific Columbia–Snake watershed annually. Most held within an easy cast from shore, waiting for your fly.

I had never imagined such an impossibly powerful setting, in part, because it ceased to exist in the 1950s. The Wenatchee junction pool is now submerged under a listless reservoir. Steelhead access to Canada is blocked irretrievably by a 1,000-foot wall of concrete at Grand Coulee. *Middle and upper Columbia steelhead are now an endangered creature, numbering a few hundred rather than a few hundred thousand.*

Ken McLeod, my early steelhead mentor, not only imagined this setting but experienced it by fishing here in the 1930s and '40s. Ken made casts to these waiting throngs of wild summer-runs before the Columbia River was converted from a river to a series of slackwater impoundments from tide to its headwaters. Its wild steelhead teeter on the brink of extinction displaced by fake hatchery steelhead. Steelheaders no longer even mourn the losses that are now permanent features of the management and angling landscape even though these changes occurred, for the most part, within only the last 60 years—in my angling lifetime.

Steelheadom is much the poorer without these scores of thousands of wild steelhead filling hundreds of miles of riffles and rips now buried. We are poorer still because that past is now a forgotten legacy. My good friend Jack de Yonge used to fish the beautiful runs and riffles that marked the passage of the Snake River from Lewiston to its junction with the Columbia. The river and its wild steelhead are all gone.

. . .

There are, of course, a few good steelhead rivers left: Oregon's Umpqua and John Day; Washington's Quileute and Queets; British Columbia's Dean and Skeena; Alaska's Karluk and Situk; and a handful of rivers in western Kamchatka. Missing altogether, however, is the broad array of rivers where steelhead were abundant in living memory—Eel, Russian, Carmel, Willamette, Skykomish, Skagit, Clearwater, Klamath, Thompson, Squamish, Nimpkish, Gold, along with scores of greater and lesser rivers, streams, creeks, and rivulets from Baja California to Kamchatka's Cape Utkholok.

This diversity is critical to both the species and us. For anglers, the diversity is what provides the wide range of angling destinations and seasonal variations. As we reduce this diversity through human activities, including hatchery programs, we deprive ourselves of the rich assemblage of steelhead races upon which our fishing depends. This dismantling of a once-complex coastal resource affects not only the rivers destroyed. Crowding on the splendid Skeena system, for instance, is a hot topic among anglers and managers alike. We would do well to reflect on the reasons for present crowding even though there are fewer steelhead anglers today fishing in Canada than a generation ago. If there are fewer anglers, why is the Skeena crowded? Simple: It is about the only place left in the province with decent numbers of fish. Thus, instead of spreading anglers across scores of systems, they are all packed onto the Skeena.

If the Eel, Trinity, Klamath, Rogue, Umpqua, Deschutes, Wind, Klickitat, Clearwater, Queets, Thompson, *et al.* were teeming with steelhead as they were just 50 years ago, I doubt that the Skeena would be so crowded. When it is the only show in North America left in September and October, small wonder that everyone who wants to fish steelhead is there.

Compare, for example, my angling calendar from 20 years ago to the present. Note that most of these destinations were not more than a five-hour drive from Seattle, which meant that I could fish frequently in systems that attracted substantial runs.

WINTER: (*December-March*)
In Washington alone, there were many dozens of rivers that offered excellent angling for winter steelhead providing anglers with a rich menu from which to select a day astream depending upon current river conditions. I was especially partial to the Skagit and Sauk, Hoh, Pilchuck, and Quileute systems. The Skagit, particularly the Birdsview–Concrete area, had fishable numbers of fresh steelhead every month of the year. Sometime after Thanksgiving, the first big push of winter steelhead could be counted on to show and provide continuous high-quality angling through May.

The Hoh River was my favorite on the Washington coast and a top choice for the Christmas-to-New-Year's break. The Quileute system also provided spectacular winter steelhead angling on uncrowded rivers. I was especially attracted to the Sol Duc where the rough whitewater limited angling competition. As recently as the mid-1980s, few boatsmen other than guides risked the Sol Duc's nasty drops.

Closer to home, the little Pilchuck was a consistent producer of fine, early-run winter steelhead. I landed my very first steelhead here from the Tavern Run. The Pilchuck was also an excellent choice in March.

Present: While some of these systems remain open to angling, the early return component of the wild winter run is virtually extinct in all these systems. Wild fish do not now begin to show even in the Olympic Peninsula rivers until early March. For much of the winter season, we're left to fish for hatchery rags. The Pilchuck is closed to angling in March, once the very best month.

Angling opportunity has been radically altered from one where anglers had a wide range of choices about where to prospect for wild steelhead to the present situation where there are not *any* nearby rivers that provide consistent quality steelhead angling during the winter.

Through the late 1980s, Vancouver Island was my destination of choice for extended trips for winter steelhead. It presented a wonderful collection of productive fisheries and extremely low angling pressure. There were many, many interesting rivers to choose from. My favorite was the Gold River, especially a day or two after heavy rain. The sea pool, half a mile downstream from the pump house, was perhaps the best fly hole in all Steelheadom—hordes of large, sea-bright steelhead holding in perfect fly water. High tide backed up to the riffle below the tailout of the sea pool. You often saw fresh steelhead push up over the riffle into the tailout. Launching an inflatable raft at the pump house allowed access to the opposite side of the river in the sea pool. It was an easy cast to the holding lies for the couple hours that the sea pool fished well on each flood tide. Once the tide started back out, you rowed the mile or so to the saltwater boat ramp. Fifteen to 20 hookups were not out of the ordinary.

It is no longer worth the long drive to Gold or, for that matter, any stream on Vancouver Island. Although closed to kill fisheries for more than 20 years, steelhead populations there have collapsed. Vancouver Island's east coast rivers are closed and the rest have critically low returns. Some runs are reduced to a pathetic few individual specimens. Having explored these rivers in their glory, their impoverishment is heartbreaking.

SPRING: (April-May)

These two months, along with September–October, have always been my favorites—lengthening daylight; budding red alder and willow; strong pushes of late-winter steelhead and the first summer runs. Fishing was so good near home that I seldom made trips to distant destinations. In fact, I used to travel from the East Coast and Europe to fish the Skykomish and Skagit. Washington was the destination with a host of rivers offering exceptionally good steelheading.

The Skykomish River was my personal favorite. As recently as a dozen years or so ago, the "Sky" was, in my opinion, the very best spring steelhead fly fishing river anywhere. It combined beautiful scenery, a robust population of steelhead, and clear, shallow fly water—all just 30 minutes from home.

Today, the Sky is still there, beckoning as ever, but the steelhead population has collapsed and the spring catch-and-release fishery is closed. Last year, for the first time in 35 years, I did not land a single steelhead from the Sky. Depressing. The Sky was not the only choice. Others included:

- Nisqually River: Hosting a strong run (6,000 to 8,000 through the late 1980s) of late winter steelhead, the run including included a high proportion of very large fish. Present: The run is in a death spiral and has dwindled to near extinction levels (190 in 2005). There are no plans to recover the Nisqually.
- Skagit and Sauk rivers: In words and pictures, Dec has already told you about how good the Skagit was. Present: I have a guide friend who fished it for 30 consecutive days last year March–April without hooking a steelhead.
- Washington coast: Again take your pick—Quinault, Queets, Hoh, and Quileute produced quality angling for exceptionally large late-winter-run steelhead, especially the Quinault. The upper Quinault is one of the most beautiful steelhead rivers and was, historically, home to outsized steelhead. Indeed, if I had to pick a single American river with the best chance of hooking a 25- to 30-pound steelhead it would have been the upper Quinault in April. It was and is an unusually clear river best fished after a serious rain event, which pulled shoals of fresh steelhead out of Lake Quinault into the upper river. I first visited the upper Quinault in April 1972. At the county line pool, the county had secured huge old-growth trees with cables to the bank to protect the roadbed. After running along the log rip-rap, the river spread out into an inviting pool where, on that first visit, I could clearly see a dozen large steelhead holding in shallow tailout. The fish would have been best approached from the other shore, but the river was not fordable.

My only choice was to creep out carefully on a large log and make a long cast down and across to the fish. I was worried about how I might land a fish on the log without falling in. This turned out to be a needless worry. During the next half hour, I hooked five very large steelhead with identical outcomes—after taking the fly, each fish turned and burned out of the pool through the riffle. Since I could not follow the fish, I broke off each steelhead in turn.

Today, the run into the upper Quinault has declined dramatically. On the other coastal rivers, steelhead populations have declined by 50 percent during the last five years. Olympic Peninsula rivers are now the last streams open to killing wild steelhead legally in Oregon, Washington, Idaho, British Columbia, and Alaska. Predictably, these rivers face an unrelenting onslaught of harvest-motivated anglers with equally predictable outcomes: dramatic decline in escapements as well as rapid erosion of the angling experience. The Hoh has failed to meet escapement goals for the last three years running. One reason is that the official Washington Department of Fish and Wildlife–tribal fishing plan, shockingly, is predicated on harvesting below the set escapement goal, which itself is set at only four percent of historic abundance—even though most of the Hoh water-shed remains in pristine condition because it is protected within Olympic National Park. Unbelievable.

North of the border, the Squamish River near Whistler produced superior fly fishing for large, aggressive steelhead throughout April and much of May. I once fished this with a friend when, on arriving on the river, I discovered that I had left my reel bag back at his house. Generously, he agreed to share his rod with me. Throughout the day, we traded runs as we floated the river. With a half a rod, I had my best day ever on the Squamish, landing nine fish to 17 pounds.

Today, coastal Canadian steelhead populations, including the Squamish, have tanked completely. The Squamish run has collapsed from some thousands to a total run numbering no more than a few hundred fish. There are no plans to recover the Squamish.

...

I won't tire you with a full litany of my summer and fall destinations, but a few examples com-

Step 3. Length-and-girth measurements are used to estimate the weight of a fish. Based upon 12 years of data collection, weight (in pounds) for Kvachina steelhead = (length inches X girth inches X girth inches) divided by 690.

plete the picture painted above of the steady erosion of angling opportunity up and down the West Coast. There is, of course, only one Dean River and every steelheader dreams of fishing this wilderness river. Its habitat is largely intact. Angling pressure is strictly regulated. Nevertheless, its steelhead population is stressed by the "incidental by-catch" in the chum and chinook commercial fisheries in the approaches to the Dean. Some experts peg the by-catch in the range of 8,000 to 12,000 steelhead annually in commercial fisheries targeting a fish that sells for a few cents a pound. No wonder Dean steelhead numbers continue to decline without any plan to assure the future of this unmatched race of steelhead.

For five decades, the Thompson River, an important tributary to the Fraser, was *the* October–November destination for dedicated steelheaders. Its source at Kamloops Lake insured that its water stayed relatively warm and open right into the cold of winter. Its thundering whitewater lower reaches and the migratory maelstrom of the Fraser canyon evolved a giant race of steelhead, my largest a magnificent 44-inch male that came to a skittered surface fly then succumbed to a tiny Blue Charm wet swung in the surface film. Although still open to angling, the run is down to a tiny fraction of what it was in the 1950s. There are no plans for recovery.

...

As my own experience illustrates, the long-term prospects for abundant, native steelhead runs are doubtful. Historical experience does not give us much reason to hope for a brighter future. As so poignantly cataloged by David R. Montgomery in his *King of Fish: A Thousand-Year Run of Salmon* (2003), salmon and western Man have not—with rare exceptions—mixed. We exterminated European Atlantic salmon in about 300 years. In North America, we accomplished the same outcome more efficiently—200 years to mostly wipe out *Salmo salar* on the eastern seaboard.

In the case of Pacific salmon, the causes for the previous two mass extinctions were well understood—habitat alterations, deforestation, dams, over-fishing, inadequate escapement, and so on. Nonetheless, on the Pacific Coast, Americans and Canadians wasted no time out doing the plunder of the Atlantic salmon resource by virtually extinguishing salmon and steelhead from much of their coastal range in about 100 years. By 1990 Nehlsen, Williams and Lichatowich in their important "Salmon at the Crossroads" report for the American Fisheries Society estimated that salmon and steelhead had been eliminated from about one-third of their native habitat in the contiguous United States, and most of the remaining stocks were at elevated risk of extinction.

The Columbia was, in its native state, the greatest salmon river on earth. In a 40-year orgy of dam construction, the Columbia and Snake rivers ceased to exist. Eighteen mainstem dams converted these prolific rivers to a series of lakes, blocked salmon access to much of the watershed, and created a diabolical obstacle course for migrating adults and juveniles alike. Incredibly, state and federal agencies justified construction of many of these dams on the basis of increased "recreational opportunity." Think of trading 50,000 wild North Fork Clearwater steelhead—magnificent leaping fish to 30 pounds—for the chance to jet ski and catch crappie behind Dworshak Dam.

Little wonder then that Columbia–Snake runs are approximately 2 percent of historic levels. In fact, most stocks are already extinct and all that remain are listed as threatened or endangered under the Endangered Species Act. As if this were not shameful enough, the very public agencies responsible for stewardship in most cases simply looked the other way or worse yet provided bogus, politically motivated pseudo-science assurances that everything would be just fine.

Even though salmon and steelhead are carefully identified and counted as they pass each of the Columbia–Snake dams, the National Marine Fisheries Service (the federal agency responsible for salmon management) failed to take any action in response to the observed steep declines in coho and sockeye salmon, and steelhead. In the case of coho, NMFS did absolutely nothing while the Snake River population vanished. Coho did not disappear mysteriously. Their numbers were diligently tabulated until there were none, but no state or federal agency took any action to prevent what the numbers predicted.

Similarly, NMFS took no action in the 1980s as the counts of sockeye salmon passing the dams enroute to Redfish Lake, Idaho (near Stanley, Idaho some 950 miles from and 5,000 feet above the sea) dwindled from thousands of fish annually to hundreds, to scores, and finally to individual specimens. Again, neither NMFS nor any other state or federal agency did anything. Instead, citizens had to petition the government to list Redfish Lake sockeye as endangered under the Endangered Species Act. Not only did NMFS avoid leadership, but the agency actually resisted the petition when filed by desperate citizens who cared about the future of wild salmon.

I witnessed similar bureaucratic inertia on a smaller scale. The Washington Department of Fish and Wildlife operates a steelhead hatchery on Tokul Creek, a small tributary to the Snoqualmie River east of Seattle. WDFW built a weir some five to six feet high across the creek to steer returning hatchery winter-run steelhead into the hatchery. To prevent steelhead from simply jumping the weir, the department extended a cement apron downstream from the weir that regulated the water depth to a few inches so that fish could not secure enough purchase to make the leap. The department also installed a by-pass to the weir to permit passage of wild steelhead and salmon native to Tokul Creek including a small population of wild summer-run steelhead. Summer steelhead passed the weir and held in the plunge pool at the base of the 10- to 12-foot waterfall obstacle half a mile upstream from the hatchery. These fish could negotiate the falls only under extremely precise flow regimes.

First, the water regime must be exactly right—just warm enough to give the fish their greatest leaping capacity—probably about 10 vertical feet with just enough flow to permit successful ascent. The steelhead needed a summer or early fall rainstorm to increase the flow over the falls sufficiently for the fish to jump into the water stream coming over the lip of the falls, and then power up the last couple of feet of the water column to the creek above the falls. All this had to happen at a time when water temperatures that coincided with steelhead's maximum metabolic rate.

I used to watch the fish try. Most fish leapt unsuccessfully, missing the water column altogether or failing to power over the lip to crash back into the creek below the falls. However, some fish did make it. In 1989, western Washington was deluged with two back-to-back massive rainstorms that caused widespread flooding. This washed out the fish passage around the weir and blocked access to the falls in plain view of officials of the public agency responsible for steelhead management. The passage facilities were never repaired. Every day, WDFW employees went to work ignoring the blockage. Consequently, Tokul Creek summer runs are now extinct. Unfortunately, Tokul Creek is not an isolated case. The nonprofit organization Washington Trout reviewed hatchery facilities in Washington and found that 38 hatcheries obstructed migration of wild salmon and steelhead.

If the agencies responsible for protecting our anadromous legacy did nothing when the evidence was plainly before their eyes, I suggest it is naively optimistic to think that they will act without prodding in the future.

Salmon and steelhead are either extinct or greatly reduced in many of the most productive North American rivers—San Joaquin, Eel, Sacramento, Skagit, Fraser, and even the Skeena in Canadian north country. Historically, California was the epicenter of steelhead abundance with millions of wild fish returning annually. Water diversions, clear-cut logging and massive over-harvest have forever altered this picture. Up through the mid-1950s, anglers routinely harvested 30,000 wild steelhead from the Eel River alone. Today, the entire wild run in the Eel amounts to about 2 to 3 percent of the annual harvest from just 50 years ago. Sadly, this bleak picture is not limited to our continent. Salmon populations in the western Pacific are following a similar trajectory. Wild salmon are essentially extinct in Japan, Korea, southern Siberia and most of the upper Amur River system in China and Russia. Steelhead are listed as a "rare and disappearing" species in the Russian Red Book—the approximate equivalent of "threatened" under the U.S. Endangered Species Act.

Billions of dollars have been spent on salmon conservation and restoration projects, yet there is little to show for these expensive efforts. Most monitored stocks continue to decline. Especially discouraging, there is virtually no evidence supporting the efficacy of restoration programs (viable,

Step 4. Taking scale samples. If you look closely, you will see six to eight scales on Soverel's lower left sleeve. Analysis of scales reveals the fish's life history: age, length of pre-smolt river residence; smolt age, saltwater residency. Kamchatkan steelhead, which are a completely natural population—never exposed to hatchery influences—display remarkable diversity of life histories. Utkholok River steelhead display at least 19 different life histories.

self-sustaining wild runs in the river), at least as currently practiced.

Perhaps most distressing of all—none of this sneaked up on us unawares. It is not that we did not know what we were doing or were uncertain as to the probable consequences of contemplated options. Further, we had the sad history of Atlantic salmon as a guide. No, we knew exactly what we were doing, and what would happen. And yet we did it and are still doing it.

When I cast my first fly for steelhead in the winter of 1969, the harvest of wild winter steelhead in Washington totaled some 90,000 fish. These fish were taken from rivers throughout the state. Although harvest records are, at best, approximations of abundance, cumulatively they show a continuing decline of wild populations. By 2001, the statewide wild winter run harvest had declined to a mere 6,601 fish—a 95 percent decline in wild winter steelhead populations, with early returning wild stocks virtually extinguished in about 50 years. The loss of the early-run component certainly means that significant portions of river systems are not utilized by steelhead with the resulting loss of vital productivity.

In spite of these horribly low numbers and continuing declines in abundance, diversity, and resiliency of wild stocks up and down the West Coast, fish-management agencies insist on management policies targeting wild stocks for harvest while compromising their productivity with ill-considered hatchery practices. You would think that even the most stodgy bureaucracies and bureaucrats would accept that past management practices have been completely ineffective, perhaps even criminally negligent. Not so.

Business as usual has been the by-word and, incredibly, anglers and the public have accepted this unbroken record of disaster without effective complaint. In Washington State, for example, the Fish and Wildlife Commission insisted on a kill fishery on the very last marginally numerous wild steelhead populations on the Washington Olympic Peninsula's north coast. Never mind that citizens overwhelmingly asked the commission to enact no-kill regulations. Never mind that these runs have declined by about 50 percent over just the past few years. Never mind the accumulated evidence from the other 140-plus rivers where kill fisheries had been practiced in Washington for the past 50 years. Nope. The commission said, *keep killing 'em.* Wow.

Paraphrasing federal Judge Marsh (ruling on the efficacy of the federal biological opinion on federal recovery plans for the Snake–Columbia watershed), if the past is a guide to the future, the steelhead's future is a bleak indeed because the agencies responsible for managing these fish have consistently denied the biological and ecological needs of the fish. You know the story: dams, obliterated forests, culverts, shopping malls, hatchery introductions, etc. It is a shameful record of profligacy and irresponsible public policy unmatched in human history. As detailed above, wild steelhead are but a faint shadow of their former abundance—hundreds of stocks are extinct, most of those that remain are at elevated risk of extinction.

Viewed against the backdrop of what Lewis and Clark encountered less than three human life-times ago, there is cause for profound pessimism about the future of steelhead angling. Absent a sea change in how we relate to and manage fish, it is a future without either fish or steelhead anglers.

That's the bad news. The good news is that the fish themselves offer hope of balancing the negatives.

. . .

Parasalmo mykiss—of which steelhead represent the anadromous life form—occupy the most diverse habitat of all the Pacific salmonids. These animals are found from the mouth of the Amur River in Siberia down the west coast of Kamchatka, up its east coast, across the Pacific along the Aleutian chain, through western Alaska and down the west coast of North America to the Sierra San Pedro mountains in Baja California and interior mountains of Nevada, Utah, and Arizona.

The breathtaking diversity of life histories represented in the species reflect the incredible ecological diversity of the places where they live. Imagine steelhead in seasonal streams in southern California, Snake River tributaries in Nevada, the icy headwaters of British Columbia's Stikine River, Bering Sea tributaries such as the Bear River, and small tundra rivers of western Kamchatka. These fish know how to adapt and survive. As we look to the future, we can build on the hardiness of the fish we love. There are some hopeful building blocks:

- Steelhead themselves are resilient, adaptable, fecund and prolific.
- We more fully understand steelhead biology and the ecological requirements for sustainability which should provide the basis for sound management regimes.
- Much of their remaining habitat around the entire Pacific Rim is publicly owned providing us (steelhead anglers and people who care about anadromous salmonids) the opportunity to implement land-use management practices that are fish friendly.
- We are at the beginning of a predicted 30- to 40-year era of favorable ocean conditions which can magnify salmon friendly actions.

. . .

If given a reasonable chance, wild steelhead are fully capable of dramatic recoveries over short time spans. However, their resiliency, adaptability, and capacity for recovery are threatened by intrusive hatchery practices. Based upon incontrovertible scientific evidence, hatchery steelhead pose the most serious threat to steelhead life-history diversity—and therefore the future of the species itself. In the wild, the most valuable steelhead is the returning wild adult. The life history of this fish has allowed it to survive to adulthood and return to its natal gravel. This fish has made it through a host of environmental bottlenecks:

- The parents had spawned at the right time so that the eggs where not washed away or silted over;
- The fish hatched at a time when, as an alevin, it could feed and grow to a fingerling;
- It found the right places in the river system to grow to smolt size over-wintering twice while avoiding flushing winter flows;
- It out-migrated reaching the estuary and ocean at the right times to take advantage of the best feeding opportunities while avoiding the host of predators;
- It went to the right places at sea to grow to adulthood;
- Finally, it returned to its river at the proper time which facilitated migration to its natal gravel bed.

On arrival at that final destination after four to seven years of successful survival at each stage of its life, it links with another wild fish that has also made the same journey that weeded out the unfit. These are the fittest fish adapted for particular river reaches where individual variations, however slight compared to other specimens, give these individuals a cumulative survival advantage. The others have not survived. The progeny of these, the fittest, will return. Charles Darwin described the process well:

> Can it be, then . . . that other variations useful in some way to each being in the great and complex battle of life, should occur in the course of many successive generations? If such do occur, can we doubt (remembering that many more individuals are born than possible survive) that individuals having any advantage, however slight, over others, would have the best chance of surviving and procreating their kind. . . . Hence, I look at individual differences, though of small interest to the systematist, as of the highest importance for us, as being the first steps towards such slight varieties as barely thought worth recording in works on natural history.

What happens if, instead of joining with another wild fish that has passed through the same environmental lenses, this survivor meets and spawns with a hatchery steelhead? We should expect that their progeny would survive at a lower level because they lack the fitness of progeny from wild–wild pairings. Thirty years of field research by Washington Department of Fish and Wildlife scientists focused exactly on this issue confirmed our expectation. The study compared the reproductive success of different pairing possibilities between wild and hatchery Kalama River steelhead:

- Native Kalama summer runs (both parents are native Kalama fish);
- Mixed parentage (hatchery male–native female or native male–hatchery female);
- Hatchery-only parentage (both parents hatchery-origin fish).

The findings? Only native–native pairings produced returning adult steelhead. The contribution of all other pairings to the returning adult populations, in the techno-speak of the study, could not be statistical distinguished from "zero." In other words, the hatchery–hatchery, hatchery–wild, and wild–hatchery progeny were so ill-adapted—so unfit for the environmental challenges they faced over their lifetime—that none of them survived to adulthood. As predicted by Darwin, differences count in life.

The results of this careful, long-term scientific study make clear two essential facts. First, hatchery fish are not the same as nor are they an acceptable substitute for wild fish. Second, permitting hatchery fish to interact with wild fish has the effect of dramatically decreasing the productivity of the wild fish. Let us suppose that hatchery fish comprise only 10 percent of the wild spawning population. This very low percentage of hatchery fish reduces the productivity of the remnant wild population by 20 percent. Of course, almost nowhere in the lower 48 do hatchery fish comprise only 10 percent of the population. More typically, hatchery fish represent 30 to 90 percent of the population. In the upper Snake system, hatchery fish account for about 90 percent of the total population. And, as a consequence, the productivity of the already dangerously depressed Snake River wild stocks that are on the precipice of extinction is reduced to about 1 percent of their inherent productivity. It should come as no surprise then that Snake–Clearwater wild stocks continue to decline precipitously under such wrong-headed management regimes.

This means that when the most precious of all steelhead—the survivor of the many environmental bottlenecks—meets and mates with a hatchery fish, all the adaptive characteristics inherent in the wild steelhead are washed away. The wild fish's entire life is wasted in the futile, unproductive coupling with its unfit cousin because that pairing will produce no adult offspring. Insidiously, as wild stocks decline, the ratio of hatchery fish spawning with wild steelhead increases, further decreasing wild reproductive success.

In spite of clear appreciation and understanding of these consequences, public agencies have continued to base steelhead management on hatchery production. It is a certain recipe for extinction. Our managers know it is harming wild stocks. Yet many anglers and politicians continue to insist on large-scale hatchery programs, and managers persist in stocking tens of millions of harmful hatchery steelhead anyway. Think about it.

The impacts of hatcheries on the productivity of wild fish are not some mystery or highly classified secret known to only a few. These impacts are well documented. They are cited as a principal contributing factor to declines and extinctions of wild populations. Yet the very agencies responsible for managing steelhead continue to plant scores of millions of hatchery fish annually with the full knowledge of the impacts on wild fish. If this is not cause for pessimism, I am not sure what would qualify.

Hunters get it; many, perhaps even most, anglers and steelhead managers don't. Think of an elk fenced in pastures without access to the mountains, forests, meadows, and alder thickets—or risk from predators. This is not really an elk. It is a zoo animal. It may superficially look like an elk, but it is not a real one. The Boone and Crocket Club, established by Theodore Roosevelt in 1887 and the respected keeper of records of North American big game, distinguishes between wild animals and penned animals. Similarly, a steelhead born in a tray and reared in a swimming pool is no more a real steelhead than the zoo elk is a real one. It may look like the real thing but it is not. Neither the zoo elk nor hatchery steelhead are viable in the wild nor are they a substitute for the real McCoy. While this may sound simplistic, the implications for steelhead management are profound.

...

The picture is discouraging. Instead of having many hundreds of productive rivers to explore for steelhead, the angling public has been robbed. We are confined increasingly to a smaller and smaller selection of rivers with fewer and fewer steelhead:

- California's San Joaquin River (historic run: 1,000,000+; present-day run: 0);
- Sacramento River (historic: 1,000,000+; present: fewer than 5000);

- Central California coast (historic 150,000+; present: a few hundred);
- Russian River (historic: 30,000 to 45,000; present: a few hundred);
- Eel River (historic: 50,000 to 75,000; present: perhaps a few thousand);
- Klamath River (historic: 750,000 to 900,000; present: perhaps a few thousand);
- Columbia–Snake rivers and tributaries (historic: 1,000,000 to 2,500,000; present: fewer than 75,000);
- Puget Sound, Washington, probably in the range of 750,000 to 1,300,000 (note: these estimates are based upon cannery records from the nineteenth century where I have divided the total poundage by nine pounds and estimated the catch was about 50 percent of the total run. It is important to note that these records reflect only those fish that were canned and not sold fresh. However, winter steelhead were frequently sold fresh.) Present abundance, while not known precisely, is certainly fewer than 20,000 spawners or about 2 percent of historic abundance.

As can be seen, throughout their range on the West Coast, steelhead are either already extinct or, where they persist, are present at only about 1 to 2 percent of historic abundance. In other words, annually, there are approximately 5.6 million fewer steelhead in California, Oregon, Idaho, and Washington than were swimming within living memory.

Even on storied steelhead waters such as the Dean and Skeena, the runs are generally depressed, even severely depressed. The species no longer exists in huge swaths of what was once steelhead country. Steelhead are functionally extinct over much of their historic North American range (middle Columbia, upper Snake, California coast, Vancouver Island, and so on). That is, while not technically extinct, steelhead are now present in ones and twos rather than the hundreds of thousands that returned annually less than a century ago.

The record is neither pretty nor hopeful. Absent dramatic changes in the way we manage steelhead, continued extinctions and reduced angling opportunity are the certain outcomes.

First, all of us need to accept that anadromous salmonids in the southern and central reaches of their ranges on both sides of the Pacific are at imminent risk of extinction (fractionated habitat, extirpation of meta-populations, loss of genetic and life history diversity, and so on.). Second, we must acknowledge that our current management practices and policies have been ineffective, even harmful to wild steelhead. Actually, our management practices have CONTRIBUTED directly to steelhead declines and extinctions. Absent these acknowledgements and a determination to make dramatic changes, you and your friends will be the last steelheaders.

Based on the record described briefly above, the greatest challenge to the future of steelhead are those very officials and agencies responsible for fish and habitat management and their political bosses. Salmon urgently need a basic management ethos founded on the biological needs of wild fish and the habitat that supports those fish. For well over a century, we have tried, without success, to use technological or industrial manipulations to offset anthropogenic impacts on wild populations or, what Jim Lichatowich so presciently labeled, *Salmon Without Rivers: A History of the Pacific Salmon Crisis* (1999).

Currently, spending for endangered species, hatchery operations and "mitigation" dominate fish-management budgets. These expenditures, while staggering (something on the order of $750 million to $1 billion annually) are of little benefit to wild fish. Indeed, most of the programs supported by such expenditures are actually harmful to wild steelhead. Measured against wild fish returning these monies have had no discernable positive effect and have, instead, diminished wild

Step 5. Tagging. Tagging helps determine migration patterns as well as approximations of overall abundance based upon the ratio of tagged to untagged fish in the catch. This fish is one of 249 steelhead landed by Pete Soverel, Tom Pero, Serge Karpovich, and Dave Goodhart in one three-week period from the Kvachina and Snotalvayam rivers. Only two tagged fish were recaptured—indicating a very large overall population. In previous years, steelhead tagged on a spawning migration in one river have been recaptured in completely different watersheds in subsequent years, confounding the notion that steelhead return faithfully to their native river.

populations.

Paraphrasing Jerry McGuire ("show me the money"), these spending patterns illustrate the wrong-headed priorities of management agencies. More insidious, the fish divisions of state fish and wildlife agencies are dependent upon the various "mitigation" payments from federal agencies and dam operators. The result is a highly skewed approach to fish management:

- Most state and federal salmon money is spent on artificial production and/or restoration programs on river systems that will almost certainly never support healthy wild runs any time soon or, more likely, never.
- Most attention is devoted to threatened and/or endangered populations.
- Relatively little money and attention are devoted to wild populations and the habitat that supports them.

The Oregon Department of Fish and Wildlife's 2003–2005 budget, for example, allocated only $6.3 million to habitat programs and a whopping $45.9 million to artificial production. Habitat work is likely to provide long-term benefits to wild fish; hatcheries are known to be harmful to wild fish.

A similar situation prevails in Washington State. There, demonstrating that old ways die hard, the legislature keeps insisting the Department of Fish and Wildlife construct a *new* production hatchery on the Skagit system, one of the last rivers to host fishable numbers of wild steelhead in the state. Only the determined efforts of conservation organizations such as Washington Trout and the Federation of Fly Fishers have blocked the construction on the Skagit which is a federally recognized Wild and Scenic River attracting a famous wintering population of bald eagles. What do you suppose the reaction of responsible biologists and citizens would be to a proposal that wild eagles be "supplemented" with cage-reared birds? An absurd notion, perhaps, but why accept cage-reared steelhead?

The addiction to hatcheries among managers and legislators is hard to break. Given the overwhelming evidence of the pernicious, harmful, impacts of hatcheries, their defenders now propose hatchery "reform," usually in the guise of using native brood stock and "integrated" hatcheries that are supposed to help wild stocks recover. Never mind that there is not a shred of evidence that such reforms can deliver the promise. Indeed, the Independent Scientific Advisory Board, after reviewing 97 such integrated–conservation hatcheries (i.e "reformed" hatcheries), reported in 2005 to the Northwest Power Planning and Conservation Council that none of these operations increased wild runs. Think of it: "O fer 97". . . and this is the future?

In the Northwest, what passes for salmon and steelhead conservation and management has focused on artificial production and costly recovery efforts. We have already seen the consequences of the former. Recovery programs hinge on two unknowns:

- Can an ecosystem be restored to support steelhead abundance—can those factors which limit steelhead productivity be removed or reduced sufficiently so that steelhead might thrive?
- If an ecosystem has been fixed, will salmon and steelhead actually re-establish abundant populations?

Neither outcome is certain. Recovery programs might work. That is, salmon stocks might recover. The salmon restoration program on the Columbia and Snake is a textbook example of what is wrong with most salmon conservation spending and management. It is business as usual. And it threatens the future of wild salmon and steelhead. No one is in charge or coordinating the efforts of different agencies. For all the talk about adaptive management, there are no rigorous monitoring protocols to measure the effects of various conservation and restoration efforts. In just the past six years, the feds and states have spent at least $2 billion on futile Columbia River salmon recovery programs—programs which have consistently been rejected as inadequate by federal courts. The outcome says it all: Columbia and Snake wild salmon and steelhead continue their slide toward certain extinction.

What is the matter with this picture? Well, just about everything. Columbia salmon recovery has no chance of succeeding absent removal of the root cause of impending extinctions, in this case the series of mainstem dams. It is also crystal clear that dam removal is not on the table. Absent removal of the root cause, we might just as well put Columbia salmon recovery money in a wheelbarrow and light it on fire. Instead, we persist with programs that demonstrably do not work. Consequently, we can predict with some degree of certainty:

- Columbia salmon recovery programs will continue wasting unimaginable quantities of money.
- Columbia–Snake wild salmon and steelhead now functionally extinct will soon become technically extinct.
- And, we will have squandered billions of dollars that could have been used to good effect elsewhere.

In other words, the Columbia and many other recovery programs are bad investments simply because recovery is highly unlikely. We would never use such a model in business or battle squandering most of our assets on actions that have the least likelihood of success. The military adage applies: never reinforce failure. Instead, we would make investments that have the highest probability of success—reinforce success. Applied to steelhead conservation, such an approach would lead us in the direction of protecting places that are not already compromised or to systems where recovery has the highest chance of succeeding.

If steelhead and other salmonids are to have a future, we need to apply bold discipline to conservation spending and reverse the current hierarchy of spending. Currently, most monies are targeted on systems with the lowest probability of success while those systems that offer the greatest probability of success have the lowest budgetary priorities. The Columbia–Snake is, of course, the penultimate example of the wrong-headed approach, but is not the only one. For instance, in Puget Sound, approximately $13 million is spent annually on Cedar River (a small, dammed, urban tributary to Lake Washington) recovery programs but only about one-quarter of that amount is directed toward salmon conservation on the Skagit–Sauk with a much higher potential for recovery and wild production. In other words, we spend a disproportional amount of available resources on the sickest systems.

If salmon and steelhead are to have a sustainable future, we must focus much more attention and money on ecosystems with the highest production potential. The best outcome would be additional monies to fix broken systems *and* recover and protect the best remaining systems. The reality, however, is that more money is not likely to be made available. In recognizing this reality, society needs to use available resources in ways *most likely* to assure healthy wild runs for the future.

We need a different approach. We need a strategy of managing salmon and steelhead based on the production and potential for recovery of individual river systems. The most valuable systems are the ones that are in the best condition with the healthiest runs of fish. The least valuable systems are those that are so permanently compromised that they will never again produce abundant populations of wild fish. I envision three categories:

I. PERMANENTLY COMPROMISED ECOSYSTEMS

The causes of salmon and steelhead declines are not mysteries. We understand that rivers and their steelhead populations are broken for a variety of reasons related to degraded habitat (urbanization, land use practices, water withdrawals, etc.), over-harvest, hydroelectric development, and hatchery introduction. Some of these factors can be reversed, but some, especially those related to hydro–irrigation development and urbanization, cannot. In those cases, recovery of wild stocks is highly unlikely no matter how much money and political capital are expended. In these systems, there are measures that can and should be taken to facilitate adult and juvenile passage, make the downstream water quality more hospitable to salmon and steelhead, and so on, but the reality is that the many dams on these systems are permanent features.

Similarly, habitat degradation caused by urbanization presents daunting challenges to recovering wild populations. The reality is that these systems are not likely candidates for recovery. Shoreline and wetlands management can reduce further erosion of salmon and steelhead habitat by limiting future development in these sensitive areas, but, as with most dams, it is most unlikely that we will recover habitat compromised by urban development.

Thus, while there may be important social considerations for insuring persistence of wild fish in urban streams, these systems will never again realize the former reproductive potential. In these sorts of circumstances, since the ecosystems cannot practically be restored, there is virtually no likelihood that wild steelhead can ever become abundant or perhaps even avoid local extirpation. Because these systems are unable to support significant wild production, hatcheries will play an

The real McCoy—a perfect, native Snotalvayam hen steelhead right off the tide, tagged and ready for safe release. This is what we must save.

important role. This is not quite the same as writing off these systems entirely, but we should exercise great care in resource allocation to insure that we preserve sufficient resources to invest in those systems that offer the greatest return on investment.

Instead, those entities which profit from the destruction and extinction of stocks (dam operators, irrigation districts, levee districts, county commissions, timber companies) should be taxed for the existence value of the salmon and steelhead in those systems that their activities compromise. For example, on the Columbia River, electric-rate payers, irrigators, barge operators, and so on would be taxed something on the order of $600 million (current salmon recovery budgets) annually forever. If wild fish should become extinct, as in the case of Snake River coho, upper Snake steelhead and chinook (above Hells Canyon Dam), upper Columbia chinook and steelhead (above Grand Coulee), none of the those revenues would be spent in the basin where the fish became extinct. Rather, these monies would be used to protect or restore more healthy systems elsewhere where the probability of success is much higher. In the event that local stocks should be extirpated, those responsible should make annual payments forever, perhaps through a performance bond, for the extinctions. Such a system would also remove any extinction incentives by imposing real penalties for extinctions rather than an economic escape route.

II. PROTECT THE BEST

Without question, the highest return on investment will be on those systems that are not already broken and which, ideally, support robust populations of steelhead and salmon. Even in those instances where abundance has been reduced by over-harvest, these systems still represent the best investments to assure the future. These rivers are generally wilderness waters (Siberia, Kamchatka, Alaska, and northern British Columbia) or rivers with low human populations which, in turn, means that conservation of these ecosystems carry the lowest cost. They do not require expensive habitat restoration programs (dismantling hatcheries, dam and levee removal, land use changes, and so on). Their populations of salmon and steelhead are already robust or at least not teetering on the verge of extinction.

Protecting these rivers and their populations must be the core of an effective international conservation strategy. A strategy focused on preserving the best remaining ecosystems is both the least expensive and the most certain to assure long term abundance of salmon and steelhead in at least a portion of their historic range.

Investing significant sums now will insure the productivity of these systems and anchor robust, abundant populations into the distant future.

III. RESTORE

Restore ecosystems where wild salmon and steelhead are most likely to recover. In river systems where hydro development and urbanization have not already compromised the system's ability to support wild populations, there are *three factors that we control* that determine steelhead abundance and wild production potential: harvest, rural-forest habitat, and hatcheries. We can decide not to plant artificial steelhead. We can decide on less-harmful land use practices, especially on the millions of acres of publicly owned timber and grazing lands in steelhead country. We can decide to retire logging roads. We can decide to install culverts that do not block fish passage. We can decide on lower harvest rates and greater escapements. These are all choices open to us and which will determine the fate and future of steelhead.

The probability of success will be related to realistic assessments of: factors limiting steelhead abundance in specific river systems; can those factors be ameliorated; if they were, will steelhead populations thrive or at least recover to a level capable of supporting angling? By way of illustration, let's examine how such an approach might work on specific river systems.

The Thompson River, a high-desert tributary to the Fraser in southern British Columbia, is a productive system especially for pink, chinook and coho salmon, but its steelhead population is extremely depressed (less than 2 percent of historic abundance). That's the bad news. On the positive side, there is no hydro development or hatchery supplementation. There is no directed harvest of Thompson steelhead. The watershed is primarily forested or in cattle production with relatively low human densities. Agricultural water withdrawals from a relatively small number of ranches for hay production appears to be the principal factor limiting the steelhead population.

Thompson steelhead recovery primarily needs to address water withdrawals and, to a lesser extent, by-catch in the Indian and commercial Fraser River salmon fisheries: hardly insuperable or even very expensive obstacles. A few millions of dollars would secure the Thompson for future generations. Recovering the Thompson is straightforward: single factor limiting abundance, low cost, and low human density equals high likelihood of success.

In other systems, such as the Hoh River on the Olympic Peninsula discussed below, with more factors limiting abundance, recovery programs would, of course, face greater challenges. The Hoh is an attractive but challenging recovery candidate. Hoh runs are composed of native stocks well adapted to the Hoh. While these populations are extremely depressed compared to historic—even recent—abundance (10 to 15 percent of estimated historic abundance of 30,000 to 50,000 winter steelhead), most of the watershed is both pristine and protected forever. Three-quarters of the Hoh watershed is inside Olympic National Park. Most of the land outside the park is forestland, and much of that is owned by Washington State or the Hoh River Trust, a conservation landowner. The human density is low: 230 souls. Thus, the Hoh habitat has good potential for natural production. However, this potential cannot be realized until:
  • Timber harvest practices in the forestlands in the lower river are significantly modified— greater riparian setbacks, longer rotation cycles, and conservation easements. The public already owns much of the land, which means that we control how it is used.
  • Spawning escapements are dramatically increased. The Hoh tribe and the Washington Department of Fish and Wildlife proposed and the federal court ordered spawning escapement goals for different species. These court-approved goals are set far below levels that would allow the Hoh to reach its production potential. The goals need to be adjusted upwards significantly, perhaps as much as tenfold. Again, however, this is a process that we largely control although it will require cooperation from the Hoh tribe.
  • Intense tribal- and sport-fishing pressure and systematic over-harvest has prevented Hoh chinook and steelhead from reaching even the unsustainably low escapement goals.
  • Annual introductions of hatchery steelhead significantly reduce the reproduction potential of the already extremely depressed wild stocks.

As can be seen, the public controls most of the factors influencing the abundance of salmon and steelhead in the Hoh River. There are many other rivers in California, Oregon, Washington, and British Columbia with similarly high potential to restore steelhead abundance: Tillamook Bay rivers, Umpqua, Queets, Quileute, Squamish, Skeena, et al.

The question is, will recovery work? In the case of steelhead, there is plenty of evidence that it can.

Puget Sound steelhead stocks were subjected to intense commercial fisheries from the late 1880s until 1932. As early as 1895, most stocks were already in steep decline, even though, throughout the region, overall abundance remained, by current standards, enormous—totaling 750,000 to 1,000,000 fish annually, by reasonable calculation. For instance, based upon U. S. Fish Commission records, the reconstructed 1895 winter steelhead run in the relatively small Stillaguamish system was a staggering 90,000 fish. Forty years later (1932), when the citizens of Washington prohibited commercial fishing for steelhead, Puget Sound stocks were severely depressed, but there was little directed harvest due to low abundance. Over the next 20 years, in spite of rapid degradation of habitat and increase in sport-fishing harvest, steelhead rebounded dramatically. By way of illustration, the Skagit, Puyallup, Green, and Cowlitz rivers each supported kill fisheries with annual catches of 8,000 to 16,000 steelhead during the early 1950s. These were all wild fish.

Deer Creek summer runs provide a more recent example. Deer Creek is a tributary to the North Fork Stillaguamish River, famous for its native summer-run steelhead. Virtually all these summer-entry fish spawn and rear in Deer Creek. The entire Deer Creek watershed was clear cut which, in turn, led to massive slope failures. Summer steelhead escapements plummeted from 1,000 or so fish to a few score by the late 1970s. Since virtually all the trees had already been cut, logging and road building largely ended, permitting the habitat to recover. The state did not attempt to use hatcheries to recover the population, properly leaving the job to the fish. Finally, there is no angling permitted in Deer Creek itself and angling in the Stilly is restricted to fly fishing only. Under these conditions, Deer Creek itself happily recovered as did its native steelhead, rebounding to about 1,000 adults over a 10- to 15-year period.

The Wind River in southwestern Washington offers a similarly hopeful example. Historically the Wind, which runs into the lower Columbia, had a strong run of early returning summer steelhead. The fish ascended Sheppard Falls, penetrating deep into the river's upper watershed. Mike Kennedy and Enos Bradner, pioneering Northwest fly fishers, had largely quit fishing the Wind by the mid-1920s, deeming the run too depressed to make the journey worthwhile. U. S. Fish and Wildlife Service data from the same period put the run at 2,500 to 3,000 fish. In ignorance, the state constructed a fish-passage facility at Sheppard Falls and stocked hatchery steelhead above the falls.

Under a management regime that facilitated passage of inferior fish, hatchery stockings and a robust kill fishery, Wind River wild steelhead counts at Sheppard Falls declined to 150 to 200 adults by the end of the century. To help restore the wild population, the Department of Fish and Wildlife adopted a series of enlightened management procedures: closed angling for summer steelhead and stopped planting hatchery fish above the falls, and—perhaps most important—trapped returning hatchery adults in the passage facility and returned them to the lower river. In only three years, wild summer steelhead spawning escapement to the upper Wind soared to more than 1,000 adults. Although annual escapements have declined somewhat since then (600 to 700), the projections for 2006 and 2007 are 1,000 and 1,200 fish respectively. Notice the dramatic impact of simply removing hatchery fish—*a five-fold increase in a single generation*. The fish can recover if we will let them.

Consider the history of steelhead in Alaska's Situk River. Over the last 70 years or so, steelhead populations in this short but remarkably productive river have fluctuated wildly. Through the 1930s, local canneries paid a bounty on rainbow trout (steelhead) and dolly varden in the mistaken belief that predation by these species limited salmon abundance. In 1934 alone, 142,547 "trout" were killed under the bounty program which paid $672.81 (roughly half a cent each). When the funding for this program dried up, the bounty-hunting effort waned. Not surprisingly, the steelhead population recovered quickly, peaking at 20,000 to 26,000 in 1952. It has subsequently declined to 6,000 to 9,000.

In 1994, as Chairman of the Wild Salmon Center, I initiated, in cooperation with Moscow State University a long-term program to monitor steelhead populations in the Kvachina, Snotalvayam, and Utkholok rivers in Kamchatka, Russia—the Kamchatka Steelhead Project (KSP). Professor Ksenya Savvaitova of Moscow State University (MGU) had first documented the life history structures of these populations in the 1960s, and then fought successfully to have Kamchatkan steelhead listed as a protected species under the Russian Red Book of Rare and Disappearing species. Why were these steelhead populations in uninhabited, wilderness rivers with pristine habitat in rapid decline? Simple: over-harvest by illegal poaching.

We discovered on our first expedition in 1994 that the steelhead populations in both the Kvachina and Snotalvayam were severely depressed and their life history structure had been altered dramatically from historic conditions. During the next dozen years, our expeditions provided a law-enforcement presence on these rivers, effectively eliminating commercial poaching.

The steelhead population responded immediately. By 2003, the life-history structure duplicated the historic structure and the overall population had exploded. That year these rivers were at extremely low flows so that although steelhead had entered the tidal zone, no fish were migrating into the river proper. Under these conditions, I along with three or four other anglers (including Tom Pero, publisher of this book) brought to hand and tagged 249 steelhead. Approximately 500 additional fish were hooked but not landed. All of the tagged fish, unable to migrate upstream into the river proper, remained available for recapture. Yet only two tagged fish were recaptured (less than 1 percent exploitation rate), suggesting an extraordinarily robust total population certainly measuring in some thousands of fish.

There are some common factors in each of these recovery examples:
- Wild steelhead are designed to take advantage of habitat opportunities. The fish have high fecundity. There is a high egg-to-smolt survival rate, especially in underutilized systems, where the overall spawner-to-recruit ratios can be three-to five-to-one (three to five adults return for each spawning parent). Thus, if we allow only wild fish, even small numbers, to spawn without interactions from hatchery fish, the species is able to quickly utilize available ecological niches and restore itself.
- Second, most obvious and most important factor is the complete absence of hatchery fish in each of these bright stories of recovery. We can conclude, given the known harmful impacts of hatchery fish described in some detail above, that the absence of hatchery fish in these examples is critical in preserving the locally adapted steelhead population upon which recovery and future abundance will depend.
- Third, increased escapements lead immediately to dramatic increases in overall abundance as was evidenced by the 2002–2003 Kvachina and Snotalvayam escapements which had recovered dramatically and numbered in the thousands of fish.

Based upon these examples, we see that a management approach focusing on protecting and restoring the best rivers, eliminating intrusive hatcheries, and fostering increased survival of wild spawners works. The fish themselves provide the key. They can recover if we change our bad behavior. However, the opposite is also true. It is obvious from the foregoing that if we do not make the necessary changes in management paradigms, then, based on a single lifetime of experience in the Pacific Northwest, there is much cause for concern.

Pacific steelhead and salmon on the West Coast are in a crisis—not because we do not understand the causes for their declines. Instead, we know perfectly well what needs to be done but have insisted on following management practices that we know are harmful: excessive harvest, inadequate escapements, hatchery introductions, land use practices that are both unsustainable and detrimental to steelhead, and so on. We have further compounded the crisis by focusing our money and efforts on the stocks that are at the highest risk while largely ignoring other stocks less at risk, all the while continuing to apply management regimes known to be harmful. We also have examples of what will work if we have the courage to trust in the resilience of the fish themselves while providing for their basic requirements.

In short, the problem is not the fish. We and the manner in which we manage steelhead are the problem. Unless and until we change the basic management paradigms, we can be certain that, in the lifetime of all you reading this beautiful new book celebrating steelhead, the species will be functionally extinct in what is now their already greatly diminished range. We can also be confident that if implemented, the changes outlined above will result in recovery of salmon and steelhead stocks in scores of rivers up and down the West Coast. However, each of the required changes represents a sea change in management paradigms—threatening careers, budgets, ways of thinking, etc. Absent these sorts of changes, the future for steelhead angling is bleak indeed.

In my angling lifetime, we have learned how to effectively fish for steelhead during winter, spring, summer and fall. During that same angling lifetime, we have also greatly diminished our angling opportunity. Preserving that opportunity means rescuing what's left of wild runs and unbroken rivers. It will involve a colossal fight. Are we up for it?

PETER W. SOVEREL
EDMONDS, WASHINGTON
January 2006

STEWARDSHIP

The following government agencies, operating with public funds, are responsible for the future of healthy runs of wild steelhead throughout their historic range on the West Coast of North America. Wild River Press urges concerned anglers to become actively involved in meaningful efforts to rescue what remains of this precious anadromous legacy.

Alaska Department of Fish and Game
1255 West Eighth Street
Juneau, Alaska 99811
Telephone 907-465-4100
Web site www.adfg.state.ak.us

Alaska Region
National Marine Fisheries Service
Post Office Box 21668
Juneau, Alaska 99802
Telephone 907-586-7221
Web site www.fakr.noaa.gov

British Columbia Ministry of Environment
Post Office Box 9339
Station Provincial Government
Victoria, British Columbia V8W 9M1
Telephone 250-387-1161
Web site www.env.gov.bc.ca

Pacific Region
Department of Fisheries and Oceans
401 Burrard Street, Suite 200
Vancouver, British Columbia V6C 3S4
Telephone 604-666-0384
Web site www.dfo-mpo.gc.ca

Washington Department of Fish and Wildlife
600 Capitol Way North
Olympia, Washington 98501
Telephone 360-902-2200
Web site www.wdfw.wa.gov

Northwest Region
National Marine Fisheries Service
7600 Sand Point Way
Seattle, Washington 98115
Telephone 206-526-6150
Web site www.nwr.noaa.gov

Idaho Fish and Game
600 South Walnut Street
Boise, Idaho 83712
Telephone 208-334-3700
Web site www.fishandgame.idaho.gov

Pacific Region
U. S. Fish and Wildlife Service
911 Northeast 11th Avenue
Portland, Oregon 97232
Telephone 503-231-6828
Web site www.fws.gov/pacific

Oregon Department of Fish and Wildlife
3406 Cherry Avenue NE
Salem, Oregon 97303
Telephone 503-947-6000
Web site www.dfw.state.or.us

California Department of Fish and Game
1416 Ninth Street
Sacramento, California 95814
Telephone 916-445-0411
Web site www.dfg.ca.gov

SPECIAL OPPORTUNITY FOR COLLECTORS

FOR COLLECTORS interested in a beautifully framed photographic print from *A Passion for Steelhead*, signed by Dec Hogan and exquisitely mounted with an original spey fly tied by Dec, Wild River Press has arranged with the author and Angler's Choice Framing—the foremost museum-quality framer of flies in America—to produce a series of limited-edition shadowbox presentations. Each fly is tied personally and with meticulous care by Dec Hogan. A limited edition copy of this book, signed by the author and with matching number, accompanies each framed piece. These special books are handsomely bound in silver-embossed, handmade lambskin covers. For more information about these and other fine products related to the series **Masters on the Fly**, please visit www.wildriverpress.com or e-mail premium@wildriverpress.com.

Wild River Press
Post Office Box 13360
Mill Creek, Washington 98082
USA

MODERN SPEY CASTING AND MORE WITH DEC HOGAN

Watching this exciting new DVD is the next best thing to a personal casting lesson from the master himself! Stand beside Dec Hogan on British Columbia's *nonpareil* Dean River as the author of *A Passion for Steelhead* takes you through a step-by-step casting clinic with the two-handed rod. Dec's techniques are an original combination of old and new styles adapted to maximize the performance of today's modern spey rods and progressive tapered lines. This film—expertly shot by noted filmmaker and avid steelheader Jeff Mishler of Portland, Oregon—takes the viewer through the complete arsenal of casts Dec uses while fishing the various conditions he encounters during a day's fishing. Dec then takes you out on the water to show the practical application of the casts demonstrated in the clinic. Flies, presentation, and Dec's fishing philosophies—to say nothing of a few chrome-bright wild steelhead—are more of what you'll discover in this entertaining 45-minute DVD.

To order copies of the DVD *Modern Spey Casting and More with Dec Hogan*, send a check (or telephone with credit card information) in the amount of $24.95 each plus $5 shipping and handling ($15 to addresses outside the U.S.) to:

Wild River Press
Post Office Box 13360
Mill Creek, Washington 98082
USA
Telephone 425-486-3638

Photography in this Book

The photograph of Dec Hogan on the cover jacket was made by Keith Balfourd.

Photographs of the life cycle of a steelhead appearing in the Introduction, "A Migratory Wonder," pages 8–37, were made by Richard T. Grost—the underwater image of two steelhead that opens Chapter 5, "How a Steelhead Takes Your Fly," pages 198–199, was also made by him.

The sequential images of spawning steelhead in the Introduction are taken from a digital underwater video shot by John McMillan. Also in the Introduction, Don Baccus made the cormorant photograph, Nate Chappel made the common merganser photograph, Dennis Frates made the Douglas fir forest photograph, Willie Holdman made the northern rain forest and Pacific Northwest beach photographs, Zafer Kizikaya made the squid photograph, Miguel Lasa made the osprey photograph, Bob Lauth of National Marine Fisheries Service made the underwater Atka mackerel photograph, Randy Morse made the underwater harbor seal and California sea lion photographs, Alan Murphy made the belted kingfisher photograph, and Dan Walters made the great blue heron photograph.

Photographic portraits of Dec Hogan on pages 39, 58, 90–91, and 201 were made by Walter Hodges.

The close-up photographs of flies tied by the author in Chapter 2, "Flies That Take Steelhead," pages 52–89, were made by Ted Fauceglia, except the image of Ed Ward's Intruder from *Fish & Fly* Magazine.

Studio photographs of the fly rods in Chapter 6, "Tackling Steelhead," pages 210–231 were made by Juan Calvillo. All other product shots are courtesy of the manufacturers.

Photographs of Pete Soverel in Russia appearing in the Afterword, "The Future of Our Sport," pages 282–307, were made by Thomas R. Pero.

All other photographs throughout *A Passion for Steelhead* were made by the author.